Docker in Practice

Docker in Practice

IAN MIELL
AIDAN HOBSON SAYERS

MANNING
SHELTER ISLAND

Manning Publications Co.
20 Baldwin Road
PO Box 761
Shelter Island, NY 11964

Development editor:	Cynthia Kane
Technical development editors:	Alain Couniot
	and Robert Wenner
Copyeditor:	Andy Carroll
Proofreader:	Melody Dolab
Technical proofreader:	José San Leandro
Typesetter:	Gordan Salinovic
Cover designer:	Marija Tudor

ISBN 9781617292729
Printed in the United States of America
1 2 3 4 5 6 7 8 9 10 – EBM – 21 20 19 18 17 16

brief contents

contents

PART 3   DOCKER AND DEVOPS 143

6 Continuous integration: speeding up your development pipeline   145

7 Continuous delivery: a perfect fit for Docker principles   169

foreword

I might be biased, but Docker is a pretty big deal.

It wasn't long ago that applications were large and monolithic, sitting alone inside lumps of steel and silicon. They would stew away for a few years, resisting change, not wanting to move. This was a problem for organizations that wanted to move fast, so it's no surprise that virtual machines caught on. Applications were no longer tied to these pieces of hardware, allowing everything to move more quickly and be more flexible.

Unfortunately, virtual machines are very complicated. They simulate an entire computer inside of another computer, and this virtual computer is still very complex and needs managing. And because virtual machines are smaller and easier to create, there are far more of them around that need managing.

How do we manage all of that complexity? With configuration management, of course—another extremely complex system for managing complexity.

Docker takes a different approach. If you put your software inside a container, it separates the complexity of your application from the infrastructure underneath, making the infrastructure simpler and the application easier to ship around. On top of this organizational efficiency, the leap in technical speed and efficiency compared to virtual machines is dramatic. Containers boot in milliseconds, not minutes. Memory is shared, not allocated. This makes your application much cheaper to run, but also means that you can architect your application in the way that you want to, not in the way that fits the constraints of slow, inflexible infrastructure.

When I first saw Solomon Hykes, creator of Docker, talking about Docker and its analogy to the shipping container, I knew he was on to something big. The complex state of the worldwide shipping industry before standardization is an apt analogy for the complex state of managing software before containers. Solomon's insight was so convincing that I started a company building tools around Docker, which was eventually acquired by Docker, Inc. and turned into what we now know as Docker Compose.

I first met Ian at some of the Docker meetups we organized in London. Back then, we insistently said, "Docker is not ready for production; please don't use it!" but Ian was the sort of person who would disregard this sensible advice and go ahead and run it in production anyway. Back then, he was working for the betting services company OpenBet alongside Aidan, and the amount of money they must have been processing with the code we had at that time makes me feel a bit light-headed.

Ian and Aidan both saw that the value they got from using Docker outweighed the inconveniences of working with it in its beta state. They jumped on the technology early, and therefore have a unique perspective on how best to apply it. The tooling they built at OpenBet has pointed out stuff that was missing in Docker, and our informal chats have had a real influence on the design and direction we've taken it.

Docker has moved along quite a bit since Ian and Aidan first started using it, and thousands of organizations are now using it to solve real problems: shipping software faster, managing its daunting complexity, improving the efficiency of infrastructure, fixing "works on my machine" problems, and so on. This is causing a huge shift in how we build, deploy, and manage software, and a whole new landscape of tools and ideas is forming around it. The bright future of containerization is exciting, but is also intimidatingly different from what we are used to.

For you, it might be hard to see how to get from here to there, but this book contains a deluge of practical advice about how to apply Docker to problems you're having right now. Follow this advice, and your organization will keep on moving quickly. And—perhaps more importantly—building and deploying your applications will become a lot more enjoyable.

BEN FIRSHMAN
DIRECTOR OF PRODUCT MANAGEMENT, DOCKER, INC.
COCREATOR OF DOCKER COMPOSE

preface

In September 2013, while browsing Hacker News, I stumbled across an article in *Wired* about a new technology called "Docker."[1] As I read it, I became increasingly excited as I realized Docker's revolutionary potential.

The company I'd worked at for over a decade was struggling to deliver software quickly enough. Provisioning environments was a costly, time-consuming, manual, and inelegant affair. Continuous integration was barely existent, and setting up development environments was an exercise in patience. As my job title included the words "DevOps Manager," I was peculiarly motivated to solve these problems!

I recruited a couple of motivated coworkers (one of them now my coauthor) via a company mailing list, and together our skunkworks team labored to turn a beta tool into a business advantage, reducing the high costs of VMs and enabling new ways of thinking about building and deploying software. We even built and open sourced an automation tool (ShutIt) to suit our organization's delivery needs.

Docker gave us a packaged and maintained tool that solved many problems that would have been effectively insuperable had we taken it upon ourselves to solve them. This was open source at its best, empowering us to take on a challenge using our spare time, overcoming technical debt, and learning lessons daily. Lessons not only about Docker, but about continuous integration, continuous delivery, packaging, automation, and how people respond to speedy and disruptive technological change.

---

[1] http://www.wired.com/2013/09/docker/

For us, Docker is a remarkably broad tool. Wherever you run software using Linux, Docker can impact it. This makes writing a book on the subject challenging, because the landscape is as broad as software itself. The task is made more onerous by the extraordinary rate at which the Docker ecosystem is producing solutions to meet the needs that emerge from such a fundamental change in software production. Over time, the shape of problems and solutions became familiar to us, and in this book we've endeavored to pass on this experience. This will enable you to figure out solutions to your particular technical and business constraints.

When giving talks at meetups, we're struck by how quickly Docker has become effective within organizations willing to embrace it. This book mirrors how we used Docker, going from our desktops, through the DevOps pipeline, and all the way to production. As a consequence, this book is sometimes unorthodox, but as engineers we believe that purity must sometimes give way to practicality, especially when it comes to saving money! Everything in this book is based on real lessons from the field, and we hope you benefit from our hard-won experience.

IAN MIELL

acknowledgments

This book couldn't have been written without the support, sacrifice, and patience of those closest to us. Special mention is due to Stephen Hazleton, whose tireless efforts with us to make Docker useful for our customers informed much of the book's contents.

Several Docker contributors and staff were kind enough to review the book at different stages and provided much useful feedback, including the following people who read the book in manuscript form: Benoit Benedetti, Burkhard Nestmann, Chad Davis, David Moravec, Ernesto Cárdenas Cangahuala, Fernando Rodrigues, José San Leandro, Kirk Brattkus, Pethuru Raj, Scott Bates, Steven Lembark, Stuart Woodward, Ticean Bennett, Valmiky Arquissandas, and Wil Moore III.

Finally, this book also owes a great deal to the Manning editorial team, who went out of their way to push us into making the book not just good enough, but the best it could be. We hope the pride they took in their work rubbed off on us.

Ian Miell   To Sarah, Isaac, and Rachel for putting up with the late-night coding, a father glued to a laptop screen, and the eternal "Docker this, Docker that, Docker blah, blah," and to my parents for encouraging me from an early age to question the status quo. And buying me that Spectrum.

Aidan Hobson Sayers   To Mona for the support and encouragement, my parents for their wisdom and motivating words, and my coauthor for that fateful "Has anyone tried this Docker thing?" e-mail.

about this book

Docker is arguably the fastest-growing software project ever. Open sourced in March 2013, by 2016 it had gained nearly 30,000 GitHub stars and over 7,500 forks. It has accepted significant numbers of pull requests from the likes of Red Hat, IBM, Microsoft, Google, Cisco and VMware.

Docker has hit this critical mass by responding to a critical need for many software organizations: the ability to build software in an open and flexible way and then deploy it reliably and consistently in different contexts. You don't need to learn a new programming language, buy expensive hardware, or do much in the way of installation or configuration to build, ship, and run applications portably.

Docker in Practice takes you through real-world examples of Docker usage using techniques we've employed in various contexts. Where possible, we've tried to elucidate these techniques without requiring knowledge of other technologies before reading. We've assumed the reader has an understanding of basic development techniques and concepts such as the ability to develop some structured code, as well as some awareness of software development and deployment processes. In addition, we've assumed a knowledge of core source control ideas and a basic understanding of network fundamentals such as TCP/IP, HTTP, and ports. Anything less mainstream is explained as we go.

Starting with a rundown of Docker fundamentals in part one, in part two we focus on using Docker in development on a single machine. In part three, we move on to Docker usage within a DevOps pipeline, covering continuous integration, continuous delivery, and testing. The last part covers Docker in production, focusing on your options relating to orchestration.

Docker is such a broad, flexible, and dynamic tool that keeping up with its fast-evolving landscape is not for the faint-hearted. We've endeavored to give you an understanding of critical concepts through real-world applications and examples, with the aim of giving you the power to critically evaluate future tools and technologies within the Docker ecosystem with confidence. We've tried to make the book an enjoyable tour of the many ways we've seen Docker make our lives easier and even fun. Immersing ourselves in Docker has introduced us to many interesting software techniques spanning the entire software life cycle in a stimulating way, and we hope that this is an experience shared by the reader.

Roadmap

This book consists of 12 chapters divided into four parts.

Part 1 lays the groundwork for the rest of the book, introducing Docker and getting you to run some basic Docker commands. In chapter 2 some time is spent getting you familiar with Docker's client-server architecture and how to debug it, which can be useful for identifying issues with unconventional Docker setups.

Part 2 focuses on familiarization with Docker and getting the most out of Docker on your own machine. An analogy with a concept you may be familiar with, virtual machines, is used as the basis for chapter 3 to provide an introduction to Docker use. Chapter 4 then details a number of Docker techniques we've found ourselves using every day. The final chapter in this part explores the topic of building images in more depth.

Part 3 begins by looking at uses of Docker in a DevOps context, from using it for automation of software builds and tests to moving your built software to different places. This part concludes with a chapter on the Docker virtual network, introduces Docker Compose, and covers some more-advanced networking topics, like network simulation and Docker network plugins.

Part 4 covers a number of topics for using Docker effectively in a production environment. It begins with chapter 9, where we survey some of the most popular tools for orchestrating containers and note what scenarios they tend to be used in. Chapter 10 addresses the important topic of security, explaining how to lock down processes running inside a container and how to restrict access to an externally exposed Docker daemon. The final two chapters go into detail on some key practical information for running Docker in production. Chapter 11 demonstrates how to apply classic sysadmin knowledge in the context of containers, from logging to resource limits, while chapter 12 looks at some problems you may encounter and provides steps for debugging and resolution.

The appendixes contain details on installing, using, and configuring Docker in different ways, including inside a virtual machine and on Windows.

Code

The source code for all tools, applications, and Docker images created by the authors for use in this book is available for download from the publisher's website at www .manning.com/books/docker-in-practice and also on GitHub under the docker-in-practice organization: https://github.com/docker-in-practice/. Images on the Docker Hub under the dockerinpractice user (https://hub.docker.com/u/dockerinpractice/) are typically automated builds from one of the GitHub repositories. Where we've felt the reader may be interested in further study of some source code behind a technique, a link to the relevant repository has been inserted in the technique discussion.

A significant number of the code listings in the book illustrate a terminal session for the reader to follow, along with corresponding output from commands. There are a couple of things to note about these sessions.

Long terminal commands may use the shell line continuation character (\) to split a command over multiple lines. Although this will work in your shell if you type it out, you may also omit it and type the whole command on one line.

Where a section of output doesn't provide extra useful information to a reader, it may be omitted and an ellipsis ([...]) inserted in its place.

Author Online

Purchase of *Docker in Practice* includes free access to a private web forum run by Manning Publications where you can make comments about the book, ask technical questions, and receive help from the lead author and from other users. To access the forum and subscribe to it, point your web browser to www.manning.com/books/docker-in-practice. This page provides information on how to get on the forum once you are registered, what kind of help is available, and the rules of conduct on the forum.

Manning's commitment to our readers is to provide a venue where a meaningful dialog between individual readers and between readers and the authors can take place. It is not a commitment to any specific amount of participation on the part of the authors, whose contribution to the forum remains voluntary (and unpaid). We suggest you try asking their some challenging questions lest them interest stray! The Author Online forum and the archives of previous discussions will be accessible from the publisher's website as long as the book is in print.

about the cover illustration

The figure on the cover of *Docker in Practice* is captioned "Man from Selce, Croatia." The illustration is taken from a reproduction of an album of Croatian traditional costumes from the mid-nineteenth century by Nikola Arsenovic, published by the Ethnographic Museum in Split, Croatia, in 2003. The illustrations were obtained from a helpful librarian at the Ethnographic Museum in Split, itself situated in the Roman core of the medieval center of the town: the ruins of Emperor Diocletian's retirement palace from around AD 304. The book includes finely colored illustrations of figures from different regions of Croatia, accompanied by descriptions of the costumes and of everyday life.

Dress codes and lifestyles have changed over the last 200 years, and the diversity by region, so rich at the time, has faded away. It's now hard to tell apart the inhabitants of different continents, let alone of different hamlets or towns separated by only a few miles. Perhaps we have traded cultural diversity for a more varied personal life—certainly for a more varied and fast-paced technological life.

Manning celebrates the inventiveness and initiative of the computer business with book covers based on the rich diversity of regional life of two centuries ago, brought back to life by illustrations from old books and collections like this one.

about the Cover Illustration

Part 1

Docker fundamentals

Part 1 of this book consists of chapters 1 and 2, which get you started using Docker and cover its fundamentals. Chapter 1 explains the origin of Docker along with its core concepts such as images, containers, and layering. Finally, you get your hands dirty by creating your first image with a Dockerfile. Chapter 2 introduces some useful techniques to give you a deeper understanding of Docker's architecture. Taking each major component in turn, we cover the relationship between the Docker daemon and its client, the Docker registry, and the Docker Hub. By the end of part 1 you'll be comfortable with core Docker concepts and will be able to demonstrate some useful techniques, laying a firm foundation of understanding for the remainder of the book.

Discovering Docker *1*

This chapter covers

- What Docker is
- The uses of Docker and how it can save you time and money
- The differences between containers and images
- Docker's layering feature
- Building and running a to-do application using Docker

Docker is a platform that allows you to "build, ship, and run any app, anywhere." It has come a long way in an incredibly short time and is now considered a standard way of solving one of the costliest aspects of software: deployment.

Before Docker came along, the development pipeline typically consisted of combinations of various technologies for managing the movement of software, such as virtual machines, configuration management tools, different package management systems, and complex webs of library dependencies. All these tools needed to be managed and maintained by specialist engineers, and most had their own unique ways of being configured.

Docker has changed all of this, allowing different engineers involved in this process to effectively speak one language, making working together a breeze. Everything goes through a common pipeline to a single output that can be used on any target—there's no need to continue maintaining a bewildering array of tool configurations, as shown in figure 1.1.

At the same time, there's no need to throw away your existing software stack if it works for you—you can package it up in a Docker container as-is for others to consume. As a bonus, you can see how these containers were built, so if you need to dig into the details, you can.

This book is aimed at intermediate developers with some knowledge of Docker. If you're OK with the basics, feel free to skip to the later chapters. The goal of this book is to expose the real-world challenges that Docker brings and show how they can be overcome. But first we're going to provide a quick refresher on Docker itself. If you want a more thorough treatment of Docker's basics, take a look at *Docker in Action* by Jeff Nickoloff (Manning Publications, 2016).

In chapter 2 you'll be introduced to Docker's architecture more deeply with the aid of some techniques that demonstrate its power. In this chapter you're going to learn what Docker is, see why it's important, and start using it.

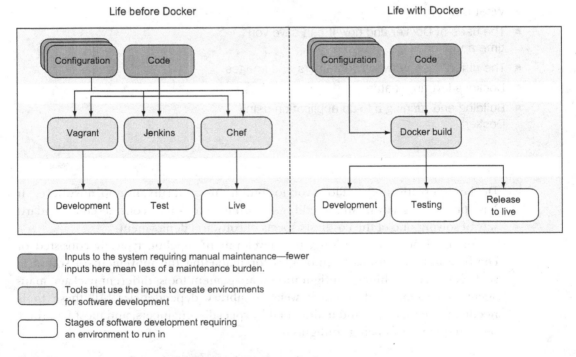

Figure 1.1 How Docker has eased the tool maintenance burden

1.1 The what and why of Docker

Before we get our hands dirty, we're going to discuss Docker a little so that you understand its context, where the name "Docker" came from, and why we're using it at all!

1.1.1 What is Docker?

To understand what Docker is, it's easier to start with a metaphor than a technical explanation, and the Docker metaphor is a powerful one. A docker was a labourer who moved commercial goods into and out of ships when they docked at ports. There were boxes and items of differing sizes and shapes, and experienced dockers were prized for their ability to fit goods into ships by hand in cost-effective ways (see figure 1.2). Hiring people to move stuff around wasn't cheap, but there was no alternative.

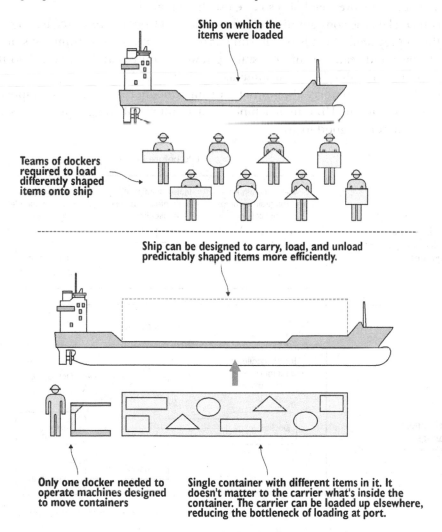

Figure 1.2   Shipping before and after standardized containers

This should sound familiar to anyone working in software. Much time and intellectual energy is spent getting metaphorically odd-shaped software into different sized metaphorical ships full of other odd-shaped software, so they can be sold to users or businesses elsewhere.

Figure 1.3 shows how time and money can be saved with the Docker concept.

Before Docker, deploying software to different environments required significant effort. Even if you weren't hand-running scripts to provision software on different machines (and plenty of people still do exactly that), you'd still have to wrestle with configuration management tools that manage state on what are increasingly fast-moving environments starved of resources. Even when these efforts were encapsulated in VMs, a lot of time was spent managing the deployment of these VMs, waiting for them to boot, and managing the overhead of resource use they created.

With Docker, the configuration effort is separated from the resource management, and the deployment effort is trivial: run docker run, and the environment's image is pulled down and ready to run, consuming fewer resources and contained so that it doesn't interfere with other environments.

You don't need to worry about whether your container is going to be shipped to a RedHat machine, an Ubuntu machine, or a CentOS VM image; as long as it has Docker on it, it'll be good to go.

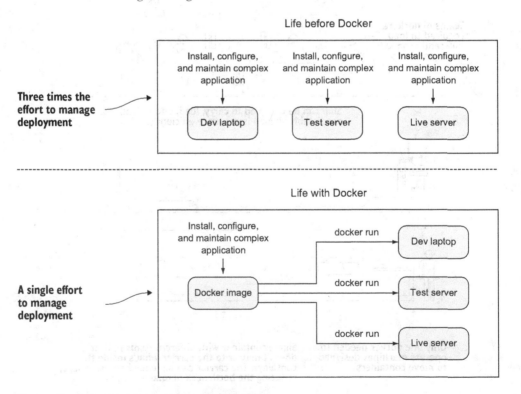

Figure 1.3 Software delivery before and after Docker

1.1.2 What is Docker good for?

Some crucial practical questions arise: why would you use Docker, and for what? The short answer to the "why" is that for a modicum of effort, Docker can save your business a lot of money quickly. Some of these ways (and by no means all) are discussed in the following subsections. We've seen all of these benefits first-hand in real working contexts.

REPLACES VIRTUAL MACHINES (VMS)

Docker can be used to replace VMs in many situations. If you only care about the application, not the operating system, Docker can replace the VM, and you can leave worrying about the OS to someone else. Not only is Docker quicker than a VM to spin up, it's more lightweight to move around, and due to its layered filesystem, it's much easier and quicker to share changes with others. It's also firmly rooted in the command line and is eminently scriptable.

PROTOTYPING SOFTWARE

If you want to quickly experiment with software without either disrupting your existing setup or going through the hassle of provisioning a VM, Docker can give you a sandbox environment in milliseconds. The liberating effect of this is difficult to grasp until you experience it for yourself.

PACKAGING SOFTWARE

Because a Docker image has effectively no dependencies for a Linux user, it's a great way to package software. You can build your image and be sure that it can run on any modern Linux machine—think Java, without the need for a JVM.

ENABLING A MICROSERVICES ARCHITECTURE

Docker facilitates the decomposition of a complex system to a series of composable parts, which allows you to reason about your services in a more discrete way. This can allow you to restructure your software to make its parts more manageable and pluggable without affecting the whole.

MODELLING NETWORKS

Because you can spin up hundreds (even thousands) of isolated containers on one machine, modelling a network is a breeze. This can be great for testing real-world scenarios without breaking the bank.

ENABLING FULL-STACK PRODUCTIVITY WHEN OFFLINE

Because you can bundle all the parts of your system into Docker containers, you can orchestrate these to run on your laptop and work on the move, even when offline.

REDUCING DEBUGGING OVERHEAD

Complex negotiations between different teams about software delivered is commonplace within the industry. We've personally experienced countless discussions about broken libraries; problematic dependencies; updates applied wrongly, or in the wrong order, or even not performed at all; unreproducible bugs, and so on. It's likely you have too. Docker allows you to state clearly (even in script form) the steps for debugging a problem on a system with known properties, making bug and environment reproduction a much simpler affair, and one normally separated from the host environment provided.

DOCUMENTING SOFTWARE DEPENDENCIES AND TOUCHPOINTS

By building your images in a structured way, ready to be moved to different environments, Docker forces you to document your software dependencies explicitly from a base starting point. Even if you decide not to use Docker everywhere, this need to document can help you install your software in other places.

ENABLING CONTINUOUS DELIVERY

Continuous delivery (CD) is a paradigm for software delivery based on a pipeline that rebuilds the system on every change and then delivers to production (or "live") through an automated (or partly automated) process.

Because you can control the build environment's state more exactly, Docker builds are more reproducible and replicable than traditional software building methods. This makes implementing CD much easier. Standard CD techniques such as Blue/Green deployment (where "live" and "last" deployments are maintained on live) and Phoenix Deployment (where whole systems are rebuilt on each release) are made trivial by implementing a reproducible Docker-centric build process.

Now you know a bit about how Docker can help you. Before we dive into a real example, let's go over a couple of core concepts.

1.1.3 Key concepts

In this section we're going to cover some key Docker concepts, which are illustrated in figure 1.4.

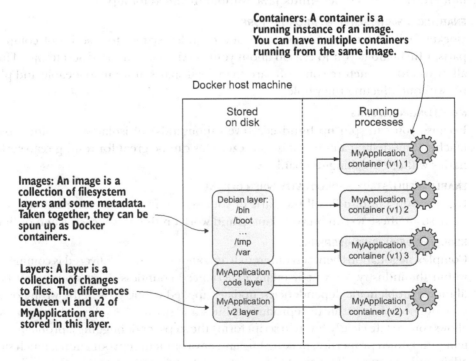

Figure 1.4   Core Docker concepts

It's most useful to get the concepts of images, containers, and layers clear in your mind before you start running Docker commands. In short, *containers* are running systems defined by *images*. These images are made up of one or more *layers* (or sets of diffs) plus some metadata for Docker.

Let's look at some of the core Docker commands. We'll turn images into containers, change them, and add layers to new images that we'll commit. Don't worry if all of this sounds confusing. By the end of the chapter it will all be much clearer!

KEY DOCKER COMMANDS

Docker's central function is to build, ship, and run software in any location that has Docker.

To the end user, Docker is a command-line program that you run. Like git (or any source control tool), this program has subcommands that perform different operations.

The principal Docker subcommands you'll use on your host are listed in table 1.1.

Table 1.1 Docker subcommands

Command	Purpose
docker build	Build a Docker image.
docker run	Run a Docker image as a container.
docker commit	Commit a Docker container as an image.
docker tag	Tag a Docker image.

IMAGES AND CONTAINERS

If you're unfamiliar with Docker, this may be the first time you've come across the words "container" and "image" in this context. They're probably the most important concepts in Docker, so it's worth spending a bit of time to make sure the difference is clear.

In figure 1.5 you'll see an illustration of these concepts, with three containers started up from one base image.

One way to look at images and containers is to see them as analogous to programs and processes. In the same way a process can be seen as an application being executed, a Docker container can be viewed as a Docker image in execution.

If you're familiar with object-oriented principles, another way to look at images and containers is to view images as classes and containers as objects. In the same way that objects are concrete instantiations of classes, containers are instantiations of images. You can create multiple containers from a single image, and they are all isolated from one another in the same way objects are. Whatever you change in the object, it won't affect the class definition—they're fundamentally different things.

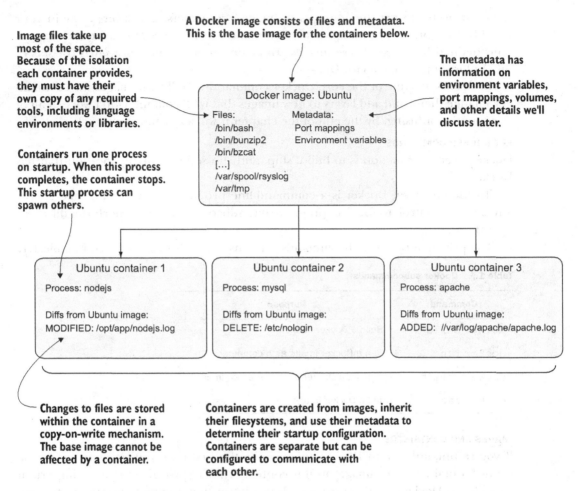

Image files take up most of the space. Because of the isolation each container provides, they must have their own copy of any required tools, including language environments or libraries.

A Docker image consists of files and metadata. This is the base image for the containers below.

The metadata has information on environment variables, port mappings, volumes, and other details we'll discuss later.

Containers run one process on startup. When this process completes, the container stops. This startup process can spawn others.

Changes to files are stored within the container in a copy-on-write mechanism. The base image cannot be affected by a container.

Containers are created from images, inherit their filesystems, and use their metadata to determine their startup configuration. Containers are separate but can be configured to communicate with each other.

Figure 1.5   Docker images and containers

1.2   *Building a Docker application*

We're going to get our hands dirty now by building a simple "to-do" application (todo-app) image with Docker. In the process, you'll see some key Docker features like Dockerfiles, image re-use, port exposure, and build automation. Here's what you'll learn in the next 10 minutes:

- How to create a Docker image using a Dockerfile
- How to tag a Docker image for easy reference
- How to run your new Docker image

A to-do app is one that helps you keep track of things you want to get done. The app we'll build will store and display short strings of information that can be marked as done, presented in a simple web interface.

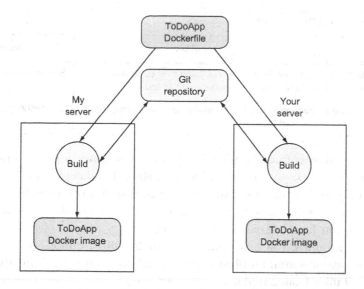

Figure 1.6   Building a Docker application

Figure 1.6 shows what we'll achieve by doing this.

The details of the application are unimportant. We're going to demonstrate that from the single short Dockerfile we're about to give you, you can reliably build, run, stop, and start an application in the same way on both your host and ours without needing to worry about application installations or dependencies. This is a key part of what Docker gives us—reliably reproduced and easily managed and shared development environments. This means no more complex or ambiguous installation instructions to follow and potentially get lost in.

> **THE TO-DO APPLICATION**   This to-do application will be used a few times throughout the book, and it's quite a useful one to play with and demonstrate, so it's worth familiarizing yourself with it.

1.2.1   Ways to create a new Docker image

There are four standard ways to create Docker images. Table 1.2 itemizes these methods.

Table 1.2   Options for creating Docker images

Method	Description	See technique
Docker commands / "By hand"	Fire up a container with `docker run` and input the commands to create your image on the command line. Create a new image with `docker commit`.	See technique 14.
Dockerfile	Build from a known base image, and specify build with a limited set of simple commands.	Discussed shortly.

Table 1.2 Options for creating Docker images (*continued*)

Method	Description	See technique
Dockerfile and configuration management (CM) tool	Same as Dockerfile, but hand over control of the build to a more sophisticated CM tool.	See technique 47.
Scratch image and import a set of files	From an empty image, import a TAR file with the required files.	See technique 10.

The first "by hand" option is fine if you're doing proofs of concept to see whether your installation process works. At the same time, you should be keeping notes about the steps you're taking so that you can return to the same point if you need to.

At some point you're going to want to define the steps for creating your image. This is the second option (and the one we'll use here).

For more complex builds, you may want to go for the third option, particularly when the Dockerfile features aren't sophisticated enough for your image's needs.

The final option builds from a null image by overlaying the set of files required to run the image. This is useful if you want to import a set of self-contained files created elsewhere, but it's rarely seen in mainstream use.

We'll look at the Dockerfile method now; the other methods will be covered later in the book.

1.2.2 *Writing a Dockerfile*

A Dockerfile is a text file with a series of commands in it. Here's the Dockerfile we're going to use for this example:

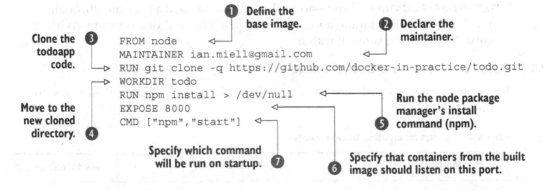

You begin the Dockerfile by defining the base image with the FROM command ❶. This example uses a Node.js image so you have access to the Node.js binaries. The official Node.js image is called node.

Next, you declare the maintainer with the MAINTAINER command ❷. In this case, we're using one of our email addresses, but you can replace this with your own reference because it's your Dockerfile now. This line isn't required to make a working Docker image, but it's good practice to include one. At this point, the build has inherited the state of the node container, and you're ready to work on top of it.

Next, you clone the todoapp code with a RUN command ❸. This uses the specified command to retrieve the code for the application, running git within the container. Git is installed inside the base node image in this case, but you can't take this kind of thing for granted.

Now you move to the new cloned directory with a WORKDIR command ❹. Not only does this change directory within the build context, but the last WORKDIR command determines which directory you're in by default when you start up your container from your built image.

Next, you run the node package manager's install command (npm) ❺. This will set up the dependencies for your application. You aren't interested in the output here, so you redirect it to /dev/null.

Because port 8000 is used by the application, you use the EXPOSE command to tell Docker that containers from the built image should listen on this port ❻.

Finally, you use the CMD command to tell Docker which command will be run on startup of the container ❼.

This simple example illustrates several key features of Docker and Dockerfiles. A Dockerfile is a simple sequence of a limited set of commands run in strict order. They affect the files and metadata of the resulting image. Here the RUN command affects the filesystem by checking out and installing applications, and the EXPOSE, CMD, and WORKDIR commands affect the metadata of the image.

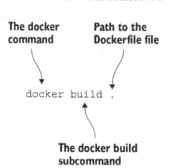

Figure 1.7 Docker build command

1.2.3 Building a Docker Image

You've defined your Dockerfile's build steps. Now you're going to build the Docker image from it by typing the command in figure 1.7.

The output you'll see will be similar to this:

Docker uploads the files and directories under the path supplied to the docker build command.

Each command results in a new image being created, and the image ID is output.

```
Sending build context to Docker daemon 178.7 kB
Sending build context to Docker daemon
Step 0 : FROM node
 ---> fc81e574af43
Step 1 : MAINTAINER ian.miell@gmail.com
 ---> Running in 21af1aad6950
 ---> 8f32669fe435
Removing intermediate container 21af1aad6950
Step 2 : RUN git clone https://github.com/ianmiell/todo.git
 ---> Running in 0a030ee746ea
Cloning into 'todo'...
```

Each build step is numbered sequentially from 0 and output with the command.

To save space, each intermediate container is removed before continuing.

```
  ---> 783c68b2e3fc
Removing intermediate container 0a030ee746ea
Step 3 : WORKDIR todo
  ---> Running in 2e59f5df7152
  ---> 8686b344b124
Removing intermediate container 2e59f5df7152
Step 4 : RUN npm install
  ---> Running in bdf07a308fca
npm info it worked if it ends with ok
[...]
npm info ok
  ---> 6cf8f3633306
Removing intermediate container bdf07a308fca
Step 5 : RUN chmod -R 777 /todo
  ---> Running in c03f27789768
  ---> 2c0ededd3a5e
Removing intermediate container c03f27789768
Step 6 : EXPOSE 8000
  ---> Running in 46685ea97b8f
  ---> f1c29feca036
Removing intermediate container 46685ea97b8f
Step 7 : CMD npm start
  ---> Running in 7b4c1a9ed6af
  ---> 439b172f994e
Removing intermediate container 7b4c1a9ed6af
Successfully built 439b172f994e
```

Debug of the build is output here (and edited out of this listing). ←

Final image ID for this build, ready to tag ←

You now have a Docker image with an image ID ("66c76cea05bb" in the preceding example, but your ID will be different). It can be cumbersome to keep referring to this ID, so you can tag it for easier reference.

Type the preceding command, replacing the 66c76cea05bb with whatever image ID was generated for you.

You can now build your own copy of a Docker image from a Dockerfile, reproducing an environment defined by someone else!

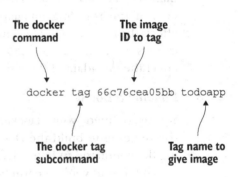

The docker command

The image ID to tag

```
docker tag 66c76cea05bb todoapp
```

The docker tag subcommand

Tag name to give image

Figure 1.8   Docker `tag` command

1.2.4   *Running a Docker container*

You've built and tagged your Docker image. Now you can run it as a container:

```
docker run -p 8000:8000 --name example1 todoapp
npm install
npm info it worked if it ends with ok
npm info using npm@2.14.4
npm info using node@v4.1.1
npm info prestart todomvc-swarm@0.0.1

> todomvc-swarm@0.0.1 prestart /todo
> make all
```

The output of the container's starting process is sent to the terminal.

The docker run subcommand starts the container, -p maps the container's port 8000 to the port 8000 on the host machine, --name gives the container a unique name, and the last argument is the image. ❶

```
npm install
npm info it worked if it ends with ok
npm info using npm@2.14.4
npm info using node@v4.1.1
npm WARN package.json todomvc-swarm@0.0.1 No repository field.
npm WARN package.json todomvc-swarm@0.0.1 license should be a
➥ valid SPDX license expression
npm info preinstall todomvc-swarm@0.0.1
npm info package.json statics@0.1.0 license should be a valid
➥ SPDX license expression
npm info package.json react-tools@0.11.2 No license field.
npm info package.json react@0.11.2 No license field.
npm info package.json node-jsx@0.11.0 license should be a valid
➥ SPDX license expression
npm info package.json ws@0.4.32 No license field.
npm info build /todo
npm info linkStuff todomvc-swarm@0.0.1
npm info install todomvc-swarm@0.0.1
npm info postinstall todomvc-swarm@0.0.1
npm info prepublish todomvc-swarm@0.0.1
npm info ok
if [ ! -e dist/ ]; then mkdir dist, fi
cp node_modules/react/dist/react.min.js dist/react.min.js

LocalTodoApp.js:9:      // TODO: default english version
LocalTodoApp.js:84:           twdList =
➥ this.host.get('/TodoList#'+listId); // TODO fn+id sig
TodoApp.js:117:         // TODO scroll into view
TodoApp.js:176:          if (i>=list.length()) { i=list.length()-1; }
➥ // TODO .length
local.html:30:    <!-- TODO 2-split, 3-split -->
model/TodoList.js:29:
➥ // TODO one op - repeated spec? long spec?
view/Footer.jsx:61:       // TODO: show the entry's metadata
view/Footer.jsx:80:            todoList.addObject(new TodoItem());
➥ // TODO create default
view/Header.jsx:25:
➥ // TODO list some meaningful header (apart from the id)

npm info start todomvc-swarm@0.0.1
```

Hit Ctrl-C ❷ here to terminate the process and the container.

```
> todomvc-swarm@0.0.1 start /todo
> node TodoAppServer.js
```

❸ Run this command to see containers that have been started and removed, along with an ID and status (like a process).

```
Swarm server started port 8000
^C
$ docker ps -a
CONTAINER ID   IMAGE            COMMAND      CREATED
➥ STATUS                      PORTS   NAMES
b9db5ada0461   todoapp:latest   "npm start"  2 minutes ago
➥ Exited (130) 2 minutes ago  example1
$ docker start example1
```

Restart the container, this time in the background. ❹

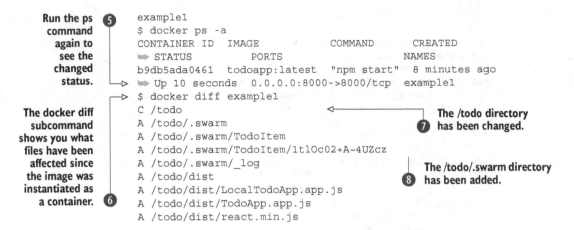

Run the ps **⑤**
command
again to
see the
changed
status.

The docker diff
subcommand
shows you what
files have been
affected since
the image was
instantiated as
a container. **⑥**

```
example1
$ docker ps -a
CONTAINER ID   IMAGE           COMMAND        CREATED
➥ STATUS         PORTS                         NAMES
b9db5ada0461   todoapp:latest  "npm start"    8 minutes ago
➥ Up 10 seconds   0.0.0.0:8000->8000/tcp   example1
$ docker diff example1
C /todo
A /todo/.swarm
A /todo/.swarm/TodoItem
A /todo/.swarm/TodoItem/1t1Oc02+A~4UZcz
A /todo/.swarm/_log
A /todo/dist
A /todo/dist/LocalTodoApp.app.js
A /todo/dist/TodoApp.app.js
A /todo/dist/react.min.js
```

The /todo directory
⑦ has been changed.

The /todo/.swarm directory
⑧ has been added.

The docker run subcommand starts up the container **①**. The -p flag maps the container's port 8000 to the port 8000 on the host machine, so you should now be able to navigate with your browser to http://localhost:8000 to view the application. The --name flag gives the container a unique name you can refer to later for convenience. The last argument is the image name.

Once the container was started, we hit CTRL-C to terminate the process and the container **②**. You can run the ps command to see the containers that have been started but not removed **③**. Note that each container has its own container ID and status, analogous to a process. Its status is Exited, but you can restart it **④**. After you do, notice how the status has changed to Up and the port mapping from container to host machine is now displayed **⑤**.

The docker diff subcommand shows you which files have been affected since the image was instantiated as a container **⑥**. In this case, the todo directory has been changed **⑦** and the other listed files have been added **⑧**. No files have been deleted, which is the other possibility.

As you can see, the fact that Docker "contains" your environment means that you can treat it as an entity on which actions can be predictably performed. This gives Docker its breadth of power—you can affect the software lifecycle from development to production and maintenance. These changes are what this book will cover, showing you in practical terms what can be done with Docker.

Next you're going to learn about layering, another key concept in Docker.

1.2.5 *Docker layering*

Docker layering helps you manage a big problem that arises when you use containers at scale. Imagine what would happen if you started up hundreds—or even thousands—of the to-do app, and each of those required a copy of the files to be stored somewhere.

As you can imagine, disk space would run out pretty quickly! By default, Docker internally uses a copy-on-write mechanism to reduce the amount of disk space required

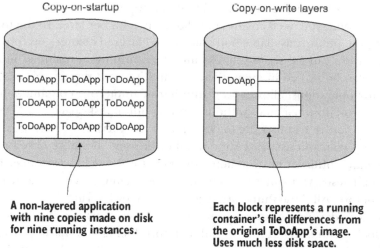

Copy-on-startup

Copy-on-write layers

A non-layered application with nine copies made on disk for nine running instances.

Each block represents a running container's file differences from the original ToDoApp's image. Uses much less disk space.

Figure 1.9 Copy-on-startup vs copy-on-write

(see figure 1.9). Whenever a running container needs to write to a file, it records the change by copying the item to a new area of disk. When a Docker commit is performed, this new area of disk is frozen and recorded as a layer with its own identifier.

This partly explains how Docker containers can start up so quickly—they have nothing to copy because all the data has already been stored as the image.

COPY-ON-WRITE Copy-on-write is a standard optimization strategy used in computing. When you create a new object (of any type) from a template, rather than copying the entire set of data required, you only copy data over when it's changed. Depending on the use case, this can save considerable resources.

Figure 1.10 illustrates that the to-do app you've built has three layers you're interested in.

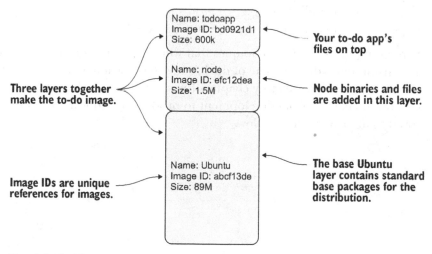

Three layers together make the to-do image.

Image IDs are unique references for images.

Name: todoapp
Image ID: bd0921d1
Size: 600k

Your to-do app's files on top

Name: node
Image ID: efc12dea
Size: 1.5M

Node binaries and files are added in this layer.

Name: Ubuntu
Image ID: abcf13de
Size: 89M

The base Ubuntu layer contains standard base packages for the distribution.

Figure 1.10 The to-do app's filesystem layering in Docker

Because the layers are static, you only need build on top of the image you wish to take as a reference, should you need anything to change in a higher layer. In the to-do app, you built from the publicly available node image and layered changes on top.

All three layers can be shared across multiple running containers, much as a shared library can be shared in memory across multiple running processes. This is a vital feature for operations, allowing the running of numerous containers based on different images on host machines without running out of disk space.

Imagine that you're running the to-do app as a live service for paying customers. You can scale up your offering to a large number of users. If you're developing, you can spin up many different environments on your local machine at once. If you're moving through tests, you can run many more tests simultaneously, and far more quickly than before. All these things are made possible by layering.

By building and running an application with Docker, you've begun to see the power that Docker can bring to your workflow. Reproducing and sharing specific environments and being able to land these in various places gives you both flexibility and control over development.

1.3   Summary

Depending on your previous experience with Docker, this chapter might have been a steep learning curve. We've covered a lot of ground in a short time.

You should now

- Understand what a Docker image is
- Know what Docker layering is, and why it's useful
- Be able to commit a new Docker image from a base image
- Know what a Dockerfile is

We've used this knowledge to

- Create a useful application
- Reproduce state in an application with minimal effort

Next we're going to introduce techniques that will help you understand how Docker works and, from there, discuss some of the broader technical debate around Docker's usage. These first two introductory chapters form the basis for the remainder of the book, which will take you from development to production, showing you how Docker can be used to improve your workflow.

Understanding Docker—inside the engine room

This chapter covers

- Docker's architecture
- Tracing the internals of Docker on your host
- Using the Docker Hub to find and download images
- Setting up your own Docker registry
- Getting containers to communicate with each other

Grasping Docker's architecture is key to understanding Docker more fully. In this chapter you'll get an overview of Docker's major components on your machine and on the network, and you'll learn some techniques that will develop this understanding.

In the process, you'll learn some nifty tricks that will help you use Docker (and Linux) more effectively. Many of the later and more advanced techniques will be based on what you see here, so pay special attention to what follows.

2.1   *Docker's architecture*

Figure 2.1 lays out Docker's architecture, and that will be the centrepiece of this chapter. We're going to start with a high-level look and then focus on each part with techniques designed to cement your understanding.

Docker on your host machine is (at the time of writing) split into two parts—a daemon with a RESTful API and a client that talks to the daemon. Figure 2.1 shows your host machine running the Docker client and daemon.

> **RESTFUL**   A RESTful API is one that uses standard HTTP request types such as GET, POST, DELETE, and others to perform functions that usually correspond to those intended by HTTP's designers.

You invoke the Docker client to get information from or give instructions to the daemon; the daemon is a server that receives requests and returns responses from the client using the HTTP protocol. In turn, it will make requests to other services to send and receive images, also using the HTTP protocol. The server will accept requests from the command-line client or anyone else authorized to connect. The daemon is

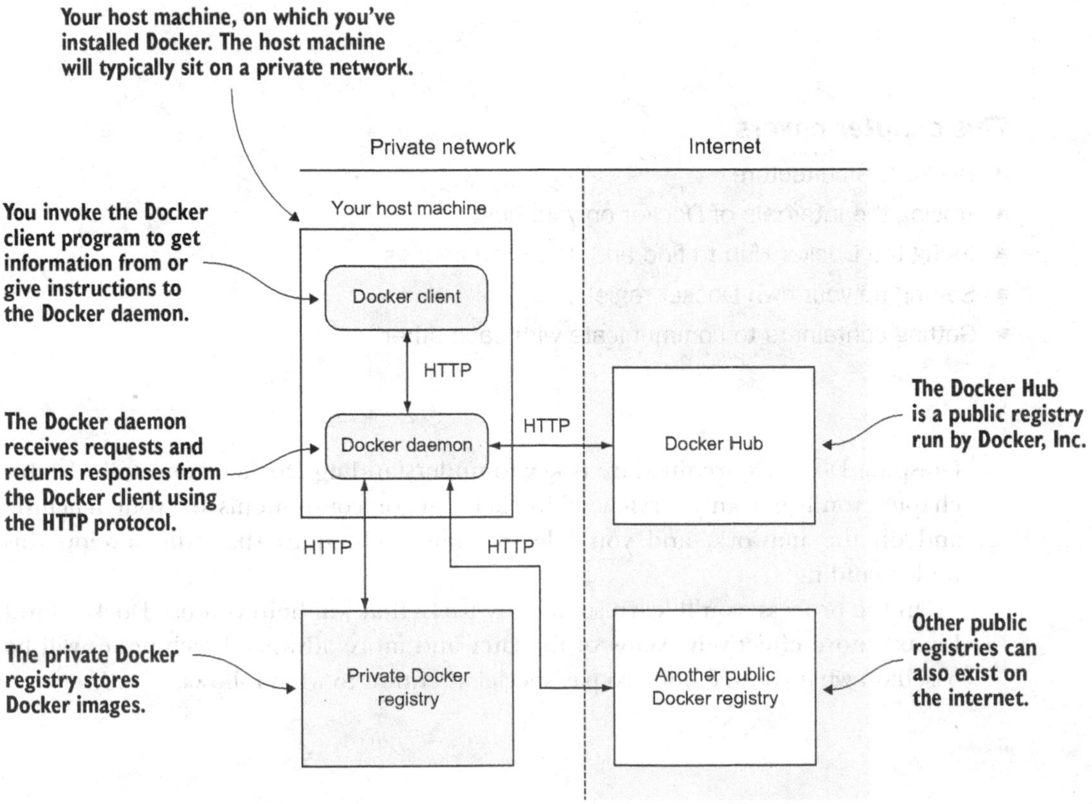

Figure 2.1   Overview of Docker architecture

also responsible for taking care of your images and containers behind the scenes, whereas the client acts as the intermediary between you and the RESTful API.

The private Docker registry is a service that stores Docker images. These can be requested from any Docker daemon that has the relevant access. This registry is on an internal network and isn't publicly accessible, so it's considered private.

Your host machine will typically sit on a private network. The Docker daemon will call out to the internet to retrieve images, if requested.

The Docker Hub is a public registry run by Docker, Inc. Other public registries can also exist on the internet, and your Docker daemon can interact with them.

In the first chapter we said that Docker containers can be shipped to anywhere you can run Docker—this isn't strictly true. In fact, only if the *daemon* can be installed on a machine will containers run on the machine. This is most obviously shown by the fact that the Docker client will run on Windows, but the daemon won't (yet).

The key point to take from this image is that when you run Docker on your machine, you may be interacting with other processes on your machine, or even services running on your network or the internet.

Now that you have a picture of how Docker is laid out, we'll introduce various techniques relating to the different parts of the figure.

2.2 The Docker daemon

The Docker daemon (see figure 2.2) is the hub of your interactions with Docker, and as such is the best place to start gaining an understanding of all the relevant pieces. It controls access to Docker on your machine, manages the state of your containers and images, and brokers interactions with the outside world.

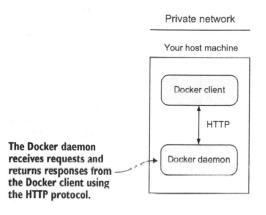

The Docker daemon receives requests and returns responses from the Docker client using the HTTP protocol.

Figure 2.2   The Docker daemon

> **DAEMONS AND SERVERS** A *daemon* is a process that runs in the background rather than under the direct control of the user. A *server* is a process that takes requests from a client and performs the actions required to fulfil the requests. Daemons are frequently also servers that accept requests from clients to perform actions for them. The docker command is a client, and the Docker daemon acts as the server doing the processing on your Docker containers and images.

Let's look at a couple of techniques that illustrate that Docker effectively runs as a daemon, and that your interactions with it using the docker command are limited to simple requests to perform actions, much like interactions with a web server. The first technique allows others to connect to your Docker daemon and perform the same actions you might on your host machine, and the second illustrates that Docker containers are managed by the daemon, not your shell session.

TECHNIQUE 1   **Open your Docker daemon to the world**

Although by default your Docker daemon is accessible only on your host, there can be good reason to allow others to access it. You might have a problem that you want someone to debug remotely, or you may want to allow another part of your DevOps workflow to kick off a process on a host machine.

> **INSECURE!**   Although this can be a powerful and useful technique, it's considered insecure. An open Docker daemon can be exploited by someone who stumbles on it and gets escalated privileges.

PROBLEM
You want to open your Docker server up for others to access.

SOLUTION
Start the Docker daemon with an open TCP address.

DISCUSSION
Figure 2.3 gives an overview of this technique's workings.

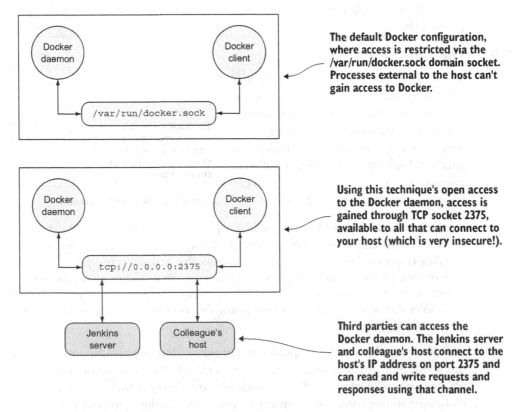

Figure 2.3   Docker accessibility: normal and opened up

Before you open up the Docker daemon, you must first shut the running one down. How you do this will vary depending on your operating system. If you're not sure how to do this, you can first try this command:

```
$ sudo service docker stop
```

If you get a message that looks like this,

```
The service command supports only basic LSB actions (start, stop, restart,
try-restart, reload, force-reload, status). For other actions, please try
to use systemctl.
```

then you have a systemctl-based startup system. Try this command:

```
$ systemctl stop docker
```

If this works, you shouldn't see any output from this command:

```
ps -ef | grep -E 'docker (-d|daemon)\b' | grep -v grep
```

Once the Docker dacmon has been stopped, you can restart it manually and open it up to outside users with the following command:

```
docker daemon -H tcp://0.0.0.0:2375
```

This command starts docker as a daemon (`docker daemon`), defines the host server with the -H flag, uses the TCP protocol, opens up to all IP addresses (with `0.0.0.0`), and opens on the standard Docker server port (`2375`). If Docker complains about daemon not being a valid subcommand, try using the older -d argument instead.

You can connect from outside with the following command:

```
$ docker -H tcp://<your host's ip>:2375
```

Note that you'll also need to do this from inside your local machine because Docker is no longer listening in the default location.

If you want to make this change permanent on your host, you'll need to configure your startup system. See appendix B for information on how to do this.

USE IP RESTRICTIONS   If you open your daemon up, be sure to open up to a specific IP range only, and not to `0.0.0.0`, which is highly insecure!

TECHNIQUE 2   **Running containers as daemons**

As you get familiar with Docker (and if you're anything like us), you'll start to think of other use cases for Docker, and one of the first of these is to run Docker containers as running services.

Running Docker containers as services with predictable behaviour through software isolation is one of the principal use cases for Docker. This technique will allow you to manage services in a way that works for your operation.

PROBLEM

You want to run a Docker container in the background as a service.

SOLUTION

Use the -d flag to the docker run command, and use related container-management flags to define the service characteristics.

DISCUSSION

Docker containers—like most processes—will run by default in the foreground. The most obvious way to run a Docker container in the background is to use the standard & control operator. Although this works, you can run into problems if you log out of your terminal session, necessitating that you use the nohup flag, which creates a file in your local directory with output that you have to manage… You get the idea: it's far neater to use the Docker daemon's functionality for this.

To do this, you use the -d flag.

```
$ docker run -d -i -p 1234:1234 --name daemon ubuntu nc -l 1234
```

The -d flag, when used with docker run, runs the container as a daemon. The -i flag gives this container the ability to interact with your Telnet session. With -p you publish the 1234 port from the container to the host. The --name flag lets you give the container a name so you can refer to it later. Finally, you run a simple listening echo server on port 1234 with netcat (nc).

If you now connect to it and send messages with Telnet, you can see that the container has received the message by using the docker logs command, as shown in the following listing.

> **Listing 2.1   Connecting to the container netcat server with Telnet**

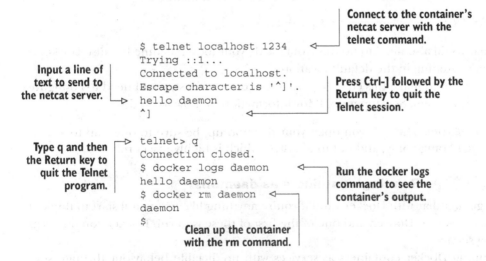

Connect to the container's netcat server with the telnet command.

```
$ telnet localhost 1234
Trying ::1...
Connected to localhost.
Escape character is '^]'.
hello daemon
^]
```

Input a line of text to send to the netcat server.

Press Ctrl-] followed by the Return key to quit the Telnet session.

Type q and then the Return key to quit the Telnet program.

```
telnet> q
Connection closed.
$ docker logs daemon
hello daemon
$ docker rm daemon
daemon
$
```

Run the docker logs command to see the container's output.

Clean up the container with the rm command.

You can see that running a container as a daemon is simple enough, but operationally some questions remain to be answered:

- What happens to the service if it fails?
- What happens to the service when it terminates?
- What happens if the service keeps failing over and over?

Fortunately Docker provides flags for each of these questions!

FLAGS NOT REQUIRED Although restart flags are used most often with the daemon flag (-d), technically it's not a requirement to run these flags with -d.

THE RESTART FLAG

The docker run --restart flag allows you to apply a set of rules to be followed (a
so-called "restart policy") when the container terminates (see table 2.1).

Table 2.1 Restart policies

Policy	Description
no	Do not restart when container exits
always	Always restart when container exits
on-failure[:max-retry]	Restart only on failure

The no policy is simple: when the container exits, it is not restarted. This is the default.

The always policy is also simple, but it's worth discussing briefly:

```
$ docker run -d --restart=always ubuntu echo done
```

This command runs the container as a daemon (-d) and always restarts the container
on termination (--restart=always). It issues a simple echo command that completes
quickly, exiting the container.

If you run the preceding command and then run a docker ps command, you'll see
output similar to this:

```
$ docker ps
CONTAINER ID        IMAGE           COMMAND         CREATED
  STATUS            PORTS                           NAMES
69828b118ec3        ubuntu:14.04    "echo done"       4 seconds ago
  Restarting  (0) Less than a second ago            sick_brattain
```

The docker ps command lists all the running containers and information about
them, including the following:

- When the container was created (CREATED).
- The current status of the container—usually this will be Restarting, as it will
  only run for a short time (STATUS).
- The exit code of the container's previous run (also under STATUS). 0 means the
  run was successful.
- The container name. By default Docker names containers by concatenating two
  random words. Sometimes this produces odd results!

Note that the STATUS column also informed us that the container exited less than a second ago and is restarting. This is because the echo done command exits immediately, and Docker must continually restart the container.

It's important to note that Docker reuses the container ID. It doesn't change on restart and there will only ever be one entry in the ps table for this Docker invocation.

Finally, the on-failure policy restarts only when the container returns a non-zero (which normally means failing) exit code from its main process:

```
$ docker run -d --restart=on-failure:10 ubuntu /bin/false
```

This command runs the container as a daemon (-d) and sets a limit on the number of restart attempts (--restart=on-failure:10), exiting if this is exceeded. It runs a simple command (/bin/false) that completes quickly and will definitely fail.

If you run the preceding command and wait a minute, and then run docker ps -a, you'll see output similar to this:

```
$ docker ps -a
CONTAINER ID          IMAGE              COMMAND           CREATED
➥ STATUS                       PORTS            NAMES
b0f40c410fe3          ubuntu:14.04       "/bin/false"      2 minutes ago
➥ Exited (1) 25 seconds ago                   loving_rosalind
```

TECHNIQUE 3   Moving Docker to a different partition

Docker stores all the data relating to your containers and images under a folder. As it can store a potentially large number of different images, this folder can get big fast!

If your host machine has different partitions (as is common in enterprise Linux workstations), you may encounter space limitations more quickly. In these cases, you may want to move the directory from which Docker operates.

PROBLEM

You want to move where Docker stores its data.

SOLUTION

Stop and start the Docker daemon, specifying the new location with the -g flag.

DISCUSSION

First you'll need to stop your Docker daemon (see appendix B for a discussion of this).

Imagine you want to run Docker from /home/dockeruser/mydocker. When you run

```
docker daemon -g /home/dockeruser/mydocker
```

a new set of folders and files will be created in this directory. These folders are internal to Docker, so play with them at your peril (as we've discovered!).

You should be aware that this will appear to wipe the containers and images from your previous Docker daemon. But don't despair. If you kill the Docker process you just ran and restart your Docker service, your Docker client will be pointed back at its original location and your containers and images will be returned to you.

If you want to make this move permanent, you'll need to configure your host system's startup process accordingly.

2.3 The Docker client

The Docker client (see figure 2.4) is the simplest component in the Docker architecture. It's what you run when you type commands like docker run or docker pull on your machine. Its job is to communicate with the Docker daemon via HTTP requests.

In this section you're going to see how you can snoop on messages between the Docker client and server. You'll also see a couple of basic techniques to do with port mapping that represent baby steps towards the orchestration section later in the book and a way of using your browser as a Docker client.

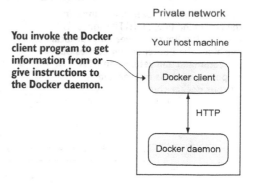

You invoke the Docker client program to get information from or give instructions to the Docker daemon.

Figure 2.4   The Docker client

TECHNIQUE 4	**Use socat to monitor Docker API traffic**

Occasionally the docker command may not work as you expect. Most often, some aspect of the command-line arguments hasn't been understood, but occasionally there are more serious setup problems, such as the Docker binary being out of date. In order to diagnose the problem, it can be useful to view the flow of data to and from the Docker daemon you are communicating with.

> **DOCKER IS NOT UNSTABLE** Don't panic! The presence of this technique doesn't indicate that Docker needs to be debugged often, or is in any way unstable! This technique is here as a tool for understanding Docker's architecture, and also to introduce you to socat, a powerful tool. If, like us, you use Docker in a lot of different locations, there will be differences in the Docker versions you use. As with any software, different versions will have different features and flags, which can catch you out.

PROBLEM

You want to debug a problem with a Docker command.

SOLUTION

Use a traffic snooper to inspect the API calls and craft your own.

DISCUSSION

In this technique you'll insert a proxy Unix domain socket between your request and the server's socket and see what passes through it (as shown in figure 2.5). Note that you'll need root or sudo privileges to make this work.

To create this proxy, you'll use socat.

> **SOCAT** socat is a powerful command that allows you to relay data between two data channels of almost any type. If you're familiar with netcat, you can think of it as netcat on steroids.

```
$ sudo socat -v UNIX-LISTEN:/tmp/dockerapi.sock \
  UNIX-CONNECT:/var/run/docker.sock &
```

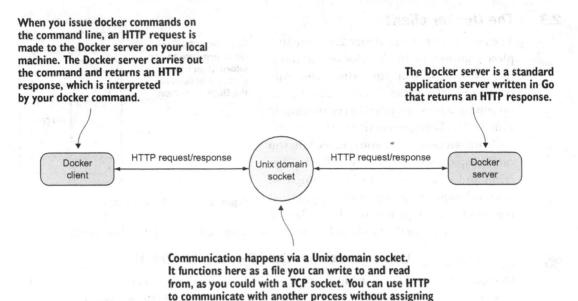

When you issue docker commands on the command line, an HTTP request is made to the Docker server on your local machine. The Docker server carries out the command and returns an HTTP response, which is interpreted by your docker command.

The Docker server is a standard application server written in Go that returns an HTTP response.

Communication happens via a Unix domain socket. It functions here as a file you can write to and read from, as you could with a TCP socket. You can use HTTP to communicate with another process without assigning a port, and use the filesystem directory structure.

Figure 2.5   Docker's client-server architecture on your host

In this command, -v makes the output readable, with indications of the flow of data. The UNIX-LISTEN part tells socat to listen on a Unix socket, and UNIX-CONNECT tells socat to connect to Docker's Unix socket. '&' specifies that the command runs in the background.

The new route that your requests to the daemon will travel can be seen in figure 2.6. All traffic traveling in each direction will be seen by socat and logged to your terminal, in addition to any output that the Docker client provides.

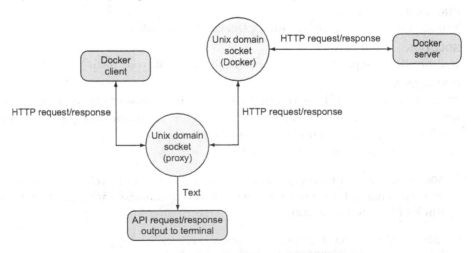

Figure 2.6   Docker client and server with socat inserted as a proxy

The output of a simple `docker` command will now look similar to this:

The command you issue to see the request and response

The HTTP request begins here, with the right angle bracket on the left.

```
$ docker -H unix:///tmp/dockerapi.sock ps -a                    ←
> 2015/01/12 04:34:38.790706  length=105 from=0 to=104          ←
GET /v1.16/containers/json?all=1 HTTP/1.1\r
Host: /tmp/dockerapi.sock\r
User-Agent: Docker-Client/1.4.1\r
\r
< 2015/01/12 04:34:38.792516  length=544 from=0 to=543          ←
HTTP/1.1 200 OK\r
Content-Type: application/json\r
Date: Mon, 12 Jan 2015 09:34:38 GMT\r
Content-Length: 435\r
\r
[{"Command":"/bin/bash","Created":1420731043,"Id":
  "4eec1b50dc6db7901d3b3c5a8d607f2576829fd6902c7f658735c3bc0a09a39c",
  "Image":"debian:jessie","Names":["/lonely_mclean"],"Ports":[],
  "Status":"Exited (0) 3 days ago"}                             ←
,{"Command":"/bin/bash","Created":1420729129,"Id":
  "029851aeccc887ecf9152de97f524d30659b3fa4b0dcc3c3fe09467cd0164da5",
  "Image":"debian:jessie","Names":["/suspicious_torvalds"],"Ports":[],
  "Status":"Exited (130) 3 days ago"}
]CONTAINER ID        IMAGE               COMMAND             CREATED
  STATUS                        PORTS               NAMES           ←
4eec1b50dc6d        debian:jessie       "/bin/bash"         3 days ago
  Exited (0) 3 days ago                             lonely_mclean
029851aeccc8        debian:jessie       "/bin/bash"         3 days ago
  Exited (130) 3 days ago                           suspicious_torvalds
```

The HTTP response begins here, with the left angle bracket on the left.

The JSON content of the response from the Docker server

The output as normally seen by the user, interpreted by the Docker client from the preceding JSON

BEWARE If you ran socat as root in the previous example, you'll need to use sudo to run the 'docker -H' command. This is because the dockerapi.sock file is owned by root.

Using socat is a powerful way to debug not only Docker, but any other network services you might come across in the course of your work.

TECHNIQUE 5   **Using ports to connect to containers**

Docker containers have been designed from the outset to run services. In the majority of cases, these will be HTTP services of one kind or another. A significant proportion of these will be web services accessible through the browser.

This leads to a problem. If you have multiple Docker containers running on port 80 in their internal environment, they can't all be accessible on port 80 on your host machine. The next technique shows how you can manage this common scenario by exposing and mapping a port from your container.

PROBLEM

You want to make multiple Docker container services available on a port from your host machine.

SOLUTION

Use Docker's -p flag to map a container's port to your host machine.

DISCUSSION

In this example we're going to use the tutum-wordpress image. Let's say you want to run two of these on your host machine to serve different blogs.

Because a number of people have wanted to do this before, someone has prepared an image that anyone can acquire and start up. To obtain images from external locations, you'll use the docker pull command. By default, images will be downloaded from the Docker Hub:

```
$ docker pull tutum/wordpress
```

To run the first blog, use the following command:

```
$ docker run -d -p 10001:80 --name blog1 tutum/wordpress
```

This docker run command runs the container as a daemon (-d) with the publish flag (-p). It identifies the host port (10001) to map to the container port (80) and gives the container a name to identify it (--name blog1 tutum/wordpress).

You'd do the same for the second blog:

```
$ docker run -d -p 10002:80 --name blog2 tutum/wordpress
```

If you now run this command,

```
$ docker ps -a | grep blog
```

you'll see the two blog containers listed, with their port mappings, looking something like this:

```
9afb95ad3617 tutum/wordpress:latest "/run.sh"
➡ 9 seconds ago Up 9 seconds
3306/tcp, 0.0.0.0:10001->80/tcp blog1 31ddc8a7a2fd tutum/wordpress:latest
➡ "/run.sh" 17 seconds ago Up 16 seconds 3306/tcp, 0.0.0.0:10002->80/tcp blog2
```

You'll now be able to access your containers by navigating to http://localhost:10001 and http://localhost:10002.

To remove the containers when you're finished (assuming you don't want to keep them), run this command:

```
$ docker rm -f blog1 blog2
```

You should now be able to run multiple identical images and services on your host by managing the port allocations yourself, if necessary.

REMEMBERING THE ORDER OF ARGUMENTS FOR THE -P FLAG   It can be easy to forget which port is the host's and which port is the container's when using the -p flag. We think of it as being like reading a sentence from left to right. The user connects to the host (-p) and that host port is passed to the container port (host_port:container_port). It's also the same format as SSH's port-forwarding commands, if you're familiar with them.

TECHNIQUE 6   **Linking containers for port isolation**

The last technique showed how to open up your containers to the host network by exposing ports. You won't always want to expose your services to the host machine or the outside world, but you will want to connect containers to one another.

This next technique shows how you can achieve this by using Docker's link flag, ensuring outsiders can't access your internal services.

PROBLEM

You want to allow communication between containers for internal purposes.

SOLUTION

Use Docker's linking functionality to allow the containers to communicate with each other.

DISCUSSION

Continuing in our quest to set up WordPress, we're going to separate the mysql database tier from the wordpress container, and link these to each other without port configuration. Figure 2.7 gives an overview of the final state.

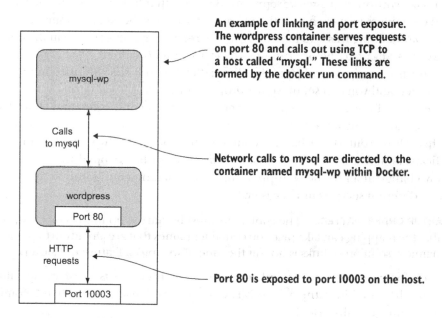

Figure 2.7   WordPress setup with linked containers

WHY IS THIS USEFUL?   Why bother with linking if you can already expose ports to the host and use that? Linking allows you to encapsulate and define the relationships between containers without exposing services to the host's network (and potentially, to the outside world). You might want to do this for security reasons, for example.

Run your containers like so, in the following order, pausing for about a minute between the first and second commands:

```
$ docker run --name wp-mysql \
  -e MYSQL_ROOT_PASSWORD=yoursecretpassword -d mysql    ❶
$ docker run --name wordpress \
  --link wp-mysql:mysql -p 10003:80 -d  wordpress       ❷
```

First you give the mysql container the name wp-mysql so you can refer to it later ❶. You also must supply an environment variable so the mysql container can initialize the database (-e MYSQL_ROOT_PASSWORD=yoursecretpassword). You run both containers as daemons (-d) and use the Docker Hub reference for the official mysql image.

In the second command ❷ you give the wordpress image the name wordpress, in case you want to refer to it later. You also link the wp-mysql container to the wordpress container (--link wp-mysql:mysql). References to a mysql server within the wordpress container will be sent to the container named wp-mysql. You also use a local port mapping (-p 10003:80), as discussed in technique 5, and add the Docker Hub reference for the official wordpress image (wordpress). Be aware that links won't wait for services in linked containers to start; hence the instruction to pause between commands. A more precise way of doing this is to look for mysqid: ready for connections in the output of docker logs wp-mysql before running the wordpress container.

If you now navigate to http://localhost:10003, you'll see the introductory wordpress screen and you can set up your wordpress instance.

The meat of this example is the --link flag in the second command. This flag sets up the container's host file so that the wordpress container can refer to a mysql server, and this will be routed to whatever container has the name "wp-mysql." This has the significant benefit that different mysql containers can be swapped in without requiring any change at all to the wordpress container, making configuration management of these different services much easier.

STARTUP ORDER MATTERS   The containers must be started up in the correct order so that the mapping can take place on container names that are already in existence. Dynamic resolution of links is not (at the time of writing) a feature of Docker.

In order for containers to be linked in this way, their ports must be specified as exposed when building the images. This is achieved using the EXPOSE command within the image build's Dockerfile.

You have now seen a simple example of Docker orchestration, and you've taken a step toward a microservices architecture. In this case, you could perform work on the mysql container while leaving the wordpress container untouched, or vice versa. This fine-grained control over running services is one of the key operational benefits of a microservices architecture.

Using Docker in your browser

It can be difficult to sell new technologies, so simple and effective demonstrations are invaluable. Making the demo hands-on is even better, which is why we've found that creating a web page with the ability to interact with a container in your browser is a great technique for giving newcomers their first taste of Docker in an easily accessible way. The significant "wow factor" doesn't hurt either!

PROBLEM

You want to be able to demonstrate the power of Docker without requiring users to install it themselves or run commands they don't understand.

SOLUTION

Start the Docker daemon with an open port and CORS enabled. Then serve the docker-terminal repository in your web server of choice.

DISCUSSION

The most common use of a REST API is to expose it on a server and use JavaScript on a web page to make calls to it. Because Docker happens to perform all interaction via a REST API, you should be able to control Docker in the same way. Although it may initially seem surprising, this control extends all the way to being able to interact with a container via a terminal in your browser.

We've already discussed how to start the daemon on port 2375 in technique 1, so we won't go into any detail on that. Additionally, CORS is too much to go into here if you're unfamiliar with it (you might want to refer to *CORS in Action* by Monsur Hossain [Manning Publications, 2014])—the short of it is that it's a mechanism that carefully bypasses the usual restriction of JavaScript that limits you to only accessing the current domain. In this case, it allows the daemon to listen on a different port from where you serve your Docker Terminal page. To enable it, you need to start the Docker daemon with the option `--api-enable-cors` alongside the option to make it listen on a port.

Now that the prerequisites are sorted, let's get this running. First, you need to get the code:

```
git clone https://github.com/aidanhs/Docker-Terminal.git
cd Docker-Terminal
```

Then you need to serve the files:

```
python2 -m SimpleHTTPServer 8000
```

The preceding command uses a module built into Python to serve static files from a directory. Feel free to use any equivalent you prefer.

Now you can visit http://localhost:8000 in your browser and start a container.

Figure 2.8 shows how the Docker terminal connects up. The page is hosted on your local computer and connects to the Docker daemon on your local computer to perform any operations.

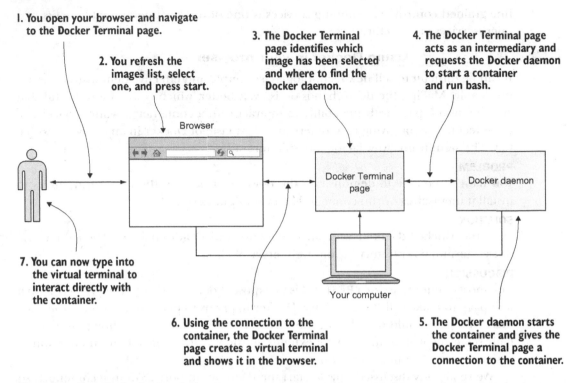

1. You open your browser and navigate to the Docker Terminal page.

2. You refresh the images list, select one, and press start.

3. The Docker Terminal page identifies which image has been selected and where to find the Docker daemon.

4. The Docker Terminal page acts as an intermediary and requests the Docker daemon to start a container and run bash.

Browser

Docker Terminal page

Docker daemon

7. You can now type into the virtual terminal to interact directly with the container.

Your computer

6. Using the connection to the container, the Docker Terminal page creates a virtual terminal and shows it in the browser.

5. The Docker daemon starts the container and gives the Docker Terminal page a connection to the container.

Figure 2.8 How the Docker terminal works

It's worth being aware of the following points if you want to give this link to other people:

- The other person must not be using a proxy of any kind. This is the most common source of errors we've seen—Docker terminal uses Websockets, which don't currently work through proxies.
- Giving a link to localhost obviously won't work—you'll need to give out the external IP address.
- Docker Terminal needs to know where to find the Docker API—it should do this automatically based on the address you're visiting in the browser, but it's something to be aware of.

WHY NOT USE DOCKER FOR THIS?   If you're more experienced with Docker, you might wonder why we haven't used Docker in this technique. The reason is that we're still introducing Docker and didn't want to add to the complexity for readers new to Docker. Dockerizing this technique is left as an exercise for the reader.

2.4 *Docker registries*

Once you've created your images, you may want to share them with other users. This is where the concept of the Docker registry comes in.

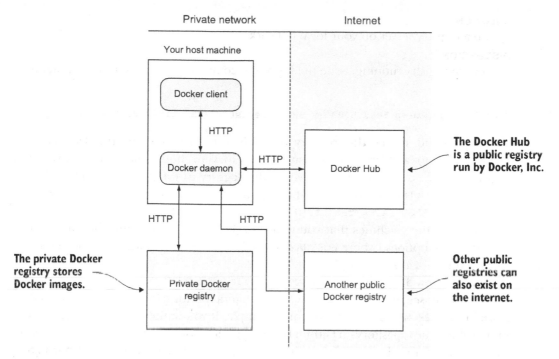

Figure 2.9   A Docker registry

The three registries in figure 2.9 differ in their accessibility. One is on a private network, one is open on a public network, and another is public but accessible only to those registered with Docker. They all perform the same function with the same API, and this is how the Docker daemon knows how to communicate with them interchangeably.

A Docker registry allows multiple users to push and pull images from a central store using a RESTful API.

The registry code is, like Docker itself, open source. Many companies (such as ours) set up private registries to store and share their proprietary images internally. This is what we'll discuss here before looking more closely at Docker Inc.'s registry.

TECHNIQUE 8   Setting up a local Docker registry

You've seen that Docker, Inc. has a service where people can share their images publicly (and you can pay if you want to do it privately). But there are a number of reasons you may want to share images without going via the Hub—some businesses like to keep as much in-house as possible, or maybe your images are large and transferring them over the internet will be too slow, or perhaps you want to keep your images private while you experiment and don't want to commit to paying. Whatever the reason, there is happily a simple solution.

PROBLEM

You want a way to host your images locally.

SOLUTION

Set up a registry server on your local network.

DISCUSSION

To get the registry running, issue the following command on a machine with plenty of disk space:

```
$ docker run -d -p 5000:5000 -v $HOME/registry:/var/lib/registry registry:2
```

This command makes the registry available on port 5000 of the Docker host (-p 5000:5000) and uses the registry folder in your home directory at /var/lib/registry in the container, which is where the registry in the container will store files by default. It also specifies that the registry in the container will store files at /registry (STORAGE_PATH=/registry).

On all of the machines that you want to access this registry, add the following to your daemon options (where HOSTNAME is the hostname or IP address of your new registry server): --insecure-registry HOSTNAME.

You can now docker push HOSTNAME:5000/image:tag.

As you can see, the most basic level of configuration for a local registry, with all data stored in the $HOME/registry directory, is simple. If you wanted to scale up or make it more robust, the repository on Github (https://github.com/docker/distribution/blob/v2.2.1/docs/storagedrivers.md) outlines some options, like storing data in Amazon S3.

You may be wondering about the --insecure-registry option. In order to help users remain secure, Docker will only allow you to pull from registries with a signed HTTPS certificate. We've overridden this because we're fairly comfortable trusting our local network. It goes without saying, though, that you should be much more cautious about doing this over the internet!

> **REGISTRY ROADMAP** As with a lot of things in the Docker ecosystem, the registry is undergoing some changes. Although the registry image will remain available and stable, it will eventually be replaced with a new tool called distribution (see https://github.com/docker/distribution).

2.5 *The Docker Hub*

The Docker Hub (see figure 2.10) is a registry maintained by Docker, Inc. It has tens of thousands of images on it ready to download and run. Any Docker user can set up a free account and public Docker images there. In addition to user-supplied images, there are official images maintained for reference purposes.

Your images are protected by user authentication, and there's a starring system for popularity, similar to Github's.

These official images can be representations of Linux distributions like Ubuntu or CentOS, or preinstalled software packages like Node.js, or whole software stacks like WordPress.

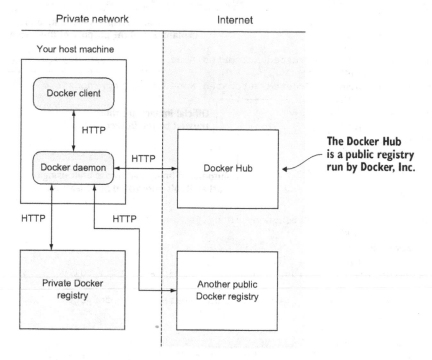

Figure 2.10   The Docker Hub

<hr/>

TECHNIQUE 9   **Finding and running a Docker image**

Docker registries enable a social coding culture similar to GitHub. If you're interested in trying out a new software application, or looking for a new one that serves a particular purpose, then Docker images can be an easy way to experiment without interfering with your host machine, provisioning a VM, or having to worry about installation steps.

PROBLEM

You want to find an application or tool as a Docker image and try it out.

SOLUTION

Use the docker search command to find the image to pull, and then run it.

DISCUSSION

Let's say you're interested in playing with Node.js. In the following code we searched for images matching "node" with the docker search command:

```
$ docker search node
NAME                            DESCRIPTION
⟹ STARS     OFFICIAL   AUTOMATED
node                                Node.js is a JavaScript-based platform for...
⟹ 432       [OK]
```

The output of docker search is ordered by the number of stars.

**The description is the uploader's
explanation of the purpose of the image.**

dockerfile/nodejs
➡ 57   [OK]   Trusted automated Node.js (http://nodejs.o...
dockerfile/nodejs-bower-grunt   Trusted automated Node.js (http://nodejs.o...
➡ 17   [OK]
nodesource/node   **Official images are those
➡ 9   [OK]   trusted by the Docker Hub.**
selenium/node-firefox
➡ 5   [OK]
selenium/node-chrome
➡ 5   [OK]   **Automated images are those built using
selenium/node-base   Docker Hub's automated build feature.**
➡ 3   [OK]
strongloop/node   StrongLoop, Node.js, and tools.
➡ 3   [OK]
selenium/node-chrome-debug
➡ 3   [OK]
dockerfile/nodejs-runtime   Trusted automated Node.js runtime Build ..
➡ 3   [OK]
jprjr/stackbrew-node   A stackbrew/ubuntu-based image for Docker,...
➡ 2   [OK]
selenium/node-firefox-debug
➡ 2   [OK]
maccam912/tahoe-node   Follow "The Easy Way" in the description t...
➡ 1   [OK]
homme/node-mapserv   The latest checkouts of Mapserver and its ...
➡ 1   [OK]
maxexcloo/nodejs   Docker framework container with Node.js an...
➡ 1   [OK]
brownman/node-0.10
➡ 0   [OK]
kivra/node   Image with build dependencies for frontend...
➡ 0   [OK]
thenativeweb/node
➡ 0   [OK]
thomaswelton/node
➡ 0   [OK]
siomiz/node-opencv   _/node + node-opencv
➡ 0   [OK]
bradegler/node
➡ 0   [OK]
tcnksm/centos-node   Dockerfile for CentOS packaging node
➡ 0   [OK]
azukiapp/node
➡ 0   [OK]
onesysadmin/node-imagetools
➡ 0   [OK]
fishead/node
➡ 0   [OK]

Once you've chosen an image, you can download it by performing a docker pull
command on the name:

```
$ docker pull node
node:latest: The image you are pulling has been verified
81c86d8c1e0c: Downloading
81c86d8c1e0c: Pull complete
3a20d8faf171: Pull complete
c7a7a01d634e: Pull complete
2a13c2a76de1: Pull complete
4cc808131c54: Pull complete
bf2afba3f5e4: Pull complete
0cba665db8d0: Pull complete
322af6f234b2: Pull complete
9787c55efe92: Pull complete
511136ea3c5a: Already exists
bce696e097dc: Already exists
58052b122b60: Already exists
Status: Downloaded newer image for node:latest
```

Pull the image named node from the Docker Hub.

This message is seen if Docker has pulled a new image (as opposed to identifying that there's no newer image than the one you already have). Your output may be different.

Then you can run it interactively using the -t and -i flags. The -t flag creates a tty device (a terminal) for you, and the -i flag specifies that this Docker session is interactive:

```
$ docker run -t -i node /bin/bash
root@c267ae999646:/# node
> process.version
'v0.12.0'
>
```

> **THE -TI FLAG IDIOM** You can save keystrokes by replacing -t -i with -ti in the preceding call to docker run. You'll see this throughout the book from here on.

Often there will be specific advice from the image maintainers about how the image should be run. Searching for the image on the http://hub.docker.com website will take you to the page for the image. The Description tab may give you more information.

> **DO YOU TRUST THE IMAGE?** If you download an image and run it, you are running code that you may not be able to fully verify. Although there is relative safety in using trusted images, nothing can guarantee 100% security when downloading and running software over the internet.

Armed with this knowledge and experience, you can now tap the enormous resources available on the Docker Hub. With literally tens of thousands of images to try out, there is much to learn. Enjoy!

2.6 Summary

In this chapter you've learned how Docker hangs together, and you've used this understanding to manipulate the various components.

These were the principal areas covered:

- Opening up your Docker daemon to outsiders over TCP or a web browser
- Running containers as service daemons
- Linking containers together via the Docker daemon
- Snooping the Docker daemon API
- Setting up your own registry
- Using the Docker Hub to find and download images

These first two chapters have covered the basics (though hopefully you've learned something new, even if you're familiar with Docker). We'll now move on to part 2, where we'll look at the role of Docker in the world of software development.

Part 2

Docker and development

In part 1, you learned Docker's core concepts and architecture by example. Part 2 will take from you from this base to demonstrate ways Docker can be used in development.

Chapter 3 covers using Docker as a lightweight virtual machine. This is a controversial area. While there are critical differences between virtual machines and Docker containers, development can be sped up considerably in many cases by using Docker. It is also an effective means of getting familiar with Docker before we move into more advanced Docker usage. Chapter 4 explains over twenty techniques to make day-to-day development with Docker more effective and efficient. In addition to building and running containers, you'll learn about persisting data with volumes and keeping your Docker host in order. Chapter 5 covers the important area of configuration management. You'll use Dockerfiles and traditional configuration management tools to get control of your Docker builds. We also cover the creation and curation of minimal Docker images to reduce image bloat. By the end of this part you'll have a wealth of useful techniques for single-use Docker and be ready to take Docker into a DevOps context.

Using Docker as a
lightweight virtual machine

This chapter covers

- Converting a virtual machine to a Docker image
- Managing the startup of your container's services
- Saving your work as you go
- Managing Docker images on your machine
- Sharing images on the Docker Hub
- Playing—and winning—at 2048 with Docker

Virtual machines (VMs) have become ubiquitous in software development and deployment since the turn of the century. The abstraction of machines to software has made the movement and control of software and services in the internet age easier and cheaper.

VIRTUAL MACHINES A virtual machine is an application that emulates a computer, usually to run an operating system and applications. It can be placed on any (compatible) physical resources that are available. The end user experiences the software as though it were on a physical machine, but those managing the hardware can focus on larger-scale resource allocation.

Docker isn't a VM technology. It doesn't simulate a machine's hardware and it doesn't include an operating system. A Docker container is not by default constrained to specific hardware limits. If Docker virtualizes anything, it virtualizes the environment in which services run, not the machine. Moreover, Docker can't easily run Windows software (or even that written for other UNIX-derived operating systems).

From some standpoints, though, Docker can be used much as a VM. For developers and testers in the internet age, the fact that there's no init process or direct hardware interaction is not usually of great significance. And there are significant commonalities, such as its isolation from the surrounding hardware and its amenability to more fine-grained approaches to software delivery.

This chapter will take you through the scenarios in which you could use Docker as you might previously have used a VM. Using Docker will not give you any obvious functional advantages over a VM, but the speed and convenience Docker brings to the movement and tracking of environments can be a game-changer for your development pipeline.

3.1 *From VM to container*

In an ideal world, moving from VMs to containers would be a simple matter of running your configuration management scripts against a Docker image from a distribution similar to the VM's. For those of us who are not in that happy state of affairs, this section shows how you can convert a VM to a container.

TECHNIQUE 10 Converting your VM to a container

The Docker Hub doesn't have all possible base images, so for some niche Linux distributions and use cases, people need to create their own. The same principle applies if you have an existing state in a VM you want to put inside Docker to iterate on top of or to benefit from the Docker ecosystem.

Ideally you'd want to build an equivalent of your VM from scratch using standard Docker techniques, such as Dockerfiles combined with standard configuration management tools (see chapter 5). The reality, though, is that many VMs are not carefully configuration-managed. This might happen because a VM has grown organically as people have used it, and the investment needed to recreate it in a more structured way isn't worth it.

PROBLEM
You have a VM you want to convert to a Docker image.

SOLUTION
Create a TAR file of your VM filesystem, using either `qemu-nbd`, `tar` over `ssh`, or another method, and use the `ADD` command in a Dockerfile on your TAR to create your image.

DISCUSSION
First we're going to divide VMs into two broad groups: local (VM disk image lives on and VM execution happens on your computer) and remote (VM disk image storage and VM execution happen somewhere else).

The principle for both groups of VMs (and anything else you want to create a Docker image from) is the same—you get a TAR of the filesystem and ADD the TAR file to / of the scratch image.

THE ADD COMMAND   The ADD Dockerfile command (unlike its sibling command COPY) unpacks TAR files (as well as gzipped files and other similar file types) when placed in an image like this.

THE SCRATCH IMAGE   The *scratch* image is a zero-byte pseudo-image you can build on top of. Typically it's used in cases like this where you want to copy (or add) a complete filesystem using a Dockerfile.

We'll now look at a case where you have a local Virtualbox VM.

Before we get started, you need to do the following:

- Install the qemu-nbd tool (available as part of the qemu-utils package on Ubuntu).
- Identify the path to your VM disk image.
- Shut down your VM.

If your VM disk image is in the .vdi or .vmdk format, this technique should work well. Other formats may experience mixed success.

The following code demonstrates how to turn your VM file into a virtual disk, which allows you to then copy all the files from it:

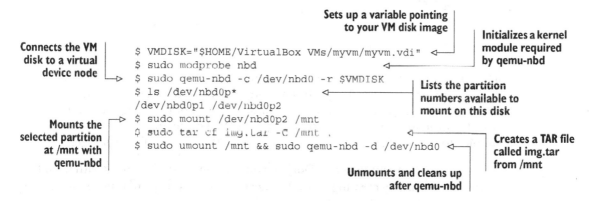

CHOOSING A PARTITION   To choose which partition to mount, run sudo cfdisk /dev/nbd0 to see what's available. Note that if you see LVM anywhere, your disk has a non-trivial partitioning scheme and you'll need to do some additional research into how to mount LVM partitions.

If your VM is kept remotely, you have a choice: either shut down the VM and ask your operations team to perform a dump of the partition you want, or create a TAR of your VM while it's still running.

If you get a partition dump, you can mount this fairly easily and then turn it into a TAR file as follows:

```
$ sudo mount -o loop partition.dump /mnt
$ sudo tar cf $(pwd)/img.tar -C /mnt .
$ sudo umount /mnt
```

Alternatively, you can create a TAR file from a running system. This is quite simple after logging into the system:

```
$ cd /
$ sudo tar cf /img.tar --exclude=/img.tar --one-file-system /
```

You now have a TAR of the filesystem image that you can transfer to a different machine with scp.

> **RISK OF STATE CORRUPTION!**   Creating a TAR from a running system may seem like the easiest option (no shutdowns, installing software, or making requests to other teams) but it has a severe downside—you could copy a file in an inconsistent state and hit strange problems when trying to use your new Docker image. If you must go this route, stop as many applications and services as possible.

Once you've got the TAR of your filesystem, you can add it to your image. This is the easiest step of the process and consists of a two-line Dockerfile:

```
FROM scratch
ADD img.tar /
```

You can now run docker build . and you have your image!

> **IMPORT FROM TAR**   Docker provides an alternative to ADD in the form of the docker import command, which you can use with cat img.tar | docker import - new_image_name. However, building on top of the image with additional instructions will require you to create a Dockerfile anyway, so it may be simpler to go the ADD route so you can easily see the history of your image.

Because you now have an image in Docker, you can start experimenting with it. In this case, you might start by creating a new Dockerfile based on your new image to experiment with stripping out files and packages.

Once you've done this and are happy with your results, you can use docker export on a running container to export a new, slimmer TAR that you can use as the basis for a newer image, and repeat the process until you get an image you're happy with.

The flowchart in figure 3.1 demonstrates this process.

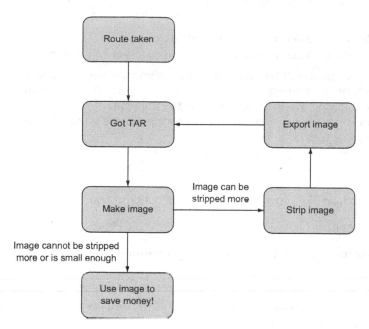

Figure 3.1 The container-slimming process

A host-like container

We'll now move on to one of the more contentious areas of discussion within the Docker community—running a host-like image, with multiple processes running from the get-go.

This is considered bad form in parts of the Docker community. Containers are not virtual machines—there are significant differences—and pretending there aren't can cause confusion and issues down the line.

For good or ill, this technique will show you how to run a host-like image and discuss some of the issues around doing this.

A GRADUAL ONBOARDING Running a host-like image can be a good way to persuade Docker refuseniks that Docker is useful. As they use it more, they'll understand the paradigm better and the microservices approach will make more sense to them. At the company we introduced Docker into, we found that this monolithic approach was a great way to move people from developing on dev servers and laptops to a more contained and manageable environment. From there, moving Docker into testing, continuous integration, escrow, and devOps workflows was trivial.

Differences between VMs and Docker containers

These are a few of the differences between VMs and Docker containers:

- Docker is application-oriented, whereas VMs are operating-system-oriented.
- Docker containers share an operating system with other Docker containers. In contrast, VMs each have their own operating system managed by a hypervisor.
- Docker containers are designed to run one principal process, not manage multiple sets of processes.

PROBLEM

You want a normal host-like environment for your container with multiple processes and services set up.

SOLUTION

Use an image designed to simulate a host, and provision it with the applications you need.

DISCUSSION

For this discussion we're going to use the phusion/baseimage Docker image, an image designed to run multiple processes.

The first steps are to start the image and jump into it with docker exec:

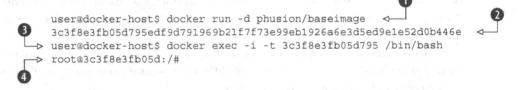

```
user@docker-host$ docker run -d phusion/baseimage        <-- 1
3c3f8e3fb05d795edf9d791969b21f7f73e99eb1926a6e3d5ed9e1e52d0b446e  <-- 2
user@docker-host$ docker exec -i -t 3c3f8e3fb05d795 /bin/bash   -- 3
root@3c3f8e3fb05d:/#                                       -- 4
```

In this code, docker run will start the image in the background ❶, starting the default command for the image and returning the ID of the newly created container ❷.

You then pass this container ID to docker exec ❸, which is a command that starts a new process inside an already running container. The -i flag allows you to interact with the new process, and -t indicates that you want to set up a TTY to allow you to start a terminal (/bin/bash) inside the container ❹.

If you wait a minute and then look at the processes table, your output will look something like the following.

Listing 3.1 Processes running in a host-like container

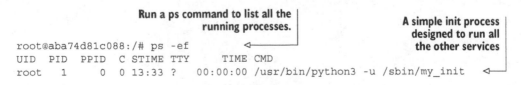

Run a ps command to list all the running processes.

A simple init process designed to run all the other services

```
root@aba74d81c088:/# ps -ef      <--
UID  PID  PPID  C STIME TTY      TIME CMD
root   1    0   0 13:33 ?     00:00:00 /usr/bin/python3 -u /sbin/my_init   <--
```

The bash process started by docker exec and acting as the shell | runsvdir runs the services defined in the passed-in /etc/service directory.

```
root     7     0  0 13:33 ?   00:00:00 /bin/bash  ◄─┘
root   111     1  0 13:33 ?   00:00:00 /usr/bin/runsvdir -P /etc/service   ◄─┘
root   112   111  0 13:33 ?   00:00:00 runsv cron  ◄─────────
root   113   111  0 13:33 ?   00:00:00 runsv sshd
root   114   111  0 13:33 ?   00:00:00 runsv syslog-ng
root   115   112  0 13:33 ?   00:00:00 /usr/sbin/cron -f
root   116   114  0 13:33 ?   00:00:00 syslog-ng -F -p
  ➡ /var/run/syslog-ng.pid --no-caps
root   117   113  0 13:33 ?   00:00:00 /usr/sbin/sshd -D
root   125     7  0 13:38 ?   00:00:00 ps -ef   ◄───────
```

The three standard services (cron, sshd, and syslog) are started here with the runsv command.

The ps command currently being run

You can see that the container starts up much like a host, initializing services such as cron and sshd that make it appear similar to a standard Linux host. This can be useful for initial demos for engineers new to Docker.

Whether this constitutes a violation of the microservices principle of "one service per container" is a matter of debate within the Docker community. Proponents of the host-like image approach argue that this doesn't violate that principle, as the container can still fulfil a single discrete function for the system within which it runs.

TECHNIQUE 12 Splitting a system into microservice containers

We've explored how to use a container as a monolithic entity (like a classical server) and explained that it can be a great way to quickly move a system architecture onto Docker. In the Docker world, however, it's generally considered best practice to split up your system as much as possible until you have one "service" running per container, and have all containers connected by links. Because this is the recommended Docker way, you'll find that most of the containers you get from the Docker Hub follow this approach, and understanding how to build images in this way is important for interacting with the rest of the Docker ecosystem.

The primary reason for using one service per container is easier separation of concerns through the single-responsibility principle. If you have one container doing one job, then it's easier to put that container through the software development lifecycle of dev, test, and production while worrying less about its interactions with other components. This makes for more agile deliveries and more scalable software projects. It does create management overhead, though, so it's good to consider whether it's worth it for your use case.

Putting aside the discussion of which approach is better for you right now, the best-practice approach has one clear advantage—experimentation and rebuilds are much faster when using Dockerfiles, as you'll see.

PROBLEM

You want to break your application up into distinct and more manageable services.

SOLUTION

Use Docker to break your application stack up into container-based services.

DISCUSSION

Within the Docker community, there's some debate about how strictly the "service per container" rule should be followed, with part of this stemming from a disagreement over the definitions—is it a single process, or a collection of processes that combine to fulfil a need? It often boils down to a statement that given the ability to redesign a system from scratch, microservices is the route most would chose. But sometimes practicality beats idealism—when evaluating Docker for our organization, we found ourselves in the position of having to go the monolithic route in order get Docker working as quickly and easily as possible.

Let's take a look at one of the concrete disadvantages of using monoliths inside Docker. First we need to show how you'd build a monolith with a database, application, and web server, as shown in the next listing.

> **SIMPLIFIED DOCKERFILES** These examples are for elucidation purposes and have been simplified accordingly. Trying to run them directly won't necessarily work.

Listing 3.2   Setting up a simple PostgreSQL, NodeJS, and Nginx application

```
FROM ubuntu:14.04
RUN apt-get update && apt-get install postgresql nodejs npm nginx
WORKDIR /opt
COPY . /opt/                                  # {*}
RUN service postgresql start && \
    cat db/schema.sql | psql && \
    service postgresql stop
RUN cd app && npm install
RUN cp conf/mysite /etc/nginx/sites-available/ && \
    cd /etc/nginx/sites-enabled && \
    ln -s ../sites-available/mysite
```

> **WHEN TO USE COMMAND CHAINING IN YOUR RUN STATEMENTS** Using && in your RUN statements effectively ensures that several commands get run as one command. This is useful because it can keep your images small. Each Dockerfile command creates a single new layer on top of the previous one. If you run a package update command like `apt-get update` with an install command in this way, you ensure that whenever the packages are installed they'll be from an updated package cache.

The preceding example is a conceptually simple Dockerfile that installs everything we need inside the container and then sets up the database, application, and web server. Unfortunately, there's a problem if you want to quickly rebuild your container—any change to any file under your repository will rebuild everything starting from the {*} onwards because the cache can't be reused. If you have some slow steps (database creation or `npm install`), you could be waiting for a while for the container to rebuild.

The solution to this is to split up the COPY . /opt/ instruction into the individual aspects of the application (database, app, and web setup):

```
FROM ubuntu:14.04
RUN apt-get update && apt-get install postgresql nodejs npm nginx
WORKDIR /opt
COPY db /opt/db                                      -+
RUN service postgresql start && \                    |-    <----- db setup
    cat db/schema.sql | psql && \                    |
    service postgresql stop                          -+
COPY app /opt/app                                    -+
RUN cd app && npm install                            |-    <----- app setup
RUN cd app && ./minify_static.sh                     -+
COPY conf /opt/conf                                  -+
RUN cp conf/mysite /etc/nginx/sites-available/ && \  +
    cd /etc/nginx/sites-enabled && \                 |-    <----- web setup
    ln -s ../sites-available/mysite                  -+
```

In the preceding code, the COPY command is split into two separate instructions. This means the database won't be rebuilt every time code changes, as the cache can be reused for the unchanged files delivered before the code.

Unfortunately, because the caching functionality is fairly simple, the container still has to be completely rebuilt every time a change is made to the schema scripts—the only way to resolve this is to move away from sequential setup steps and create multiple Dockerfiles, as shown in the following three listings.

Listing 3.3 Database Dockerfile

```
FROM ubuntu:14.04
RUN apt-get update && apt-get install postgresql
WORKDIR /opt
COPY db /opt/db
RUN service postgresql start && \
    cat db/schema.sql | psql && \
    service postgresql stop
```

Listing 3.4 App Dockerfile

```
FROM ubuntu:14.04
RUN apt-get update && apt-get install nodejs npm
WORKDIR /opt
COPY app /opt/app
RUN cd app && npm install
RUN cd app && ./minify_static.sh
```

Listing 3.5 Web server Dockerfile

```
FROM ubuntu:14.04
RUN apt-get update && apt-get install nginx
WORKDIR /opt
COPY conf /opt/conf
```

```
RUN cp conf/mysite /etc/nginx/sites-available/ && \
    cd /etc/nginx/sites-enabled && \
    ln -s ../sites-available/mysite
```

Whenever one of the db, app, or conf folders changes, only one container will need to be rebuilt. This is particularly useful when you have many more than three containers or there are time-intensive setup steps—with some care you can add the bare minimum of files necessary for each step and get more useful Dockerfile caching as a result. In the app Dockerfile (listing 3.4) the operation of npm install is defined by a single file, package.json, so we can alter our Dockerfile to take advantage of dockerfile layer caching and only rebuild the slow npm install step when necessary, as follows.

> **Listing 3.6 Reordered Dockerfile to perform npm install earlier**

```
FROM ubuntu:14.04
RUN apt-get update && apt-get install nodejs npm
WORKDIR /opt
COPY app/package.json /opt/app/package.json
RUN cd app && npm install
COPY app /opt/app
RUN cd app && ./minify_static.sh
```

Unfortunately, there's no such thing as a free lunch—you've traded a single simple Dockerfile for multiple Dockerfiles with duplication. You can address this partially by adding another Dockerfile to act as your base image, but some duplication is not uncommon. Additionally, there is now some complexity in starting your image—in addition to EXPOSE steps making appropriate ports available for linking, and altering of Postgres configuration, you need to be sure to link the containers every time they start up. Fortunately there's tooling for this called *docker-compose* (formerly *fig*), which we'll cover in technique 68.

3.2 *Managing services on your containers*

As is made clear throughout the Docker literature, a Docker container is not a VM. One of the key differences between a Docker container and a VM is that a container is designed to run one process. When that process finishes, the container exits. This is different from a Linux VM (or any Linux OS) in that it doesn't have an init process.

The init process runs on a Linux OS with a process ID of 1 and a parent process ID of 0. This init process might be called "init" or "systemd". Whatever it's called, its job is to manage the housekeeping for all other processes running on that operating system.

If you start to experiment with Docker, you may find that you want to start multiple processes. You might want to run cron jobs to tidy up your local application log files, for example, or set up an internal memcached server within the container. If you take this path, you may end up writing shell scripts to manage the startup of these subprocesses. In effect, you'll be emulating the work of the init process. Don't do that! The many problems arising from process management have been encountered by others before and have been solved in prepackaged systems.

TECHNIQUE 13 Managing the startup of your container's services

Running multiple services inside your container may be a convenience when trying out Docker as a VM replacement, or it may be a necessity for running vital services after the initial conversion of a VM to a container.

Whatever your reason, it's important to avoid reinventing the wheel when trying to manage processes inside a container.

PROBLEM

You want to manage multiple processes within a container.

SOLUTION

Use the Supervisor application (http://supervisord.org/) to manage process startup for you.

DISCUSSION

We're going to show you how to provision a container with Tomcat and an Apache web server, and have it start up and run in a managed way with Supervisor.

First, create your Dockerfile in a new and empty directory, as the next listing shows.

Listing 3.7 Example Supervisor Dockerfile

Installs python-pip (to install Supervisor), apache2, and tomcat7 →

Starts from ubuntu:14.04 →

Sets an environment variable to indicate this session is non-interactive →

```
FROM ubuntu:14.04
RUN apt-get update && apt-get install -y python-pip apache2 tomcat7
ENV DEBIAN_FRONTEND noninteractive
RUN pip install supervisor
RUN mkdir -p /var/lock/apache2
RUN mkdir -p /var/run/apache2
RUN mkdir -p /var/log/tomcat
RUN echo_supervisord_conf > /etc/supervisord.conf
ADD ./supervisord_add.conf /tmp/supervisord_add.conf
RUN cat /tmp/supervisord_add.conf >> /etc/
   supervisord.conf
RUN rm /tmp/supervisord_add.conf
CMD ["supervisord","-c","/etc/supervisord.conf"]
```

Installs Supervisor with pip →

Creates housekeeping directories needed to run the applications

Creates a default supervisord configuration file with the echo_supervisord_conf utility →

Copies the Apache and Tomcat supervisord configuration settings into the image, ready to add to the default configuration →

Appends the Apache and Tomcat supervisord configuration settings to the supervisord configuration file

You only need to run Supervisor now on container startup.

Removes the file you uploaded, as it's no longer needed

You'll also need configuration for Supervisor to instruct it what applications it needs to start up, as shown in the next listing.

Listing 3.8 supervisord_add.conf

Declares the global configuration section for supervisord →

```
[supervisord]
nodaemon=true
```

← Doesn't daemonize the Supervisor process, as it's the foreground process for the container.

Section declaration for a new program

Commands to start up the programs declared in the section

Configuration pertaining to logging

```
# apache
[program:apache2]
command=/bin/bash -c "source /etc/apache2/envvars &&
   exec /usr/sbin/apache2 -DFOREGROUND"

# tomcat
[program:tomcat]
command=service start tomcat
redirect_stderr=true
stdout_logfile=/var/log/tomcat/supervisor.log
stderr_logfile=/var/log/tomcat/supervisor.error_log
```

Building your image uses the standard single-command Docker process, as you're using a Dockerfile:

```
docker build -t supervised .
```

You can now run your image!

Maps the container's port 80 to the host's port 9000, gives the container a name, and specifies the image name you're running, as tagged with the build command previously

Starts up the Supervisor process

Starts up the managed processes

```
$ docker run -p 9000:80 --name supervised supervised
2015-02-
      06 10:42:20,336 CRIT Supervisor running as root (no user in config file)
2015-02-06 10:42:20,344 INFO RPC interface 'supervisor' initialized
2015-02-06 10:42:20,344 CRIT Server 'unix_http_server' running
   without any HTTP authentication checking
2015-02-06 10:42:20,344 INFO supervisord started with pid 1
2015-02-06 10:42:21,346 INFO spawned: 'tomcat' with pid 12
2015-02-06 10:42:21,348 INFO spawned: 'apache2' with pid 13
2015-02-06 10:42:21,368 INFO reaped unknown pid 29
2015-02-06 10:42:21,403 INFO reaped unknown pid 30
2015-02-06 10:42:22,404 INFO success: tomcat entered RUNNING state,
   process has stayed up for > than 1 seconds (startsecs)
2015-02-06 10:42:22,404 INFO success: apache2 entered RUNNING state,
   process has stayed up for > than 1 seconds (startsecs)
```

Managed processes have been deemed by Supervisor to have successfully started

If you navigate to http://localhost:9000, you should see the default page of the Apache server you started up.

To clean up the container, run the following command:

```
docker rm -f supervised
```

If you're interested in alternatives to Supervisor, there is also runit, used by the Phusion baseimage covered in technique 11.

3.3   Saving and restoring your work

Some people say that code isn't written until it's committed to source control—it doesn't always hurt to have the same attitude about containers. It's possible to save state with VMs by using snapshots, but Docker takes a much more active approach in encouraging the saving and reusing of your existing work.

We'll cover the "save game" approach to development, the niceties of tagging, using the Docker Hub, and referring to specific images in your builds. Because these operations are considered so fundamental, Docker makes them relatively simple and quick.

Nonetheless, this can still be a confusing topic for Docker newbies, so in this section we'll take you through the steps to a fuller understanding of this subject.

<hr>

TECHNIQUE 14   **The "save game" approach to development**

<hr>

If you've ever developed any kind of software, you've likely exclaimed, "I'm sure it was working before!" at least once. Perhaps your language was not as sober as this. The inability to restore a system to a known good (or maybe only "better") state as you're hurriedly hacking away at code to hit a deadline or fix a bug is the cause of many broken keyboards.

Source control has helped significantly with this, but there are two problems in this particular case:

- The source may not reflect the state of your "working" environment's filesystem.
- You may not be willing to commit the code yet.

The first problem is more significant than the second. Although modern source control tools like Git can easily create local throwaway branches, capturing the state of your entire development filesystem is not the purpose of source control.

Docker provides a cheap and quick way to store the state of your container's development filesystem through its commit functionality, and that's what we're going to explore here.

PROBLEM
You want to save the state of your development environment.

SOLUTION
Use docker commit to save state.

DISCUSSION
Let's imagine you want to make a change to your to-do application from chapter 1. The CEO of ToDoCorp is not happy and wants the title of the browser to show "ToDoCorp's ToDo App" instead of "Swarm+React - TodoMVC."

You're not sure how to achieve this, so you probably want fire up your application and experiment by changing files to see what happens:

```
$ docker run -d -p 8000:8000 --name todobug1 dockerinpractice/todoapp     <--- ❶
3c3d5d3ffd70d17e7e47e90801af7d12d6fc0b8b14a8b33131fc708423ee4372
$ docker exec -i -t todobug1 /bin/bash     <------ ❷
```

The docker run command ❶ starts the to-do application in a container in the background (-d), maps the container's port 8000 to port 8000 on the host (-p 8000:8000), names it todobug1 (--name todobug1) for easy reference, and returns the container ID. The command started in the container will be the default command specified at build time of the dockerinpractice/todoapp image, which we have built for you and made available on the Docker Hub.

The second command ❷ will start /bin/bash in the running container. The name todobug1 is used, but you can also use the container ID. -i makes this exec run interactive, and -t makes sure that the exec will work as a terminal would.

Now you're in the container, so the first step in experimenting is to install an editor. We prefer vim, so we used these commands:

```
apt-get update
apt-get install vim
```

After a little effort you realize that the file you need to change is local.html. You therefore change line 5 as follows:

```
<title>ToDoCorp's ToDo App</title>
```

Then word comes through that the CEO might want the title to be in lowercase, as she's heard that it looks more modern. You want to be ready either way, so you commit what you have at the moment. In another terminal you run the following command:

Turn the container
you created earlier
into an image.

The new
image ID of the
container you've
committed

```
$ docker commit todobug1          ⟵
ca76b45144f2cb31fda6a31e55f784c93df8c9d4c96bbeacd73cad9cd55d2970  ⟵
```

You have now committed your container to an image that you can run from later.

STATE IS NOT CAPTURED! Committing a container only stores the state of the filesystem at the time of commit, not the processes. Docker containers are not VMs, remember. If your environment's state depends on the state of running processes that aren't recoverable through standard files, this technique won't store the state as you need it. In this case, you'll probably want to look at making your development processes recoverable.

Next you change local.html to the other possible required value:

```
<title>todocorp's todo app</title>
```

Commit again:

```
$ docker commit todobug1
071f6a36c23a19801285b82eafc99333c76f63ea0aa0b44902c6bae482a6e036
```

You now have two image IDs (ca76b45144f2cb31fda6a31e55f784c93df8c9d4c96bbeac-d73cad9cd55d2970 and 071f6a36c23a19801285b82eafc99333c76f63ea0aa0b44902c6-bae482a6e036 in our case, but yours will be different) that represent the two options. When the CEO comes in to evaluate which one she wants, you can run up either image and let her decide which one to commit.

You do this by opening up new terminals and running the following commands:

> **Maps the container's port 8000 to the host's port 800I and specifies the lowercase image ID**

```
$ docker run -p 8001:8000 \
  ca76b45144f2cb31fda6a31e55f784c93df8c9d4c96bbeacd73cad9cd55d2970 ◄
$ docker run -p 8002:8000 \
  071f6a36c23a19801285b82eafc99333c76f63ea0aa0b44902c6bae482a6e036        ◄
```

> **Maps the container's port 8000 to the host's port 8002 and specifies the uppercase image ID**

In this way you can present the uppercase option as available on http://localhost:8001 and the lowercase option on http://localhost:8002.

You're no doubt wondering whether there's a better way to reference images than with long random strings of characters. The next technique will look at giving these containers names you can more easily reference.

We find this to be a useful technique when we've negotiated a tricky sequence of commands to set up an application. Committing the container, once successful, records our bash session history, meaning that a set of steps for regaining the state of our system is available. This can save a *lot* of time! It's also useful when you're experimenting with a new feature and are unsure whether you're finished, or when you've recreated a bug and want to be as sure as possible that you can return to the broken state.

> **EXTERNAL DEPENDENCIES NOT CAPTURED!** Any dependencies external to the container (such as databases, Docker volumes, or other services called) are not stored on commit. This technique doesn't have any external dependencies so we don't need to worry about this.

TECHNIQUE 15 Docker tagging

You've now saved the state of your container by committing, and you have a random string as the ID of your image. It's obviously difficult to remember and manage the large numbers of these image IDs. It would be helpful to use Docker's tagging functionality to give readable names (and tags) to your images and remind you what they were created for.

Mastering this technique will allow you to see what your images are for at a glance, making image management on your machine far simpler.

PROBLEM

You want to conveniently reference and store a Docker commit.

SOLUTION

Use docker tag to name your commit.

DISCUSSION

In its basic form, tagging is simple:

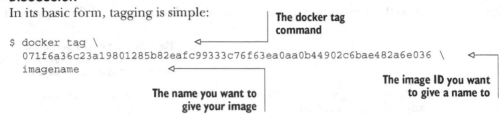

This gives your image a name that you can refer to, like so:

```
docker run imagename
```

This is much easier than remembering random strings of letters and numbers!

If you want to share your images with others, there's more to tagging than this, though. Unfortunately, the terminology around tags can be rather confusing. Terms such as *image, name,* and *repository* are used interchangeably. Table 3.1 provides some definitions.

Table 3.1 Docker tagging terms

Term	Meaning
Image	A read-only layer.
Name	The name of your image, such as "todoapp."
Tag	As a verb, it refers to giving an image a name. As a noun, it's a modifier for your image name.
Repository	A hosted collection of tagged images that together create the filesystem for a container.

Perhaps the most confusing terms in this table are *image* and *repository*. We've been using the term *image* loosely to mean a collection of layers that we spawn a container from, but technically an image is a single layer that refers to its parent layer recursively. A repository is hosted, meaning that it's stored somewhere (either on your Docker daemon or on a registry). In addition, a repository is a collection of tagged images that make up the filesystem for a container.

An analogy with Git can be helpful here. When cloning a Git repository, you check out the state of the files at the point you requested. This is analogous to an image. The repository is the entire history of the files at each commit, going back to the initial commit. You therefore check out the repository at the head's layer. The other layers (or commits) are all there in the repository you've cloned.

In practice, the terms *image* and *repository* are used more or less interchangeably, so don't worry too much about this. But be aware that these terms exist and are used similarly.

What you've seen so far is how to give an image ID a name. Confusingly, this name isn't the image's *tag*, although people often refer to it as that. We distinguish between the action to *tag* (verb) and the *tag* you can give to the image name (noun). This tag (noun) allows you to name a specific version of the image. You might add a tag to manage references to different versions of the same image. You could tag with a version name or the date of commit, for example.

A good example of a repository with multiple tags is the Ubuntu image. If you pull the Ubuntu image and then run docker images, you'll get output similar to the following listing.

Listing 3.9   An image with multiple tags

```
$ docker images
REPOSITORY   TAG        IMAGE ID       CREATED       VIRTUAL SIZE
ubuntu       trusty     8eaa4ff06b53   4 weeks ago   192.7 MB
ubuntu       14.04      8eaa4ff06b53   4 weeks ago   192.7 MB
ubuntu       14.04.1    8eaa4ff06b53   4 weeks ago   192.7 MB
ubuntu       latest     8eaa4ff06b53   4 weeks ago   192.7 MB
```

The Repository column lists the hosted collection of layers called "ubuntu." Often this is referred to as the image. The Tag column here lists four different names (trusty, 14.04, 14.04.1, and latest). The Image ID column lists identical image IDs. This is because these differently tagged images are identical.

This shows that you can have a repository with multiple tags from the same image ID. In theory, though, these tags could later point to different image IDs. If "trusty" gets a security update, for example, the image ID may be changed with a new commit by the maintainers and tagged with "trusty," "14.04.2," and "latest."

The default is to give your image a tag of "latest" if no tag is specified.

MEANING OF THE "LATEST" TAG   The "latest" tag has no special significance in Docker—it's a default for tagging and pulling. It doesn't necessarily mean that this was the last tag set for this image. The "latest" tag of your image may be an old version of the image, as versions built later may have been tagged with a specific tag like "v1.2.3."

TECHNIQUE 16   Sharing images on the Docker Hub

Tagging images with descriptive names would be even more helpful if you could share these names (and images) with other people. To satisfy this need, Docker comes with the ability to easily move images to other places, and Docker, Inc. created the Docker Hub as a free service to encourage this sharing.

DOCKER HUB ACCOUNT NEEDED   To follow this technique, you'll need a Docker Hub account that you have logged into previously by running `docker login` on your host machine. If you haven't set one up, you can do so at http://hub.docker.com. Just follow the instructions to register.

PROBLEM

You want to share a Docker image publicly.

SOLUTION

Use the Docker Hub registry to share your image.

DISCUSSION

As with tagging, the terminology around registries can be confusing. Table 3.2 should help you understand how the terms are used.

Table 3.2   Docker registry terms

Term	Meaning
Username	Your Docker registry username.
Registry	Registries hold images. A registry is a store you can upload images to or download them from. Registries can be public or private.
Registry host	The host on which the Docker registry runs.
Docker Hub	The default public registry hosted at https://hub.docker.com.
Index	The same as a registry host. It appears to be a deprecated term.

As you've seen previously, it's possible to tag an image as many times as you like. This is useful for copying over an image so that you have control of it.

Let's say your username on the Docker Hub is "adev." The following three commands show how to copy the `debian:wheezy` image from the Docker Hub to be under your own account.

Listing 3.10   Copying a public image and pushing to adev's Docker Hub account

```
docker pull debian:wheezy
docker tag debian:wheezy adev/debian:mywheezy1
docker push adev/debian:mywheezy1
```

Pull the Debian image from the Docker Hub.

Tag the wheezy image with your own username (adev) and tag (mywheezy1).

Push the newly created tag.

You now have a reference to the Debian wheezy image you downloaded that you can maintain, refer to, and build on.

If you have a private repository to push to, the process is identical except that you must specify the address of the registry before the tag. Let's say you have a repository that's served from http://mycorp.private.dockerregistry. The following listing will tag and push the image.

Listing 3.11 Copying a public image and pushing to adev's private registry

Pull the Debian image from the Docker Hub.

```
docker pull debian
docker tag debian:wheezy \
mycorp.private.dockerregistry/adev/debian:mywheezy1
docker push mycorp.private.dockerregistry/adev/debian:mywheezy1
```

Tag the wheezy image with your registry (mycorp.private.dockerregistry), username (adev), and tag (mywheezyl).

Push the newly created tag to the private registry. Note that the private registry server's address is required both when tagging and pushing, so that Docker can be sure it's pushing to the right place.

The preceding commands won't push the image to the public Docker Hub but will push it to the private repository, so that anyone with access to resources on that service can pull it.

You now have the ability to share your images with others. This is a great way to share work, ideas, or even issues you are facing with other engineers.

TECHNIQUE 17 Referring to a specific image in builds

Most of the time you'll be referring to generic image names in your builds, such as "node" or "ubuntu" and will proceed without problem.

If you refer to an image name, then it's possible that the image can change while the tag remains the same. As paradoxical as it sounds, this is indeed the case! The repository name is only a reference, and it may be altered to point at a different underlying image. Specifying a tag with the colon notation (such as ubuntu:trusty) doesn't remove this risk, either, as security updates can use the same tag to automatically rebuild vulnerable images.

Most of the time you'll want this—the maintainers of the image may have found an improvement, and patching security holes is generally a good thing. Occasionally, though, this can cause you pain. And this is not merely a theoretical risk: this has happened to us on a number of occasions, breaking continuous delivery builds in a way that's difficult to debug. In the early days of Docker, packages would be added to and removed from the most popular images regularly (including, on one memorable occasion, the disappearance of the passwd command!), making builds that previously worked suddenly break.

PROBLEM

You want to be sure that your build is from a specific and unchanging image.

SOLUTION

Build from a specific image ID.

DISCUSSION

For the times when you want to be absolutely certain that you're building against a given set of files, you can specify a specific image ID in your Dockerfile.

Here's an example (which will likely not work for you):

Build from a specific image (or layer) ID.

```
FROM 8eaa4ff06b53
RUN echo "Built from image id:" > /etc/buildinfo
RUN echo "8eaa4ff06b53" >> /etc/buildinfo
RUN echo "an ubuntu 14.4.01 image" >> /etc/buildinfo
CMD ["echo","/etc/buildinfo"]
```

The built image will by default output the information you recorded in the /etc/buildinfo file.

Run a command within this image to record the image you built from within a file in the new image.

To build from a specific image (or layer) ID like this, the image ID must be stored locally on your Docker daemon. The Docker registry will not perform any kind of lookup to find the image ID in layers of images available to you on the Docker Hub, or in any other registry you may be configured to use.

Note that the image you refer to need not be tagged—it could be any layer you have locally. You can begin your build from any layer you wish. This might be useful for certain surgical or experimental procedures you want to perform for Dockerfile build analysis.

If you want to persist the image remotely, then it's best to tag and push the image to a repository that's under your control in a remote registry.

DOCKER IMAGES CAN STOP WORKING! It's worth pointing out that almost the opposite problem can occur when a Docker image that was previously working suddenly does not. Usually this is because something on the network has changed. One memorable example of this was when our builds failed to apt-get update one morning. We assumed it was a problem with our local deb cache and tried debugging without success until a friendly sysadmin pointed out that the particular version of Ubuntu we were building from was no longer supported. This meant that the network calls to apt-get update were returning an HTTP error.

3.4   *Environments as processes*

One way of viewing Docker is to see it as turning environments into processes. Again, VMs can be treated in the same way, but Docker makes this much more convenient and efficient.

To illustrate this, we'll show you how the speedy spin-up, storage, and recreation of container state can allow you to do something otherwise (almost) impossible—to win at 2048!

TECHNIQUE 18   **The "save game" approach to development**

This technique is designed to provide you with a little light relief while showing you how Docker can be used to revert state easily. If you're not familiar with 2048, it's an addictive game where you push numbers around a board. The original version is available online at http://gabrielecirulli.github.io/2048 if you want to get acquainted with it first.

PROBLEM

You want to save container state regularly in order to revert to a known state if necessary.

SOLUTION

Use docker commit to "save game" whenever you are unsure whether you will survive.

DISCUSSION

We've created a monolithic image on which you can play 2048 within a Docker container that contains a VNC server and Firefox.

To use this image you'll need to install a VNC client. Popular implementations include TigerVNC and VNC Viewer. If you don't have one, then a quick search for "vnc client" on the package manager on your host should yield useful results.

To start up the container, run the following commands.

Listing 3.12   Start the 2048 container

```
$ docker run -d -p 5901:5901 -p 6080:6080 --name win2048 \
    imiell/win2048                                                    ❶
$ vncviewer localhost:1                    ◄───── ❷
```

First you run a container from the imiell/win2048 image, which we've prepared for you ❶. You start this in the background and specify that it should open two ports (5901 and 6080) to the host. These ports will be used by the VNC server started automatically inside the container. You also give the container a name for easy use later: win2048.

You can now run your VNC viewer (the executable may differ depending on what you have installed) and instruct it to connect to your local computer ❷. Because the appropriate ports have been exposed from the container, connecting to localhost will actually connect to the container. The :1 after localhost is appropriate if you have no X displays on your host other than a standard desktop—if you do, you may need to choose a different number and look at the documentation for your VNC viewer to manually specify the VNC port as 5901.

Once you're connected to the VNC server you'll be prompted for a password. The password for VNC on this image is vncpass.

You'll see a window with a Firefox tab and a 2048 table preloaded. Click on it to give it focus, and play until you're ready to save the game.

To save the game, you tag the named container after committing it:

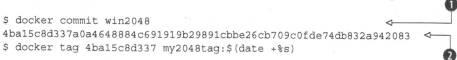

```
$ docker commit win2048                                            ◄─────── ❶
4ba15c8d337a0a4648884c691919b29891cbbe26cb709c0fde74db832a942083   ◄─┐
$ docker tag 4ba15c8d337 my2048tag:$(date +%s)                       ❷
```

An image ID ❷ was generated by committing the win2048 container ❶, and now you want to give it a unique name (because you may be creating a number of these images). To do this, we'll use the output of date +%s as the part of the image name, which outputs the number of seconds since the first day of 1970, providing a unique (for our purposes), constantly increasing value. The $(command) syntax just substitutes the output of command at that position. If you prefer, you can run the date +%s manually and paste the output as part of the image name instead.

You can then continue playing until you lose. Now comes the magic! You can return to your save point with the following commands.

Listing 3.13   Return to the saved game

```
$ docker rm -f win2048
$ docker run -d -p 5901:5901 -p 6080:6080 --name win2048 my2048tag:$mytag
```

$mytag is a tag selected from the docker images command. Repeat the tag, rm, and run steps until you complete 2048.

3.5   Summary

In this chapter you've seen how Docker can take the place of VMs for many use cases. Although Docker is not a VM technology and there are important distinctions between VMs and containers, the convenience of Docker can speed up your development process.

This chapter has built on the first two by showing how Docker's architecture lays the foundations for the greater convenience that it can bring to your work.

We covered these principal points:

- It's relatively easy to convert a VM to a Docker image to make the initial move to Docker.
- You can supervise services on your containers to mimic their previous VM-like operation.
- Committing is the correct way to save your work as you go.
- You can name your images and share them with the world on the Docker Hub for free.

Developing within a new paradigm will always introduce you to some routine tasks and daily trials, In the next chapter we'll examine some of the more important of these.

Day-to-day Docker

As you develop software with Docker you will discover you have various needs that arise. You may grapple with running GUIs from a container, run into confusion around the Dockerfile build cache, want to manipulate your containers directly while in use, wonder about the lineage of your images, want to reference data from an external source, and so on.

This chapter takes you through techniques that show you how to handle these and other concerns that may arise. Think of it as your Docker toolbox!

4.1   *Volumes—a persistent problem*

Containers are a powerful concept, but sometimes not everything you want to access is ready to be encapsulated. You may have a reference Oracle database stored on a large cluster that you want to connect to for testing. Or maybe you have a large legacy server already set up with binaries that can't easily be reproduced.

When you begin working with Docker, most of the things you'll want to access will likely be data and programs external to your container. We'll take you from the straightforward mounting of files from your host to more sophisticated container patterns: the data container and the dev tools container. We'll also demonstrate a pragmatic favorite of ours for remote mounting across a network that requires only an SSH connection to work, and a means of sharing data with other users via the BitTorrent protocol.

Volumes are a core part of Docker, and the issue of external data reference is yet another fast-changing area of the Docker ecosystem.

TECHNIQUE 19   Docker volumes—problems of persistence

Much of the power of containers comes from the fact that they encapsulate as much of the state of the environment's filesystem as is useful.

Sometimes, though, you don't want to put files into a container. You might have some large files that you want to share across containers or manage separately. The classic example is the large, centralized database that you want your container to access, but you also want other (perhaps more traditional) clients to access alongside your new-fangled containers.

The solution is *volumes*, Docker's mechanism for managing files outside the lifecycle of the container. Although this goes against the philosophy of containers being "deployed anywhere" (you won't be able to deploy your database-dependent container where there's no compatible database available to mount, for example), it's a useful feature for real-world Docker use.

PROBLEM
You want to access files on the host from within a container.

SOLUTION
Use Docker's volume flag to access host files from within the container.

DISCUSSION
Figure 4.1 illustrates the use of a volume flag to interact with the host's filesystem.

The following command shows the host's /var/db/tables directory being mounted on /var/data1, and it could be run to start the container in figure 4.1:

```
$ docker run -v /var/db/tables:/var/data1 -it debian bash
```

The -v flag (--volume in longhand) indicates that a volume external to the container is required. The subsequent argument gives the volume specification in the form of two directories separated by a colon, instructing Docker to map the external /var/db/tables directory to the container's /var/data1 directory. Both the external and container directories will be created if they don't exist.

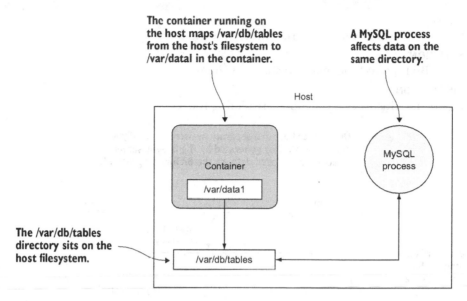

Figure 4.1 A volume inside a container

Beware of mapping over existing directories. The container's directory will be mapped even if it already exists in the image. This means that the directory you're mapping to within the container will effectively disappear. Fun things happen if you try to map a key directory! Try mounting an empty directory over /bin, for example.

Also note that volumes are assumed not to persist in Dockerfiles. If you add a volume and then make changes to that folder within a Dockerfile, the changes won't be persisted to the resulting image.

> **SELINUX ISSUES?** You may run into difficulties if your host runs SELinux. If SELinux policy is enforced, the container may not be able to write to the /var/db/tables directory. You'll see a "permission denied" error. If you need to work around this, you'll need to talk to your sysadmin (if you have one) or switch off SELinux (for development purposes only). See technique 101 for more on SELinux.

TECHNIQUE 20   **Distributed volumes with BitTorrent Sync**

When experimenting with Docker in a team, you may want to be able to share large quantities of data among team members, but you may not be allocated the resources for a shared server with sufficient capacity. The lazy solution to this is copying the latest files from other team members when you need them—this quickly gets out of hand for a larger team.

The solution is to use a decentralized tool for sharing files—no dedicated resource required.

PROBLEM

You want to share volumes across hosts over the internet.

SOLUTION

Use a BitTorrent Sync image to share a volume.

DISCUSSION

Figure 4.2 illustrates the setup we're aiming for.

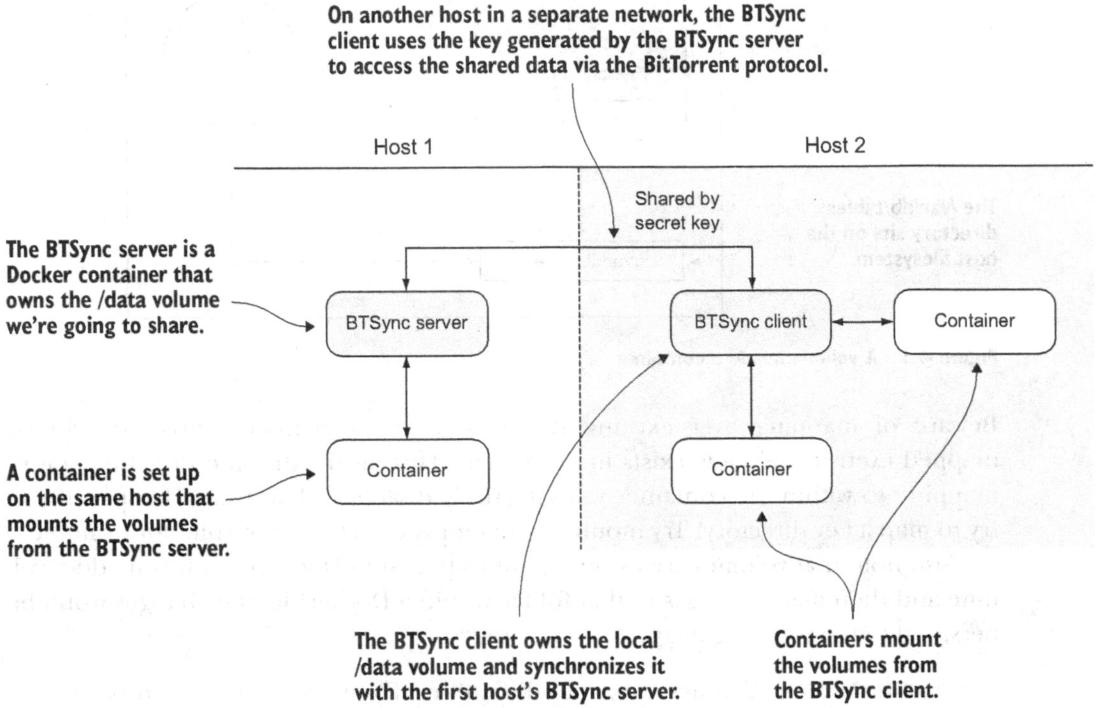

On another host in a separate network, the BTSync
client uses the key generated by the BTSync server
to access the shared data via the BitTorrent protocol.

The BTSync server is a
Docker container that
owns the /data volume
we're going to share.

A container is set up
on the same host that
mounts the volumes
from the BTSync server.

The BTSync client owns the local
/data volume and synchronizes it
with the first host's BTSync server.

Containers mount
the volumes from
the BTSync client.

Figure 4.2 **Using BitTorrent Sync**

The end result is a volume (/data) conveniently synchronized over the internet without requiring any complicated setup.

On your primary server, run the following commands to set up the containers on
the first host:

Runs the published ctlc/btsync image
as a daemon container, calls btsync,
and opens the required ports

Gets the
output of the
btsync
container so
you can make a
note of the key

Make a note of this key—it
will be different for your run.

```
[host1]$ docker run -d -p 8888:8888 -p 55555:55555 \
--name btsync ctlc/btsync
$ docker logs btsync
Starting btsync with secret: \
ALSVEUABQQ5ILRS2OQJKAOKCU5SIIP6A3
By using this application, you agree to our Privacy Policy and Terms.
http://www.bittorrent.com/legal/privacy
http://www.bittorrent.com/legal/terms-of-use
```

```
                      total physical memory 536870912 max disk cache 2097152
                      Using IP address 172.17.4.121
```

<table>
<tr>
<td>Adds a file
to the /data
volume</td>
<td>

```
[host1]$ docker run -i -t --volumes-from btsync \
ubuntu /bin/bash
$ touch /data/shared_from_server_one
$ ls /data
shared_from_server_one
```

</td>
<td>Starts up an
interactive container
with the volumes from
the btsync server</td>
</tr>
</table>

On the second server, open up a terminal and run these commands to synchronize
the volume:

<table>
<tr>
<td></td>
<td></td>
<td>Starts a btsync client container as a
daemon with the key generated by
the daemon run on host1</td>
</tr>
<tr>
<td>Starts an
interactive
container that
mounts the
volumes from
your client
daemon</td>
<td>

```
[host2]$ docker run -d --name btsync-client -p 8888:8888 \
-p 55555:55555 \
ctlc/btsync ALSVEUABQQ5ILRS2OQJKAOKCU5SIIP6A3
[host2]$ docker run -i -t --volumes-from btsync-client \
ubuntu bash
$ ls /data
shared_from_server_one
$ touch /data/shared_from_server_two
$ ls /data
shared_from_server_one   shared_from_server_two
```

</td>
<td></td>
</tr>
</table>

The file created on
host1 has been
transferred to host2.

Creates a
second file
on host2

Back on host1's running container, you should see that the file has been synchronized
between the hosts exactly as the first file was:

```
[host1]$ ls /data
shared_from_server_one   shared_from_server_two
```

The synchronization of files comes with no timing guarantees, so you may have to wait
for the data to sync. This is particularly the case for larger files.

> **NO GUARANTEES OF GOOD BEHAVIOR**   As the data may be sent over the internet and
> is processed by a protocol over which you have no control, you shouldn't rely on
> this if you have any meaningful security, scalability, or performance constraints.

TECHNIQUE 21 Retain your container's bash history

Experimenting inside a container with the knowledge that you can wipe everything
out when you're done can be a liberating experience. But there are some conve-
niences that you lose when doing this. One that we've hit many times is an inability to
recall a sequence of commands we've run inside a container.

PROBLEM
You want to share your container's bash history with your host's history.

SOLUTION
Alias your docker run command to share your bash history with the host's history.

DISCUSSION

To understand this problem, we're going to show you a simple scenario where not having this is plain annoying.

Imagine you are experimenting in Docker containers, and in the midst of your work you do something interesting and reusable. Here we'll use a simple echo command, but it could be a long and complex concatenation of programs that results in a useful output:

```
$ docker run -ti --rm ubuntu /bin/bash
$ echo my amazing command
$ exit
```

After some time, you want to recall the incredible echo command you ran earlier. Unfortunately, you can't recall it, and you no longer have the terminal session on your screen to scroll to. Out of habit you try looking through your bash history on the host:

```
$ history | grep amazing
```

Nothing comes back, because the bash history is kept within the now-removed container and not the host you were returned to.

To share your bash history with the host, you can use a volume mount when running your Docker images. Here's an example:

```
$ docker run -e HIST_FILE=/root/.bash_history \      ◀──┐  Sets the environment variable
 -v=$HOME/.bash_history:/root/.bash_history \        ◀──   picked up by bash. This
 -ti ubuntu /bin/bash                                      ensures the bash history file
                                                           used is the one you mount.

                                                     Maps the container's
                                                     root's bash history
                                                     file to the host's
```

SEPARATE CONTAINER BASH HISTORY FILE You may want to separate the container's bash history from your host's. One way to do this is to change the value for the first part of the preceding -v argument.

This is quite a handful to type every time, so to make this more user-friendly you can set up an alias by putting this into your ~/.bashrc file:

```
$ alias dockbash='docker run -e HIST_FILE=/root/.bash_history \
 -v=$HOME/.bash_history:/root/.bash_history
```

This is still not seamless, as you have to remember to type dockbash if you want to perform a docker run command. For a more seamless experience, you can add these to your ~/.bashrc file:

```
                                          Create a bash function called basher
                                          that will handle the docker command.
function basher() {              ◀──
Determine whether  │    if [[ $1 = 'run' ]]
the first argument to │    then                     ...remove that argument from the list
basher/docker is   │      shift         ◀──────────  of arguments you've passed in.
'run'. If it is... │
```

Run the docker run command you ran earlier, invoking the absolute path to the Docker runtime to avoid confusion with the following docker alias. Find out by running the which docker command on your host before implementing this solution.

Pass the arguments after "run" to the Docker runtime.

Run the docker command with the original arguments intact.

```
    /usr/bin/docker run \
      -e HIST_FILE=/root/.bash_history \
      -v $HOME/.bash_history:/root/.bash_history "$@"
    else
      /usr/bin/docker "$@"
    fi
  }
  alias docker=basher
```

Alias the docker command when invoked on the command line to the basher function you've created. This ensures that the call to docker is caught before bash finds the docker binary on the path.

Now when you next open a bash shell and run any docker run command, the commands that are run within that container will be added to your host's bash history. Make sure the path to Docker is correct. It might be located in /bin/docker, for example.

> **REMEMBER TO LOG OUT OF THE HOST BASH SESSION** You'll need to log out of your host's original bash session for the history file to be updated. This is due to a subtlety of bash and how it updates the bash history it keeps in memory. If in doubt, exit all bash sessions you're aware of, and then start one up to ensure your history is as up-to-date as possible.

TECHNIQUE 22 Data containers

If you use volumes a lot on a host, managing the container's startup can get tricky. You may also want the data to be managed by Docker exclusively, and not be generally accessible on the host. One way to manage these things more cleanly is to use the data-only container design pattern.

PROBLEM

You want to use an external volume within a container but you only want Docker to access the files.

SOLUTION

Start up a data container and use the --volumes-from flag when running other containers.

DISCUSSION

Figure 4.3 shows the structure of the data container pattern and explains how it works. The key thing to note is that in the second host, the containers don't need to know where the data is located on disk. All they need to know is the name of the data container and they're good to go. This can make the operation of containers more portable.

Another benefit of this approach over the straightforward mapping of host directories is that access to these files is managed by Docker, which means that it's less likely that a non-Docker process will affect the contents.

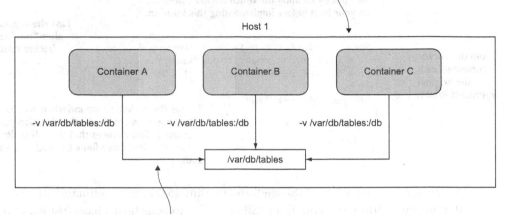

This host is running three containers, each pointed at the host's /var/db/tables directory with the –volume/-v flag. No data container exists here.

Each container has mounted the directory separately, so if the location of the folder changes or the mount needs to be moved, each container has to be reconfigured.

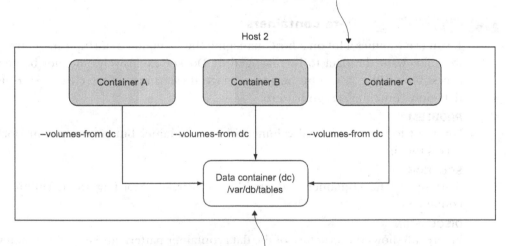

This host is running four containers. The three containers from the previous host are run with the –volumes-from flags all pointing at the data container.

This single data container mounts the host's volume, creating a single point of responsibility for data mounts on the host.

Figure 4.3   The data container pattern

DATA-ONLY CONTAINER DOESN'T NEED TO RUN! A common source of confusion is whether the data-only container needs to run. It doesn't! It merely needs to exist, to have been run on the host and not deleted.

Let's go through a simple example so you can get a feel for how to use this technique. First you run your data container:

```
$ docker run -v /shared-data --name dc busybox \
  touch /shared-data/somefile
```

The -v argument doesn't map the volume to a host directory, so it creates the directory within the scope of this container's responsibility. This directory is populated with a single file with touch, and the container immediately exists—a data container need not be running to be used. We've used the small but functional busybox image to reduce the amount of extra baggage our data container needs.

Then you run up another container to access the file you just created:

```
docker run -t -i --volumes-from dc busybox /bin/sh
/ # ls /shared-data
somefile
```

The --volumes-from flag allows you to reference the files from the data container by mounting them in the current container—you just need to pass it the ID of a container with volumes defined. The busybox image doesn't have bash, so you need to start up a simpler shell to verify that the /shared-data folder from the dc container is available to you.

You can start up any number of containers all reading from and writing to the specified data container's volumes.

VOLUMES PERSIST! It's important to understand that using this pattern can result in heavy disk usage that can be relatively difficult to debug. Because Docker manages the volume within the data-only container, and does not delete the volume when the last container referencing it has exited, any data on a volume will persist. This is to prevent undesired data loss. For advice on managing this, see technique 35.

Using this pattern isn't required to use volumes—you may find this approach harder to manage than a straightforward mount of a host directory. If, however, you like to cleanly delegate responsibility for managing data to a single point managed within Docker and uncontaminated by other host processes, then data containers may be useful for you.

FIGHTING OVER FILE PATHS If your application is logging from multiple containers to the same data container, it's important to ensure that each container log file writes to a unique file path. If you don't ensure this, different containers might overwrite or truncate the file, resulting in lost data, or might write interleaved data, which is less easy to analyze. Similarly, if you invoke --volumes-from from a data container, you allow that container to potentially overlay directories over yours, so be careful of name clashes here also.

TECHNIQUE 23   **Remote volume mounting using sshfs**

We've discussed mounting local files, but soon the question of how to mount remote filesystems arises. Perhaps you want to share a reference database on a remote server and treat it as if it were local, for example.

Although it's theoretically possible to set up NFS on your host system and the server and then access the filesystem by mounting that directory, there's a quicker and simpler way for most users that requires no setup on the server side (as long as there is SSH access).

> **ROOT PRIVILEGES REQUIRED** You'll need root privileges for this technique to work, and you'll need FUSE (Linux's "Filesystem in Userspace" kernel module) installed. You can determine whether you have the latter by running `ls /dev/fuse` in a terminal to see whether the file exists.

PROBLEM

You want to mount a remote filesystem without requiring any server-side configuration.

SOLUTION

Use SSHFS to mount the remote filesystem.

DISCUSSION

This technique works by using a FUSE kernel module with SSH to give you a standard interface to a filesystem, while in the background doing all communications via SSH. SSHFS also provides various behind-the-scenes features (such as remote file read-ahead) to facilitate the illusion that the files are local. The upshot is that once a user is logged into the remote server, they'll see the files as if they were local. Figure 4.4 helps explain this.

> **CHANGES WON'T PERSIST ON THE CONTAINER** Although this technique doesn't use the Docker volumes functionality, and the files are visible through the filesystem, this technique doesn't give you any container-level persistence. Any changes made take place on the remote server's filesystem only.

You can get started by running the following commands, adjusted for your environment.

The first step is to start up a container with `--privileged` on your host machine:

```
$ docker run -t -i --privileged debian /bin/bash
```

Then, when it's started up, run `apt-get update && apt-get install sshfs` from within the container to install SSHFS.

When SSHFS is successfully installed, log on to the remote host as follows:

Replace the values here with your remote host username, remote host address, and remote path.

Choose a directory to mount the remote location into.

Create the local directory to mount into.

```
$ LOCALPATH=/path/to/local/directory
$ mkdir $LOCALPATH
$ sshfs user@host:/path/to/remote/directory $LOCALPATH
```

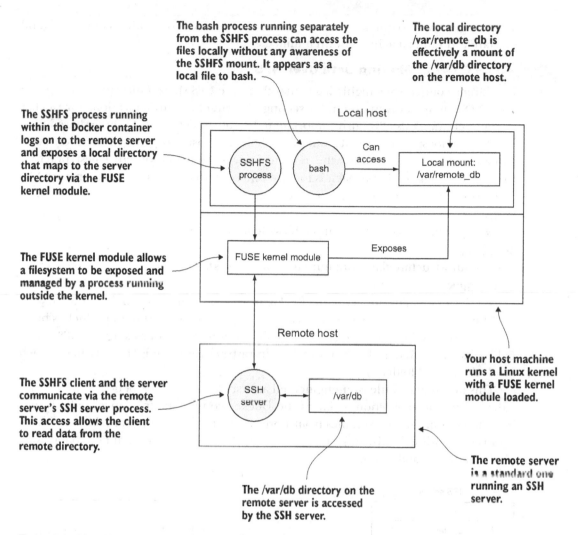

The bash process running separately from the SSHFS process can access the files locally without any awareness of the SSHFS mount. It appears as a local file to bash.

The local directory /var/remote_db is effectively a mount of the /var/db directory on the remote host.

The SSHFS process running within the Docker container logs on to the remote server and exposes a local directory that maps to the server directory via the FUSE kernel module.

Local host

SSHFS process

bash

Can access

Local mount: /var/remote_db

The FUSE kernel module allows a filesystem to be exposed and managed by a process running outside the kernel.

FUSE kernel module

Exposes

Remote host

The SSHFS client and the server communicate via the remote server's SSH server process. This access allows the client to read data from the remote directory.

SSH server

/var/db

Your host machine runs a Linux kernel with a FUSE kernel module loaded.

The remote server is a standard one running an SSH server.

The /var/db directory on the remote server is accessed by the SSH server.

Figure 4.4   Mounting a remote filesystem with SSHFS

You'll now see the contents of the path on the remote server in the folder you've just created.

> **MOUNT PRE-EXISTING DIRECTORIES WITH THE NONEMPTY OPTION**   It's simplest to mount to a directory that you've newly created, but it's also possible to mount a pre-existing directory with files already present if you use the `-o nonempty` option. See the SSHFS man page for more information.

To cleanly unmount the files, use the `fusermount` command as follows, replacing the path as appropriate:

```
fusermount -u /path/to/local/directory
```

This is a great way to quickly get remote mounts working from within containers (and on standard Linux machines) with minimal effort.

TECHNIQUE 24   **Sharing data over NFS**

In a larger company it's highly likely that there are NFS shared directories already in use—NFS is a well-proven option for serving files out of a central location. For Docker to get traction, it's usually fairly important to be able to get access to these shared files.

Docker doesn't support NFS out of the box, and installing an NFS client on every container so you can mount the remote folders isn't considered a best practice. Instead, the suggested approach is to have one container act as a translator from NFS to a more Docker-friendly concept: volumes.

PROBLEM

You want seamless access to a remote filesystem over NFS.

SOLUTION

Use an infrastructure data container to broker access.

DISCUSSION

This technique builds on technique 22. Figure 4.5 shows the idea in the abstract.

The NFS server exposes the internal directory as the /export folder, which is bind-mounted on the host. The Docker host then mounts this folder using the NFS proto-col to its /mnt folder. Then a so-called infrastructure container is created, which binds the mount folder.

This may seem a little over-engineered at first glance, but the benefit is that it provides a level of indirection as far as the Docker containers are concerned: all they need to do is mount the volumes from a pre-agreed infrastructure container, and whoever is responsible for the infrastructure can worry about the internal plumbing, availability, network, and so on.

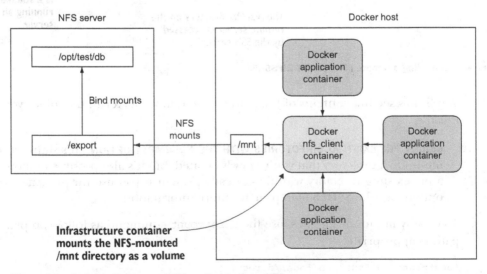

Figure 4.5   An infrastructure container that brokers NFS access

A thorough treatment of NFS is beyond the scope of this book. In this technique we're going to go through the steps of setting up such a share on a single host by having the NFS server's components on the same host as the Docker containers. This has been tested on Ubuntu 14.04.

Imagine you want to share the contents of your host's /opt/test/db folder, which contains the file mybigdb.db.

As root, install the NFS server and create an export directory with open permissions:

```
# apt-get install nfs-kernel-server
# mkdir /export
# chmod 777 /export
```

Now bind mount the db directory to your export directory:

```
# mount --bind /opt/test/db /export
```

You should now be able to see the contents of the /opt/test/db directory in /export:

> **PERSISTING THE BIND MOUNT** If you want this to persist following a reboot, add this line to your /etc/fstab file: /opt/test/db /export none bind 0 0

Now add this line to your /etc/exports file:

```
/export          127.0.0.1(ro,fsid=0,insecure,no_subtree_check,async)
```

For this proof of concept example, we're mounting locally on 127.0.0.1, which defeats the object a little. In a real-world scenario, you'd lock this down to a class of IP addresses such as 192.168.1.0/24. If you like playing with fire, you can open it up to the world with * instead of 127.0.0.1!

For safety, we're mounting read-only (ro) here, but you can mount read-write by replacing ro with rw. Remember that if you do this, you'll need to add a no_root_squash flag after the async flag there, but think about security before going outside this sandpit.

Mount the directory over NFS to the /mnt directory, export the filesystems you specified previously in /etc/exports, and then restart the NFS service to pick up the changes:

```
# mount -t nfs 127.0.0.1:/export /mnt
# exportfs -a
# service nfs-kernel-server restart
```

Now you're ready to run your infrastructure container:

```
# docker run -ti --name nfs_client --privileged -v /mnt:/mnt
  busybox /bin/true
```

And now you can run—without privileges, or knowledge of the underlying implementation—the directory you want to access:

```
# docker run -ti --volumes-from nfs_client debian /bin/bash
root@079d70f79d84:/# ls /mnt
myb
root@079d70f79d84:/# cd /mnt
root@079d70f79d84:/mnt# touch asd
touch: cannot touch `asd': Read-only file system
```

> **USE A NAMING CONVENTION FOR OPERATIONAL EFFICIENCY**   If you have a lot of these containers to manage, you can make this easier to manage by having a naming convention such as `--name nfs_client_opt_database_live` for a container that exposes the /opt/database/live path.

This pattern of a shared resource mounted with privileged access centrally for use by others in multiple containers is a powerful one that can make development workflows much simpler.

> **NOT A SUBSTITUTE FOR SECURITY**   Remember that this technique only provides security through obscurity (which is no security at all). As you'll see later, any-one that can run the Docker executable effectively has root privileges on the host.

TECHNIQUE 25   Dev tools container

If you're an engineer who often finds yourself on others' machines struggling without the programs or configuration you have on your beautiful unique-as-a-snowflake development environment, this may be for you. Similarly, if you want to share your pimped-up dev environment with others, Docker can make this easy.

PROBLEM
You want to access your development environment on others' machines.

SOLUTION
Create a container with your setup on it and place it on a registry.

DISCUSSION
As a demonstration we're going to use one of our dev tools images. You can download it by running `docker pull dockerinpractice/docker-dev-tools-image`. The repo is available on https://github.com/docker-in-practice/docker-dev-tools-image if you want to inspect the Dockerfile.

Running up the container is simple—a straightforward `docker run -t -i docker-inpractice/docker-dev-tools-image` will give you a shell in our dev environment. You can root around our dotfiles and maybe send us some advice about the setup.

The real power of this technique can be seen when combined with others. Here you can see a dev tools container used to display a GUI on the host's network and IPC stacks and to mount the host's code:

Mounts the Docker socket to give access to the host's Docker daemon →

```
docker run -t -i \
  -v /var/run/docker.sock:/var/run/docker.sock \
  -v /tmp/.X11-unix:/tmp/.X11-unix \
```

← Mounts the X server Unix domain socket to allow you to start up GUI-based applications (see technique 26)

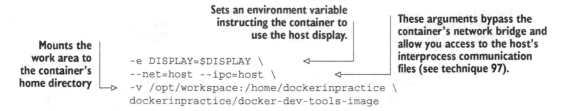

The preceding command gives you an environment with access to the host's resources:

- Network
- Docker daemon (to run normal Docker commands as though on the host)
- Inter-process communication (IPC) files
- X server to start GUI-based apps, if needed

HOST SECURITY As always when mounting host directories, be careful not to mount any vital directories, as you could do damage. Mounting any host directory under root is generally best avoided.

4.2   Running containers

Although much of this book is about running containers, there are some practical techniques related to running containers on your host that may not be immediately obvious. We'll look at how you can get GUI applications working, escape a container once started without killing it, inspect the state of containers and their source images, and shut down containers.

TECHNIQUE 26   Running GUIs within Docker

You've already seen a GUI served from within a Docker container using a VNC server in technique 14. That's one way to view applications within your Docker container, and it's self-contained, requiring only a VNC client to use.

Fortunately there's a more lightweight and well-integrated way to run GUIs on your desktop, but it requires more setup on your part. It mounts the directory on the host that manages communications with the X server so that it's accessible to the container.

PROBLEM
You want to run GUIs in a container as though they were normal desktop apps.

SOLUTION
Create an image with your user credentials and the program, and bind mount your X server to it.

DISCUSSION
Figure 4.6 shows how the final setup will work.

The container is linked to the host via the mount of the host's /tmp/.X11 directory, and this is how the container can perform actions on the host's desktop.

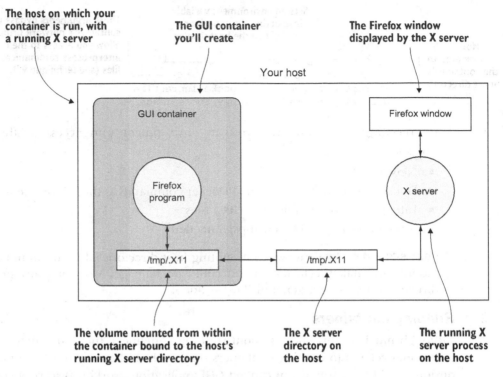

The host on which your container is run, with a running X server

The GUI container you'll create

The Firefox window displayed by the X server

Your host

GUI container

Firefox window

Firefox program

X server

/tmp/.X11   /tmp/.X11

The volume mounted from within the container bound to the host's running X server directory

The X server directory on the host

The running X server process on the host

Figure 4.6   **Communicating with the host's X server**

First make a new directory somewhere convenient, and determine your user and group IDs with the `id` command, as shown in the following listing.

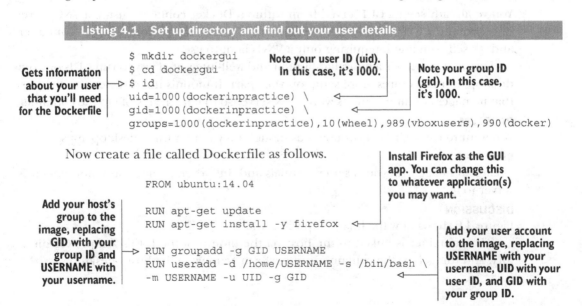

Listing 4.1   Set up directory and find out your user details

Gets information about your user that you'll need for the Dockerfile

Note your user ID (uid). In this case, it's 1000.

Note your group ID (gid). In this case, it's 1000.

```
$ mkdir dockergui
$ cd dockergui
$ id
uid=1000(dockerinpractice) \
gid=1000(dockerinpractice) \
groups=1000(dockerinpractice),10(wheel),989(vboxusers),990(docker)
```

Now create a file called Dockerfile as follows.

Install Firefox as the GUI app. You can change this to whatever application(s) you may want.

Add your host's group to the image, replacing GID with your group ID and USERNAME with your username.

Add your user account to the image, replacing USERNAME with your username, UID with your user ID, and GID with your group ID.

```
FROM ubuntu:14.04

RUN apt-get update
RUN apt-get install -y firefox

RUN groupadd -g GID USERNAME
RUN useradd -d /home/USERNAME -s /bin/bash \
-m USERNAME -u UID -g GID
```

Set the HOME variable correctly. Replace USERNAME with your username.

The image should run as the user you've created. Replace USERNAME with your username.

```
USER USERNAME
ENV HOME /home/USERNAME
CMD /usr/bin/firefox
```

Run Firefox on startup by default.

Now you can build from that Dockerfile and tag the result as "gui", as shown in the next listing.

Listing 4.2 Build the gui image

```
$ docker build -t gui .
```

Run it as shown in the following listing.

Listing 4.3 Run the gui image

```
docker run -v /tmp/.X11 unix:/tmp/.X11-unix \
-e DISPLAY=$DISPLAY gui
-h $HOSTNAME -v $HOME/.Xauthority:/home/$USER/.Xauthority
```

Bind mount the X server directory to the container ...

...set the DISPLAY variable in the container to be the same as that used in the host, so the program knows which X server to talk to...

...and give the container the appropriate credentials.

You'll see a Firefox window pop up!

You can use this technique to avoid mixing up your desktop work with your development work. With Firefox, for example, you might want to see how your application behaves with no web cache, bookmarks, or search history in a repeatable way for testing purposes. If you see error messages about being unable to open a display when trying to start the image and run Firefox, see technique 58 for more ways to allow containers to start graphical applications to be displayed on the host.

TECHNIQUE 27 Inspecting containers

Although the Docker commands give you access to information about images and containers, sometimes you want to know more about the internal metadata of these Docker objects.

PROBLEM

You want to find out a container's IP address.

SOLUTION

Use docker inspect to retrieve and filter the container's metadata.

DISCUSSION

The docker inspect command gives you access to Docker's internal metadata in JSON format. This produces a lot of output, so only a brief snippet of an image's metadata is shown in the next listing.

Listing 4.4   Raw `inspect` output on an image

```
$ docker inspect ubuntu | head
[{
    "Architecture": "amd64",
    "Author": "",
    "Comment": "",
    "Config": {
        "AttachStderr": false,
        "AttachStdin": false,
        "AttachStdout": false,
        "Cmd": [
            "/bin/bash"
$
```

You can inspect images and containers by name or ID. Obviously their metadata will differ—for example, a container will have runtime fields such as "State" that the image will lack (an image has no state).

In this case, you want to find out a container's IP address on your host. To do this, you can use the `docker inspect` command with the `format` flag (see the following listing).

Listing 4.5   Determining a container's IP address

The docker inspect command →
```
docker inspect \
--format '{{.NetworkSettings.IPAddress}}' \
0808ef13d450
```
← The ID of the Docker item you want to inspect

The format flag. This uses Go templates (not covered here) to format the output. Here, the IPAddress field is taken from the NetworkSettings field in the inspect output.

This technique can be useful for automation, as the interface is likely to be more stable than other Docker commands. The following command gives you the IP addresses of all running containers and pings them.

Listing 4.6   Get IPs of running containers and ping each in turn

Gets the container IDs of all running containers →
```
$ docker ps -q | \
xargs docker inspect --format='{{.NetworkSettings.IPAddress}}' | \
xargs -l1 ping -c1
PING 172.17.0.5 (172.17.0.5) 56(84) bytes of data.
64 bytes from 172.17.0.5: icmp_seq=1 ttl=64 time=0.095 ms

--- 172.17.0.5 ping statistics ---
1 packets transmitted, 1 received, 0% packet loss, time 0ms
rtt min/avg/max/mdev = 0.095/0.095/0.095/0.000 ms
```
← Runs the inspect command against all container IDs to get their IP addresses

Takes each IP address and runs ping against each in turn →

Note that because `ping` only accepts one IP address, we had to pass an additional argument to `xargs` telling it to run the command for each individual line.

SET UP A RUNNING CONTAINER TO TEST   If you have no running containers, run this command to get one going: docker run -d ubuntu sleep 1000.

TECHNIQUE 28   Cleanly killing containers

If the state of a container is important to you when it terminates, you may want to understand the distinction between docker kill and docker stop. This distinction can also be important if you need your applications to close gracefully in order to save data.

PROBLEM

You want to cleanly terminate a container.

SOLUTION

Use docker stop rather than docker kill.

DISCUSSION

The crucial point to understand is that docker kill doesn't behave the same way as the standard command-line kill program.

The program kill works by sending a TERM (a.k.a. signal value 15) signal to the process specified, unless directed otherwise. This signal indicates to the program that it should terminate, but doesn't force the program. Most programs will perform some kind of cleanup when this signal is handled, but the program can do what it likes—including ignoring the signal.

A KILL signal (a.k.a. signal value 9), by contrast, forces the specified program to terminate.

Confusingly, docker kill uses a KILL signal on the running process, giving the processes within it no chance to handle the termination. This means that stray files, such as files containing running process IDs, may be left in the filesystem. Depending on the application's ability to manage state, this may or may not cause problems for you if you start up the container again.

Even more confusingly, the docker stop command acts like the kill command, sending a TERM signal (see table 4.1).

Table 4.1   Stopping and killing

Command	Default signal	Default signal value
kill	TERM	15
docker kill	KILL	9
docker stop	TERM	15

In summary, don't use docker kill as you'd use kill, and you're probably best off getting into the habit of using docker stop.

TECHNIQUE 29   **Using Docker Machine to provision Docker hosts**

Setting up Docker on your local machine was probably not too difficult—there's a script you can use for convenience, or alternatively it's just a matter of a few commands to add the appropriate sources for your package manager. But this can get tedious when you're trying to manage Docker installs on other hosts.

PROBLEM

You want to spin up containers on a separate Docker host from your machine.

SOLUTION

Use Docker Machine.

DISCUSSION

This technique will be useful if you need to run Docker containers on multiple external hosts. You may want this for a number of reasons: to test networking between Docker containers by provisioning a VM to run within your own physical host; to provision containers on a more powerful machine through a VPS provider; to risk trashing a host with some kind of crazy experiment; to have the choice of running on multiple cloud providers. Whatever the reason, Docker Machine is probably the answer for you. It's also the gateway to more sophisticated orchestration tools like Docker Swarm.

WHAT DOCKER MACHINE IS

Docker Machine is mainly a convenience program. It wraps a lot of potentially tortuous instructions around provisioning external hosts and turns them into a few easy-to-use commands. If you're familiar with Vagrant, it has a similar feel: provisioning and managing other machine environments is made simpler with a consistent interface. If you cast your mind back to our architecture overview in chapter 2, one way of viewing it is to imagine that it's facilitating the management of different Docker daemons from one client (see figure 4.7).

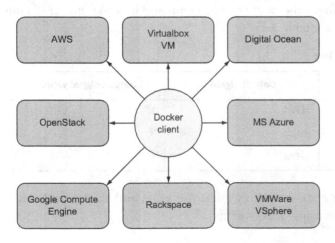

Figure 4.7   Docker Machine as a client of external hosts

The list of Docker host providers in figure 4.7 isn't exhaustive, and it's likely to grow. At the time of writing, the following drivers are available, which allow you to provision to the given host provider:

- Amazon Web Services
- Digital Ocean
- Google Compute Engine
- IBM Softlayer

- Microsoft Azure
- Microsoft Hyper-V
- Openstack
- Rackspace

- Oracle VirtualBox
- VMware Fusion
- VMware vCloud Air
- VMware vSphere

The options that must be specified to provision a machine will vary greatly depending on the functionality provided by the driver. At one end, provisioning an Oracle VirtualBox VM on your machine has only 3 flags available to the `create`, compared with OpenStack's 17.

WHAT DOCKER MACHINE IS NOT

It's worth clarifying that Docker Machine is not any kind of clustering solution for Docker. Other tools, such as Docker Swarm, fulfill that function, and we'll look at them later.

INSTALLATION

Installation is a straightforward binary. Download links and installation instructions for different architectures are available here: https://github.com/docker/machine/releases.

> **MOVE THE BINARY?** You may want to move the binary to a standard location, like /usr/bin, and ensure it's renamed or symlinked to `docker-machine` before continuing, as the downloaded file may have a longer name suffixed with the binary's architecture.

USING DOCKER MACHINE

To demonstrate Docker Machine's use, you can start by creating a VM with a Docker daemon on it that you can work with.

> **VIRTUALBOX VM MANAGER ASSUMED** You'll need to have Oracle's VirtualBox installed for this to work. It is widely available in most package managers.

Use docker-machine's create subcommand to create a new host and specify its type with the --driver flag. The host has been named host1.

```
$ docker-machine create --driver virtualbox host1
INFO[0000] Creating CA: /home/imiell/.docker/machine/certs/ca.pem
INFO[0000] Creating client certificate: /home/imiell/.docker/machine/certs/
  cert.pem
```

```
INFO[0002] Downloading boot2docker.iso to /home/imiell/.docker/machine/cache/
 boot2docker.iso...
INFO[0011] Creating VirtualBox VM...
INFO[0023] Starting VirtualBox VM...
INFO[0025] Waiting for VM to start...                    Your machine is now created.
INFO[0043] "host1" has been created and is now the active machine.
INFO[0043] To point your Docker client at it, run this in your shell:
 $(docker-machine env host1)
```

Run this command to set the DOCKER_HOST environment variable, which sets the default host that Docker commands will be run on.

Vagrant users will feel right at home here. By running this, you've created a machine that you can now manage Docker on. If you follow the instructions given in the output, you can SSH directly to the new VM:

The $() takes the output of the docker-machine env command and applies it to your environment. docker-machine env outputs a set of commands that you can use to set the default host for Docker commands.

The environment variable names are all prefixed with DOCKER_.

The DOCKER_HOST variable is the endpoint of the Docker daemon on the VM.

```
$ eval $(docker-machine env host1)
$ env | grep DOCKER
DOCKER_HOST=tcp://192.168.99.101:2376
DOCKER_TLS_VERIFY=yes
DOCKER_CERT_PATH=/home/imiell/.docker/machine/machines/host1
DOCKER_MACHINE_NAME=host1
$ docker ps -a
CONTAINER ID    IMAGE     COMMAND     CREATED     STATUS     PORTS      NAMES
$ docker-machine ssh host1
```

These variables handle the security side of connections to the new host.

The ssh subcommand will take you directly to the new VM itself.

The docker command is now pointed at the VM host you have created, not at your previously used host machine. You have created no containers on the new VM, so there is no output.

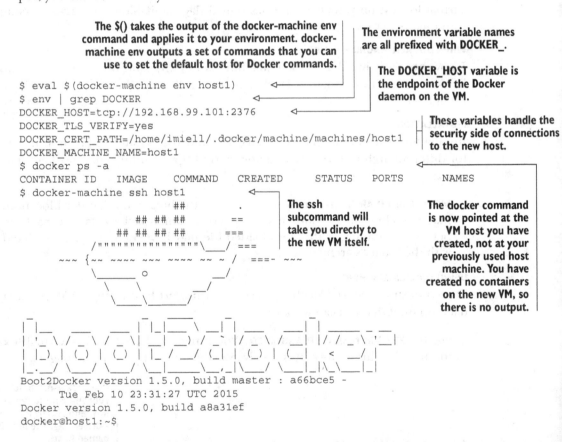

```
Boot2Docker version 1.5.0, build master : a66bce5 -
     Tue Feb 10 23:31:27 UTC 2015
Docker version 1.5.0, build a8a31ef
docker@host1:~$
```

MANAGING HOSTS

Managing multiple Docker hosts from one client machine can make it difficult to track what's going on. Docker machine comes with various management commands to make this simpler, as shown in table 4.2.

Table 4.2   List of docker machine commands

Subcommand	Action
create	Creates a new machine
ls	Lists the Docker host machines
stop	Stops the machine
start	Starts a machine
restart	Stops and starts a machine
rm	Destroys a machine
kill	Kills a machine off
inspect	Returns a JSON representation of the machine's metadata
config	Returns the configuration required to connect to the machine
ip	Returns the IP address of the machine
url	Returns a URL for the Docker daemon on the machine
upgrade	Upgrades to the latest Docker version on the host

The following example lists two machines. The active machine is listed with an asterisk, and it has a state associated with it, analogous to the state of containers or processes:

```
$ docker-machine ls
NAME    ACTIVE  DRIVER      STATE     URL                         SWARM
host1           virtualbox  Running   tcp://192.168.99.102:2376
host2   *       virtualbox  Running   tcp://192.168.99.103:2376
```

In fact, you can look at this as turning machines into processes much like Docker itself can be seen as turning environments into processes.

> **SWITCHING BACK**   You may be wondering how to switch back to your original host machine Docker instance. At the time of writing we haven't found a simple way to do this. You can either docker-machine rm all the machines, or if that's not an option, you can manually unset the environment variables previously set with unset DOCKER_HOST DOCKER_TLS_VERIFY DOCKER_CERT_PATH.

4.3   *Building images*

Although the simplicity of Dockerfiles makes them a powerful time-saving tool, there are some subtleties that can cause confusion. We'll take you over a few time-saving features and their details, starting with the ADD instruction, and then covering the Docker build cache, how it can let you down, and how you can manipulate it to your advantage.

Remember to refer to the official Docker documentation for a complete reference on Dockerfile instructions.

Injecting files into your image using ADD

Although it's possible to add files within a Dockerfile using the RUN command and basic shell primitives, this can quickly become unmanageable. The ADD command was added to the list of Dockerfile commands to address the need to put large numbers of files into an image without fuss.

PROBLEM

You want to download and unpack a tarball into your image in a concise way.

SOLUTION

Tar and compress your files, and use the ADD directive in your Dockerfile.

DISCUSSION

Create a fresh environment for this Docker build with mkdir add_example && cd add_example. Then retrieve a tarball and give it a name you can reference later:

```
$ curl \
https://www.flamingspork.com/projects/libeatmydata/libeatmydata-105.tar.gz > \
my.tar.gz
```

In this case we've used the example of a tar file from another technique, but it could be any tarball you like:

```
FROM debian
RUN mkdir -p /opt/libeatmydata
ADD my.tar.gz /opt/libeatmydata/
RUN ls -lRt /opt/libeatmydata
```

Build this Dockerfile with docker build --no-cache . and the output should look like this:

```
$ docker build --no-cache .
Sending build context to Docker daemon 422.9 kB
Sending build context to Docker daemon
Step 0 : FROM debian
 ---> c90d655b99b2
Step 1 : RUN mkdir -p /opt/libeatmydata
 ---> Running in fe04bac7df74
 ---> c0ab8c88bb46
Removing intermediate container fe04bac7df74
Step 2 : ADD my.tar.gz /opt/libeatmydata/
 ---> 06dcd7a88eb7
Removing intermediate container 3f093a1f9e33
Step 3 : RUN ls -lRt /opt/libeatmydata
 ---> Running in e3283848ad65
/opt/libeatmydata:
total 4
drwxr-xr-x 7 1000 1000 4096 Oct 29 23:02 libeatmydata-105

/opt/libeatmydata/libeatmydata-105:
total 880
```

```
drwxr-xr-x 2 1000 1000     4096 Oct 29 23:02 config
drwxr-xr-x 3 1000 1000     4096 Oct 29 23:02 debian
drwxr-xr-x 2 1000 1000     4096 Oct 29 23:02 docs
drwxr-xr-x 3 1000 1000     4096 Oct 29 23:02 libeatmydata
drwxr-xr-x 2 1000 1000     4096 Oct 29 23:02 m4
-rw-r--r-- 1 1000 1000     9803 Oct 29 23:01 config.h.in
[...edited...]
-rw-r--r-- 1 1000 1000     1824 Jun 18  2012 pandora_have_better_malloc.m4
-rw-r--r-- 1 1000 1000      742 Jun 18  2012 pandora_header_assert.m4
-rw-r--r-- 1 1000 1000      431 Jun 18  2012 pandora_version.m4
 ---> 2ee9b4c8059f
Removing intermediate container e3283848ad65
Successfully built 2ee9b4c8059f
```

You can see from this output that the tarball has been unpacked into the target directory by the Docker daemon (the extended output of all the files has been edited). Docker will unpack tarfiles of most of the standard types (.gz, .bz2, .xz, .tar).

It's worth observing that although you can download tarballs from URLs, they'll only be unpacked automatically if they're stored in the local filesystem. This can lead to confusion.

If you repeat the preceding process with the following Dockerfile, you'll notice that the file is downloaded but not unpacked:

```
FROM debian                                    The file is retrieved from
RUN mkdir -p /opt/libeatmydata                 the internet using a URL.
ADD \
https://www.flamingspork.com/projects/libeatmydata/libeatmydata-105.tar.gz \
/opt/libeatmydata/
RUN ls -lRt /opt/libeatmydata
```

The destination directory is indicated by the directory name and a trailing slash. Without the trailing slash, the argument is treated as a filename for the downloaded file.

Here is the resulting build output:

```
Sending build context to Docker daemon 422.9 kB
Sending build context to Docker daemon
Step 0 : FROM debian
 ---> c90d655b99b2
Step 1 : RUN mkdir -p /opt/libeatmydata
 ---> Running in 6ac454c52962
 ---> bdd948e413c1
Removing intermediate container 6ac454c52962
Step 2 : ADD \
https://www.flamingspork.com/projects/libeatmydata/libeatmydata-105.tar.gz \
/opt/libeatmydata/
Downloading [==================================================>] \
419.4 kB/419.4 kB
 ---> 9d8758e90b64
Removing intermediate container 02545663f13f
Step 3 : RUN ls -lRt /opt/libeatmydata
 ---> Running in a947eaa04b8e
/opt/libeatmydata:
total 412
-rw------- 1 root root 419427 Jan  1  1970 \
```

```
libeatmydata-105.tar.gz                    ◄──────┐
 ---> f18886c2418a
Removing intermediate container a947eaa04b8e
Successfully built f18886c2418a
```

> The libeatmydata-l05.tar.gz file has
> been downloaded and placed in the
> /opt/libeatmydata directory without
> being unpacked.

Note that without the trailing slash in the ADD line in the previous Dockerfile, the file would be downloaded and saved with that filename. The trailing slash indicates that the file should be downloaded and placed in the directory specified.

All new files and directories are owned by root (or whoever has group or user IDs of zero within the container).

DON'T WANT TO UNPACK?   If you want to add a compressed file from the local filesystem without it being unpacked, use the COPY command, which looks exactly like the ADD command but doesn't unpack any files.

> ### Whitespace in filenames?
> If your filenames have whitespace in them, you'll need to use the quoted form of ADD (or COPY):
>
> ```
> ADD "space file.txt" "/tmp/space file.txt"
> ```

TECHNIQUE 31   **Rebuilding without the cache**

Building with Dockerfiles takes advantage of a useful caching feature: steps that have already been built are only rebuilt if the commands have changed. The next listing shows the output of a rebuild of the to-do app from chapter 1.

Listing 4.7   Rebuilding with the cache

```
$ docker build .
Sending build context to Docker daemon  2.56 kB
Sending build context to Docker daemon
Step 0 : FROM node
 ---> 91cbcf796c2c
Step 1 : MAINTAINER ian.miell@gmail.com
 ---> Using cache           ◄─────
 ---> 8f5a8a3d9240
Step 2 : RUN git clone -q https://github.com/docker-in-practice/todo.git
 ---> Using cache
 ---> 48db97331aa2
Step 3 : WORKDIR todo
 ---> Using cache
 ---> c5c85db751d6
Step 4 : RUN npm install > /dev/null
 ---> Using cache
 ---> be943c45c55b
```

> Indicates you're
> using the cache

> Specifies the cached
> image/layer ID

```
Step 5 : EXPOSE 8000
 ---> Using cache
 ---> 805b18d28a65
Step 6 : CMD npm start
 ---> Using cache
 ---> 19525d4ec794
Successfully built 19525d4ec794
```

> The final image is "rebuilt," but in reality nothing has changed.

As useful and time-saving as this is, it's not always the behavior you want.

Taking the preceding Dockerfile as an example, imagine you'd changed your source code and pushed to the Git repository. The new code wouldn't be checked out, because the git clone command has not changed. As far as the Docker build is concerned, it's the same, so the cached image can be reused.

In these cases, you'll want to rebuild your image without using the cache.

PROBLEM

You want to rebuild your Dockerfile without using the cache.

SOLUTION

Build your image with the --no-cache flag.

DISCUSSION

To force a rebuild without using the image cache, run your docker build with the --no-cache flag. The following listing runs the previous build with --no-cache.

Listing 4.8   Forcing a rebuild without using the cache

```
$ docker build --no-cache .                          ◄
Sending build context to Docker daemon  2.56 kB
Sending build context to Docker daemon
Step 0 : FROM node
 ---> 91cbcf796c2c
Step 1 : MAINTAINER ian.miell@gmail.com
  ---> Running in ca243b77f6a1            ◄
 ---> 602f1294d7f1
Removing intermediate container ca243b77f6a1
Step 2 : RUN git clone -q https://github.com/docker-in-practice/todo.git
 ---> Running in f2c0ac021247
 ---> 04ee24faaf18
Removing intermediate container f2c0ac021247
Step 3 : WORKDIR todo
 ---> Running in c2d9cd32c182
 ---> 4e0029de9074
Removing intermediate container c2d9cd32c182
Step 4 : RUN npm install > /dev/null
 ---> Running in 79122dbf9e52
npm WARN package.json todomvc-swarm@0.0.1 No repository field.
 ---> 9b6531f2036a
Removing intermediate container 79122dbf9e52
Step 5 : EXPOSE 8000
 ---> Running in d1d58e1c4b15
 ---> f7c1b9151108
Removing intermediate container d1d58e1c4b15
```

> Rebuilds the Docker image ignoring cached layers with the --no-cache flag

> No mention of caching this time

> Intervening images have a different ID than in the previous listing.

```
Step 6 : CMD npm start
 ---> Running in 697713ebb185
 ---> 74f9ad384859
Removing intermediate container 697713ebb185
Successfully built 74f9ad384859
```

A new image is built.

The output shows no mention of caching, and each intervening layer ID is different from the output in listing 4.7.

Similar problems can occur in other situations. We were flummoxed early on using Dockerfiles when a network blip meant that a command didn't retrieve something properly from the network, but the command didn't error. We kept calling `docker build`, but the resulting bug wouldn't go away! This was because a "bad" image had found its way into the cache and we didn't understand the way Docker caching worked. Eventually we figured it out.

TECHNIQUE 32   **Busting the cache**

Using the `--no-cache` flag is often enough to get around any problems with the cache. But sometimes you'll want a more fine-grained solution. If you have a build that takes a long time, for example, you may want to use the cache up to a certain point, then invalidate it to rerun a command and create a new image.

PROBLEM

You want to invalidate the Docker build cache from a specific point in the Dockerfile build.

SOLUTION

Add a benign comment after the command to invalidate the cache.

DISCUSSION

Starting with the Dockerfile in https://github.com/docker-in-practice/todo, we've done a build and then added a comment in the Dockerfile on the line with `CMD`. You can see the output of doing `docker build` again here:

```
$ docker build .
Sending build context to Docker daemon  2.56 kB
Sending build context to Docker daemon
Step 0 : FROM node
 ---> 91cbcf796c2c
Step 1 : MAINTAINER ian.miell@gmail.com
 ---> Using cache
 ---> 8f5a8a3d9240
Step 2 : RUN git clone -q https://github.com/docker-in-practice/todo.git
 ---> Using cache
 ---> 48db97331aa2
Step 3 : WORKDIR todo
 ---> Using cache
 ---> c5c85db751d6
Step 4 : RUN npm install
 ---> Using cache
 ---> be943c45c55b
Step 5 : EXPOSE 8000
```

A "normal" docker build

Cache is used up to here.

```
    ┌─> ---> Using cache
    │   ---> 805b18d28a65
    │   Step 6 : CMD ["npm","start"] #bust the cache   <─┐
    │   ---> Running in fc6c4cd487ce
    │   ---> d66d9572115e                                <─
    Removing intermediate container fc6c4cd487ce
    Successfully built d66d9572115e
```

Cache has been invalidated but the command is effectively unchanged.

A new image has been created.

The reason this trick works is because Docker treats the non-whitespace change to the line as though it were a new command, so the cached layer is not reused.

You may be wondering (as we did when we first looked at Docker) whether you can move Docker layers from image to image, merging them at will as though they were change sets in Git. This isn't possible at present within Docker. A layer is defined as a change set from a given image only. Because of this, once the cache has been broken, it can't be reapplied for commands re-used later in the build.

For this reason, you're advised to put commands that are less likely to change nearer the top of the Dockerfile if possible.

4.4 Staying ship-shape

If you're anything like us (and if you're following this book studiously), your growing Docker addiction will mean that you start up numerous containers on, and download a variety of images to, your chosen host.

As time goes on, this Docker will take up more and more resources, and some housekeeping of containers and volumes will be required—we'll show you the how and why of this. We'll also introduce some visual tools for keeping your Docker environment clean and tidy, in case you want an escape from the command line.

TECHNIQUE 33 Running Docker without sudo

The Docker daemon runs in the background of your machine as the root user, giving it a significant amount of power, which it exposes to you, the user. Needing to use sudo is a result of this, but it can be inconvenient and make some third-party Docker tools impossible to use.

PROBLEM
You want to be able to run the docker command without having to use sudo.

SOLUTION
Add yourself to the docker group.

DISCUSSION
Docker manages permissions around the Docker Unix domain socket through a user group. For security reasons, distributions don't make you part of that group by default.

By adding yourself to this group, you'll enable the use of the docker command as yourself:

```
$ sudo addgroup -a username docker
```

Restart Docker and fully log out and in again, or reboot your machine if that's easier. Now you don't need to remember to type sudo or set up an alias to run Docker as yourself.

TECHNIQUE 34   Housekeeping containers

A frequent gripe of new Docker users is that in a short space of time you can end up with many containers on your system in various states, and there are no standard tools for managing this on the command line.

PROBLEM

You want to prune the containers on your system.

SOLUTION

Set up aliases to run the commands that tidy up old containers.

DISCUSSION

The simplest approach here is to delete all containers. Obviously, this is something of a nuclear option that should only be used if you're certain it's what you want.

The following command will remove all containers on your host machine:

> Get a list of all container IDs, both running and stopped, and pass them to...

```
$ docker ps -a -q | \
xargs --no-run-if-empty docker rm -f
```

> ...the docker rm -f command, which will remove any containers passed, even if they're running.

To briefly explain xargs, it takes each line of the input and passes them all as arguments to the subsequent command. We've passed an additional argument, --no-run-if-empty, which avoids running the command at all if there's no output from the previous command, in order to avoid an error.

If you have containers running that you may want to keep, but you want to remove all those that have exited, you can filter the items returned by the docker ps command:

> The --filter flag tells the docker ps command which containers you want returned. In this case you're restricting it to containers that have exited. Other options are running and restarting.

```
docker ps -a -q --filter status=exited | \
xargs --no-run-if-empty docker rm
```

> This time you don't force the removal of containers because they shouldn't be running, based on the filter you've given.

As an example of a more advanced use case, the following command will list all containers with a non-zero error code. You may need this if you have many containers on your system and want to automate the examination and removal of any containers that exited unexpectedly:

Finds containers with an exit code of zero, sorts them, and passes them as a file to comm

Runs the comm command to compare the contents of two files. The -3 argument suppresses lines that appear in both files (those with a zero exit code) and outputs any others.

Finds exited container IDs, sorts them, and passes them as a file to comm

```
comm -3 \
<(docker ps -a -q --filter=status=exited | sort) \
<(docker ps -a -q --filter=exited=0 | sort) | \
xargs --no-run-if-empty docker inspect > error_containers
```

Runs docker inspect against containers with a non-zero exit code (as piped in by comm), and saves the output to the error_containers file

PROCESS SUBSTITUTION IN BASH If you've not seen it before, the `<(command)` syntax is called process substitution. It allows you to treat the output of a command as a file and pass it to another command, which can be useful where piping output isn't possible.

The preceding example is rather complicated, but it shows the power you can get from combining different utilities together. It outputs all stopped container IDs, and then picks just those that have a non-zero exit code (those that exited in an unexpected way). If you're struggling to follow this, running each command separately and understanding them that way first can be helpful in learning the building blocks.

Such a command could be useful for gathering container information on production. You may want to adapt it to run a cron to clear out containers that exited in expected ways.

Make these one-liners available as commands

You can add commands as aliases so that they're more easily run whenever you log in to your host. To do this, add lines like the following to the end of your ~/.bashrc file:

```
alias dockernuke='docker ps -a -q | \
xargs --no-run-if-empty docker rm -f'
```

Then, when you next log in, running `dockernuke` from the command line will delete any Docker containers found on your system.

We've found that this saves a surprising amount of time. But be careful! It's all too easy to remove production containers this way, as we can attest. And even if you are careful enough not to remove running containers, you still might remove non-running but still useful data-only containers.

TECHNIQUE 35 **Housekeeping volumes**

Although volumes are a powerful feature of Docker, they come with a significant operational downside.

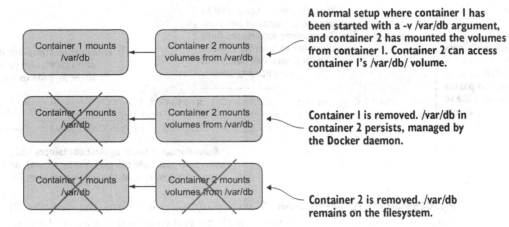

Figure 4.8   What happens to /var/db when containers are removed?

Because volumes can be shared between different containers, they can't be deleted when a container that mounted them is deleted. Imagine the scenario outlined in figure 4.8.

"Easy!" you might think, "Delete the volume when the last-referencing container is removed!" Indeed, Docker could have taken that option, and this approach is the one that garbage-collected programming languages take when they remove objects from memory: when no other object references it, it can be deleted.

But Docker judged that this could leave people open to losing valuable data accidentally, and preferred to make it a user decision as to whether a volume should be deleted on removal of the container. An unfortunate side effect of this is that, by default, volumes remain on your Docker daemon's host disk until they're removed manually.

If these volumes are full of data, your disk can fill up, so it's useful to be aware of ways to manage these orphaned volumes.

PROBLEM

You are using too much disk space because orphaned Docker mounts exist in your host.

SOLUTION

Use the -v flag when calling docker rm, or use a script to destroy them if you forget.

DISCUSSION

In the scenario in figure 4.8, you can ensure that /var/db is deleted if you always call docker rm with the -v flag. The -v flag removes any associated volumes if no other container still has it mounted. Fortunately Docker is smart enough to know whether any other container has the volume mounted, so there are no nasty surprises.

The simplest approach is to get into the habit of typing -v whenever you remove a container. That way you retain control of whether containers are removed.

The problem with this approach is that you might not want to always delete volumes. If you're writing a lot of data to these volumes, it's quite likely that you won't want to lose the data. Additionally, if you get into such a habit, it's likely to become automatic, and you'll only realize you've deleted something important when it's too late.

In these scenarios you'll need to use a script, which is—naturally— Dockerized for your convenience. Note that you'll need root permissions to run this:

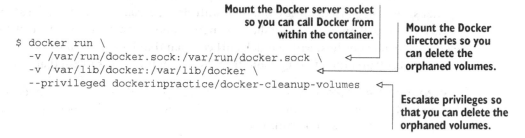

```
$ docker run \
  -v /var/run/docker.sock:/var/run/docker.sock \
  -v /var/lib/docker:/var/lib/docker \
  --privileged dockerinpractice/docker-cleanup-volumes
```

Mount the Docker server socket so you can call Docker from within the container.

Mount the Docker directories so you can delete the orphaned volumes.

Escalate privileges so that you can delete the orphaned volumes.

The preceding command will remove any volumes no longer accessed by any existing containers. The output will look like this:

```
$ docker run -v /var/run/docker.sock:/var/run/docker.sock \
  -v /var/lib/docker:/var/lib/docker --privileged 951acdb777bf

Delete unused volume directories from /var/lib/docker/volumes
Deleting 659cfdc5d394ec7ad5942862ba5feb1d24c9f67ca314462207835ef5bf657131
In use 6ae01c5524267c8f01f1d1e83933b494fdb5c709d9468122b470bfcdd5a5b03d
Deleting 73260d192a0a4d0ebc3606d9daf7137ab220e41cbbfe919ef1dded01a2f37b29

Delete unused volume directories from /var/lib/docker/vfs/dir
Deleting 659cfdc5d394ec7ad5942862ba5feb1d24c9f67ca314462207835ef5bf657131
In use 6ae01c5524267c8f01f1d1e83933b494fdb5c709d9468122b470bfcdd5a5b03d
Deleting 73260d192a0a4d0ebc3606d9daf7137ab220e41cbbfe919ef1dded01a2f37b29
```

If you're nervous about running this command and potentially deleting things you don't want to delete, you can call it with --dry-run at the end to prevent it from deleting anything.

> **RECOVERING DATA** If you want to recover data from an undeleted volume that's no longer referenced by any containers, you'll need to take a look inside the folders in /var/lib/docker/volumes as the root user.

TECHNIQUE 36 Detaching containers without stopping them

When working with Docker, you'll often find yourself in a position where you have an interactive shell, but exiting from the shell would terminate the container, as it's the container's principal process. Fortunately there's a way to detach from a container (and, if you want, you can use docker attach to connect to the container again).

PROBLEM
You want to detach from a container interaction without stopping it.

SOLUTION

Press Ctrl-P and then Ctrl-Q to detach.

DISCUSSION

Docker has helpfully implemented a key sequence that's unlikely to be needed by any other application and is also unlikely to be pressed by accident.

Let's say you started up a container with `docker run -t -i -p 9005:80 ubuntu /bin/bash` and then apt-get installed an nginx webserver. You want to test that it's accessible from your host with a quick curl command to localhost:9005.

Press Ctrl-P and then Ctrl-Q. Note that it's not all three keys pressed at once!

> **CONTAINERS RUNNING WITH --RM** If you're running with `--rm`, you'll need to hit Ctrl-C to get your terminal back once the key sequence has been pressed. The container will still be running.

TECHNIQUE 37 **Using DockerUI to manage your Docker daemon**

When demonstrating Docker, it can be difficult to demonstrate how containers and images differ—lines on a terminal aren't visual. In addition, the Docker command-line tools can be unfriendly if you want to kill and remove specific containers out of many. This problem has been solved with the creation of a point-and-click tool for managing the images and containers on your host.

PROBLEM

You want to manage containers and images on your host without using the CLI.

SOLUTION

Use DockerUI.

DISCUSSION

DockerUI is a tool created by one of the core committers to Docker—you can read about it and find the source at https://github.com/crosbymichael/dockerui, but because there are no prerequisites you can jump straight to running it:

```
$ docker run -d -p 9000:9000 --privileged \
-v /var/run/docker.sock:/var/run/docker.sock dockerui/dockerui
```

This will start the dockerui container in the background. If you now visit http://local-host:9000, you'll see the dashboard giving you at-a-glance information for Docker on your computer.

Container management functionality is probably one of the most useful pieces of functionality here—go to the Containers page and you'll see your running containers listed (including the dockerui container), with an option to display all containers. From here you can perform bulk operations on containers (such as killing them) or click on a container name to dive into more detail about the container and perform individual operations relevant to that container. For example, you'll be shown the option to remove a running container.

The Images page looks fairly similar to the Containers page and also allows you to select multiple images and perform bulk operations on them. Clicking on the image ID offers some interesting options, such as creating a container from the image and tagging the image.

Remember that DockerUI may lag behind official Docker functionality—if you want to use the latest and greatest functionality, you may be forced to resort to the command line.

TECHNIQUE 38 Generate a dependency graph of your Docker images

The file-layering system in Docker is an immensely powerful idea that can save space and make building software much quicker. But once you start using a lot of images, it can be difficult to understand how your images are related. The docker images -a command will return a list of all the layers on your system, but this isn't a user-friendly way to comprehend these relationships—it's much easier to visualize the relationships between your images by creating a tree of them as an image using Graphviz.

This is also a demonstration of Docker's power to make complicated tasks simpler. Installing all the components to produce the image on a host machine would previously have involved a long series of error-prone steps, but with Docker it can be turned into a single portable command that's far less likely to fail.

PROBLEM
You want to visualize a tree of the images stored on your host.

SOLUTION
Use an image that we've created with this functionality as a one-liner to output a PNG or get a web view.

DISCUSSION
Generating the graph involves using an image we've provided containing scripts that use Graphviz to generate the PNG image file. All you need to do in your run command is mount the Docker server socket and you're good to go, as the next listing shows.

Listing 4.9 Generating an image of your layer tree

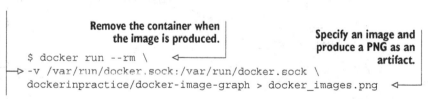

Mount the Docker server's Unix domain socket so you can access the Docker server from within the container. If you've changed the default for the Docker daemon, this will not work.

Remove the container when the image is produced.

Specify an image and produce a PNG as an artifact.

```
$ docker run --rm \
-v /var/run/docker.sock:/var/run/docker.sock \
dockerinpractice/docker-image-graph > docker_images.png
```

Figure 4.9 shows a PNG of an image tree from one of our machines.

You can see from this figure that the node and golang:1.3 images share a common root, and that the golang:runtime only shares the global root with the golang:1.3 image. Similarly, the mesosphere image is built from the same root as the ubuntu-upstart image.

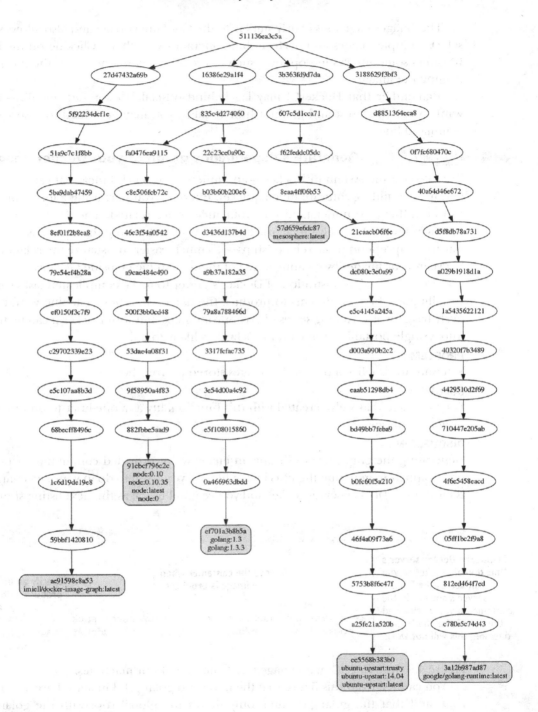

Figure 4.9   An image tree

You may be wondering what the global root node on the tree is. This is the *scratch* image, which is exactly 0 bytes in size.

Direct action—execute commands on your container

In the early days of Docker, many users added SSH servers to their images so that they could access them with a shell from outside. This was frowned upon by Docker, as it treated the container as a VM (and we know that containers are not VMs) and added a process overhead to a system that shouldn't need it. Many objected that once started, there was no easy way to get into a container. As a result, Docker introduced the exec command, which was a much neater solution to the problem of affecting and inspecting the internals of containers once started. It's this command that we'll discuss here.

PROBLEM

You want to perform commands on a running container.

SOLUTION

Use the docker exec command.

DISCUSSION

In the next listing we're going to start a container in the background (with -d) and tell it to sleep forever (do nothing). We'll name this command 'sleeper'.

Listing 4.10   Run a container to run docker exec commands on

```
docker run -d --name sleeper debian sleep infinity
```

Now that you've started a container, you can perform various actions on it using Docker's exec command. The command can be viewed as having three basic modes, listed in table 4.3.

Table 4.3   Docker exec modes

Mode	Description
Basic	Runs the command in the container synchronously on the command line
Daemon	Runs the command in the background on the container
Interactive	Runs the command and allows the user to interact with it

First we'll cover the basic mode. The following listing runs an echo command inside our 'sleeper' container.

Listing 4.11   Run an echo command from the container

```
$ docker exec sleeper echo "hello host from container"
hello host from container
```

Note that the structure of this command is very similar to the `docker run` command, but instead of the ID of an image, we give the ID of a running container. The `echo` command refers to the echo binary within the container, not outside.

The daemon mode runs the command in the background; you won't see the output in your terminal. This might be useful for regular housekeeping tasks, where you want to fire the command and forget, such as cleaning up log files as in the following listing.

Listing 4.12   Delete log files older than a week on a container

Returns immediately, regardless of how long it will take to complete

The -d flag runs the command as a daemon in the background.

Removes all files that are unchanged in the last seven days and that end with "log"

```
$ docker exec -d sleeper \
find / -ctime 7 -name '*log' -exec rm {} \;
$
```

Finally, we have the interactive mode. This allows you to run whatever commands you like from within the container. To enable this, you'll usually want to specify the shell to run interactively, which in the following code is bash:

```
$ docker exec -i -t sleeper /bin/bash
root@d46dc042480f:/#
```

The `-i` and `-t` arguments do the same thing you're familiar with from `docker run`—they make the command interactive and set up a TTY device so shells will function correctly. After running this, you'll have a prompt running inside the container.

4.5   Summary

In this chapter we've truly gone from theory to practice. You've seen the beginnings of the possibilities that Docker brings to your daily workflow. By now you'll have an understanding not only of Docker's architecture, but also of the areas where issues arise from daily use, and how to address them. It's a short step from here to the more powerful use of Docker to create artifacts that others can consume.

You learned several things in this chapter:

- You should reach for volumes if you need to get at external data from inside a container.
- SSHFS is a simple way to access data on other machines with no extra setup.
- Running GUI applications in Docker requires only a small amount of preparation of your image.
- Caching in the build process is a double-edged sword.
- You can use data containers to abstract away the location of your data.
- The `docker exec` command is the correct way to get inside a running container—resist installing SSH.

Now we'll move on from the haphazard and experimental work you might do every day to the serious business of Docker configuration management.

Configuration management— getting your house in order

5

This chapter covers

- Managing the building of images using Dockerfiles
- Building images using traditional configuration management tools
- Managing the secret information required to build images
- Reducing the size of your images for faster, lighter, and safer delivery

Configuration management is the art of managing your environments so that they're stable and predictable. Tools such as Chef and Puppet have attempted to alleviate the sysadmin burden of managing multiple machines. To an extent, Docker also reduces this burden by making the software environment isolated and portable. Even so, configuration management techniques are required to produce Docker images, and it's an important area to be aware of.

As you get more experience with Docker, these techniques will give you more tools for building images for whatever configuration needs you're trying to satisfy.

5.1   *Configuration management and Dockerfiles*

Dockerfiles are considered to be the standard way of building Docker images. Dockerfiles are often confusing in terms of what they mean for configuration management. You may have many questions (particularly if you have experience in other configuration management tools), such as

- What happens if the base image changes?
- What happens if the packages I'm installing change and I rebuild?
- Does this replace Chef/Puppet/Ansible?

In fact, Dockerfiles are quite simple: starting from a given image, a Dockerfile specifies a series of shell commands and meta-instructions to Docker, which will produce the desired final image.

Dockerfiles provide a common, simple, and universal language for provisioning Docker images. Within them, you can use anything you like to reach the desired end state. You could call out to Puppet, copy in another script, or copy in an entire filesystem!

First we'll consider how to deal with some minor challenges that Dockerfiles bring with them before moving on to the meatier issues we just outlined.

TECHNIQUE 40   Create reliable bespoke tools with ENTRYPOINT

Docker's potential for allowing you to run commands anywhere means that complex bespoke instructions or scripts run on the command line can be preconfigured and wrapped up into a packaged tool.

The easily misunderstood ENTRYPOINT instruction is a vital part of this. You're going to see how it enables you to create Docker images as tools that are well-encapsulated, clearly defined, and flexible enough to be useful.

PROBLEM

You want to define the command the container will run, but leave the command's arguments up to the user.

SOLUTION

Use the Dockerfile ENTRYPOINT instruction.

DISCUSSION

As a demonstration, we'll imagine a simple scenario in a corporation where a regular admin task is to clean up old log files. Often this is prone to error, and people accidentally delete the wrong things, so we're going to use a Docker image to reduce the risk of problems arising.

The following script (which you should name clean_log when you save it) deletes logs over a certain number of days old, where the number is passed in as a command-line option:

```
#!/bin/bash
echo "Cleaning logs over $1 days old"
find /log_dir -ctime "$1" -name '*log' -exec rm {} \;
```

Note that the log cleaning takes place on the /log_dir folder. This folder will only exist when you mount it at runtime. You may have also noticed that there's no check for whether an argument has been passed in to the script. The reason for this will be revealed as we go through the technique.

Now let's create a Dockerfile in the same directory to create an image, with the script running as the defined command, or *entrypoint*.

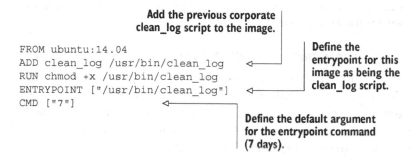

```
FROM ubuntu:14.04
ADD clean_log /usr/bin/clean_log
RUN chmod +x /usr/bin/clean_log
ENTRYPOINT ["/usr/bin/clean_log"]
CMD ["7"]
```

Add the previous corporate clean_log script to the image.

Define the entrypoint for this image as being the clean_log script.

Define the default argument for the entrypoint command (7 days).

BEST PRACTICE—ALWAYS USE ARRAY MODE You'll observe that we generally prefer the array form for CMD and ENTRYPOINT (for example, CMD ["/usr/bin/command"]) over the shell form (CMD /usr/bin/command). This is because the shell form automatically prepends a /bin/bash -c command to the command you supply, which can result in unexpected behaviour. Sometimes, however, the shell form is more useful (see technique 47).

The difference between ENTRYPOINT and CMD often confuses people. The key point to understand is that an entrypoint will always be run when the image is started, even if a command is supplied to the docker run invocation. If you try to supply a command, it will add that as an argument to the entrypoint, replacing the default defined in the CMD instruction. You can only override the entrypoint if you explicitly pass in an --entrypoint flag to the docker run command.

This means that running the image with a /bin/bash command will not give you a shell; rather it will supply /bin/bash as an argument to the clean_log script.

The fact that a default argument is defined by the CMD instruction means that the argument supplied need not be checked.

Here's how you might build and invoke this tool:

```
docker build -t log-cleaner .
docker run -v /var/log/myapplogs:/log_dir log-cleaner 365
```

After building the image, the image is invoked by mounting /var/log/myapplogs into the directory the script will use and passing 365 to remove log files over a year old, rather than a week.

If someone tries to use the image incorrectly by not specifying a day, they'll be given an error message:

```
$ docker run -ti log-cleaner /bin/bash
Cleaning logs over /bin/bash days old
find: invalid argument `-name' to `-ctime'
```

This example is quite trivial, but you can imagine that a corporation could apply it to centrally manage scripts used across its estate such that they could be maintained and distributed safely with a private registry.

> **IMAGE AVAILABLE**   This image is available to view and use as dockerinpractice/log-cleaner on the Docker Hub.

TECHNIQUE 41   **Avoid package drift by specifying versions in your build**

Dockerfiles have simple syntax and limited functionality, they can help greatly to clarify your build's requirements, and they can aid the stability of image production, but they can't guarantee repeatable builds. We're going to explore one of the numerous approaches to solving this problem and reducing the risk of nasty surprises when the underlying package management dependencies change.

This technique is helpful for avoiding those "it worked yesterday" moments, and it may be familiar if you've used classic configuration management tools. Building Docker images is fundamentally quite different from maintaining a server, but some hard-learned lessons are still applicable.

> **DEBIAN-BASED IMAGES ONLY**   This technique will only work for Debian-based images, such as Ubuntu.

PROBLEM

You want to ensure that your deb packages are the versions you expect.

SOLUTION

Run a script to capture the versions of all dependent packages on a verified installed system and capture the dependent versions. Install the specific versions in your Dockerfile.

DISCUSSION

A basic check for versions can be performed with an apt-cache call on a system you've verified as OK:

```
$ apt-cache show nginx | grep ^Version:
Version: 1.4.6-1ubuntu3
```

You can then specify the version in your Dockerfile like this:

```
RUN apt-get -y install nginx=1.4.6-1ubuntu3
```

This may be enough for your needs. What this doesn't do is guarantee that all dependencies from this version of nginx have the same versions that you originally verified. You can get information about all of those dependencies by adding a --recurse flag to the argument:

```
apt-cache --recurse depends nginx
```

The output of this command is intimidatingly large, so getting a list of version require-ments is tricky. Fortunately, we maintain a Docker image (what else?) to make this eas-ier for you. It outputs the RUN line you need to put into your Dockerfile to ensure that the versions of all the dependencies are correct:

```
$ docker run -ti dockerinpractice/get-versions vim
RUN apt-get install -y \
vim=2:7.4.052-1ubuntu3 vim-common=2:7.4.052-1ubuntu3 \
vim-runtime=2:7.4.052-1ubuntu3 libacl1:amd64=2.2.52-1 \
libc6:amd64=2.19-0ubuntu6.5 libc6:amd64=2.19-0ubuntu6.5 \
libgpm2:amd64=1.20.4-6.1 libpython2.7:amd64=2.7.6-8 \
libselinux1:amd64=2.2.2-1ubuntu0.1 libselinux1:amd64=2.2.2-1ubuntu0.1 \
libtinfo5:amd64=5.9+20140118-1ubuntu1 libattr1:amd64=1:2.4.47-1ubuntu1 \
libgcc1:amd64=1:4.9.1-0ubuntu1 libgcc1:amd64=1:4.9.1-0ubuntu1 \
libpython2.7-stdlib:amd64=2.7.6-8 zlib1g:amd64=1:1.2.8.dfsg-1ubuntu1 \
libpcre3:amd64=1:8.31-2ubuntu2 gcc-4.9-base:amd64=4.9.1-0ubuntu1 \
gcc-4.9-base:amd64=4.9.1-0ubuntu1 libpython2.7-minimal:amd64=2.7.6-8 \
mime-support=3.54ubuntu1.1 mime-support=3.54ubuntu1.1 \
libbz2-1.0:amd64=1.0.6-5 libdb5.3:amd64=5.3.28-3ubuntu3 \
libexpat1:amd64=2.1.0-4ubuntu1 libffi6:amd64=3.1~rc1+r3.0.13-12 \
libncursesw5:amd64=5.9+20140118-1ubuntu1 libreadline6:amd64=6.3-4ubuntu2 \
libsqlite3-0:amd64=3.8.2-1ubuntu2 libssl1.0.0:amd64=1.0.1f-1ubuntu2.8 \
libssl1.0.0:amd64=1.0.1f-1ubuntu2.8 readline-common=6.3-4ubuntu2 \
debconf=1.5.51ubuntu2 dpkg=1.17.5ubuntu5.3 dpkg=1.17.5ubuntu5.3 \
libnewt0.52:amd64=0.52.15-2ubuntu5 libslang2:amd64=2.2.4-15ubuntu1 \
vim=2:7.4.052-1ubuntu3
```

At some point your build will fail because the version is no longer available. When this happens, you'll be able to see which package has changed and review the change to determine whether it's OK for your particular image's needs.

This example assumes that you're using ubuntu:14.04. If you're using a different flavour of Debian, then fork the repo and change the Dockerfile's FROM instruction and build it. The repo is available here: https://github.com/docker-in-practice/get-versions.git.

Although this technique can help you with the stability of your build, it does noth-ing in terms of security, as you're still downloading packages from a repository you have no direct control over.

TECHNIQUE 42 **Replacing text with perl -p -i -e**

It's not uncommon when building images with Dockerfiles to need to replace specific items of text across multiple files. Numerous solutions for this exist, but we'll intro-duce a somewhat unusual favorite that's particularly handy in Dockerfiles.

PROBLEM
You want to alter specific lines in files during a build.

SOLUTION
Use perl -p -i -e.

DISCUSSION

We like this command for a few reasons:

- Unlike sed -i (a command with a similar syntax and effect), this works on multiple files out of the box, even if it encounters a problem with one of the files. This means you can run it across a directory with a '*' glob without fear that it will suddenly break when a directory is added in a later revision of the package.
- As with sed, you can replace the forward slashes in the search and replace commands with other characters.
- It's easy to remember (we refer to it as the "perl pie" command).

KNOWLEDGE OF REGULAR EXPRESSIONS ASSUMED This technique assumes an understanding of regular expressions. If you're not familiar with regular expressions, there are plenty of websites available to help you.

Here's a typical example of this command's use:

```
perl -p -i -e 's/127\.0\.0\.1/0.0.0.0/g' *
```

In this command, the -p flag asks perl to assume a loop while it processes all the lines seen. The -i flag asks perl to update the matched lines in place, and the -e flag asks perl to treat the supplied string as a perl program. The s is an instruction to perl to search and replace strings as they're matched in the input. Here 127.0.0.1 is replaced with 0.0.0.0. The g modifier ensures that all matches are updated, not just the first on any given line. Finally, the asterisk (*) applies the update to all files in this directory.

The preceding command performs a fairly common action for Docker containers. It replaces the standard localhost IP address (127.0.0.1) with one that indicates "any" IPv4 address (0.0.0.0) when used as an address to listen on. Many applications restrict access to the localhost IP by only listening on that address, and frequently you'll want to change this in their config files to the "any" address because you'll be accessing the application from your host, which appears to the container to be an external machine.

APPLICATION IN CONTAINER NOT ACCESSIBLE? If an application within a Docker container appears not to be accessible to you from the host machine despite the port being open, it can be worth trying to update the addresses to listen on to 0.0.0.0 in the application config file and restarting. It may be that the application is rejecting you because you're not coming from its localhost. Using --net=host (covered later in technique 97) when running your image can help confirm this hypothesis.

Another nice feature of perl -p -i -e (and sed) is that you can use other characters to replace the forward slashes if escaping the slashes gets awkward. Here's a real-world example from one of the authors' scripts that adds some directives to the default Apache site file:

This awkward command,

```
perl -p -i -e 's/\/usr\/share\/www\/\/var\/www\/html/g' /etc/apache2/*
```

becomes this:

```
perl -p -i -e 's@/usr/share/www@/var/www/html/@g' /etc/apache2/*
```

In the rare cases that you want to match or replace both the / and @ characters, you can try other characters such as | or #.

TECHNIQUE 43   **Flattening images**

A consequence of the design of Dockerfiles and their production of Docker images is that the final image contains the data state at each step in the Dockerfile. In the course of building your images, secrets may need to be copied in to ensure the build can work. These secrets may be SSH keys, certificates, or password files. Deleting these secrets before committing your image doesn't provide you with any real protection, as they'll be present in higher layers of the final image, and a malicious user could easily extract them from the image.

One way of handling this problem is to flatten the resulting image.

PROBLEM

You want to remove secret information from the layer history of your image.

SOLUTION

Create a container with the image, export it and import it, and then tag it with the original image ID.

DISCUSSION

To demonstrate a scenario where this could be useful, let's create a simple Dockerfile in a new directory that contains a Big Secret. Run `mkdir secrets && cd secrets` and then create a Dockerfile in that folder with the following contents:

```
                                                      Place a file with
                                                      some secret
                                                      information within
      FROM debian                                     your build.
      RUN echo "My Big Secret" >> /tmp/secret_key  ◄─┘
Remove the │  RUN cat /tmp/secret_key  ◄─┐
secret file. └─> RUN rm /tmp/secret_key  │  Do something with the secret file. This Dockerfile
                                         │  only cats the file, but yours might SSH to another
                                         │  server or encrypt that secret within the image.
```

Now run `docker build -t mysecret .` to build and tag that Dockerfile.

Once it's built, you can examine the layers of the resulting Docker image with the `docker history` command:

```
                                         Runs the docker history command against
                                         the name of the image you created
$ docker history mysecret  ◄─────────┘
IMAGE           CREATED          CREATED BY
➥ SIZE
55f3c131a35d   25 seconds ago    /bin/sh -c rm /tmp/secret_key
```

The layer where you removed the secret key

The layer where you added the secret key

```
⇒ 0 B
5b376ff3d7cd   26 seconds ago      /bin/sh -c cat /tmp/secret_key
⇒ 0 B
5e39caf7560f   27 seconds ago      /bin/sh -c echo "My Big Secret" >> /tmp/secre
⇒ 14 B
c90d655b99b2   2 weeks ago         /bin/sh -c #(nop) CMD [/bin/bash]
⇒ 0 B
30d39e59ffe2   2 weeks ago         /bin/sh -c #(nop) ADD file:3f1a40df75bc5673ce
⇒ 85.01 MB
511136ea3c5a   20 months ago
⇒ 0 B
```

The scratch (empty) layer

The layer that added the Debian filesystem. Note that this layer is the largest one in the history.

Now imagine that you've downloaded this image from a public registry. You could inspect the layer history and then run the following command to reveal the secret information:

```
$ docker run 5b376ff3d7cd cat /tmp/secret_key
My Big Secret
```

Here we've run a specific layer and instructed it to cat the secret key we removed at a higher layer. As you can see, the file is accessible.

Now you have a "dangerous" container with a secret inside that you've seen can be hacked to reveal its secrets. To make this image safe, you'll need to *flatten* it. This means you'll keep the same data in the image, but remove the intermediate layering information. To achieve this you need to export the image as a trivially run container and then re-import and tag the resulting image:

Runs a trivial command to allow the container to exit quickly, because you don't need it to be running

The docker history output now shows only one layer with the final set of files.

```
$ docker run -d mysecret /bin/true
28cde380f0195b24b33e19e132e81a4f58d2f055a42fa8406e755b2ef283630f
$ docker export 28cde380f | docker import - mysecret
$ docker history mysecret
IMAGE              CREATED          CREATED BY   SIZE
fdbeae08751b   13 seconds ago                   85.01 MB
```

Runs docker export, taking a container ID as an argument and outputting a TAR file of the filesystem contents. This is piped to docker import, which takes a TAR file and creates an image from the contents.

The - argument to the docker import command indicates you wish to read the TAR file from the command's standard input. The final argument to docker import indicates how the imported image should be tagged. In this case you're overwriting the previous tag.

Because there's now only one layer in the image, there's no record of the layers that contained the secrets. No secrets can now be extracted from the image.

TECHNIQUE 44   **Managing foreign packages with alien**

Although most Dockerfile examples in this book (and on the internet) use a Debian-based image, the reality of software development means that many people won't be dealing with them exclusively.

Fortunately tools exist to help you with this.

PROBLEM

You want to install a package from a foreign distribution.

SOLUTION

Use an alien-based Docker image to convert the package.

DISCUSSION

Alien is a command-line utility designed to convert package files between various formats, listed in table 5.1. On more than one occasion, we've been required to make packages from foreign package management systems work, such as .deb files in centos, and .rpm files in non-Red-Hat-based systems.

Table 5.1 Package formats supported by Alien

Extension	Description
.deb	Debian package
.rpm	Red Hat package management
.tgz	Slackware gzipped TAR file
.pkg	Solaris pkg package
slp	Stampede package

> **SOLARIS AND STAMPEDE PACKAGES NOT COVERED**   For the purposes of this technique, Solaris and Stampede packages aren't fully covered. Solaris requires software peculiar to Solaris, and Stampede is an abandoned project.

Researching this book, we discovered it could be a little fiddly to install Alien on non-Debian-based distributions. This being a Docker book, we've naturally decided to provide a conversion tool in the format of a Docker image. As a bonus, this tool uses the ENTRYPOINT command from technique 40 to make using the tools simpler.

As an example, let's take the eatmydata package, which will be used in technique 56:

Create an empty directory to work in.

Retrieve the package files you want to convert.

```
$ mkdir tmp && cd tmp
$ wget \
http://mirrors.kernel.org/ubuntu/pool/main/libe/libeatmydata/
➥ eatmydata_26-2_i386.deb
```

The container informs you of its actions as it runs its Alien wrapper script.

```
$ docker run -v $(pwd):/io dockerinpractice/alienate
Examining eatmydata_26-2_i386.deb from /io
eatmydata_26-2_i386.deb appears to be a Debian package
eatmydata-26-3.i386.rpm generated
eatmydata-26.slp generated
eatmydata-26.tgz generated
====================================================================
/io now contains:
eatmydata-26-3.i386.rpm
eatmydata-26.slp
eatmydata-26.tgz
eatmydata_26-2_i386.deb

====================================================================
$ ls -1
eatmydata_26-2_i386.deb
eatmydata-26-3.i386.rpm
eatmydata-26.slp
eatmydata-26.tgz
```

Run the dockerinpractice/alienate image, mounting the current directory to the container's /io path. The container will examine that directory and try to convert any valid files it finds.

The files have been converted to RPM, Slackware tgz, and Stampede files.

Alternatively, you can pass the URL directly to the docker run command:

```
$ mkdir tmp && cd tmp
$ docker run -v $(pwd):/io dockerinpractice/alienate \
http://mirrors.kernel.org/ubuntu/pool/main/libe/
➥ libeatmydata/eatmydata_26-2_i386.deb
wgetting http://mirrors.kernel.org/ubuntu/pool/main/libe/
➥ libeatmydata/eatmydata_26-2_i386.deb
--2015-02-26 10:57:28--  http://mirrors.kernel.org/ubuntu/pool/main/libe/
➥ libeatmydata/eatmydata_26-2_i386.deb
Resolving mirrors.kernel.org (mirrors.kernel.org)...
➥ 198.145.20.143, 149.20.37.36, 2001:4f8:4:6f:0:1994:3:14, ...
Connecting to mirrors.kernel.org (mirrors.kernel.org)
➥ |198.145.20.143|:80... connected.
HTTP request sent, awaiting response... 200 OK
Length: 7782 (7.6K) [application/octet-stream]
Saving to: 'eatmydata_26-2_i386.deb'

    OK .......                                        100% 2.58M=0.003s

2015-02-26 10:57:28 (2.58 MB/s) - 'eatmydata_26-2_i386.deb' saved [7782/7782]

Examining eatmydata_26-2_i386.deb from /io
eatmydata_26-2_i386.deb appears to be a Debian package
eatmydata-26-3.i386.rpm generated
eatmydata-26.slp generated
eatmydata-26.tgz generated
====================================================================
/io now contains:
eatmydata-26-3.i386.rpm
eatmydata-26.slp
eatmydata-26.tgz
eatmydata_26-2_i386.deb
====================================================================
$ ls -1
```

```
eatmydata 26-2 i386.deb
eatmydata-26-3.i386.rpm
eatmydata-26.slp
atmydata-26.tgz
```

If you want to run Alien in a container yourself, you can start up the container with this:

```
docker run -ti --entrypoint /bin/bash dockerinpractice/alienate
```

> **NOT GUARANTEED TO WORK** Alien is a "best effort" tool, and it's not guaranteed to work with the packages you give it.

TECHNIQUE 45   Reverse-engineer a Dockerfile from an image

You may find yourself in a situation where someone has created an image with a Dockerfile that you have access to, but the original Dockerfile has been lost. We've found ourselves in this position on more than one occasion. Being able to recover information about the build steps can sidestep a lengthy process of rediscovering them for yourself.

PROBLEM

You have an image and you want to reverse-engineer the original Dockerfile.

SOLUTION

Use the docker history command and inspect layers to try to determine what changed.

DISCUSSION

Although it's impossible to completely reverse-engineer a Docker image in every case, you have a good chance of working out how it was put together if it was substantially created with a Dockerfile (hopefully enough of a chance to reconstruct the image sufficiently for your purposes).

In this technique we're going to use the following Dockerfile as an example. It contains as many different types of instructions as we could fit in the shortest number of steps. You're going to build this Dockerfile, then run a simple shell command to give you an idea of how the technique works, and we'll finally look at a neater Dockerized solution.

> **LABEL INSTRUCTION MAY NOT WORK** The LABEL instruction is relatively new to Docker at the time of writing, so it may not have made it to your installation yet.

```
FROM busybox
MAINTAINER ian.miell@gmail.com
ENV myenvname myenvvalue
LABEL mylabelname mylabelvalue
WORKDIR /opt
RUN mkdir -p copied
COPY Dockerfile copied/Dockerfile
RUN mkdir -p added
```

```
ADD Dockerfile added/Dockerfile
RUN touch /tmp/afile
ADD Dockerfile /
EXPOSE 80
VOLUME /data
ONBUILD touch /tmp/built
ENTRYPOINT /bin/bash
CMD -r
```

First, you need to build this example image, giving the resulting image the name reverseme:

```
$ docker build -t reverseme .
```

SHELL SOLUTION

This shell-based implementation is mostly here for instruction, and is less complete than the upcoming Dockerized solution. This solution uses docker inspect to extract the metadata for the command, for example.

> **JQ REQUIRED** To run this solution, you may need to install the jq program. This allows you to query and manipulate JSON data.

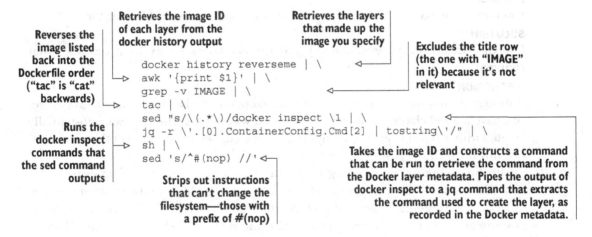

The output will look like this:

```
MAINTAINER Jérôme Petazzoni <jerome@docker.com>
ADD file:8cf517d90fe79547c474641cc1e6425850e04abbd8856718f7e4a184ea878538 in /
CMD ["/bin/sh"]
MAINTAINER ian.miell@gmail.com
ENV myenvname=myenvvalue
WORKDIR /opt
mkdir -p copied
COPY file:d0fb99565b15f8dfec37ea1cf3f9c4440b95b1766d179c11458e31b5d08a2ced in
➥ copied/Dockerfile
mkdir -p added
ADD file:d0fb99565b15f8dfec37ea1cf3f9c4440b95b1766d179c11458e31b5d08a2ced in
```

```
⮡ added/Dockerfile
touch /tmp/afile
ADD file:d0fb99565b15f8dfec37ea1cf3f9c4440b95b1766d179c11458e31b5d08a2ced in /
COPY dir:9cc240dcc0e31ce1b68951d230ee03fc6d3b834e2ae459f4ad7b7d023845e834 in /
COPY file:97bc58d5eaefdf65278cf82674906836613be10af02e4c02c81f6c8c7eb44868 in /
EXPOSE 80/tcp
VOLUME [/data]
ONBUILD touch /tmp/built
ENTRYPOINT [/bin/sh -c /bin/bash]
CMD [/bin/sh -c -r]
```

This output looks similar to our original Dockerfile with a few differences. The FROM command has been replaced with the three commands that made up the layers to create the BusyBox image. The ADD and COPY commands reference a checksum and the location the file or files were unpacked to. This is because the original build context isn't preserved in the metadata. Finally, the CMD and ENTRYPOINT instructions are changed to a canonical square bracket form.

> **WHAT IS A BUILD CONTEXT?**   A Docker *build context* is the set of files at and under the location of the directory passed in with the docker build command. This context is where Docker looks for files to ADD or COPY into Dockerfiles.

Because the lack of build context makes the ADD and COPY instructions invalid, this Dockerfile can't be run in as is. Unfortunately, if you have these in your reverse-engineered Dockerfile, you'll have to try to work out what file or files were added from the context information. For example, in the preceding output, if you run up the reverseme image as a container and then look at copied/Dockerfile, you should be able to extract the file and add it to your new build context.

A DOCKERIZED SOLUTION

Although the preceding solution is a useful and instructive way to get information about the image you're interested in (and relatively easy to modify for your own needs), there's a cleaner way to achieve the same thing—a way that's more likely to be maintained. As a bonus, this solution also gives you (if it can) a FROM command similar to the one in your original Dockerfile:

```
$ docker run -v /var/run/docker.sock:/var/run/docker.sock \
  dockerinpractice/dockerfile-from-image reverseme
FROM busybox:buildroot-2014.02
MAINTAINER ian.miell@gmail.com
ENV myenvname=myenvvalue
WORKDIR /opt
RUN mkdir -p copied
COPY file:43a582585c738bb8fd3f03f29b18caaf3b0829d3ceb13956b3071c5f0befcbfc \
in copied/Dockerfile
RUN mkdir -p added
ADD file:43a582585c738bb8fd3f03f29b18caaf3b0829d3ceb13956b3071c5f0befcbfc \
in added/Dockerfile
RUN touch /tmp/afile
ADD \
```

```
file:43a582585c738bb8fd3f03f29b18caaf3b0829d3ceb13956b3071c5f0befcbfc in /
EXPOSE 80/tcp
VOLUME [/data]
ONBUILD touch /tmp/built
ENTRYPOINT [/bin/sh -c /bin/bash]
CMD [/bin/sh -c -r]
```

This technique has got us out of a couple of tight spots at work!

> **ONLY APPLIES TO DOCKERFILE-CREATED IMAGES** If the image was properly created with a Dockerfile, this technique should work as described. If it was hand-crafted and then committed, the differences between the images won't be available in the image metadata.

5.2   *Traditional configuration management tools with Docker*

Now we'll move on to how Dockerfiles can work alongside more traditional configuration management tools.

We'll look here at traditional configuration management with make, show you how you can use your existing Chef scripts to provision your images with Chef Solo, and look at a shell script framework built to help non-Docker experts build images.

TECHNIQUE 46   Traditional: using make with Docker

At some point you might find that having a bunch of Dockerfiles is limiting your build process. For example, it's impossible to produce any output files if you limit yourself to running docker build, and there's no way to have variables in Dockerfiles.

This requirement for additional tooling can be achieved by a number of tools (including plain shell scripts). In this technique we'll look at how you can twist the venerable make tool to work with Docker.

PROBLEM
You want to add additional tasks around docker build execution.

SOLUTION
Wrap your image creation inside make.

DISCUSSION
In case you haven't used it before, make is a tool that takes one or more input files and produces an output file, but it can also be used as a task runner. Here's a simple example (note that all indents must be tabs):

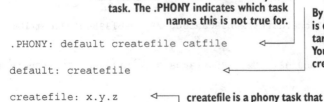

By default, make assumes that all targets are filenames that will be created by the task. The .PHONY indicates which task names this is not true for.

By convention, the first target in a Makefile is default. When run without an explicit target, make will choose the first in the file. You can see that default will execute createfile as its only dependency.

```
.PHONY: default createfile catfile

default: createfile

createfile: x.y.z
```

createfile is a phony task that depends on the x.y.z task.

```
catfile:
    cat x.y.z
```
◄──────┐ **catfile is a phony task that
        │ runs a single command.**

```
x.y.z:
    echo "About to create the file x.y.z"
    echo abc > x.y.z
```
◄──────┐ **x.y.z is a file task that runs
        │ two commands and creates
        │ the target x.y.z file.**

> **SPACING IS IMPORTANT** All indents in a Makefile must be tabs, and each command in a target is run in a different shell (so environment variables will not be carried across).

Once you have the preceding content in a file called Makefile, you can invoke any target with a command like make createfile.

Now we can look at some useful patterns in a Makefile—the rest of the targets we'll talk about will be phony, as it's difficult (although possible) to use file change tracking to trigger Docker builds automatically. Dockerfiles use a cache of layers, so builds tend to be fast.

The first step is to run a Dockerfile. Because a Makefile consists of shell commands, this is easy:

```
base:
    docker build -t corp/base .
```

Normal variations of this work as you'd expect (such as piping the file to docker build to remove the context, or using -f to use a differently named Dockerfile) and you can use the dependencies feature of make to automatically build base images (used in FROM) where necessary. For example, if you checked out a number of repositories into a subdirectory called repos (also easily doable with make), you could add a target like this:

```
app1: base
    cd repos/app1 && docker build -t corp/app1 .
```

The downside of this is that every time your base image needs rebuilding, Docker will upload a build context that includes all of your repos. You can fix this by explicitly passing a build context TAR file to Docker:

```
base:
    tar -cvf - file1 file2 Dockerfile | docker build -t corp/base .
```

This explicit statement of dependencies will provide a significant speed increase if your directory contains a large number of files that are irrelevant to the build. You can slightly modify this target if you want to keep all your build dependencies in a different directory:

```
base:
    tar --transform 's/^deps\///' -cf - deps/* Dockerfile | \
docker build -t corp/base .
```

Here you add everything in the deps directory to the build context, and use the --transform option to tar (available in recent tar versions on Linux) to strip any leading "deps/" from filenames. In this particular case, a better approach would have been to put the deps and Dockerfile in a directory of their own to permit a normal docker build, but it's useful to be aware of this advanced usage as it can come in handy in the most unlikely places. Always think carefully before using it, though, as it adds complexity to your build process.

Simple variable substitution is a relatively simple matter, but (as with --transform previously) think carefully before you use it—Dockerfiles deliberately don't support variables in order to keep builds easily reproducible. Here we're going to use variables passed to make and substitute using sed, but you can pass and substitute however you like:

```
VAR1 ?= defaultvalue
base:
    cp Dockerfile.in Dockerfile
    sed -i 's/{VAR1}/$(VAR1)/' Dockerfile
    docker build -t corp/base .
```

The Dockerfile will be regenerated every time the base target is run, and you can add more variable substitutions by adding more sed -i lines. To override the default value of VAR1, you run make VAR1=newvalue base. If your variables include slashes you may need to choose a different sed seperator, like sed -i 's#{VAR1}#$(VAR1)#' Dockerfile.

Finally, if you've been using Docker as a build tool, you need to know how to get files back out of Docker. We'll present a couple of different possibilities, depending on your use case:

```
singlefile: base
    docker run --rm corp/base cat /path/to/myfile > outfile
multifile: base
    docker run --rm -v $(pwd)/outdir:/out corp/base sh \
-c "cp -r /path/to/dir/* /out/"
```

Here, singlefile runs cat on a file and pipes the output to a new file. This approach has the advantage of automatically setting the correct owner of the file, but it becomes cumbersome for more than one file. The multifile approach mounts a volume in the container and copies all files from a directory to the volume. You can follow this up with a chown command to set the correct owner on the files, but bear in mind that you'll probably need to invoke it with sudo.

The Docker project itself uses the volume-mounting approach when building Docker from source.

TECHNIQUE 47   Building images with Chef Solo

One of the things that confuses newcomers to Docker is whether Dockerfiles are the only supported configuration management tool, and whether existing configuration management tools should ported to Dockerfiles. Neither of these is true.

Although Dockerfiles are designed to be a simple and portable means of provisioning images, they are also flexible enough to allow any other configuration management tool to take over. In short, if you can run it in a terminal, you can run it in a Dockerfile.

As a demonstration of this, we'll show you how to get up and running with Chef, arguably the most established configuration management tool, in a Dockerfile. Using a tool like Chef can reduce the amount of work required for you to configure images.

PROBLEM

You want to reduce configuration effort by using Chef.

SOLUTION

Install Chef in your container and run recipes to provision it.

DISCUSSION

In this example we're going to provision a simple "Hello World!" Apache website using Chef. This will give you a taste of what Chef can do for your configuration.

For this example we're using Chef Solo, which requires no external Chef server setup. If you're already familiar with Chef, this example can easily be adapted for your pre-existing scripts.

We're going to walk through the creation of this Chef example, but if you want to download the working code, it's available as a Git repository. To download it, run this command:

```
git clone https://github.com/docker-in-practice/docker-chef-solo-example.git
```

We'll begin with the simple aim of setting up a webserver with Apache that outputs "Hello World!" (what else?) when you hit it. The site is going to be served from mysite.com, and a mysiteuser user will be set up on the image.

To begin, create a directory and set it up with the files you'll need for Chef configuration:

The Chef config file, which sets some base variables for the Chef configuration

The Dockerfile that will build the image

The Chef attributes file, which defines the variables for this image (or node, in Chef parlance), will contain the recipes in the run-list for this image, and other information.

Create the default recipe folder, which stores the Chef instructions for building the image.

Create the templates for the dynamically configured content.

```
$ mkdir chef_example
$ cd chef_example
$ touch attributes.json
$ touch config.rb
$ touch Dockerfile
$ mkdir -p cookbooks/mysite/recipes
$ touch cookbooks/mysite/recipes/default.rb
$ mkdir -p cookbooks/mysite/templates/default
$ touch cookbooks/mysite/templates/default/message.erb
```

First we'll fill out attributes.json in the following listing.

Listing 5.1   attributes.json

```
{
    "run_list": [
            "recipe[apache2::default]",
            "recipe[mysite::default]"
    ]
}
```

This file sets out the recipes that you're going to run. The apache2 recipes will be retrieved from a public repository; the mysite recipes will be written here.

Next, populate your config.rb with some basic information, as shown in the next listing.

Listing 5.2   config.rb

```
base_dir         "/chef/"
file_cache_path base_dir + "cache/"
cookbook_path    base_dir + "cookbooks/"
verify_api_cert true
```

This file sets up basic information about the location, and adds the configuration setting `verify_api_cert` to suppress an irrelevant error.

Now we get to the meat of the work: the image's Chef recipe. Each stanza terminated by an end in the code block defines a Chef resource (see the following listing).

Listing 5.3   cookbooks/mysite/recipes/default.rb

```
user "mysiteuser" do          ⟵────── Creates a user
    comment "mysite user"
    home "/home/mysiteuser"
    shell "/bin/bash"
    supports :manage_home => true
end

directory "/var/www/html/mysite" do    ⟵  Creates a
    owner "mysiteuser"                          directory for the
    group "mysiteuser"                          web content
    mode 0755
    action :create
end                                        Defines a file that will be placed
                                           in the web folder. This file will be
template "/var/www/html/mysite/index.html" do  ⟵  created from a template defined
    source "message.erb"                            in the "source" attribute.
    variables(
        :message => "Hello World!"
    )
    user "mysiteuser"
    group "mysiteuser"
    mode 0755
```

```
end

web_app "mysite" do        ←——————⌐ Defines a web app
    server_name "mysite.com"              for apache2
    server_aliases ["www.mysite.com","mysite.com"] ←
    docroot "/var/www/html/mysite"
    cookbook 'apache2'
end
```

> **Defines a web app for apache2**

> **In a real scenario you'd have to change these references from "mysite" to your website's name. If you're accessing or testing from your host, this doesn't matter.**

The content of the website is contained within the template file. It contains one line, which Chef will read, substituting in the "Hello World!" message from config.rb and then writing the substituted file out to the template target (/var/www/html/mysite/index.html). This uses a templating language that we're not going to cover here.

Listing 5.4   cookbooks/mysite/templates/default/message.erb

```
<%= @message %>
```

Finally, you put everything together with the Dockerfile, which sets up the Chef prerequisites and runs Chef to configure the image, as shown in the following listing.

Listing 5.5   Dockerfile

```
FROM ubuntu:14.04

RUN apt-get update && apt-get install y git curl

RUN curl -L \
https://opscode-omnibus-packages.s3.amazonaws.com/
➥ ubuntu/12.04/x86_64/chefdk_0.3.5-1_amd64.deb \
-o chef.deb
RUN dpkg -i chef.deb && rm chef.deb        ←

COPY . /chef        ←

WORKDIR /chef/cookbooks
RUN knife cookbook site download apache2
RUN knife cookbook site download iptables
RUN knife cookbook site download logrotate

RUN /bin/bash -c 'for f in $(ls *gz); do tar -zxf $f; rm $f; done'  ←

RUN chef-solo -c /chef/config.rb -j /chef/attributes.json  ←

CMD /usr/sbin/service apache2 start && sleep infinity  ←
```

> **Download and install Chef. If this download doesn't work for you, check the latest code in the docker-chef-solo-example mentioned earlier in this discussion, as a later version of Chef may now be required.**

> **Copy the contents of the working folder into the /chef folder on the image.**

> **Move to the cookbooks folder and download the apache2 cookbook and its dependencies as tarballs using Chef's knife utility.**

> **Extract the downloaded tarballs and remove them.**

> **Run the chef command to configure your image. Supply it with the attributes and config files you already created.**

> **Define the default command for the image. The sleep infinity command ensures that the container doesn't exit as soon as the service command has finished its work.**

You're now ready to build and run the image:

```
docker build -t chef-example .
docker run -ti -p 8080:80 chef-example
```

If you now navigate to http://localhost:8080, you should see your "Hello World!" message.

TIMEOUTS ON DOCKER HUB If your Chef build takes a long time and you're using the Docker Hub workflow, the build can time out. If this happens, you can perform the build on a machine you control, pay for a supported service, or break the build steps into smaller chunks so that each individual step in the Dockerfile takes less time to return.

Although this is a trivial example, the benefits of using this approach should be clear. With relatively straightforward configuration files, the details of getting the image into a desired state are taken care of by the configuration management tool. This doesn't mean that you can forget about the details of configuration; changing the values will require you to understand the semantics to ensure you don't break anything. But this approach can save you much time and effort, particularly in projects where you don't need to get into the details too much.

TECHNIQUE 48   Source-to-image builds

We've looked at a few options for building Docker images, but the only one designed from scratch to take advantage of Docker's features is the Dockerfile. However, there are alternatives that can make life much easier for a developer uninterested in Docker, or that can provide more power to the build process.

PROBLEM
You want to give users a means of creating a Docker image without them needing to understand Docker.

SOLUTION
Use Red Hat's Source to Image (S2I, or STI) framework for building Docker images.

DISCUSSION
Source to Image is a means of creating Docker images by depositing source code into a separately defined Docker image that's responsible for building the image.

You may be wondering why such a build method was conceived. The principal reason is that it allows application developers to make changes to their code without being concerned with the details of Dockerfiles, or even Docker images. If the image is delivered to an aPaaS (application platform as a service), the individual engineer need not know about Docker at all to contribute to the project. This is useful in an enterprise environment where there are large numbers of people who have specific areas of expertise and are not directly concerned with the build process of their project.

S2I IS ALSO KNOWN AS STI The Source to Image method of building is known by two names in both its source code and documentation: the older STI, and the newer S2I. They're the same thing.

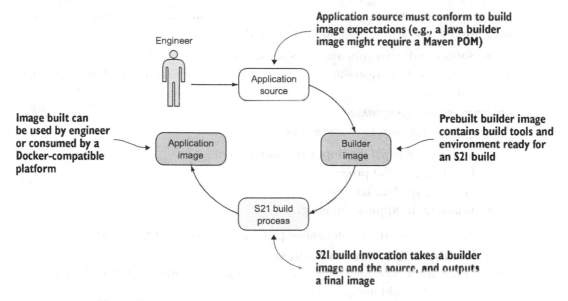

Figure 5.1   The Source to Image workflow

Figure 5.1 shows the S2I workflow in its core outline.

Once the process is set up, the engineer need only be concerned about the changes they want to make to their source code in order to progress it to different environments. Everything else is driven by the `sti` tool that enables the process.

OTHER BENEFITS

The advantages of this approach break down into a number of areas:

- *Flexibility*—This process can easily be plugged into any existing software delivery process, and it can use almost any Docker image as its base layer.
- *Speed*—This method of building can be faster than Dockerfile builds, as any number of complex operations can be added to the build process without creating a new layer at each step. S2I also gives you the capability to reuse artifacts between builds to save time.
- *Separation of concerns*—Because source code and Docker image are cleanly and strongly separated, developers can be concerned with code while infrastructure can be concerned with Docker images and delivery. As the base underlying image is separated from the code, upgrades and patches are more easily delivered.
- *Security*—This process can restrict the operations performed in the build to a specific user, unlike Dockerfiles, which allow arbitrary commands to be run as root.
- *Ecosystem*—The structure of this framework allows for a shared ecosystem of image and code separation patterns for easier large-scale operations.

This technique will show you how to build one such pattern, albeit a simple and somewhat limited one. Our application pattern will consist of

- Source code that contains one shell script
- A builder that creates an image that takes that shell script, makes it runnable, and runs it

CREATING YOUR OWN S2I IMAGE

There are several steps to creating your own S2I image:

1. Starting up an S2I development environment
2. Creating your Git project
3. Creating the builder image
4. Building the application image

Once you've created the image, making changes and rebuilding is easy.

START UP AN S2I DEVELOPMENT ENVIRONMENT

To help ensure a consistent experience, you can use a maintained environment to develop your S2I build image and project:

```
$ docker run -ti \
-v /var/run/docker.sock:/var/run/docker.sock \
dockerinpractice/shutit-s2i
```

Ensure the host's Docker daemon is available within the container (see technique 25).

Use a maintained S2I build environment.

> **PROBLEMS? SELINUX ENABLED?** If you're running in an selinux-enabled environment, you may have problems running Docker within a container. See technique 88.

CREATE YOUR GIT PROJECT

You could use a Git project built elsewhere and placed on GitHub, but to keep this example simple and self-contained, we're going to create a project locally in our S2I development environment. As mentioned earlier, the source code consists of one shell script that outputs "Hello World" to the terminal:

```
mkdir /root/myproject
cd /root/myproject
git init
git config --global user.email "you@example.com"
git config --global user.name "Your Name"
cat > app.sh <<< "echo 'Hello World'"
git add .
git commit -am 'Initial commit'
```

CREATE THE BUILDER IMAGE

To create the builder image, we're going get sti to create a skeleton for us to modify:

```
sti create sti-simple-shell /opt/sti-simple-shell
cd /opt/sti-simple-shell
```

This S2I command creates several files. To get our workflow working, we're going to focus on editing these files:

- Makefile
- Dockerfile
- .sti/bin/assemble
- .sti/bin/run

Taking the Dockerfile first, change its contents to match the following:

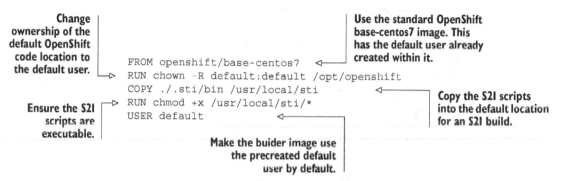

Change ownership of the default OpenShift code location to the default user.

Use the standard OpenShift base-centos7 image. This has the default user already created within it.

Ensure the S2I scripts are executable.

Copy the S2I scripts into the default location for an S2I build.

Make the builder image use the precreated default user by default.

```
FROM openshift/base-centos7
RUN chown -R default:default /opt/openshift
COPY ./.sti/bin /usr/local/sti
RUN chmod +x /usr/local/sti/*
USER default
```

Next you create the assemble script, which is responsible for taking the source code and compiling it so it's ready to run. The following is a simplified, but feature-complete, version of this bash script for you to use:

Run as a bash script and exit on any failure.

If the usage flag is passed in, print the usage.

If possible, restore any artifacts saved from previous builds.

Install the application source into the default directory.

Build the application from source. In this case, the build is the simple step of making the app.sh file executable.

```
#!/bin/bash -e
if [ "$1" = "-h" ]; then
    exec /usr/local/sti/usage
fi
if [ "$(ls /tmp/artifacts/ 2>/dev/null)" ]; then
  echo "---> Restoring build artifacts"
  mv /tmp/artifacts/* ./
fi
echo "---> Installing application source"
cp -Rf /tmp/src/. ./
echo "---> Building application from source"
chmod +x /opt/openshift/src/app.sh
```

The run script of your S2I build is responsible for running your application. It's the script that the image will run by default:

```
#!/bin/bash -e
exec /opt/openshift/src/app.sh
```

Now that your builder is ready, you run make to build your S2I builder image. It will create a Docker image called sti-simple-shell, which will provide the environment for your application image to be built—the one that includes the software project you made earlier. The output of your make call should look similar to this:

```
$ make
imiell@osboxes:/space/git/sti-simple-shell$ make
docker build --no-cache -t sti-simple-shell .
Sending build context to Docker daemon 153.1 kB
Sending build context to Docker daemon
Step 0 : FROM openshift/base-centos7
 ---> f20de2f94385
Step 1 : RUN chown -R default:default /opt/openshift
 ---> Running in f25904e8f204
 ---> 3fb9a927c2f1
Removing intermediate container f25904e8f204
Step 2 : COPY ./.sti/bin /usr/local/sti
 ---> c8a73262914e
Removing intermediate container 93ab040d323e
Step 3 : RUN chmod +x /usr/local/sti/*
 ---> Running in d71fab9bbae8
 ---> 39e81901d87c
Removing intermediate container d71fab9bbae8
Step 4 : USER default
 ---> Running in 5d305966309f
 ---> ca3f5e3edc32
Removing intermediate container 5d305966309f
Successfully built ca3f5e3edc32
```

If you run docker images, you should now see an image called sti-simple-shell stored locally on your host.

BUILD THE APPLICATION IMAGE

Looking back at figure 5.1, you now have the three things you need for an S2I build:

- Source code
- A builder image that provides an environment for building and running the source code
- The sti program

These three things are located in one place in this walkthrough, but the only one that needs to be local to your run is the sti program. The builder image can be fetched from a registry, and the source code can be fetched from a Git repository such as GitHub.

As you have all three parts in place, you can trigger the build process with the sti program:

**Runs the build with S2I's build subcommand,
disabling the default force-pulling of the image
(the image is only available locally) and
increasing logging to a useful level (you can
increment the number for more verbosity)**

**Directs the build to the source code
Git repository and passes both the
S2I builder image reference for this
source code and the desired tag for
the application image produced**

**General debug
information about the
details of the build**

```
$ sti build --force-pull=false --loglevel=1 \
file:///root/myproject sti-simple-shell final-image-1
I0608 13:02:00.727125 00119 sti.go:112] Building final-image-1
I0608 13:02:00.843933 00119 sti.go:182] Using assemble from image:///usr/local/sti
I0608 13:02:00.843961 00119 sti.go:182] Using run from image:///usr/local/sti
I0608 13:02:00.843976 00119 sti.go:182] Using save-artifacts from image:///
➥ usr/local/sti
I0608 13:02:00.843989 00119 sti.go:120] Clean build will be performed
I0608 13:02:00.844003 00119 sti.go:130] Building final-image-1
I0608 13:02:00.844026 00119 sti.go:330] No .sti/environment provided
➥ (no evironment file found in application sources)
I0608 13:02:01.178553 00119 sti.go:388] ---> Installing application source
I0608 13:02:01.179582 00119 sti.go:388] ---> Building application from source
I0608 13:02:01.294598 00119 sti.go:216] No .sti/environment provided
➥ (no evironment file found in application sources)
I0608 13:02:01.353449 00119 sti.go:246] Successfully built final-image-1 )
```

**Details of application
image build**

**General debug information about the
application of the source within the build image**

In this example, the Git repository is stored locally (hence the `file://` prefix), but you could also refer to it with a URL to a repository served online with https://gitserver .example.com/yourusername/yourproject or git@gitserver.example.com:yourusername/ yourproject.

You can now run your built image with the source code applied to it:

```
$ docker run final-image-1
Hello World
```

CHANGE AND REBUILD

It's easier to see the purpose of this build method now that you have a working example. Imagine you're a new developer ready to contribute to the project. You can make changes to the Git repository and run a simple command to rebuild the image without knowing anything about Docker:

```
$ cd /root/myproject
$ cat > app.sh <<< "echo 'Hello S2I!'"
$ git commit -am 'new message'
$ sti build --force-pull=false file:///root/myproject sti-simple-shell \
  final-image-2
```

Running this image shows the new message you set in the preceding code:

```
$ docker run final-image-2
Hello S21!
```

This technique demonstrated a simple example, but it's easy to imagine how this framework could be adapted to your particular requirements. What you end up with is a means for developers to push changes out to other consumers of their software without caring about the details of Docker image production.

Other techniques can be used in combination with this one to facilitate DevOps processes. For example, by using Git post-commit hooks you can automate the S2I build call on check-in.

5.3   *Small is beautiful*

If you're creating lots of images and sending them hither and thither, the issue of image size will be more likely to arise. Although Docker's use of image layering can help with this, you may have such a panoply of images on your estate that this isn't practical to manage.

In these cases, it can be helpful to have some best practices in your organization relating to reducing images to as small a size as possible. In this section we'll show you some of these, and even how a standard utility image can be reduced from 96 MB to only 6.5 MB—a much smaller size of object to fling around your network.

TECHNIQUE 49   Dockerfile tricks for keeping your build small

Because Dockerfiles are the recommended way to build images, it's natural that the community would focus on them when coming up with ideas to reduce image size. The result is a number of suggestions for taking advantage of Dockerfile features and working around some limitations.

PROBLEM

You want to reduce the size of your Dockerfile image.

SOLUTION

Reduce the layer overhead of the Docker build.

DISCUSSION

We're going to start with a fairly typical Dockerfile to build OSQuery, a tool to report on system performance using a SQL interface, as shown in the next listing.

Listing 5.6   OSQuery Dockerfile

```
FROM ubuntu:14.04
RUN apt-get update && apt-get upgrade -y
RUN apt-get install -y git
RUN apt-get install -y wget
RUN git clone https://github.com/facebook/osquery.git
```

Initialize Ubuntu container and upgrade to latest packages.

Install required packages.

Check out the OSQuery Git repository.

```
WORKDIR /osquery
RUN git checkout 1.0.3
RUN ./tools/provision.sh
RUN make
RUN make package
RUN dpkg -i \
./build/linux/osquery-0.0.1-trusty.amd64.deb
CMD ["/usr/bin/osqueryi"]
```

Build version I.0.3 of OSQuery as a deb package.

Install the created deb package.

Default the container to start the OSQuery tool.

Building this image gave us an image with a reported size of 2.377 GB—a fairly hefty image to cart around!

USE A SMALLER BASE IMAGE

The simplest way to reduce the size of your final image is to build from a smaller base. For this example, we'll change the FROM line to base our build on the stackbrew :ubuntu:14.04 image rather than the official ubuntu:14.04 one.

Keep in mind that a smaller base image means that you may be missing software previously installed in the larger image. These packages might include sudo, wget, and so on. In this technique we don't consider this.

Performing this step reduced the size of our image by about 10% to 2.186 GB.

CLEAN UP AFTER YOURSELF

You can reduce the size of the image further by removing packages and information from the image. Adding these lines to listing 5.6 before the CMD instruction will reduce the files on the container significantly, as the next listing shows.

Listing 5.7 OSQuery Dockerfile purge fragment

```
RUN SUDO_FORCE_REMOVE=yes apt-get purge -y git wget sudo
RUN rm -rf /var/lib/apt/lists/*
RUN apt-get autoremove -y
RUN apt-get clean
RUN cd
RUN rm -rf /osquery
```

Our image size is now bigger than the last version, at 2.19 GB! Due to Docker's layering, each RUN command creates a new copy-on-write layer in the final image, increasing the image's size, even though we're removing files. That leads us to our next improvement.

> **WHAT IS COPY-ON-WRITE?** Copy-on-write is a technique for minimizing resource usage when dealing with files. Processes that only want to read a file will look at the file from the topmost layer it's present in—processes in different containers could be looking at the same underlying file, as long as their images share a layer. This significantly reduces the amount of disk space that's required on most systems. When a container wishes to modify a file, that file must be copied into the container layer before it can be changed (otherwise other containers might see the changes), hence *copy-on-write*.

COLLATE SETS OF COMMANDS TO ONE LINE

Although you can flatten the image manually (see technique 43), you can achieve the same result within your Dockerfile by placing all the commands within one RUN instruction, as shown in the following listing.

Listing 5.8   OSQuery Dockerfile with a single RUN instruction

```
FROM stackbrew/ubuntu:14.04
RUN apt-get update && apt-get upgrade -y && \
    apt-get install -y git wget sudo && \
    git clone https://github.com/facebook/osquery.git && \
    cd /osquery && \
    git checkout 1.0.3 && \
    ./tools/provision.sh && \
    make && \
    make package && \
    dpkg -i ./build/linux/osquery-0.0.1-trusty.amd64.deb && \
    SUDO_FORCE_REMOVE=yes apt-get purge -y git wget sudo && \
    rm -rf /var/lib/apt/lists/* && \
    apt-get autoremove -y && \
    apt-get clean && \
    cd / && \
    rm -rf /osquery
CMD ["/usr/bin/osqueryi"]
```

> The entire install is reduced to a single RUN instruction.

Success! The reported size of the built image is now 1.05 GB. We've more than halved the size of original image.

WRITE A SCRIPT TO DO THE INSTALL

Having done all this, you might consider the resulting Dockerfile a bit unreadable. A friendlier way to achieve the same result with only a tiny overhead is to turn the RUN command into a script that you copy in and run, as shown in the following two listings.

Listing 5.9   OSQuery Dockerfile installed from a shell script

```
FROM stackbrew/ubuntu:14.04
COPY install.sh /install.sh
RUN /bin/bash /install.sh && rm /install.sh
CMD ["/usr/bin/osqueryi"]
```

Listing 5.10   install.sh

```
#!/bin/bash
set -o errexit
apt-get update
apt-get upgrade -y
apt-get install -y git wget sudo
git clone https://github.com/facebook/osquery.git
cd /osquery
git checkout 1.0.3
```

> Configure the bash script to throw an error if any of the commands within it return a non-zero exit code.

```
./tools/provision.sh
make
make package
dpkg -i ./build/linux/osquery-0.0.1-trusty.amd64.deb
SUDO_FORCE_REMOVE=yes apt-get purge -y git wget sudo
rm -rf /var/lib/apt/lists/*
apt-get autoremove -y
apt-get clean
cd /
rm -rf /osquery
```

The reported size of the built image is unchanged at 1.05 GB.

> **TRADING ONE PROBLEM FOR ANOTHER** By making these changes, you lose many beneficial features that Dockerfiles bring to the table. For example, the time-saving benefits of the build cache are rendered null and void by the reduction of work to a single instruction. As ever, there's a trade-off between image size, build flexibility, and build time.

Using these few simple tricks you can reduce the size of your resulting image significantly. This isn't the end of the story, though, as you can put images on much stricter diets with the more radical techniques that follow.

TECHNIQUE 50 Tricks for making an image smaller

Let's say you've been given an image by a third party, and you want to make the image smaller. The simplest approach is to start with an image that works and remove the unnecessary files.

Classic configuration management tools tend not to remove things unless explicitly instructed to do so—instead they start from a non-working state and add new configurations and files. This leads to *snowflake* systems crafted for a particular purpose, which may look very different from what you'd get if you ran your configuration management tool against a fresh server, especially if the configuration has evolved over time. Courtesy of layering and lightweight images in Docker, you can perform the reverse of this process and experiment with removing things.

PROBLEM
You want to make your images smaller.

SOLUTION
Remove unnecessary packages and doc files.

DISCUSSION
This technique will follow these steps to reduce the size of an image:

1 Run the image.
2 Enter the container.
3 Remove unnecessary files.
4 Commit the container as a new image (see technique 14).
5 Flatten the image (see technique 43).

The last two steps have been covered earlier in the book, so we're only going to cover the first three here.

To illustrate how to use this, we're going to take the image created in technique 40 and try and make that image smaller.

First, run up the image as a container:

```
docker run -ti --name smaller --entrypoint /bin/bash \
dockerinpractice/log-cleaner
```

Because this is a Debian-based image, you can start by seeing which packages you might not need and removing them. Run `dpkg -l | awk '{print $2}'` and you will get a list of installed packages on the system.

You can then go through those packages running `apt-get purge -y package _name` on them. If there's a scary message warning you that "You are about to do something potentially harmful," then hit Return to continue.

Once you've removed all the packages that can safely be removed, you can run these commands to clean up the apt cache:

```
apt-get autoremove
apt-get clean
```

This is a relatively safe way to reduce space usage in your images.

Further significant savings can be made by removing docs. For example, running `rm -rf /usr/share/doc/* /usr/share/man/* /usr/share/info/*` will often remove sizeable files you'll probably never need. And you can take this to the next level by manually running `rm` on binaries and libraries you don't need.

Another area for rich pickings is the /var folder, which should contain temporary data, or data not essential to the running of programs.

This command will get rid of all files with the suffix .log:

```
find /var | grep '\.log$' | xargs rm -v
```

Using this somewhat manual process, you can get the original dockerinpractice/ log-cleaner image down to a few dozen MB quite easily, and even make it smaller if you have the motivation. Remember that due to Docker's layering, you'll need to export and import the image as explained in technique 43.

RELATED TECHNIQUE   Technique 53 will show you a much more effective (but risky) way to significantly reduce the size of your images.

Due to Docker's layering, the image size can only get bigger as you act on it. To finalise your reduced image, use the image flattening technique outlined in technique 43.

MAINTAINED EXAMPLE   An example of the commands described here is maintained at https://github.com/docker-in-practice/log-cleaner-purged, and can be Docker pulled from dockerinpractice/log-cleaner-purged.

| TECHNIQUE 51 | **Tiny Docker images with BusyBox and Alpine** |

Small, usable OSs that can be embedded onto a low-power or cheap computer have existed since Linux began. Fortunately, the efforts of these projects have been repurposed to produce small Docker images for use where image size is important.

PROBLEM

You want a small, functional image.

SOLUTION

Use a minimal Linux build, such as BusyBox or Alpine.

DISCUSSION

This is another area where the state of the art is fast changing. The two popular choices are BusyBox and Alpine, and each has different characteristics.

If lean but useful is your aim, then BusyBox may fit the bill. If you start up a BusyBox image with the following command, something surprising happens:

```
$ docker run -ti busybox /bin/bash
exec: "/bin/bash": stat /bin/bash: no such file or directory2015/02/23
➥ 09:55:38 Error response from daemon: Cannot start container
➥ 73f45e34145647cd1996ae29d8028e7b06d514d0d32dec9a68ce9428446faa19: exec:
➥ "/bin/bash": stat /bin/bash: no such file or directory
```

BusyBox is so lean it has no bash! Instead it uses ash, which is a posix-compliant shell—effectively a limited version of more advanced shells such as bash and ksh:

```
$ docker run -ti busybox /bin/ash
/ #
```

As the result of many decisions like this, the BusyBox image weighs in at under 2.5 MB!

> **NON-GNU VERSIONS OF STANDARD UTILITIES** BusyBox can contain some other nasty surprises. The `tar` version, for example, will have difficulty untarring TAR files created with GNU `tar`.

This is great if you want to write a small script that only requires simple tools, but if you want to run anything else you'll have to install it yourself. BusyBox comes with no package management.

Other maintainers have added package management functionality to BusyBox. For example, progrium/busybox might not be the smallest BusyBox container (it's currently a little under 5 MB), but it has opkg, which means you can easily install other common packages while keeping the image size to an absolute minimum. If you're missing bash, for example, you can install it like this:

```
$ docker run -ti progrium/busybox /bin/ash
/ # opkg-install bash > /dev/null
/ # bash
bash-4.3#
```

When committed, this results in a 6 MB image.

A less-established but interesting Docker image (which may replace progrium/ busybox) is gliderlabs/alpine. It's similar to BusyBox but has a more extensive range of packages that you can browse at http://forum.alpinelinux.org/packages.

The packages are designed to be lean on install. To take a concrete example, the next listing shows a Dockerfile that results in an image that's one-third of a gigabyte.

Listing 5.11   Ubuntu plus mysql-client

```
FROM ubuntu:14.04
RUN apt-get update -q \
&& DEBIAN_FRONTEND=noninteractive apt-get install -qy mysql-client \
&& apt-get clean && rm -rf /var/lib/apt
ENTRYPOINT ["mysql"]
```

> **AVOID INTERACTIONS WITH DEBIAN_FRONTEND=NONINTERACTIVE** The DEBIAN_ FRONTEND=noninteractive before the apt-get install ensures that the install doesn't prompt for any input during the install. As you can't easily engi-neer responses to questions when running commands, this is often useful in Dockerfiles.

By contrast, this results in an image that's a little over 16 MB:

```
FROM gliderlabs/alpine:3.1
RUN apk-install mysql-client
ENTRYPOINT ["mysql"]
```

TECHNIQUE 52   **The Go model of minimal containers**

Although it can be illuminating to winnow down your working containers by remov-ing redundant files, there's another option—compiling minimal binaries without dependencies.

Doing this radically simplifies the task of configuration management—if there's only one file to deploy and no packages required, a significant amount of configura-tion management tooling becomes redundant.

PROBLEM

You want to build binary Docker images with no external dependencies.

SOLUTION

Build a statically linked binary.

DISCUSSION

To demonstrate how this can be useful, we'll first create a small "Hello world" image with a small C program. Then we'll go on to show you how to do something equivalent for a more useful application.

A MINIMAL HELLO WORLD BINARY

First, create a new directory and create a Dockerfile, as shown in the following listing.

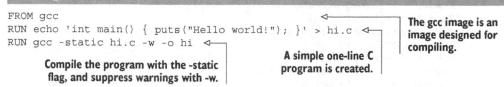

Listing 5.12   Hello Dockerfile

```
FROM gcc
RUN echo 'int main() { puts("Hello world!"); }' > hi.c
RUN gcc -static hi.c -w -o hi
```

The gcc image is an image designed for compiling.

A simple one-line C program is created.

Compile the program with the -static flag, and suppress warnings with -w.

The preceding Dockerfile compiles a simple "Hello world" program without dependencies. You can now build it and extract that binary from the container, as shown in the next listing.

Listing 5.13   Extract the binary from the image

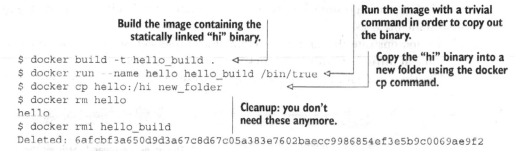

Build the image containing the statically linked "hi" binary.

Run the image with a trivial command in order to copy out the binary.

Copy the "hi" binary into a new folder using the docker cp command.

```
$ docker build -t hello_build .
$ docker run --name hello hello_build /bin/true
$ docker cp hello:/hi new_folder
$ docker rm hello
hello
$ docker rmi hello_build
Deleted: 6afcbf3a650d9d3a67c8d67c05a383e7602baecc9986854ef3e5b9c0069ae9f2
```

Cleanup: you don't need these anymore.

You now have a statically built binary in a fresh directory. Move to it with this command:

```
$ cd new_folder
```

Now create another Dockerfile, as shown in the next listing.

Listing 5.14   Minimal Hello Dockerfile

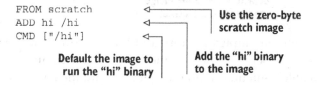

```
FROM scratch
ADD hi /hi
CMD ["/hi"]
```

Use the zero-byte scratch image

Add the "hi" binary to the image

Default the image to run the "hi" binary

Build and run it as shown in the following listing.

Listing 5.15   Create the minimal container

```
$ docker build -t hello_world .
Sending build context to Docker daemon 931.3 kB
Sending build context to Docker daemon
Step 0 : FROM scratch
 --->
Step 1 : ADD hi /hi
```

```
---> 2fe834f724f8
Removing intermediate container 01f73ea277fb
Step 2 : ENTRYPOINT /hi
 ---> Running in 045e32673c7f
 ---> 5f8802ae5443
Removing intermediate container 045e32673c7f
Successfully built 5f8802ae5443
$ docker run hello_world
Hello world!
$ docker images | grep hello_world
hello_world      latest    5f8802ae5443   24 seconds ago  928.3 kB
```

The image builds, runs, and weighs in at under 1 MB!

A MINIMAL GO WEB SERVER IMAGE

This is a relatively trivial example, but you can apply the same principle to programs built in Go. An interesting feature of the Go language is that it's relatively easy to build such static binaries.

To demonstrate this ability, we created a simple web server in Go whose code is available at https://github.com/docker-in-practice/go-web-server.

The Dockerfile for building this simple web server is shown in the following listing.

Listing 5.16 Dockerfile to statically compile a Go web server

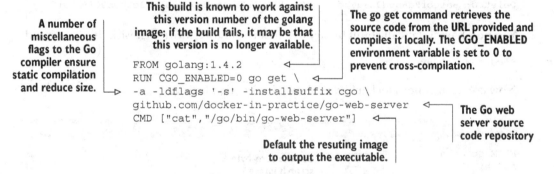

A number of miscellaneous flags to the Go compiler ensure static compilation and reduce size.

This build is known to work against this version number of the golang image; if the build fails, it may be that this version is no longer available.

The go get command retrieves the source code from the URL provided and compiles it locally. The CGO_ENABLED environment variable is set to 0 to prevent cross-compilation.

```
FROM golang:1.4.2
RUN CGO_ENABLED=0 go get \
-a -ldflags '-s' -installsuffix cgo \
github.com/docker-in-practice/go-web-server
CMD ["cat","/go/bin/go-web-server"]
```

The Go web server source code repository

Default the resuting image to output the executable.

If you save this Dockerfile into an empty directory and build it, you'll now have an image containing the program. Because you specified the default command of the image to output the executable content, you now just need to run the image and send the output to a file on your host, as the following listing shows.

Listing 5.17 Get the Go web server from the image

Runs the image and redirects the binary output to a file

Builds and tags the image

Makes and moves into a fresh directory to deposit the binary

```
$ docker build -t go-web-server .
$ mkdir -p go-web-server && cd go-web-server
$ docker run go-web-server > go-web-server
$ chmod +x go-web-server
```

Makes the binary executable

Now, as with the "hi" binary, you have a binary with no library dependencies or need to access the filesystem. We're therefore going to create a Dockerfile from the zero-byte scratch image and add the binary to it, as before:

```
FROM scratch
ADD go-web-server /go-web-server
ENTRYPOINT ["/go-web-server"]
```

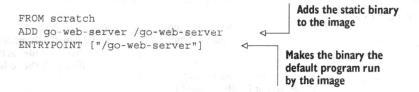

Adds the static binary
to the image

Makes the binary the
default program run
by the image

Now build it and run the image. The resulting image is a little over 4 MB in size:

```
$ docker build -t go-web-server .
$ docker images | grep go-web-server
go-web-server    latest    de1187ee87f3   3 seconds ago    4.156 MB
$ docker run -p 8080:8080 go-web-server -port 8080
```

You can access it on http://localhost:8080. If the port is already in use, you can replace the 8080s in the preceding code with a port of your choice.

DOCKER REDUNDANT?

If you can bundle applications into one binary, why bother with Docker at all? You can move the binary around, run multiple copies, and so on.

You can do so if you want, but you'd lose the following:

- All the container management tools in the Docker ecosystem
- The metadata within the Docker images that document significant application information, such as ports, volumes, and labels
- The isolation that gives Docker its operational power

TECHNIQUE 53   Using inotifywait to slim containers

We're now going to take slimming our containers to the next level by using a nifty tool that tells us what files are being referenced when we run a container.

This could be called the nuclear option, as it can be quite risky to implement on production. But it can be an instructive means of learning about your system, even if you don't follow through with using it for real—a crucial part of configuration management is understanding what your application requires to operate correctly.

PROBLEM

You want to reduce your container to the smallest possible set of files and permissions.

SOLUTION

Use inotify-tools to identify which files are needed, and then remove all others.

DISCUSSION

At a high level, you need to know what files are being accessed when you run a command in a container. If you remove all the other files on the container filesystem, you'll theoretically still have everything you need.

In this walkthrough, you're going to use the log-cleaner-purged image from technique 50. You'll install inotify-tools, and then run `inotifywait` to get a report on which files were accessed. You'll then run a simulation of the image's entrypoint (the log_clean script). Then, using the file report generated, you'll remove any file that hasn't been accessed:

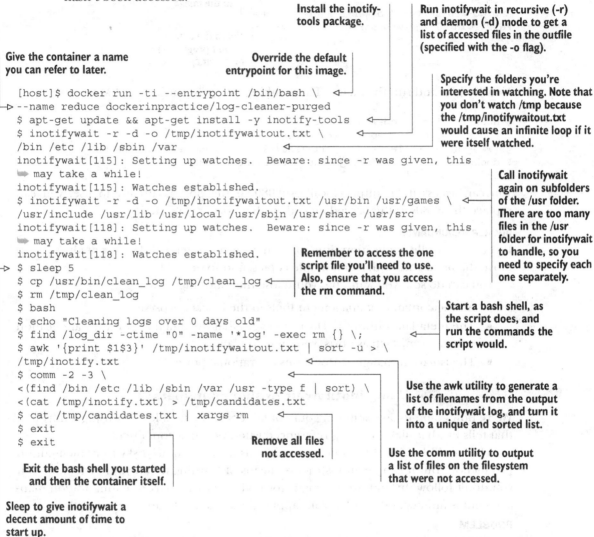

Install the inotify-tools package.

Run inotifywait in recursive (-r) and daemon (-d) mode to get a list of accessed files in the outfile (specified with the -o flag).

Give the container a name you can refer to later.

Override the default entrypoint for this image.

Specify the folders you're interested in watching. Note that you don't watch /tmp because the /tmp/inotifywaitout.txt would cause an infinite loop if it were itself watched.

```
[host]$ docker run -ti --entrypoint /bin/bash \
--name reduce dockerinpractice/log-cleaner-purged
$ apt-get update && apt-get install -y inotify-tools
$ inotifywait -r -d -o /tmp/inotifywaitout.txt \
/bin /etc /lib /sbin /var
inotifywait[115]: Setting up watches.  Beware: since -r was given, this
  may take a while!
inotifywait[115]: Watches established.
$ inotifywait -r -d -o /tmp/inotifywaitout.txt /usr/bin /usr/games \
/usr/include /usr/lib /usr/local /usr/sbin /usr/share /usr/src
inotifywait[118]: Setting up watches.  Beware: since -r was given, this
  may take a while!
inotifywait[118]: Watches established.
$ sleep 5
$ cp /usr/bin/clean_log /tmp/clean_log
$ rm /tmp/clean_log
$ bash
$ echo "Cleaning logs over 0 days old"
$ find /log_dir -ctime "0" -name '*log' -exec rm {} \;
$ awk '{print $1$3}' /tmp/inotifywaitout.txt | sort -u > \
/tmp/inotify.txt
$ comm -2 -3 \
<(find /bin /etc /lib /sbin /var /usr -type f | sort) \
<(cat /tmp/inotify.txt) > /tmp/candidates.txt
$ cat /tmp/candidates.txt | xargs rm
$ exit
$ exit
```

Call inotifywait again on subfolders of the /usr folder. There are too many files in the /usr folder for inotifywait to handle, so you need to specify each one separately.

Remember to access the one script file you'll need to use. Also, ensure that you access the rm command.

Start a bash shell, as the script does, and run the commands the script would.

Use the awk utility to generate a list of filenames from the output of the inotifywait log, and turn it into a unique and sorted list.

Remove all files not accessed.

Exit the bash shell you started and then the container itself.

Use the comm utility to output a list of files on the filesystem that were not accessed.

Sleep to give inotifywait a decent amount of time to start up.

At this point you've

- Placed a watch on files to see what files are being accessed
- Run all the commands to simulate the running of the script
- Run commands to ensure you access the script you'll definitely need, and the rm utility

- Gained a list of all files not accessed during the run
- Removed all the non-accessed files

Now you can flatten this container (see technique 43) to create a new image and test that it still works:

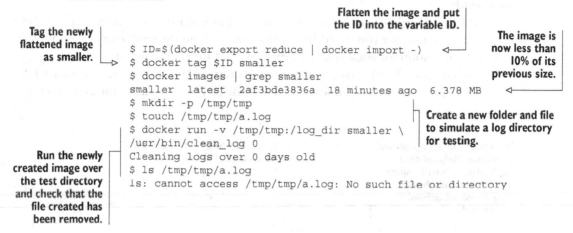

We reduced the size of this image from 96 MB to around 6.5 MB, and it still appears to work. Quite a saving!

> **RISKY!** This technique, like overclocking your CPU, is not an optimization for the unwary. This particular example works well because it's an application that's quite limited in scope, but your mission-critical business application is likely to be more complex and dynamic in how it accesses files. You could easily remove a file that wasn't accessed on your run, but that is needed at some other point.

If you're a little nervous of potentially breaking your image by removing files you'll need later, you can use the /tmp/candidates.txt file to get a list of the biggest files that were untouched, like this:

```
cat /tmp/candidates.txt | xargs wc -c | sort -n | tail
```

You can then remove the larger files that you're sure won't be needed by your application. There can be big wins here, too!

TECHNIQUE 54 Big can be beautiful

Although this section is about keeping images small, it's worth remembering that small is not necessarily better. As we'll discuss, a relatively large monolithic image can be more efficient than a small one.

PROBLEM

You want to reduce disk space usage and network bandwidth due to Docker images.

SOLUTION

Create a universal, large, monolithic base image for your organization.

DISCUSSION

It's paradoxical, but a large monolithic image could save you disk space and network bandwidth.

Recall that Docker uses a copy-on-write mechanism when its containers are running. This means that you could have hundreds of Ubuntu containers running, but only a small amount of additional disk space is used for each container started.

If you have lots of different, smaller images on your Docker server, as in figure 5.2, more disk space may be used than if you have one larger monolithic image with everything you need in it.

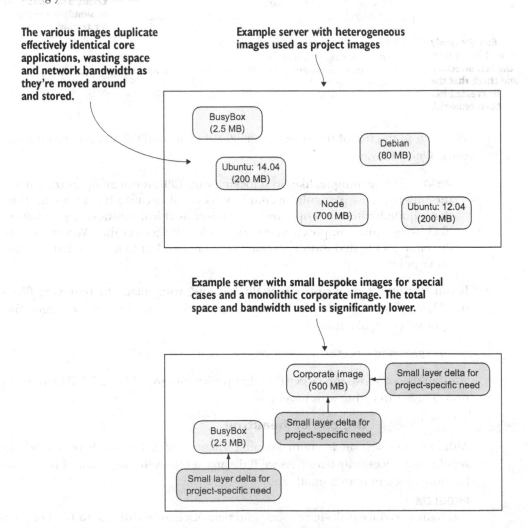

The various images duplicate effectively identical core applications, wasting space and network bandwidth as they're moved around and stored.

Example server with heterogeneous images used as project images

BusyBox (2.5 MB)

Debian (80 MB)

Ubuntu: 14.04 (200 MB)

Node (700 MB)

Ubuntu: 12.04 (200 MB)

Example server with small bespoke images for special cases and a monolithic corporate image. The total space and bandwidth used is significantly lower.

Corporate image (500 MB)

Small layer delta for project-specific need

Small layer delta for project-specific need

BusyBox (2.5 MB)

Small layer delta for project-specific need

Figure 5.2   Many small base images vs. fewer large base images

You may be reminded of the principle of a shared library. A shared library can be loaded by multiple applications at once, reducing the amount of disk and memory needed to run the required programs. In the same way, a shared base image for your organization can save space, as it only needs to be downloaded once and should contain everything you need. Programs and libraries previously required in multiple images are now only required once.

In addition, there can be other benefits of having a monolithic, centrally managed image shared across teams. The maintenance of this image can be centralized, improvements can be shared, and issues with the build need only be solved once.

If you're going to adopt this technique, here are some things to watch out for:

- The base image should be reliable first. If it doesn't behave consistently, the users will avoid using it.
- Changes to the base image must be tracked somewhere that's visible so that users can debug problems themselves.
- Regression tests are essential to reduce confusion when updating the vanilla image.
- Be careful about what you add to the base—once it's in the base image, it's hard to remove, and the image can bloat fast.

We used this technique to great effect in our 600-strong development company. A monthly build of core applications was bundled into a large image and published on the internal Docker registry. Teams would build on the so-called "vanilla" corporate image by default, and create bespoke layers if necessary on top of that.

5.4   Summary

This chapter has shown how you can manage the configuration of your Docker images, a key aspect of any Docker workflow. We looked at how you can use your existing processes within the official Docker recommended route, and at some best practices for building your images.

We've discussed how

- You can extend the flexibility of Dockerfiles if you're feeling limited.
- It's possible to remove secrets from the lower layers of images by flattening them.
- Dockerfiles are not mutually exclusive with more traditional configuration management tools like Chef.
- You should aim to make your images as small as is reasonably possible.

Now that you've got your Docker images in some kind of order, it's time to think about how these images can be shared with others, laying the groundwork for techniques that facilitate continuous delivery and integration.

Part 3

Docker and DevOps

Now you're ready to take Docker beyond your development environment and start using it in other phases of software delivery. Build and testing automation are cornerstones of the DevOps movement. We'll demonstrate Docker's power through automation of the software delivery lifecycle, deployments, and realistic environment testing. Chapter 6 will show various techniques to deliver and improve continuous integration, making your software deliveries both more reliable and scalable. Continuous delivery is the focus of Chapter 7. We explain what continuous delivery is, and look at ways in which Docker can be used to improve this aspect of your development pipeline. Chapter 8 covers how to harness Docker's networking model to full effect, creating multi-container services, simulation of realistic networks, and creation of networks on demand. This part takes you from development all the way to the point where you can think about running Docker in production.

Continuous integration: speeding up your development pipeline

6

This chapter covers

- Using the Docker Hub workflow as a CI tool
- Speeding up your IO-heavy builds
- Using Selenium for automated testing
- Running Jenkins within Docker
- Using Docker as a Jenkins slave
- Scaling your available compute with your dev team

In this chapter we're going to look at various techniques that will use Docker to enable and improve your CI efforts.

By now you should understand how Docker is well suited to being used for automation. Its lightweight nature and the power it gives you to port environments from one place to another can make it a key enabler of continuous integration (CI). We've found the techniques in this chapter to be invaluable in making a CI process feasible within a business.

Making your build environment stable and reproducible, using testing tools requiring significant setup, and expanding your build capacity are all problems you may face, and Docker can help.

> **CONTINUOUS INTEGRATION** In case you don't know, *continuous integration* is a software lifecycle strategy used to speed up the development pipeline. By automatically rerunning tests every time a significant change is made to the codebase, you get faster and more stable deliveries because there's a base level of stability in the software being delivered.

6.1   *Docker Hub automated builds*

The Docker Hub automated build feature was mentioned in technique 9, though we didn't go into any detail on it. In short, if you point to a Git repository containing a Dockerfile, the Docker Hub will handle the process of building the image and making it available to download. An image rebuild will be triggered on any changes in the Git repository, making this quite useful as part of a CI process.

TECHNIQUE 55   Using the Docker Hub workflow

This technique introduces you to the Docker Hub workflow, which enables you to trigger rebuilds of your images.

> **DOCKER.COM ACCOUNT REQUIRED** For this section you'll need an account on docker.com linked to either a GitHub or a Bitbucket account. If you don't already have these set up and linked, instructions are available from the homepages of github.com and bitbucket.org.

PROBLEM

You want to automatically test and push changes to your image when the code changes.

SOLUTION

Set up a Docker Hub repository and link it to your code.

DISCUSSION

Although the Docker Hub build isn't complicated, there are a number of steps required, so we've broken them up into bite-sized chunks in table 6.1, which serves as an overview of the process.

Table 6.1   Setting up a linked Docker Hub repository

Number	Step
1	Create your repository on GitHub or Bitbucket
2	Clone the new Git repository
3	Add code to your Git repository
4	Commit the source
5	Push the Git repository

Table 6.1 Setting up a linked Docker Hub repository (*continued*)

Number	Step
6	Create a new repository on the Docker Hub
7	Link the Docker Hub repository to the Git repository
8	Wait for the Docker Hub build to complete
9	Commit and push a change to the source
10	Wait for the second Docker Hub build to complete

GIT AND DOCKER REPOSITORIES Both Git and Docker use the term *repository* to refer to a project. This can confuse people. A Git repository and a Docker repository are not the same thing, even though here we're linking the two types of repositories.

1. CREATE YOUR REPOSITORY ON GITHUB OR BITBUCKET

Create a new repository on GitHub or Bitbucket. You can give it any name you want.

2. CLONE THE NEW GIT REPOSITORY

Clone your new Git repository to your host machine. The command for this will be available from the Git project's homepage.

Change directory into this repository.

3. ADD CODE TO YOUR GIT REPOSITORY

Now you need to add code to the project.

You can add any Dockerfile you like, but the following listing shows an example known to work. It consists of two files representing a simple dev tools environment. It installs some preferred utilities and outputs the bash version you have.

Listing 6.1 Dockerfile—simple dev tools container

```
FROM ubuntu:14.04
ENV DEBIAN_FRONTEND noninteractive
RUN apt-get update
RUN apt-get install -y curl
RUN apt-get install -y nmap
RUN apt-get install -y socat
RUN apt-get install -y openssh-client
RUN apt-get install -y openssl
RUN apt-get install -y iotop
RUN apt-get install -y strace
RUN apt-get install -y tcpdump
RUN apt-get install -y lsof
RUN apt-get install -y inotify-tools
RUN apt-get install -y sysstat
RUN apt-get install -y build-essential
RUN echo "source /root/bash_extra" >> /root/.bashrc
ADD bash_extra /root/bash_extra
CMD ["/bin/bash"]
```

Install useful packages.

Add a line to the root's bashrc to source bash_extra.

Add bash_extra from the source to the container.

Now you need to add the bash_extra file you referenced and give it the content shown in the next listing.

```
bash --version
```

4. COMMIT THE SOURCE

To commit your source code source, use this command:

```
git commit -am "Initial commit"
```

5. PUSH THE GIT REPOSITORY

Now you can push the source to the Git server with this command:

```
git push origin master
```

6. CREATE A NEW REPOSITORY ON THE DOCKER HUB

Next you need to create a repository for this project on the Docker Hub. Go to https://hub.docker.com and ensure you're logged in. Then click on Add Repository and choose Automated Build.

7. LINK THE DOCKER HUB REPOSITORY TO THE GIT REPOSITORY

You'll see a screen with a choice of Git services. Pick the source code service you use (GitHub or Bitbucket) and select your new repository from the provided list. (If this step doesn't work for you, you may need to set up the link between your Docker Hub account and the Git service.)

You'll see a page with options for the build configuration. You can leave the defaults and click Create Repository at the bottom.

8. WAIT FOR THE DOCKER HUB BUILD TO COMPLETE

You'll see a page with a message explaining that the link worked. Click on the Build Details link.

Next, you'll see a page that shows the details of the builds. Under Builds History there will be an entry for this first build. If you don't see anything listed, you may need to press the button to trigger the build manually. The Status field next to the build ID will show Pending, Finished, Building, or Error. If all is well, you'll see one of the first three. If you see Error, then something has gone wrong and you'll need to click on the build ID to see what the error was.

> **BUILDING CAN TAKE TIME** It can take a while for the build to start, so seeing Pending for some time while waiting is perfectly normal.

Click Refresh periodically until you see that the build has completed. Once it's complete, you can pull the image with the `docker pull` command listed on the top of the same page.

9. COMMIT AND PUSH A CHANGE TO THE SOURCE

Now you decide that you want more information about your environment when you log in, so you want to output the details of the distribution you're running in. To achieve this, add these lines to your bash_extra file so that it now looks like this:

```
bash --version
cat /etc/issue
```

Then commit and push as in steps 4 and 5.

10. WAIT FOR THE (SECOND) DOCKER HUB BUILD TO COMPLETE

If you return to the build page, a new line should show up under the Builds History section, and you can follow this build as in step 8.

> **EMAIL RECEIVED ON ERROR ONLY** You'll be emailed if there's an error with your build (no email if all is OK), so once you're used to this workflow, you only need to check up on it if you receive an email.

You can now use the Docker Hub workflow! You'll quickly get used to this framework and find it invaluable for keeping your builds up to date and reducing the cognitive load of rebuilding Dockerfiles by hand.

6.2   *More efficient builds*

CI implies a more frequent rebuilding of your software and tests. Although Docker makes delivering CI easier, the next problem you may bump into is the resulting increased load on your compute resources.

We'll look at ways to alleviate this pressure in terms of disk I/O, network bandwidth, and automated testing.

TECHNIQUE 56   Speed up I/O-intensive builds with eatmydata

Because Docker is a great fit for automated building, you'll likely perform a lot of disk-I/O-intensive builds as time goes on. Jenkins jobs, database rebuild scripts, and large code checkouts will all hit your disks hard. In these cases, you'll be grateful for any speed increases you can get, both to save time and to minimize the many overheads that result from resource contention.

This technique has been shown to give up to a 1/3 speed increase, and our experience backs this up. This is not to be sniffed at!

PROBLEM
You want to speed up your I/O-intensive builds.

SOLUTION
Install eatmydata on your image.

DISCUSSION
eatmydata is a program that takes your system calls to write data and makes them super-fast by bypassing work required to persist those changes. This entails some lack of safety, so it's not recommended for normal use, but it's quite useful for environments not designed to persist, such as in testing.

INSTALLATION

To install eatmydata, you have a number of options.

If you're running a deb-based distribution, you can `apt-get install` it.

If you're running an rpm-based distribution, you'll be able to `rpm --install` it by searching for it on the web and downloading it. Websites such as rpmfind.net are a good place to start.

As a last resort, and if you have a compiler installed, you can download and compile it directly as shown in the next listing.

Listing 6.3   Compile and install eatmydata

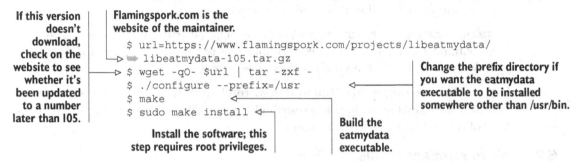

If this version doesn't download, check on the website to see whether it's been updated to a number later than 105.

Flamingspork.com is the website of the maintainer.

```
$ url=https://www.flamingspork.com/projects/libeatmydata/
  ➥ libeatmydata-105.tar.gz
$ wget -qO- $url | tar -zxf -
$ ./configure --prefix=/usr
$ make
$ sudo make install
```

Change the prefix directory if you want the eatmydata executable to be installed somewhere other than /usr/bin.

Install the software; this step requires root privileges.

Build the eatmydata executable.

USING EATMYDATA

Once libeatmydata is installed on your image (either from a package or from source), run the eatmydata wrapper script before any command to take advantage of it:

```
docker run -d mybuildautomation eatmydata /run_tests.sh
```

Figure 6.1 shows at a high level how eatmydata saves you processing time.

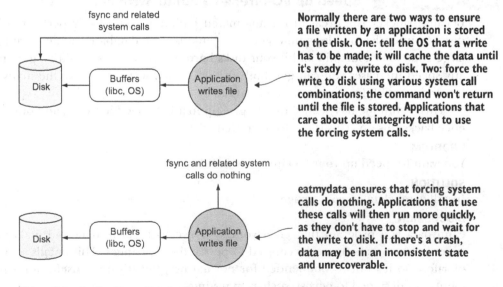

Normally there are two ways to ensure a file written by an application is stored on the disk. One: tell the OS that a write has to be made; it will cache the data until it's ready to write to disk. Two: force the write to disk using various system call combinations; the command won't return until the file is stored. Applications that care about data integrity tend to use the forcing system calls.

eatmydata ensures that forcing system calls do nothing. Applications that use these calls will then run more quickly, as they don't have to stop and wait for the write to disk. If there's a crash, data may be in an inconsistent state and unrecoverable.

Figure 6.1   Application writes to disk without and with eatmydata

USE WITH CAUTION! eatmydata skips the steps to guarantee that data is safely written to disk, so there's a risk that data will not yet be on disk when the program thinks it is. For test runs, this usually doesn't matter, because the data is disposable, but don't use eatmydata to speed up any kind of environment where the data matters!

TECHNIQUE 57   Set up a package cache for faster builds

As Docker lends itself to frequent rebuilding of services for development, testing, and production, you can quickly get to a point where you're repeatedly hitting the network a lot. One major cause is downloading package files from the internet. This can be a slow (and costly) overhead, even on a single machine. This technique shows you how to set up a local cache for your package downloads, covering apt and yum.

PROBLEM
You want to speed up your builds by reducing network I/O.

SOLUTION
Install a Squid proxy for your package manager.

DISCUSSION
Figure 6.2 illustrates how this technique works in the abstract.

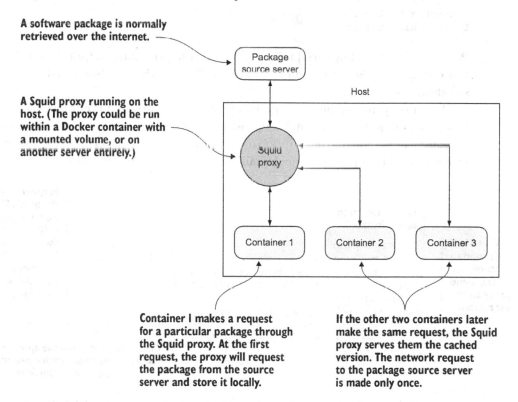

Figure 6.2   Using a Squid proxy to cache packages

Because the calls for packages go to the local Squid proxy first, and are only requested over the internet the first time, there should only be one request over the internet for each package. If you have hundreds of containers all pulling down the same large packages from the internet, this can save you a lot of time and money.

> **NETWORK SETUP!** You may have network configuration issues when setting this up on your host. Advice is given in the following sections to determine whether this is the case, but if you're unsure how to proceed, you may need to seek help from a friendly network admin.

DEBIAN

For Debian (otherwise known as apt or .deb) packages, the setup is simpler because there is a prepackaged version.

On your Debian-based host run this command:

```
sudo apt-get install squid-deb-proxy
```

Ensure that the service is started by telneting to port 8000:

```
$ telnet localhost 8000
Trying ::1...
Connected to localhost.
Escape character is '^]'.
```

Press Ctrl-] followed by Ctrl-d to quit if you see the preceding output. If you don't see this output, then Squid has either not installed properly, or it has installed on a non-standard port.

To set up your container to use this proxy, we've provided the following example Dockerfile. Bear in mind that the IP address of the host from the point of view of the container may change from run to run. You may want to convert this Dockerfile to a script to be run from within the container before installing new software:

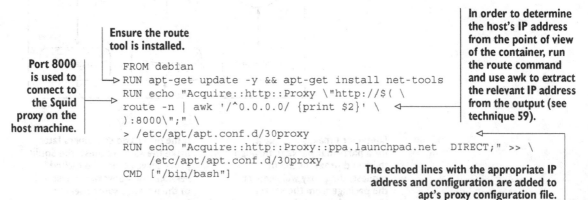

Port 8000 is used to connect to the Squid proxy on the host machine.

Ensure the route tool is installed.

In order to determine the host's IP address from the point of view of the container, run the route command and use awk to extract the relevant IP address from the output (see technique 59).

```
FROM debian
RUN apt-get update -y && apt-get install net-tools
RUN echo "Acquire::http::Proxy \"http://$( \
route -n | awk '/^0.0.0.0/ {print $2}' \
):8000\";" \
> /etc/apt/apt.conf.d/30proxy
RUN echo "Acquire::http::Proxy::ppa.launchpad.net  DIRECT;" >> \
    /etc/apt/apt.conf.d/30proxy
CMD ["/bin/bash"]
```

The echoed lines with the appropriate IP address and configuration are added to apt's proxy configuration file.

YUM

On the host, ensure Squid is installed by installing the "squid" package with your package manager.

Then you need to change the Squid configuration to create a larger cache space. Open up the /etc/squid/squid.conf file and replace the commented line beginning with #cache_dir ufs /var/spool/squid with this: cache_dir ufs /var/spool/squid 10000 16 256. This creates a space of 10,000 MB, which should be sufficient.

Ensure the service is started by telneting to port 3128:

```
$ telnet localhost 3128
Trying ::1...
Connected to localhost.
Escape character is '^]'.
```

Press Ctrl-] followed by Ctrl-d to quit if you see the preceding output. If you don't see this output, then Squid has either not installed properly, or has installed on a nonstandard port.

To set up your container to use this proxy, we've provided the following example Dockerfile. Bear in mind that the IP address of the host from the point of view of the container may change from run to run. You may want to convert this Dockerfile to a script to be run from within the container before installing new software:

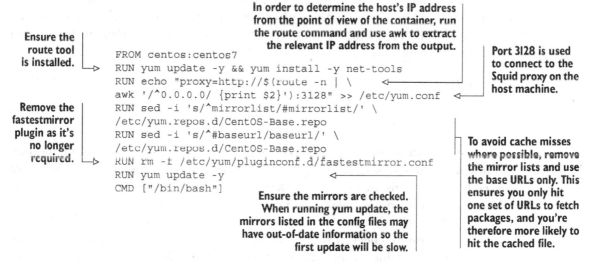

Ensure the route tool is installed.

In order to determine the host's IP address from the point of view of the container, run the route command and use awk to extract the relevant IP address from the output.

Port 3128 is used to connect to the Squid proxy on the host machine.

```
FROM centos:centos7
RUN yum update -y && yum install -y net-tools
RUN echo "proxy=http://$(route -n | \
awk '/^0.0.0.0/ {print $2}'):3128" >> /etc/yum.conf
RUN sed -i 's/^mirrorlist/#mirrorlist/' \
/etc/yum.repos.d/CentOS-Base.repo
RUN sed -i 's/^#baseurl/baseurl/' \
/etc/yum.repos.d/CentOS-Base.repo
RUN rm -f /etc/yum/pluginconf.d/fastestmirror.conf
RUN yum update -y
CMD ["/bin/bash"]
```

Remove the fastestmirror plugin as it's no longer required.

Ensure the mirrors are checked. When running yum update, the mirrors listed in the config files may have out-of-date information so the first update will be slow.

To avoid cache misses where possible, remove the mirror lists and use the base URLs only. This ensures you only hit one set of URLs to fetch packages, and you're therefore more likely to hit the cached file.

If you set up two containers this way and install the same large package on both, one after the other, you should notice that the second installation downloads its prerequisites much quicker than the first.

DOCKERIZE THE SQUID PROXY You may have observed that you can run the Squid proxy on a container rather than on the host. That option wasn't shown here to keep the explanation simple (in some cases, more steps are required to make Squid work within a container). You can read more about this, along with how to make containers automatically use the proxy, at https://github.com/jpetazzo/squid-in-a-can.

TECHNIQUE 58   Running Selenium tests inside Docker

One Docker use case we haven't yet examined in much detail is running graphical applications. In chapter 3, VNC was used to connect to containers during the "save game" approach to development (technique 14), but this can be clunky—windows are contained inside the VNC viewer window, and desktop interaction can be a little limited. We'll explore an alternative to this by demonstrating how to write graphical tests using Selenium and also show you how this image can be used to run the tests as part of your CI workflow.

PROBLEM

You want to be able to run graphical programs in your CI process while having the option to display those same graphical programs on your own screen.

SOLUTION

Share your X11 server socket to view the programs on your own screen, and use xvfb in your CI process.

DISCUSSION

No matter what other things you need to do to start your container, you must have the Unix socket that X11 uses to display your windows mounted as a volume inside the container, and you need to indicate which display your windows should be shown on. You can double-check whether these two things are set to their defaults by running the following commands:

```
~ $ ls /tmp/.X11-unix/
X0
~ $ echo $DISPLAY
:0
```

The first command checks that the X11 server Unix socket is running in the location assumed for the rest of the technique. The second command checks the environment variable applications used to find the X11 socket. If your output for these commands doesn't match the output here, you may need to alter some arguments to the commands in this technique.

Now that you've checked your machine setup, you want to get applications running inside a container to be seamlessly displayed outside the container. The main problem you need to overcome is the security that your computer puts in place to prevent other people from connecting to your machine, taking over your display, and potentially recording your keystrokes. In technique 26 you briefly saw how to do this, but we didn't talk about how it worked or look at any alternatives.

X11 has multiple ways of authenticating a container to use your X socket. First we'll look at the .Xauthority file—it should be present in your home directory. It contains hostnames along with the "secret cookie" each host must use to connect. By giving your Docker container the same hostname as your machine, you can use your existing X authority file:

```
$ ls $HOME/.Xauthority
/home/myuser/.Xauthority
$ docker run -e DISPLAY=$DISPLAY -v /tmp/.X11-unix:/tmp/.X11-unix \
    --hostname=$HOSTNAME -v $HOME/.Xauthority:/root/.Xauthority \
    -it ubuntu:14.04 bash
```

The second method of allowing Docker to access the socket is a much blunter instrument and it has security issues, as it disables all the protection X gives you. If nobody has access to your computer, this may be an acceptable solution, but you should always try to use the X authority file first. You can secure yourself again after you try the following steps by running xhost - (though this will lock out your Docker container):

```
$ xhost +
access control disabled, clients can connect from any host
$ docker run -e DISPLAY=$DISPLAY -v /tmp/.X11-unix:/tmp/.X11-unix \
    -it ubuntu:14.04 bash
```

The first line disables all access control to X, and the second runs the container. Note that you don't have to set the hostname or mount anything apart from the X socket.

Once you've started up your container, it's time to check that it works. You can do this by running the following commands:

```
root@ef351febcee4:/# apt-get update && apt-get install -y x11-apps
[...]
root@ef351febcee4:/# xeyes
```

This will start up a classic application that tests whether X is working—xeyes. You should see the eyes follow your cursor as you move it around the screen. Note that (unlike VNC) the application is integrated into your desktop—if you were to start xeyes multiple times, you'd see multiple windows.

It's time to get started with Selenium. If you've never used it before, it's a tool with the ability to automate browser actions and is commonly used to test website code—it needs a graphical display for the browser to run in. Although it's most commonly used with Java, we're going to use Python to allow more interactivity:

```
root@ef351febcee4:/# apt-get install -y python2.7 python-pip firefox
[...]
root@ef351febcee4:/# pip install selenium
Downloading/unpacking selenium==2.47.3
[...]
Successfully installed selenium==2.47.3
Cleaning up...
root@ef351febcee4:/# python
Python 2.7.6 (default, Mar 22 2014, 22:59:56)
[GCC 4.8.2] on linux2
Type "help", "copyright", "credits" or "license" for more information.
>>> from selenium import webdriver
>>> b = webdriver.Firefox()
```

As you may have noticed, Firefox has launched and appeared on your screen! All the preceding code does is install Python, Firefox, and a Python package manager. It then uses the Python package manager to install the Selenium Python package.

You can now experiment with Selenium. An example session running against GitHub follows—you'll need a basic understanding of CSS selectors to understand what's going on here. Note that websites frequently change, so this particular snippet may need modifying to work correctly:

```
>>> b.get('http://github.com')
>>> searchselector = '.js-site-search-form input[type="text"]'
>>> searchbox = b.find_element_by_css_selector(searchselector)
>>> searchbox.send_keys('docker-in-practice\n')
>>> usersxpath = '//nav//a[contains(text(), "Users")]'
>>> userslink = b.find_element_by_xpath(usersxpath)
>>> userslink.click()
>>> dlinkselector = '.user-list-info a'
>>> dlink = b.find_elements_by_css_selector(dlinkselector)[0]
>>> dlink.click()
>>> mlinkselector = '.org-header a.meta-link'
>>> mlink = b.find_element_by_css_selector(mlinkselector)
>>> mlink.click()
```

The details here aren't important. Just note that we're writing commands in Python in our container and seeing them take effect in the Firefox window running inside the container, but visible on the desktop.

This is great for debugging tests you write, but how would you integrate them into a CI pipeline with the same Docker image? A CI server typically doesn't have a graphical display, so you need to make this work without mounting your own X server socket, but Firefox still needs an X server to run on. There's a useful tool created for situations like this called xvfb, which pretends to have an X server running for applications to use, but doesn't require a monitor.

To see how this works, let's install xvfb, commit the container, tag it as `selenium`, and create a test script:

```
>>> exit()
root@ef351febcee4:/# apt-get install -y xvfb
[...]
root@ef351febcee4:/# exit
$ docker commit ef351febcee4 selenium
d1cbfbc76790cae5f4ae95805a8ca4fc4cd1353c72d7a90b90ccfb79de4f2f9b
$ cat > myscript.py << EOF
from selenium import webdriver
b = webdriver.Firefox()
print 'Visiting github'
b.get('http://github.com')
print 'Performing search'
searchselector = '.js-site-search-form input[type="text"]'
searchbox = b.find_element_by_css_selector(searchselector)
searchbox.send_keys('docker-in-practice\n')
```

```
print 'Switching to user search'
usersxpath = '//nav//a[contains(text(), "Users")]'
userslink = b.find_element_by_xpath(usersxpath)
userslink.click()
print 'Opening docker in practice user page'
dlinkselector = '.user-list-info a'
dlink = b.find_elements_by_css_selector(dlinkselector)[99]
dlink.click()
print 'Visiting docker in practice site'
mlinkselector = '.org-header a.meta-link'
mlink = b.find_element_by_css_selector(mlinkselector)
mlink.click()
print 'Done!'
EOF
```

Note the subtle difference in the assignment of the dlink variable. By attempting to get the hundredth result containing the text "Docker in Practice," you'll trigger an error, which will cause the Docker container to exit with a non-zero status and trigger failures in the CI pipeline.

Time to try it out:

```
$ docker run --rm -v $(pwd):/mnt selenium sh -c \
"xvfb-run -s '-screen 0 1024x768x24 -extension RANDR'\
python /mnt/myscript.py"
Visiting github
Performing search
Switching to user search
Opening docker in practice user page
Traceback (most recent call last):
  File "myscript.py", line 15, in <module>
      dlink = b.find_elements_by_css_selector(dlinkselector)[99]
    IndexError: list index out of range
$ echo $?
1
```

You've run a self-removing container that executes the Python test script running under a virtual X server. As expected, it failed and returned a non-zero exit code.

> **CMD VS. ENTRYPOINT**   The sh -c "command string here" is an unfortunate result of how Docker treats CMD values by default. If you were to put this in a Dockerfile, you'd be able to remove the sh -c and make xvfb-run the entrypoint, allowing you to run whatever test scripts you'd like.

As has been demonstrated, Docker is a flexible tool and can be put to some initially surprising uses (graphical apps in this case). Some people run *all* of their graphical apps inside Docker, including games! We wouldn't go that far, but we've found that re-examining assumptions about Docker can lead to some surprising use cases.

6.3   *Containerizing your CI process*

Once you have a consistent development process across teams, it's important to also have a consistent build process. Randomly failing builds defeat the point of Docker.

As a result, it makes sense to *containerize* your entire CI process. This not only makes sure your builds are repeatable, it allows you to move your CI process anywhere without fear of leaving some vital piece of configuration behind (likely discovered with much frustration later).

In these techniques, we'll use Jenkins (as this is the most widely used CI tool), but the same techniques should apply to other CI tools. We don't assume a great deal of familiarity with Jenkins here, but we won't cover setting up standard tests and builds. That information is not essential to the techniques here.

TECHNIQUE 59   Containing a complex development environment

Docker's portability and lightweight nature make it an obvious choice for a CI slave (a machine the CI master connects to in order to carry out builds). A Docker CI slave is a step change from a VM slave (and is even more of a leap from bare-metal build machines). It allows you to perform builds on a multitude of environments with a single host, to quickly tear down and bring up clean environments to ensure uncontaminated builds, and to use all your familiar Docker tooling to manage your build environments.

Being able to treat the CI slave as just another Docker container is particularly interesting. Have mysterious build failures on one of your Docker CI slaves? Pull the image and try the build yourself.

PROBLEM
You want to scale and modify your Jenkins slave.

SOLUTION
Encapsulate the configuration of your slave in a Docker image, and deploy.

DISCUSSION
Many organizations set up a heavyweight Jenkins slave (often on the same host as the server), maintained by a central IT function, that serves a useful purpose for a time. As time goes on, and teams grow their codebases and diverge, requirements grow for more and more software to be installed, updated, or altered so that the jobs will run.

Figure 6.3 shows a simplified version of this scenario. Imagine hundreds of software packages and multiple new requests all giving an overworked infrastructure team headaches.

> **ILLUSTRATIVE, NON-PORTABLE EXAMPLE**   This technique has been constructed to show you the essentials of running a Jenkins slave in a container. This makes the result less portable but the lesson easier to grasp. Once you understand all the techniques in this chapter, you'll be able to make a more portable setup.

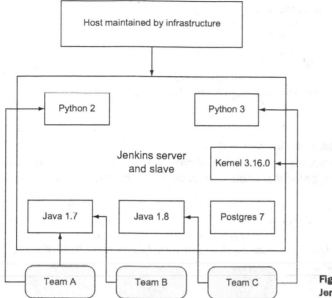

Figure 6.3 An overloaded Jenkins server

Stalemate has been known to ensue, because sysadmins may be reluctant to update their configuration management scripts for one group of people as they fear breaking another's build, and teams get increasingly frustrated over the slowness of change.

Docker (naturally) offers a solution by allowing multiple teams to use a base image for their own personal Jenkins slave, while using the same hardware as before. You can create an image with the required shared tooling on it, and allow teams to alter it to meet their own needs.

Some contributors have uploaded their own reference slaves on the Docker Hub; you can find them by searching for "jenkins slave" on the Docker Hub. The following listing is a minimal Jenkins slave Dockerfile.

Listing 6.4 Bare-bones Jenkins slave Dockerfile

```
FROM ubuntu
ENV DEBIAN_FRONTEND noninteractive
RUN groupadd -g 1000 jenkins_slave
RUN useradd -d /home/jenkins_slave -s /bin/bash \
-m jenkins_slave -u 1000 -g jenkins_slave
RUN echo jenkins_slave:jpass | chpasswd
RUN apt-get update && \
apt-get install -y openssh-server openjdk-7-jre wget
RUN mkdir -p /var/run/sshd
CMD ip route | grep "default via" \
| awk '{print $3}' && /usr/sbin/sshd -D
```

Create the Jenkins slave user and group.

Install the required software to function as a Jenkins slave.

Set the Jenkins user password to jpass. In a more sophisticated setup, you'd likely want to use other authentication methods.

On startup, output the IP address of the host machine from the point of view of the container, and start the SSH server.

Build the slave image, tagging it as jenkins_slave:

```
$ docker build -t jenkins_slave .
```

Run it with this command:

```
$ docker run --name jenkins_slave -ti -p 2222:22 jenkins_slave
172.17.42.1
```

> ## Jenkins server needs to be running
>
> If you don't have a Jenkins server already running on your host, ensure you have the Jenkins server running as in the previous technique. If you're in a hurry, run this command:
>
> ```
> $ docker run --name jenkins_server -p 8080:8080 -p 50000:50000 \
> dockerinpractice/jenkins:server
> ```
>
> This will make the Jenkins server available at http://localhost:8080 if you've run it on your local machine.

If you navigate to the Jenkins server, you'll be greeted with the page in figure 6.4.

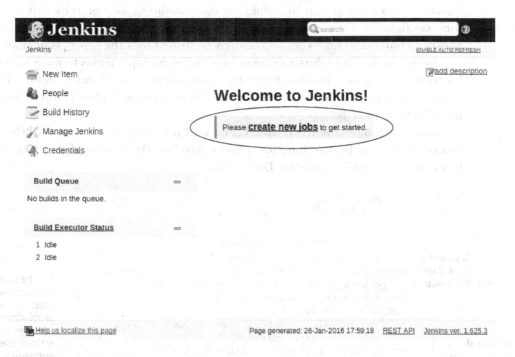

Figure 6.4   Jenkins' welcome page

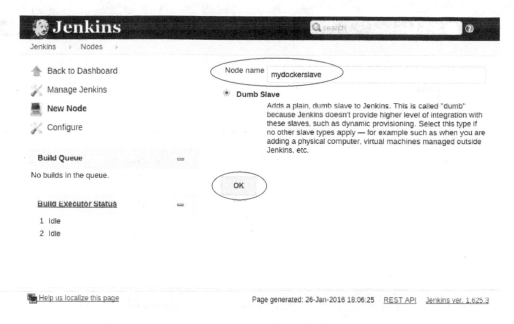

Figure 6.5   Naming a new node

You can add a slave by clicking on Build Executor Status > New Node and adding the node name as a dumb slave, as shown in figure 6.5. Call it `mydockerslave`.

Click OK and configure it with these settings, as shown in figure 6.6:

- Set Remote Root Directory to /home/jenkins_slave.
- Click Advanced to expose the port field, and set it to 2222.
- Click Add to add credentials, and set the username to `jenkins_slave` and the password to `jpass`.
- Make sure the Launch Slave Agents on Unix Machines Via SSH option is selected.
- Set the host to the route IP seen from within the container (output with the `docker run` earlier).
- Give it a Label of `dockerslave`.
- Click Save.

Now click on Launch Slave Agent (assuming this doesn't happen automatically) and you should see that the slave agent is now marked as online.

Go back to the home page by clicking on Jenkins in the top left, and click on New Item. Create a Freestyle Project called `test`, and under the Build section click on Add Build Step > Execute Shell, with the command `echo done`. Scroll up and select Restrict Where Project Can Be Run and enter the Label Expression `dockerslave`. You should see that Slaves In Label is set as `1`.

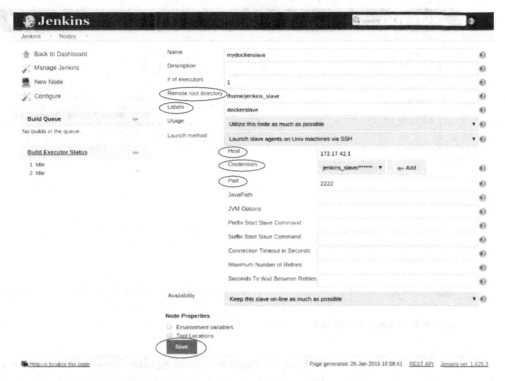

Figure 6.6   Configuring the new node

The job is now linked to the Docker slave. Click Build Now, then click the build that appears below on the left, and then click Console Output, and you should see output like this in the main window:

```
Started by user anonymous
Building remotely on testslave (dockerslave) in workspace
/home/jenkins_slave/workspace/ls
[ls] $ /bin/sh -xe /tmp/hudson4490746748063684780.sh
+ echo done
done
Finished: SUCCESS
```

Well done! You've successfully created your own Jenkins slave.

Now if you want to create your own bespoke slave, all you need to do is alter the slave image's Dockerfile to your taste, and run that instead of the example one.

> **AVAILABLE ON GITHUB**   The code for this technique and related ones is available on GitHub at https://github.com/docker-in-practice/jenkins.

TECHNIQUE 60   Running the Jenkins master within a Docker container

Putting the Jenkins master inside a container doesn't have as many benefits as doing the same for a slave, but it does give you the normal Docker win of immutable images.

We've found that being able to commit known-good master configurations and plugins eases the burden of experimentation significantly.

PROBLEM

You want a portable Jenkins server.

SOLUTION

Use a Jenkins Docker image.

DISCUSSION

Running Jenkins within a Docker container gives you some advantages over a straight-forward host install. Cries of "Don't touch my Jenkins server configuration!" or, even worse, "Who touched my Jenkins server?" aren't unheard of in our office, and being able to clone the state of a Jenkins server with a `docker export` of the running container to experiment with upgrades and changes helps silence these complaints. Similarly, backups and porting become easier.

In this technique we'll take the official Jenkins Docker image and make a few changes to facilitate some later techniques that require the ability to access the Docker socket, like doing a Docker build from Jenkins.

> **DIRECT FROM THE SOURCE** The Jenkins related examples from this book are available on GitHub: git clone https://github.com/docker-in-practice/jenkins.git.

> **A COMMON BASELINE** This Jenkins image and its run command will be used as the server in Jenkins-related techniques in this book.

BUILDING THE SERVER

We'll first prepare a list of plugins we want for the server and place it in a file called jenkins_plugins.txt:

```
swarm:1.22
```

This very short list consists of the Jenkins Swarm plugin (no relation to Docker Swarm), which we'll use in a later technique.

The following listing shows the Dockerfile for building the Jenkins server.

Listing 6.5 Jenkins server build

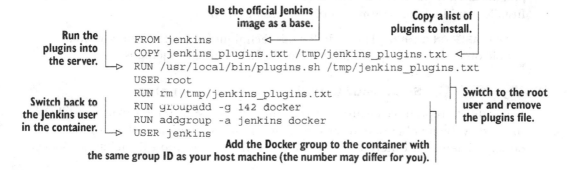

No CMD or ENTRYPOINT instruction is given because we want to inherit the startup command defined in the official Jenkins image.

The group ID for Docker may be different on your host machine. To see what the ID is for you, run this command to see the local group ID:

```
$ grep -w ^docker /etc/group
docker:x:142:imiell
```

Replace the value if it differs from 142.

> **MATCHING GROUP IDS ACROSS ENVIRONMENTS**   The group ID must match on the Jenkins server environment and your slave environment if you plan to run Docker from within the Jenkins Docker container. If you do, there will be a potential portability issue if you choose to move the server (you'd encounter the same issue on a native server install). Environment variables won't help here by themselves, as the group needs to be set up at build time rather than being dynamically configured.

To build the image in this scenario, run this command:

```
docker build -t jenkins_server .
```

RUNNING THE SERVER

Now you can run the server under Docker with this command:

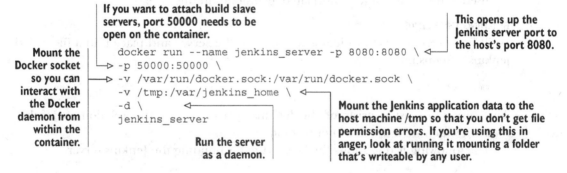

If you access http://localhost:8080, you'll see the Jenkins server ready to go with your plugins already installed. To check this, go to Manage Jenkins > Manage Plugins > Installed and look for Swarm to verify that it's installed.

> **AVAILABLE ON GITHUB**   The code for this technique and related ones is available on GitHub at https://github.com/docker-in-practice/jenkins.

TECHNIQUE 61   Scale your CI with Jenkins' Swarm plugin

Being able to reproduce environments is a big win, but your build capacity is still constrained by the number of dedicated build machines you have available. If you want to do experiments on different environments with the newfound flexibility of Docker slaves, this may become frustrating. Capacity can also become a problem for more mundane reasons—the growth of your team!

PROBLEM

You want your CI compute to scale up with your development work rate.

SOLUTION

Use Jenkins' Swarm plugin and a Docker swarm slave to dynamically provision Jenkins slaves.

DISCUSSION

Many small- to medium-sized businesses have a model for CI where there are one or more Jenkins servers devoted to supplying the resources required to run Jenkins jobs. This is illustrated in figure 6.7.

This works fine for a time, but as the CI processes become more embedded, the capacity limits are often reached. Most Jenkins workloads are triggered off check-ins to source control, so as more developers check in, the workload increases. The number of complaints to the ops team then explodes as busy developers impatiently wait for their build results.

One neat solution is to have as many Jenkins slaves as there are people checking in code, as illustrated in figure 6.8.

The Dockerfile shown in listing 6.6 creates an image with the Jenkins Swarm client plugin installed, allowing a Jenkins master with the appropriate Jenkins Swarm server

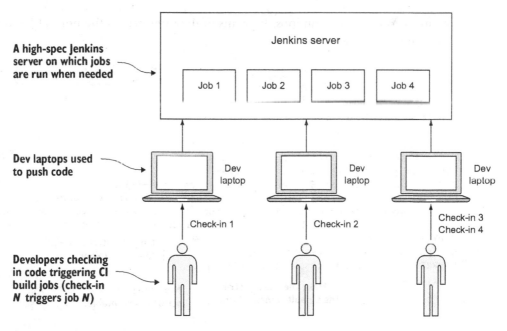

Figure 6.7   Before: Jenkins server—OK with one dev, but doesn't scale

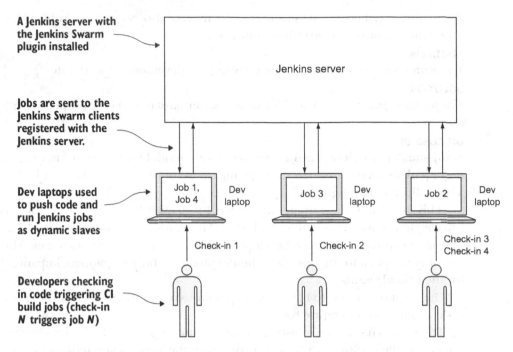

A Jenkins server with the Jenkins Swarm plugin installed

Jobs are sent to the Jenkins Swarm clients registered with the Jenkins server.

Dev laptops used to push code and run Jenkins jobs as dynamic slaves

Developers checking in code triggering CI build jobs (check-in *N* triggers job *N*)

Figure 6.8   After: compute scales with team

plugin to connect and run jobs. It begins in the same way as the normal Jenkins slave Dockerfile in the last technique.

Listing 6.6   Dockerfile

```
FROM ubuntu
ENV DEBIAN_FRONTEND noninteractive
RUN groupadd -g 1000 jenkins_slave
RUN useradd -d /home/jenkins_slave -s /bin/bash \
-m jenkins_slave -u 1000 -g jenkins_slave
RUN echo jenkins_slave:jpass | chpasswd
RUN apt-get update && apt-get install -y openjdk-7-jre wget unzip
RUN wget -O /home/jenkins_slave/swarm-client-1.22-jar-with-dependencies.jar \
http://maven.jenkins-ci.org/content/repositories/releases/org/jenkins-ci/
   plugins/swarm-client/1.22/swarm-client-1.22-jar-with-dependencies.jar
COPY startup.sh /usr/bin/startup.sh
RUN chmod +x /usr/bin/startup.sh
ENTRYPOINT ["/usr/bin/startup.sh"]
```

Retrieve the Jenkins Swarm plugin.

Copy the startup script to the container.

Make the startup script the default command run.

Mark the startup script as executable.

The following listing is the startup script copied into the preceding Dockerfile.

Listing 6.7 startup.sh

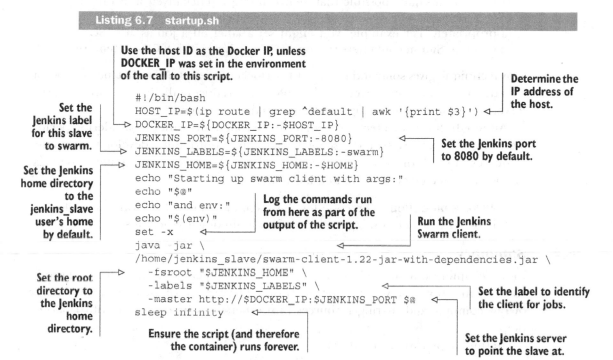

Use the host ID as the Docker IP, unless DOCKER_IP was set in the environment of the call to this script.

Determine the IP address of the host.

Set the Jenkins label for this slave to swarm.

Set the Jenkins home directory to the jenkins_slave user's home by default.

Set the root directory to the Jenkins home directory.

```
#!/bin/bash
HOST_IP=$(ip route | grep ^default | awk '{print $3}')
DOCKER_IP=${DOCKER_IP:-$HOST_IP}
JENKINS_PORT=${JENKINS_PORT:-8080}
JENKINS_LABELS=${JENKINS_LABELS:-swarm}
JENKINS_HOME=${JENKINS_HOME:-$HOME}
echo "Starting up swarm client with args:"
echo "$@"
echo "and env:"
echo "$(env)"
set -x
java jar \
/home/jenkins_slave/swarm-client-1.22-jar-with-dependencies.jar \
  -fsroot "$JENKINS_HOME" \
  -labels "$JENKINS_LABELS" \
  -master http://$DOCKER_IP:$JENKINS_PORT $@
sleep infinity
```

Set the Jenkins port to 8080 by default.

Log the commands run from here as part of the output of the script.

Run the Jenkins Swarm client.

Set the label to identify the client for jobs.

Ensure the script (and therefore the container) runs forever.

Set the Jenkins server to point the slave at.

Most of the preceding script sets up and outputs the environment for the Java call at the end. The Java call runs the Swarm client, which turns the machine on which it's run into a dynamic Jenkins slave rooted in the directory specified in the -fsroot flag, running jobs labeled with the -labels flag and pointed at the Jenkins server specified with the -master flag. The lines with echo just provide some debugging information about the arguments and environment setup.

Building and running the container is a simple matter of running what should be the now-familiar pattern:

```
$ docker build -t jenkins_swarm_slave .
$ docker run -d --name \
jenkins_swarm_slave jenkins_swarm_slave
```

Now that you have a slave set up on this machine, you can run Jenkins jobs on them. Set up a Jenkins job as normal, but add swarm as a label expression in the Restrict Where This Project Can Be Run section (see technique 59).

SET UP A SYSTEM SERVICE TO SPREAD THIS AROUND You can automate this process by setting it up as a supervised system service on all of your estate's PCs (see technique 75).

PERFORMANCE IMPACT ON SLAVE MACHINES   Jenkins jobs can be onerous processes, and it's quite possible that their running will negatively affect the laptop. If the job is a heavy one, you can set the labels on jobs and Swarm clients appropriately. For example, you might set a label on a job as 4CPU8G and match it to Swarm containers run on 4 CPU machines with 8 GB of memory.

This technique gives some indication of the Docker concept. A predictable and portable environment can be placed on multiple hosts, reducing the load on an expensive server and reducing the configuration required to a minimum.

Although this is not a technique that can be rolled out without considering performance, we think there's a lot of scope here to turn contributing developer computer resources into a form of game, increasing efficiencies with a development organization without needing expensive new hardware.

AVAILABLE ON GITHUB   The code for this technique and related ones is available on GitHub at https://github.com/docker-in-practice/jenkins.

6.4   Summary

In this chapter we've shown how Docker can be used to enable and facilitate CI within your organization. You've seen how many of the barriers to CI, such as the availability of raw compute and sharing resources with others, can be overcome with Docker's help.

In this chapter you learned that

- Builds can be sped up significantly by using eatmydata and package caches.
- You can run GUI tests (like Selenium) inside Docker.
- A Docker CI slave lets you keep complete control over your environment.
- You can farm out build processes to your whole team using Docker and Jenkins' Swarm plugin.

In the next chapter we'll move away from CI to deployment and cover techniques related to continuous delivery, another key component of the DevOps picture.

Continuous delivery: a perfect fit for Docker principles

This chapter covers

- The Docker contract between dev and ops
- Taking manual control of build availability across environments
- Moving builds between environments over low-bandwidth connections
- Centrally configuring all containers in an environment
- Achieving zero-downtime deployment with Docker

Once you're confident that all of your builds are being quality-checked with a consistent CI process, the logical next step is to start looking at deploying every good build to your users. This goal is known as continuous delivery (CD).

In this chapter we'll refer to your *CD pipeline*—the process your build goes through after it comes out of your CI pipeline. The separation can sometimes be blurred, but think of the CD pipeline as starting when you have a final image that has passed your initial tests during the build process. Figure 7.1 demonstrates how the image might progress through a CD pipeline until it (hopefully) reaches production.

It's worth repeating that last point— the image that comes out of CI should be final and unmodified throughout your

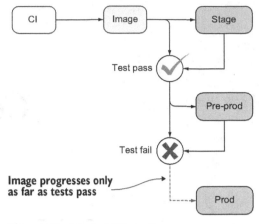

Figure 7.1   A typical CD pipeline

CD process! Docker makes this easy to enforce with immutable images and encapsulation of state, so using Docker takes you one step down the CD road already.

7.1   *Interacting with other teams during the CD pipeline*

First we're going to take a little step back and look at how Docker changes the relationship between development and operations.

Some of the biggest challenges of software development aren't technical—splitting people up into teams based on their roles and expertise is a common practice, yet this can result in communication barriers and insularity. Having a successful CD pipeline requires involvement from the teams at all stages of the process, from development to testing to production, and having a single reference point for all teams can help ease this interaction by providing structure.

TECHNIQUE 62   The Docker contract—reducing friction

One of Docker's aims is to allow easy expression of inputs and outputs as they relate to a container that contains a single application. This can provide clarity when working with other people—communication is a vital part of collaboration, and understanding how Docker can ease things by providing a single reference point can help you win over Docker unbelievers.

PROBLEM

You want cooperating teams' deliverables to be clean and unambiguous, reducing friction in your delivery pipeline.

SOLUTION

Use the *Docker contract* to facilitate clean deliverables between teams.

DISCUSSION

As companies scale, they frequently find that the flat, lean organization they once had, in which key individuals "knew the whole system," gives way to a more structured organization within which different teams have different responsibilities and competencies. We've seen this first-hand in the organizations we've worked at.

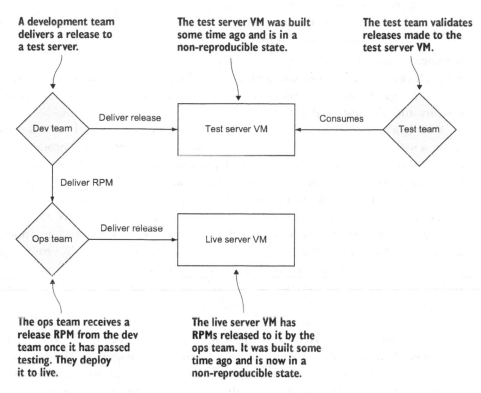

A development team
delivers a release to
a test server.

The test server VM was built
some time ago and is in a
non-reproducible state.

The test team validates
releases made to the
test server VM.

The ops team receives a
release RPM from the dev
team once it has passed
testing. They deploy
it to live.

The live server VM has
RPMs released to it by the
ops team. It was built some
time ago and is now in a
non-reproducible state.

Figure 7.2   Before: a typical software workflow

If technical investment isn't made, friction can arise as growing teams deliver to each other. Complaints of increasing complexity, "throwing the release over the wall," and buggy upgrades all become familiar. Cries of "Well, it works on our machine!" will increasingly be heard, to the frustration of all concerned. Figure 7.2 gives a simplified but representative view of this scenario.

The workflow in figure 7.2 has a number of problems that may well look familiar to you. They all boil down to the difficulties of managing state. The test team might test something on a machine that differs from what the operations team has set up. In theory, changes to all environments should be carefully documented, rolled back when problems are seen, and kept consistent. Unfortunately, the reality of commercial pressure and human behavior routinely conspire against this goal, and environmental drift is seen.

Existing solutions to this problem include VMs and RPMs. VMs can be used to reduce the surface area of environmental risk by delivering complete machine representations to other teams. The downside is that VMs are relatively monolithic entities that are difficult for teams to manipulate efficiently. At the other end, RPMs offer a standard way of packaging applications that helps define dependencies when rolling out software. This doesn't eliminate configuration management issues, and rolling out RPMs created by fellow teams is far more error-prone than using RPMs that have been battle-tested across the internet.

THE DOCKER CONTRACT

What Docker can do is give you a clean line of separation between teams, where the Docker image is both the borderline and the unit of exchange. We call this the *Docker contract*, and it's illustrated in figure 7.3.

With Docker, the reference point for all teams becomes much cleaner. Rather than dealing with sprawling monolithic virtual (or real) machines in unreproducible states, all teams are talking about the same code, whether it's on test, live, or development. In addition, there's a clean separation of data from code, which makes it easier to reason about whether problems are caused by variations in data or code.

Because Docker uses the remarkably stable Linux API as its environment, teams that deliver software have far more freedom to build software and services in whatever fashion they like, safe in the knowledge that it will run predictably in various environments. This doesn't mean that you can ignore the context in which it runs, but it does reduce the risk of environmental differences causing issues.

Various operational efficiencies result from having this single reference touchpoint. Bug reproduction becomes much easier, as all teams are able to describe and reproduce issues from a known starting point. Upgrades become the responsibility of the team delivering the change. In short, state is managed by those making the change. All these benefits greatly reduce the communications overhead and allow teams to get on with their jobs. This reduced communications overhead can also help encourage moves towards a microservices architecture.

This is no merely theoretical benefit: we've seen this improvement first-hand in a company of over 500 developers, and it's a frequent topic of discussion at Docker technical meetups.

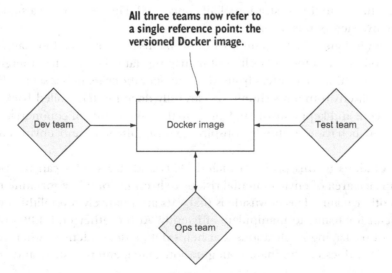

All three teams now refer to a single reference point: the versioned Docker image.

Dev team   Docker image   Test team

Ops team

Figure 7.3   After: the Docker contract

7.2   *Facilitating deployment of Docker images*

The first problem when trying to implement CD is moving the outputs of your build process to the appropriate location. If you're able to use a single registry for all stages of your CD pipeline, it may seem like this problem has been solved. But it doesn't cover a key aspect of CD.

One of the key ideas behind CD is *build promotion*. Build promotion means each stage of a pipeline (user acceptance tests, integration tests, and performance tests) can only trigger the next stage if the previous one has been successful. With multiple registries you can ensure that only *promoted* builds are used by only making them available in the next registry when a build stage passes.

We'll look at a few ways of moving your images between registries, and even at a way of sharing Docker objects without a registry.

TECHNIQUE 63   **Manually mirroring registry images**

The simplest image-mirroring scenario is when you have a machine with a high-bandwidth connection to both registries. This permits the use of normal Docker functionality to perform the image copy.

PROBLEM
You want to copy an image between two registries.

SOLUTION
Pull the image, retag it, and push.

DISCUSSION
If you have an image at test-registry.company.com and you want to move it to stage-registry.company.com, the process is simple:

```
$ IMAGE=mygroup/myimage:mytag
$ OLDREG=test-registry.company.com
$ NEWREG=stage-registry.company.com
$ docker pull $OLDREG/$MYIMAGE
[...]
$ docker tag -f $OLDREG/$MYIMAGE $NEWREG/$MYIMAGE
$ docker push $NEWREG/$MYIMAGE
$ docker rmi $OLDREG/$MYIMAGE
$ docker rmi $(docker images -q --filter dangling=true)
```

There are three important points to note about this process:

1 The new image has been force-tagged. This means that any older image with the same name on the machine (left there for layer-caching purposes) will lose the image name, so the new image can be tagged with the desired name.

2 All dangling images have been removed. Although layer caching is extremely useful for speeding up deployment, leaving unused image layers around can quickly use up disk space. In general, old layers are less likely to be used as time passes and they become more out-of-date.

3 You may need to log into your new registry with docker login.

The image is now available in the new registry for use in subsequent stages of your CD pipeline.

TECHNIQUE 64   Delivering images over constrained connections

Even with layering, pushing and pulling Docker images can be a bandwidth-hungry process. In a world of free large-bandwidth connections, this wouldn't be a problem, but sometimes reality forces us to deal with low-bandwidth connections or costly bandwidth metering between data centers. In this situation you need to find a more efficient way of transferring differences, or the CD ideal of being able to run your pipeline multiple times a day will remain out of reach.

The ideal solution is a tool that will reduce the average size of an image so it's even smaller than classic compression methods can manage.

PROBLEM
You want to copy an image between two machines with a low-bandwidth connection between them.

SOLUTION
Export the image, use bup to split it, transfer the bup chunks, and import the recombined image on the other end.

DISCUSSION
We must first introduce a new tool, *bup*. It was created as a backup tool with extremely efficient deduplication—deduplication being the ability to recognize where data is used repeatedly and only store it once. Deduplication also happens to be extremely useful in other scenarios, like transferring multiple images with very similar contents. For this technique we've created an image called dbup (short for "docker bup"), which makes it easier to use bup to deduplicate images. You can find the code behind it at https://github.com/docker-in-practice/dbup.

As a demonstration, let's see how much bandwidth we could save when upgrading from the ubuntu:14.04.1 image to ubuntu:14.04.2. Bear in mind that in practice you'd have a number of layers on top of each of these, which Docker would want to completely retransfer after a lower layer change. By contrast, this technique will recognize the significant similarities and give you much greater savings.

The first step is to pull both of those images so we can see how much is transferred over the network:

```
$ docker pull ubuntu:14.04.1 && docker pull ubuntu:14.04.2
[...]
$ docker history ubuntu:14.04.1
IMAGE          CREATED        CREATED BY                                      SIZE
5ba9dab47459   3 months ago   /bin/sh -c #(nop) CMD [/bin/bash]               0 B
51a9c7c1f8bb   3 months ago   /bin/sh -c sed -i 's/^#\s*\(deb.*universe\)$/   1.895 kB
5f92234dcf1e   3 months ago   /bin/sh -c echo '#!/bin/sh' > /usr/sbin/polic   194.5 kB
27d47432a69b   3 months ago   /bin/sh -c #(nop) ADD file:62400a49cced0d7521   188.1 MB
511136ea3c5a   23 months ago                                                  0 B
$ docker history ubuntu:14.04.2
IMAGE          CREATED        CREATED BY                                      SIZE
```

```
07f8e8c5e660   2 weeks ago    /bin/sh -c #(nop) CMD ["/bin/bash"]        0 B
37bea4ee0c81   2 weeks ago    /bin/sh -c sed -i 's/^#\s*\(deb.*universe\)$/   1.895 kB
a82efea989f9   2 weeks ago    /bin/sh -c echo '#!/bin/sh' > /usr/sbin/polic   194.5 kB
e9e06b06e14c   2 weeks ago    /bin/sh -c #(nop) ADD file:f4d7b4b3402b5c53f2   188.1 MB
$ docker save ubuntu:14.04.1 | gzip | wc -c
65970990
$ docker save ubuntu:14.04.2 | gzip | wc -c
65978132
```

This demonstrates that the Ubuntu images share no layers, so we can use the whole image size as the amount that would be transferred when pushing the new image. Also note that the Docker registry uses gzip compression to transfer layers, so we've included that in our measurement (instead of taking the size from docker history). About 65 MB is being transferred in both the initial deployment and the subsequent deployment.

In order to get started, you'll need two things—a directory to store the "pool" of data bup uses as internal storage, and the dockerinpractice/dbup image. You can then go ahead and add your image to the bup data pool:

```
$ mkdir bup_pool
$ alias dbup="docker run --rm \
    -v $(pwd)/bup_pool:/pool -v /var/run/docker.sock:/var/run/docker.sock \
    dockerinpractice/dbup"
$ dbup save ubuntu:14.04.1
Saving image!
Done!
$ du -sh bup_pool
74M     bup_pool
$ dbup save ubuntu:14.04.2
Saving image!
Done!
$ du -sh bup_pool
90M     bup_pool
```

Adding the second image to the bup data pool has only increased the size by about 15 MB. Assuming you synced the folder to another machine (possibly with rsync) after adding ubuntu:14.04.1, syncing the folder again will only transfer 15 MB (as opposed to the 65 MB before).

You then need to load the image at the other end:

```
$ dbup load ubuntu:14.04.1
Loading image!
Done!
```

The process for transferring between registries would look something like this:

1 docker pull on host1
2 dbup save on host1
3 rsync from host1 to host2
4 dbup load on host2
5 docker push on host2

This technique opens up a number of possibilities that may not have been possible previously. For example, you can now rearrange and consolidate layers without having to worry about how long it will take to transfer all of the new layers over the low-bandwidth connection.

Even when following best practices and adding your application code as the last stage, bup may be able to help—it will recognize that most of the code is unchanged and only add the difference to the data pool.

Although you may not see an immediate need for this process, keep it in mind in case your bandwidth bills start growing!

TECHNIQUE 65   Sharing Docker objects as TAR files

TAR files are a classic method of moving files around on Linux. Docker allows you to create these and ship them around manually when there's no registry available and no possibility of setting one up. Here we're going to show you the ins and outs of these commands.

PROBLEM
You want to share images and containers with others, with no available registry.

SOLUTION
Use docker export or docker save to create TAR file artifacts, and then consume them with docker import or docker load over SSH.

DISCUSSION
The distinctions between the commands can be difficult to grasp if you're using them casually, so let's take a moment to quickly go over what they do. Table 7.1 outlines the inputs and outputs of the commands.

Table 7.1   Export and import vs. save and load

Command	Creates?	Of what?	From what?
export	TAR file	Container filesystem	Container
import	Docker image	Flat filesystem	Tarball
save	TAR file	Docker image (with history)	Image
load	Docker image	Docker image (with history)	Tarball

The first two commands work with flat filesystems. The command docker export outputs a TAR file of the files that make up the state of the container. As always with Docker, the state of running processes is not stored—only the files. The command docker import creates a Docker image—with no history or metadata—from a tarball.

These commands aren't symmetrical—you can't create a container from an existing container using only import and export. This asymmetry can be useful because it allows you to docker export an image to a tarfile, and then docker import it to "lose" all the layer history and metadata. This is the image-flattening approach described in technique 43.

If you're exporting or saving to a TAR file, then the file is sent to stdout by default, so make sure you save it to a file like this:

```
docker pull debian:7:3
[...]
docker save debian:7.3 > debian7_3.tar
```

This TAR file can then be flung around the network safely, and others can use them to import images intact. They can be emailed or scp'd if you have access:

```
$ scp debian7_3.tar example.com:/tmp/debian7_3.tar
```

You can take this one step further and deliver images to other users' Docker daemons directly—assuming you have the permission:

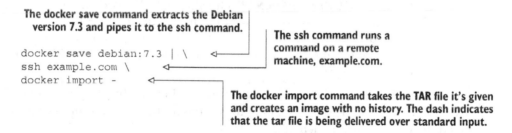

If you want to retain the history of the image, you can use load instead of import and the history will be retained on the other side's Docker daemon:

```
docker save debian:7.3 | ssh example.com docker load
```

> **DOCKER LOAD/IMPORT INCONSISTENCY** Unlike docker import, docker load doesn't require a dash at the end to indicate that the TAR file is being delivered through standard input.

7.3   Configuring your images for environments

As mentioned in the introduction to this chapter, one of the keystones of CD is the concept of "doing the same thing everywhere." Without Docker, this would mean building a deployment artifact once and using the same one everywhere. In a Docker-ized world, this means using the same image everywhere.

But environments are not all the same—there may be different URLs for external services, for example. For "normal" applications you'd be able to use environment variables to solve this problem (with the caveat that they're not easy to apply to numerous machines). The same solution can work for Docker (explicitly passing the variables in), but there's a better way of doing it with Docker that comes with some additional benefits.

Docker images are designed so they can be deployed anywhere, but you'll often want to be able to add some extra information after deployment to affect the behaviour of the application while it's running. In addition, machines running Docker may need to remain unaltered, so you may need an external source of information (making environment variables less suitable).

PROBLEM

You need an external source of configuration when running containers.

SOLUTION

Create an etcd cluster to hold your configuration, and use an etcd proxy to access it.

DISCUSSION

etcd is a distributed key-value store—it holds pieces of information and can be part of a multinode cluster for resiliency.

> **KEEPING SUCCINCT CONFIGURATION**   Each value held by etcd should be kept small—under 512 KB is a good rule of thumb; past this point you should consider doing benchmarking to verify that etcd is still performing as you'd expect. This limit is not unique to etcd. You should bear it in mind for other key-value stores like Zookeeper and Consul.

Because etcd cluster nodes need to talk to each other, the first step is to identify your external IP address. If you were going to run the nodes on different machines, you'd need the external IP for each of them:

```
$ ip addr | grep 'inet ' | grep -v 'lo$\|docker0$'
    inet 10.194.12.221/20 brd 10.194.15.255 scope global eth0
```

Here we've looked for all IPv4 interfaces and excluded loopback and Docker. This leaves us with the one IP we need (the first on the line).

We can now get started with our cluster. Be careful with the following arguments—the ports being exposed and advertised change on each line, as do the names of the cluster nodes and containers:

The external IP address of your machine

Use the external IP address of the machine in the cluster definition, giving the nodes a way to communicate with others. Because all nodes will be on the same host, the cluster ports (for connecting to other nodes) must be different.

The port for handling requests from clients

```
$ IMG=quay.io/coreos/etcd:v2.0.10
$ docker pull $IMG
[...]
$ HTTPIP=http://10.194.12.221
$ CLUSTER="etcd0=$HTTPIP:2380,etcd1=$HTTPIP:2480,etcd2=$HTTPIP:2580"
$ ARGS=
$ ARGS="$ARGS -listen-client-urls http://0.0.0.0:2379"
$ ARGS="$ARGS -listen-peer-urls http://0.0.0.0:2380"
$ ARGS="$ARGS -initial-cluster-state new"
```

The port to listen on for talking to other nodes in the cluster, corresponding to the ports specified in $CLUSTER

```
$ ARGS="$ARGS -initial-cluster $CLUSTER"
$ docker run -d -p 2379:2379 -p 2380:2380 --name etcd0 $IMG \
    $ARGS -name etcd0 -advertise-client-urls $HTTPIP:2379 \
    -initial-advertise-peer-urls $HTTPIP:2380
912390c041f8e9e71cf4cc1e51fba2a02d3cd4857d9ccd90149e21d9a5d3685b
$ docker run -d -p 2479:2379 -p 2480:2380 --name etcd1 $IMG \
    $ARGS -name etcd1 -advertise-client-urls $HTTPIP:2479 \
    -initial-advertise-peer-urls $HTTPIP:2480
446b7584a4ec747e960fe2555a9aaa2b3e2c7870097b5babe65d65cffa175dec
$ docker run -d -p 2579:2379 -p 2580:2380 --name etcd2 $IMG \
    $ARGS -name etcd2 -advertise-client-urls $HTTPIP:2579 \
    -initial-advertise-peer-urls $HTTPIP:2580
3089063b6b2ba0868e0f903a3d5b22e617a240cec22ad080dd1b497ddf4736be
$ curl -L $HTTPIP:2579/version
etcd 2.0.10
```

You've now started up the cluster and have a response from one node. In the preceding commands, anything referring to peer is controlling how the etcd nodes find and talk to each other, and anything referring to client defines how other applications can connect to etcd.

Let's see the distributed nature of etcd in action:

```
$ curl -L $HTTPIP:2579/v2/keys/mykey -XPUT -d value="test key"
{"action":"set","node": {"key":"/mykey","value":"test key",
➥ "modifiedIndex":7,"createdIndex":7}}
$ sleep 5
$ docker kill etcd2
etcd2
$ curl -L $HTTPIP:2579/v2/keys/mykey
curl: (7) couldn't connect to host
$ curl -L $HTTPIP:2379/v2/keys/mykey
{"action":"get","node": {"key":"/mykey","value":"test key",
➥ "modifiedIndex":7,"createdIndex" 7}}
```

In the preceding code, you add a key to your etcd2 node and then kill it. But etcd has automatically replicated the information to the other nodes and is able to provide you with the information anyway. Although the preceding code paused for five seconds, etcd will typically replicate in under a second (even across different machines). Feel free to docker start etcd2 now to make it available again.

You can see that the data is still available, but it's a little unfriendly to have to manually choose another node to connect to. Fortunately etcd has a solution for this—you can start a node in "proxy" mode, which means it doesn't replicate any data; rather it forwards the requests to the other nodes:

```
$ docker run -d -p 8080:8080 --restart always --name etcd-proxy $IMG \
    -proxy on -listen-client-urls http://0.0.0.0:8080 \
    -initial-cluster $CLUSTER
037c3c3dba04826a76c1d4506c922267885edbfa690e3de6188ac6b6380717ef
$ curl -L $HTTPIP:8080/v2/keys/mykey2 -XPUT -d value="t"
{"action":"set","node": {"key":"/mykey2","value":"t",
➥ "modifiedIndex":12,"createdIndex":12}}
```

```
$ docker kill etcd1 etcd2
$ curl -L $HTTPIP:8080/v2/keys/mykey2
{"action":"get","node": {"key":"/mykey2","value":"t",
➥ "modifiedIndex":12,"createdIndex":12}}
```

This now gives you some freedom to experiment with how etcd behaves when over half the nodes are offline:

```
$ curl -L $HTTPIP:8080/v2/keys/mykey3 -XPUT -d value="t"
{"message":"proxy: unable to get response from 3 endpoint(s)"}
$ docker start etcd2
etcd2
$ curl -L $HTTPIP:8080/v2/keys/mykey3 -XPUT -d value="t"
{"action":"set","node": {"key":"/mykey3","value":"t",
➥ "modifiedIndex":16,"createdIndex":16}}
```

etcd permits reading but prevents writing when half or more of the nodes are not available.

You can now see that it would be possible to start an etcd proxy on each node in a cluster to act as an "ambassador container" for retrieving centralized configuration:

```
$ docker run -it --rm --link etcd-proxy:etcd ubuntu:14.04.2 bash
root@8df11eaae71e:/# apt-get install -y wget
root@8df11eaae71e:/# wget -q -O- http://etcd:8080/v2/keys/mykey3
{"action":"get","node": {"key":"/mykey3","value":"t",
➥ "modifiedIndex":16,"createdIndex":16}}
```

> **WHAT IS AN AMBASSADOR?** An ambassador is a so-called "Docker pattern" that has some currency among Docker users. An ambassador container is placed between your application container and some external service and handles the request. It's similar to a proxy, but it has some intelligence baked into it to handle the specific requirements of the situation—much like a real-life ambassador.

Once you have an etcd running in all environments, creating a machine in an environment is just a matter of starting it up with a link to an etcd-proxy container—all CD builds to the machine will then use the correct configuration for the environment. The next technique shows how to use etcd-provided configuration to drive zero-downtime upgrades.

7.4   *Upgrading running containers*

In order to achieve the ideal of multiple deployments to production every day, it's important to reduce downtime during the final step of the deployment process—turning off the old applications and starting up the new ones. There's no point deploying four times a day if the switchover is an hour-long process each time!

Because containers provide an isolated environment, a number of problems are already mitigated. For example, you don't need to worry about two versions of an application using the same working directory and conflicting with each other, or about rereading some configuration files and picking up new values without restarting with the new code.

Unfortunately there are some downsides to this—it's no longer simple to change files in-place, so "soft-restarts" (required to pick up configuration file changes) become harder to achieve. As a result, we've found it a best practice to always perform the same upgrade process regardless of whether you're changing a few configuration files or thousands of lines of code.

Let's look at an upgrade process that will achieve the gold standard of zero-downtime deployment for web-facing applications.

TECHNIQUE 67 Using confd to enable zero-downtime switchover

Because containers can exist side by side on a host, the simple switchover approach of removing a container and starting a new one can be performed in as little as a few seconds (and it permits a similarly fast rollback).

For most applications, this may well be fast enough, but applications with a long startup time or high availability requirements need an alternative approach. Sometimes this an unavoidably complex process requiring special handling with the application itself, but web-facing applications have an option you may wish to consider first.

PROBLEM

You need to be able to upgrade web-facing applications with zero downtime.

SOLUTION

Use confd with nginx on your host to perform a two-stage switchover.

DISCUSSION

Nginx is an extremely popular web server with a crucial built-in ability—reloading configuration files without dropping connections to the server. By combining this with confd, a tool that can retrieve information from a central datastore (like etcd) and alter configuration files accordingly, you can update etcd with the latest settings and watch everything else be handled for you.

> **APACHE/HAPROXY OPTION** The Apache HTTP server and HAProxy both also offer zero-downtime reloading and can be used instead of nginx if you have existing configuration expertise.

The first step is to start an application that will serve as an old application that you'll eventually update. Python comes with Ubuntu and has a built-in web server, so we'll use it as an example:

```
$ ip addr | grep 'inet ' | grep -v 'lo$\|docker0$'
    inet 10.194.12.221/20 brd 10.194.15.255 scope global eth0
$ HTTPIP=http://10.194.12.221
$ docker run -d --name py1 -p 80 ubuntu:14.04.2 \
  sh -c 'cd / && python3 -m http.server 80'
e6b769ec3efa563a959ce771164de8337140d910de67e1df54d4960fdff74544
$ docker inspect -f '{{.NetworkSettings.Ports}}' py1
map[80/tcp:[map[HostIp:0.0.0.0 HostPort:49156]]]
$ curl -s localhost:49156 | tail
```

```
<li><a href="sbin/">sbin/</a></li>
<li><a href="srv/">srv/</a></li>
<li><a href="sys/">sys/</a></li>
<li><a href="tmp/">tmp/</a></li>
<li><a href="usr/">usr/</a></li>
<li><a href="var/">var/</a></li>
</ul>
<hr>
</body>
</html>
```

The HTTP server has started successfully, and we used the filter option of the inspect command to pull out information about what port on the host is mapped to point inside the container.

Now make sure you have etcd running—this technique assumes you're still in the same working environment as the previous technique. This time you're going to use etcdctl (short for "etcd controller") to interact with etcd (rather than curling etcd directly) for simplicity:

```
$ IMG=dockerinpractice/etcdctl
$ docker pull dockerinpractice/etcdctl
[...]
$ alias etcdctl="docker run --rm $IMG -C \"$HTTPIP:8080\""
$ etcdctl set /test value
value
$ etcdctl ls
/test
```

This has downloaded an etcdctl Docker image that we prepared, and it has set up an alias to always connect the etcd cluster set up previously. Now start up nginx:

```
$ IMG=dockerinpractice/confd-nginx
$ docker pull $IMG
[...]
$ docker run -d --name nginx -p 8000:80 $IMG $HTTPIP:8080
5a0b176586ef9e3514c5826f17d7f78ba8090537794cef06160ea7310728f7dc
```

This is an image we prepared earlier, which uses confd to retrieve information from etcd and automatically update configuration files. The parameter that we pass tells the container where it can connect to the etcd cluster. Unfortunately we haven't told it where it can find our apps yet, so the logs are filled with errors!

Let's add the appropriate information to etcd:

```
$ docker logs nginx
Using http://10.194.12.221:8080 as backend
2015-05-18T13:09:56Z fc6082e55a77 confd[14]:
➥ ERROR 100: Key not found (/app) [14]
2015-05-18T13:10:06Z fc6082e55a77 confd[14]:
➥ ERROR 100: Key not found (/app) [14]
$ echo $HTTPIP
```

```
http://10.194.12.221
$ etcdctl set /app/upstream/py1 10.194.12.221:49156
10.194.12.221:49156
$ sleep 10
$ docker logs nginx
Using http://10.194.12.221:8080 as backend
2015-05-18T13:09:56Z fc6082e55a77 confd[14]:
➥ ERROR 100: Key not found (/app) [14]
2015-05-18T13:10:06Z fc6082e55a77 confd[14]:
➥ ERROR 100: Key not found (/app) [14]
2015-05-18T13:10:16Z fc6082e55a77 confd[14]:
➥ ERROR 100: Key not found (/app) [14]
2015-05-18T13:10:26Z fc6082e55a77 confd[14]:
➥ INFO Target config /etc/nginx/conf.d/app.conf out of sync
2015-05-18T13:10:26Z fc6082e55a77 confd[14]:
➥ INFO Target config /etc/nginx/conf.d/app.conf has been updated
$ curl -s localhost:8000 | tail
<li><a href="sbin/">sbin/</a></li>
<li><a href="srv/">srv/</a></li>
<li><a href="sys/">sys/</a></li>
<li><a href="tmp/">tmp/</a></li>
<li><a href="usr/">usr/</a></li>
<li><a href="var/">var/</a></li>
</ul>
<hr>
</body>
</html>
```

The update to etcd has been read by confd and applied to the nginx configuration
file, allowing you to visit your simple file server. The `sleep` command is included
because confd has been configured to check for updates every 10 seconds. Behind the
scenes, a confd daemon running in the confd-nginx container polls for changes in the
etcd cluster, using a template within the container to regenerate the nginx configuration only when changes are detected.

Let's say we've decided we want to serve /etc rather than /. We'll now start up our
second application and add it to etcd. Because we then will have two backends, we'll
end up getting responses from each of them:

```
$ docker run -d --name py2 -p 80 ubuntu:14.04.2 \
  sh -c 'cd /etc && python3 -m http.server 80'
9b5355b9b188427abaf367a51a88c1afa2186e6179ab46830715a20eacc33660
$ docker inspect -f '{{.NetworkSettings.Ports}}' py2
map[80/tcp:[map[HostIp:0.0.0.0 HostPort:49161]]]
$ curl $HTTPIP:49161 | tail | head -n 5
<li><a href="udev/">udev/</a></li>
<li><a href="update-motd.d/">update-motd.d/</a></li>
<li><a href="upstart-xsessions">upstart-xsessions</a></li>
<li><a href="vim/">vim/</a></li>
<li><a href="vtrgb">vtrgb@</a></li>
$ etcdctl set /app/upstream/py2 $HTTPIP:49161
10.194.12.221:49161
$ etcdctl ls /app/upstream
```

```
/app/upstream/py1
/app/upstream/py2
$ curl -s localhost:8000 | tail | head -n 5
<li><a href="sbin/">sbin/</a></li>
<li><a href="srv/">srv/</a></li>
<li><a href="sys/">sys/</a></li>
<li><a href="tmp/">tmp/</a></li>
<li><a href="usr/">usr/</a></li>
$ curl -s localhost:8000 | tail | head -n 5
<li><a href="udev/">udev/</a></li>
<li><a href="update-motd.d/">update-motd.d/</a></li>
<li><a href="upstart-xsessions">upstart-xsessions</a></li>
<li><a href="vim/">vim/</a></li>
<li><a href="vtrgb">vtrgb@</a></li>
```

In the preceding process we checked that the new container came up correctly before adding it to etcd (see figure 7.4). Because of this, we could have performed the process

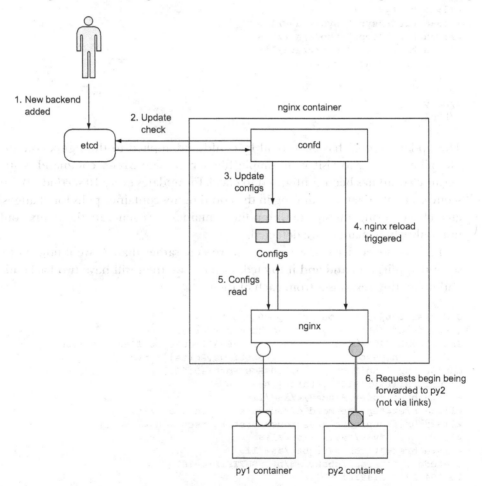

Figure 7.4 Adding the py2 container to etcd

in one step by overwriting the /app/upstream/py1 key in etcd. This is also useful if you need only one backend to be accessible at a time.

With the two-stage switchover, the final stage is to remove the old backend and container:

```
$ etcdctl rm /app/upstream/py1

$ etcdctl ls /app/upstream
/app/upstream/py2
$ docker rm -f py1
py1
```

And the new application is up and running! At no point has the application been inaccessible to users, and there has been no need to manually connect to web server machines to reload nginx.

The uses of confd extend to more than configuring web servers: if you have a file containing text that needs updating based on external values, confd is there to step in. Bear in mind from the previous technique that etcd is not designed for storing large values. And there's no reason you must use etcd with confd. There are a number of integrations available for the most popular key-value stores, so you might not need to add another moving part if you've already got something that works for you.

Later on in technique 83, when we look at using Docker in production, you'll see a method that avoids having to manually alter etcd at all if you want to update the backend servers for a service.

7.5 Summary

Using Docker puts you on the road to a streamlined CD pipeline, but in this chapter we also explored some ways you can use extra tools to complement Docker and work around some Docker limitations.

In this chapter you saw that

- Moving images between registries can be a good way to control how far builds progress through your CD pipeline.
- bup is good at squeezing image transfers even more than layers can.
- etcd can act as a central configuration store for an environment.
- Zero-downtime deployment can be achieved by combining etcd, confd, and nginx.

The next chapter will explore speeding up your CD pipeline even more by simulating networks for testing rather than requiring a full environment.

Network simulation: realistic environment testing without the pain

This chapter covers

- Coming to grips with Docker Compose
- Running a DNS server to perform basic container service discovery
- Testing your applications on troublesome networks
- Creating a substrate network for seamless communications across Docker hosts

As part of your DevOps workflow, you'll likely need to use the network in some way. Whether you're trying to find out where the local memcache container is, connecting to the outside world, or plumbing together Docker containers running on different hosts, you're likely to want to reach out to the wider network sooner or later.

In this chapter we'll show you how to simulate and manage networks by using Docker's virtual network tooling. This chapter is a small first step toward orchestration and service discovery—subjects we'll take a deeper dive into in chapter 9.

8.1   Container communication—beyond manual linking

In technique 6 you saw how to connect containers with links and we mentioned the advantages provided by a clear statement of container dependencies. Unfortunately, links have a number of disadvantages. They have to be manually specified when starting each container, containers have to be started in the correct order (so no loops in container linking), and there's no way to replace a link (if a container dies, every dependent container must be restarted to recreate the links).

Fortunately, tools exist to address these pain points.

TECHNIQUE 68   **A simple Docker Compose cluster**

Docker Compose started life as *fig*, a now-deprecated independent effort to ease the pain of starting multiple containers with appropriate arguments for linking, volumes, and ports. Docker, Inc. liked this so much that they acquired it, gave it a makeover, and released it with a new name.

This technique introduces you to Docker Compose using a simple example of Docker container orchestration.

PROBLEM
You want to coordinate linked containers on your host machine.

SOLUTION
Use Docker Compose.

DISCUSSION
Docker Compose is a tool for defining and running complex Docker applications. The central idea is that rather than wiring up complex container startup commands with complex shell scripts or makefiles, you declare the application's startup configuration and then bring the application up with a single, simple command.

At the time of writing, Docker Compose isn't recommended for use in production.

> **INSTALLATION** We assume you have Docker Compose installed. Instructions for installing are fast-changing at the time of writing, so refer to Docker's instructions (http://docs.docker.com/compose/install) for the latest advice. You may need to use sudo to run docker-compose.

In this technique we're going to keep things as simple as possible with an echo server and client. The client sends the familiar "Hello world!" message every five seconds to the echo server, and then receives the message back.

> **SOURCE CODE AVAILABLE** The source code for this technique is available at https://github.com/docker-in-practice/docker-compose-echo.

The following commands create a directory for us to work in while creating our server image:

```
$ mkdir server
$ cd server
```

Create the server Dockerfile with the code shown in the following listing.

Listing 8.1   Dockerfile—Simple echo server

```
FROM debian
RUN apt-get update && apt-get install -y nmap
CMD ncat -l 2000 -k --exec /bin/cat
```

Run the ncat program by default
when starting the image.

Install the nmap package,
which provides the ncat
program used here.

The `-l 2000` arguments instruct ncat to listen on port 2000 and `-k` tells it to accept multiple client connections simultaneously and to continue running after clients close their connections, so more clients can connect. The final arguments, `--exec /bin/cat`, will make ncat run`/bin/cat` for any incoming connections and forward any data coming over the connection to the running program.

Next, build the Dockerfile with this command:

```
$ docker build -t server .
```

Now you can set up the client image that sends messages to the server. Create a new directory and place the client.py file and Dockerfile in there:

```
$ cd ..
$ mkdir client
$ cd client
```

We'll use a simple Python program as the echo server client in the next listing.

Listing 8.2   client.py—a simple echo client

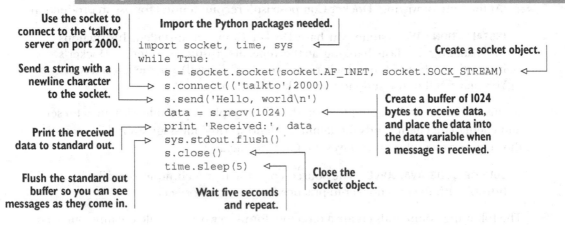

Use the socket to
connect to the 'talkto'
server on port 2000.

Import the Python packages needed.

Send a string with a
newline character
to the socket.

Print the received
data to standard out.

Flush the standard out
buffer so you can see
messages as they come in.

Create a socket object.

Create a buffer of 1024
bytes to receive data,
and place the data into
the data variable when
a message is received.

Close the
socket object.

Wait five seconds
and repeat.

```python
import socket, time, sys
while True:
    s = socket.socket(socket.AF_INET, socket.SOCK_STREAM)
    s.connect(('talkto',2000))
    s.send('Hello, world\n')
    data = s.recv(1024)
    print 'Received:', data
    sys.stdout.flush()
    s.close()
    time.sleep(5)
```

The Dockerfile for the client is straightforward. It installs Python, adds the client.py file, and then defaults it to run on startup, as shown in the following listing.

Listing 8.3   Dockerfile—a simple echo client

```
FROM debian
RUN apt-get update && apt-get install -y python
ADD client.py /client.py
CMD ["/usr/bin/python","/client.py"]
```

Build the client with this command:

```
docker build -t client .
```

To demonstrate the value of docker-compose, we'll first run these containers by hand:

```
docker run --name echo-server -d server
docker run --rm --name client --link echo-server:talkto client
```

When you're finished, Ctrl-C out of the client, and remove the containers:

```
docker rm -f client echo-server
```

Many things can go wrong even in this trivial example: starting the client first will result in the failure of the application to start; forgetting to remove the containers will result in problems when you try to restart; and naming containers incorrectly will result in failure. These kinds of orchestration problems will only increase as your containers and their architecture get more sophisticated.

Compose helps with this by encapsulating the orchestration of these containers' startup and configuration within a simple text file, managing the nuts and bolts of the startup and shutdown commands for you.

Compose takes a YAML file. You create this in a new directory:

```
cd ..
mkdir docker-compose
cd docker-compose
```

The YAML file's contents are as shown in the next listing.

Listing 8.4   docker-compose.yml—Docker Compose echo server and client YAML file

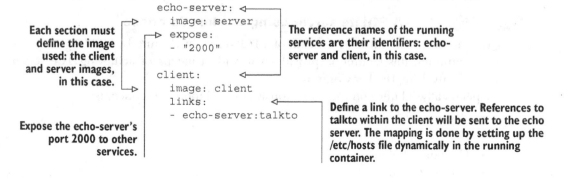

Each section must define the image used: the client and server images, in this case.

Expose the echo-server's port 2000 to other services.

```
echo-server:
  image: server
  expose:
  - "2000"

client:
  image: client
  links:
  - echo-server:talkto
```

The reference names of the running services are their identifiers: echo-server and client, in this case.

Define a link to the echo-server. References to talkto within the client will be sent to the echo server. The mapping is done by setting up the /etc/hosts file dynamically in the running container.

The syntax of docker-compose.yml is fairly easy to grasp: each service is named on the left, and its configuration is stated in an indented section underneath. Each item of configuration has a colon after its name, and attributes of these items are stated either on the same line or on the following lines, beginning with dashes at the same level of indentation.

The key item of configuration to understand here is the links within the client definition. These are created in the same way as the docker run command sets up links. In fact, most of the Docker command-line arguments have direct analogues in the docker-compose.yml syntax.

We used the image: statement in this example to define the image used for each service, but you can also get docker-compose to rebuild the required image dynamically by defining the path to the Dockerfile in a build: statement. Docker Compose will perform the build for you.

> **WHAT IS A YAML FILE?**   A YAML file is a text configuration file with a straightforward syntax. You can read more about it at http://yaml.org.

Now that all the infrastructure is set up, running the application is easy:

```
$ docker-compose up
Creating dockercompose_server_1...
Creating dockercompose_client_1...
Attaching to dockercompose_server_1, dockercompose_client_1
client_1 | Received: Hello, world
client_1 |
client_1 | Received: Hello, world
client_1 |
```

> **CAN'T CONNECT ERRORS?**   If you get an error when starting docker-compose that looks like "Couldn't connect to Docker daemon at http+unix://var/run/docker.sock—is it running?" the issue may be that you need to run it with sudo.

When you've seen enough, hit Ctrl-C a few times to exit the application. You can bring it up again at will with the same command without worrying about removing containers. Note that it will output "Recreating" rather than "Creating" if you rerun it.

Now that you've come to grips with Docker Compose, we'll move on to a more complex and real-world scenario for docker-compose: using socat, volumes, and links to add server-like functionality to a SQLite instance running on the host machine.

TECHNIQUE 69   A SQLite server using Docker Compose

SQLite doesn't come with any concept of a TCP server by default. By building on previous techniques, this technique provides you with a means of achieving TCP server functionality using Docker Compose.

Specifically, it builds on these previously covered tools and concepts:

- Volumes
- Proxying with socat
- Container linking
- Docker Compose

SQLITE VERSION 3 REQUIRED This technique requires SQLite version 3 to be installed on your host. We also suggest that you install rlwrap to make line editing friendlier when interacting with your SQLite server (though this is optional). These packages are freely available from standard package managers.

The code for this technique is available for download here: https://github.com/docker-in-practice/docker-compose-sqlite.

If you run into trouble with this technique, you may need to upgrade your version of Docker. Anything from version 1.7.0 up should work fine.

PROBLEM

You want to efficiently develop a complex application referencing external data on your host using Docker.

SOLUTION

Use Docker Compose.

DISCUSSION

Figure 8.1 gives an overview of this technique's architecture. At a high level there are two running Docker containers, one responsible for executing SQLite clients, and the other for proxying separate TCP connections to these clients. Note that the container executing SQLite isn't exposed to the host; the proxy container achieves that. This kind of separation of responsibility into discrete units is a common feature of microservices architectures.

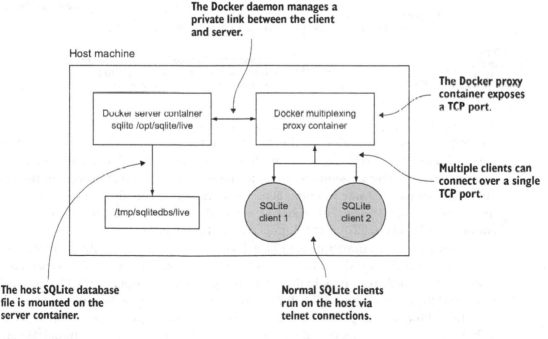

Figure 8.1 How the SQLite server works

We're going to use the same image for all our nodes. Set up the Dockerfile in the next listing.

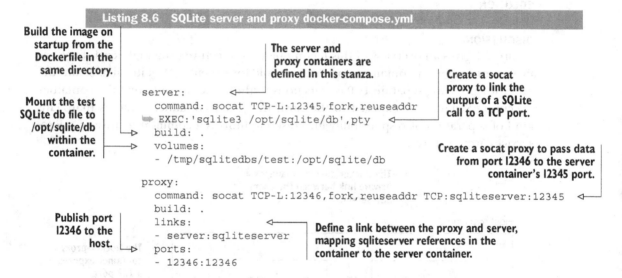

Listing 8.5   All-in-one SQLite server, client, and proxy Dockerfile

```
FROM ubuntu:14.04
RUN apt-get update && apt-get -y install rlwrap sqlite3 socat
EXPOSE 12345
```

Expose port 12345 so that the nodes can communicate via the Docker daemon.

Install required applications.

The following listing shows docker-compose.yml, which defines how the containers should be started up.

Listing 8.6   SQLite server and proxy docker-compose.yml

Build the image on startup from the Dockerfile in the same directory.

Mount the test SQLite db file to /opt/sqlite/db within the container.

The server and proxy containers are defined in this stanza.

Create a socat proxy to link the output of a SQLite call to a TCP port.

```
server:
    command: socat TCP-L:12345,fork,reuseaddr
    EXEC:'sqlite3 /opt/sqlite/db',pty
    build: .
    volumes:
        - /tmp/sqlitedbs/test:/opt/sqlite/db
proxy:
    command: socat TCP-L:12346,fork,reuseaddr TCP:sqliteserver:12345
    build: .
    links:
        - server:sqliteserver
    ports:
        - 12346:12346
```

Create a socat proxy to pass data from port 12346 to the server container's 12345 port.

Publish port 12346 to the host.

Define a link between the proxy and server, mapping sqliteserver references in the container to the server container.

The socat process in the server container will listen on port 12345 and permit multiple connections, as specified by the `TCP-L:12345,fork,reuseaddr` argument. The part following `EXEC:` tells `socat` to run SQLite on the /opt/sqlite/db file for every connection, assigning a pseudo-terminal to the process. The socat process in the client container has the same listening behavior as the server container (except on a different port), but instead of running something in response to an incoming connection, it will establish a TCP connection to the SQLite server.

Although this functionality could be achieved in one container, the server/proxy container setup allows the architecture of this system to grow more easily, as each container is responsible for one job: the server is responsible for opening SQLite connections, and the proxy is responsible for exposing the service to the host machine.

The following listing (simplified from the original in the repository, https://github.com/docker-in-practice/docker-compose-sqlite) creates two minimal SQLite databases, test and live, on your host machine.

Listing 8.7 setup_dbs.sh

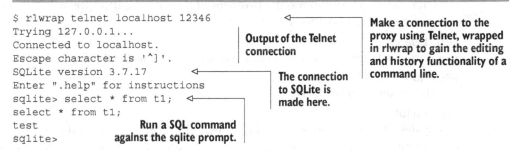

```
#!/bin/bash
echo "Creating directory"
SQLITEDIR=/tmp/sqlitedbs
rm -rf $SQLITEDIR
if [ -a $SQLITEDIR ]
then
    echo "Failed to remove $SQLITEDIR"
    exit 1
fi
mkdir -p $SQLITEDIR
cd $SQLITEDIR
echo "Creating DBs"
echo 'create table t1(c1 text);' | sqlite3 test
echo 'create table t1(c1 text);' | sqlite3 live
echo "Inserting data"
echo 'insert into t1 values ("test");' | sqlite3 test
echo 'insert into t1 values ("live");' | sqlite3 live
cd - > /dev/null 2>&1
echo "All done OK"
```

Annotations:
- **Throw an error if the directory still exists.**
- **Remove any directory from a previous run.**
- **Create the live DB with one table.**
- **Create the test DB with one table.**
- **Insert one row with the string "test" into the table.**
- **Insert one row with the string "live" into the table.**
- **Return to the previous directory.**

To run this example, set up the databases and call docker-compose up, as shown in the following listing.

Listing 8.8 Run up the Docker Compose cluster

```
$ chmod +x setup_dbs.sh
$ ./setup_dbs.sh
$ sudo docker-compose up
Creating dockercomposesqlite_server_1...
Creating dockercomposesqlite_proxy_1...
Attaching to dockercomposesqlite_server_1, dockercomposesqlite_proxy_1
```

Then, in one or more other terminals, you can run Telnet to create multiple sessions against one SQLite DB, as the next listing shows.

Listing 8.9 Connecting to the SQLite server

```
$ rlwrap telnet localhost 12346
Trying 127.0.0.1...
Connected to localhost.
Escape character is '^]'.
SQLite version 3.7.17
Enter ".help" for instructions
sqlite> select * from t1;
select * from t1;
test
sqlite>
```

Annotations:
- **Make a connection to the proxy using Telnet, wrapped in rlwrap to gain the editing and history functionality of a command line.**
- **Output of the Telnet connection**
- **The connection to SQLite is made here.**
- **Run a SQL command against the sqlite prompt.**

Now if you want to switch the server to live, you can change the configuration by changing the volumes line in docker-compose.yml from this

```
- /tmp/sqlitedbs/test:/opt/sqlite/db
```

to this:

```
- /tmp/sqlitedbs/live:/opt/sqlite/db
```

Then rerun this command:

```
$ sudo docker-compose up
```

> **NOT PRODUCTION-READY**   Although we did some basic tests with this multiplexing of SQLite clients, we make no guarantees about the data integrity or performance of this server under any kind of load.

This technique demonstrates how Docker Compose can take something relatively tricky and complicated and make it robust and straightforward. Here we've taken SQLite and given it extra server-like functionality by wiring up containers to proxy SQLite invocations to the data on the host. Managing the container complexity is made significantly easier with Docker Compose's YAML configuration, which turns the tricky matter of orchestrating containers correctly from a manual, error-prone process to a safer, automated one that can be put under source control. This is the beginning of our journey into orchestration, which you'll be hearing much more about in chapter 9.

TECHNIQUE 70   Finding containers via DNS with Resolvable

When you start containers, they are by default allocated their own IP addresses and can communicate with each other if they know the IPs of their peers— linking, both manually and as provided by Docker Compose, are a way of distributing IPs in /etc/ hosts and environment variables.

However, this method of distribution is limited—there's no way to update environment variables in a running container, and trying to dynamically update /etc/hosts could be problematic. Docker avoids both of these problems by refusing to allow you to add links to a running container.

There's a good solution to the problem of distributing IP addresses, and you probably use it every day—DNS servers!

PROBLEM

You want containers to be able to discover each other without using links.

SOLUTION

Use Resolvable as a DNS server.

DISCUSSION

Resolvable (https://github.com/gliderlabs/resolvable/) is a tool that reads information about currently running containers on a host and serves a name-to IP-address mapping in a standard way—it's a DNS server.

BUILT INTO DOCKER Some versions of Docker (newer than 1.7.1 and older than 1.9.0) provide the ability for containers to ping other containers by name without needing any external tools. But there is possibly still value in Resolvable if you want to be able to look up containers from the host, as described at the end of the technique.

There are some settings you need to identify before you can begin: the address of the docker0 interface and the DNS servers currently used when you start up containers:

```
$ ip addr | grep 'inet.*docker0'
    inet 172.17.42.1/16 scope global docker0
$ docker run --rm ubuntu:14.04.2 cat /etc/resolv.conf | grep nameserver
nameserver 8.8.8.8
nameserver 8.8.4.4
```

Both of the preceding values are the Docker defaults—if you've tweaked some settings on the Docker daemon or have some unusual configuration on your laptop, you may find they differ slightly.

You can now start up your Resolvable container with the appropriate values you just looked up:

```
$ DNSARGS="--dns 8.8.8.8 --dns 8.8.4.4"
$ PORTARGS="-p 172.17.42.1:53:53/udp"
$ VOLARGS="-v /var/run/docker.sock:/tmp/docker.sock"
$ docker run -d --name res -h resolvable $DNSARGS $PORTARGS $VOLARGS \
gliderlabs/resolvable:master
5ebbe218b297da6390b8f05c0217613e47f46fe46c04be919c415a5a1763fb11
```

Three crucial pieces of information were provided in the startup of the container:

- Resolvable needs to know who to ask if an address being requested can't be mapped to a container—the answer is upstream DNS servers. Resolvable will pick these up from /etc/resolv.conf in the container; the --dns arguments will populate /etc/resolv.conf. Although it's not strictly required here (the values specified are the defaults) you'll see how this is useful later on.
- The interface that should be listened on for DNS requests. Using the IP address of the Docker bridge has the advantages of not exposing the server to the outside world (as 0.0.0.0 would) and of being available at an unchanging IP address (unlike using container IP addresses).
- Resolvable needs the Docker socket to be able to find container names.

For every container you have running, Resolvable makes two names available: <container_name>.docker and <container_hostname>. You can test this with the dig command, available in the dnsutils package on Ubuntu or bind-utils on CentOS by looking for the Resolvable container itself:

```
$ dig +short @172.17.42.1 res.docker
172.17.0.22
$ dig +short @172.17.42.1 resolvable
172.17.0.22
```

This is interesting, but it's not entirely helpful—similar information can be obtained with docker inspect. The value comes when you start a container configured to use the new DNS server:

```
$ docker run -it --dns 172.17.42.1 ubuntu:14.04.2 bash
root@216a71584c9c:/# ping -q -c1 res.docker
PING res.docker (172.17.0.22) 56(84) bytes of data.

--- res.docker ping statistics ---
1 packets transmitted, 1 received, 0% packet loss, time 0ms
rtt min/avg/max/mdev = 0.065/0.065/0.065/0.000 ms
root@216a71584c9c:/# ping -q -c1 www.google.com
PING www.google.com (216.58.210.36) 56(84) bytes of data.

--- www.google.com ping statistics ---
1 packets transmitted, 1 received, 0% packet loss, time 0ms
rtt min/avg/max/mdev = 7.991/7.991/7.991/0.000 ms
```

Here we've verified that using the DNS server provided by Resolvable gives us access both to other containers and the outside world. But it's a bit tiresome to have to specify a --dns argument every time you start up a container. Happily there are some options you can pass to the Docker daemon to save the day. Edit your daemon arguments (using the appropriate method for your operating system) to add this:

```
--bip=172.17.42.1/16 --dns=172.17.42.1
```

> **SETTING DOCKER DAEMON ARGUMENTS** See appendix B for help on specifying Docker daemon arguments.

These values are based on the command you ran near the beginning of this technique to find out the details of the Docker bridge. You should alter them appropriately to match your results. The role of the --dns argument to the daemon is fairly straightforward—it alters the default DNS servers used by containers. Meanwhile, --bip fixes the configuration of the Docker bridge so it won't potentially change on a daemon restart (which would break DNS in all of the containers).

The DNS arguments passed when starting up Resolvable are crucial here—if you don't add them, Resolvable will use the default DNS servers for upstream lookups, which points back to itself! If this happens, huge logs will be generated and the client lookups will time out.

Once you've restarted your Docker daemon and started Resolvable, try starting a container:

```
$ docker run --rm ubuntu:14.04.2 ping -q -c1 resolvable
PING resolvable (172.17.0.1) 56(84) bytes of data.

--- resolvable ping statistics ---
1 packets transmitted, 1 received, 0% packet loss, time 0ms
rtt min/avg/max/mdev = 0.095/0.095/0.095/0.000 ms
```

There are a couple of final features Resolvable comes with that we won't go into any detail on, but we'll mention them for completeness. If you mount /etc/resolv.conf to /tmp/resolv.conf, you'll find the DNS server address is added to your host DNS servers, allowing you to ping containers by name from outside any containers. Users of systemd can get a similar integration by mounting /run/systemd to /tmp/systemd, and /var/run/dbus/system_bus_socket to the same path in the container.

Being able to easily find and connect to other containers is a hot topic when it comes to multiple hosts. We'll cover service discovery in more detail later in the book.

8.2 Using Docker to simulate real-world networking

Most people who use the internet treat it as a black box that somehow retrieves information from other places around the world and puts it on their screens. Sometimes they experience slowness or connection drops, and it's not uncommon to observe cursing of the ISP as a result.

When you build images containing applications that need to be connected, you likely have a much better grasp of which components need to connect to where, and how the overall setup looks. But one thing remains constant: you can still experience slowness and connection drops. Even large companies, with data centers they own and operate, have observed unreliable networking and the issues it causes with applications.

We'll look at a couple of ways you can experiment with flaky networks to help determine what problems you may be facing in the real world.

TECHNIQUE 71 Simulating troublesome networks with Comcast

As much as we might wish for perfect network conditions when we distribute applications across many machines, the reality is much uglier—tales of packet loss, connection drops, and network partitions abound, particularly on commodity cloud providers.

It's prudent to test your stack before it encounters these situations in the real world to see how it behaves—an application designed for high availability shouldn't grind to a halt if an external service starts experiencing significant additional latency.

PROBLEM
You want to be able to apply varying network conditions to individual containers.

SOLUTION
Use comcast (the networking tool, not the ISP).

DISCUSSION
Comcast (https://github.com/tylertreat/Comcast) is a humorously named tool for altering network interfaces on your Linux machine in order to apply unusual (or, if you're unfortunate, typical!) conditions to them.

Whenever Docker creates a container, it also creates virtual network interfaces—this is how all your containers have different IPs and can ping each other. Because these are standard network interfaces, you can use Comcast on them, as long as you can find the network interface name. This is easier said than done.

Here's a Docker image containing Comcast, all its prerequisites, and some tweaks:

```
$ IMG=dockerinpractice/comcast
$ docker pull $IMG
latest: Pulling from dockerinpractice/comcast
[...]
Status: Downloaded newer image for dockerinpractice/comcast:latest
$ alias comcast="docker run --rm --pid=host --privileged \
-v /var/run/docker.sock:/var/run/docker.sock $IMG"
$ comcast -help
Usage of comcast:
  -cont="": Container ID or name to get virtual interface of
  -default-bw=-1: Default bandwidth limit in kbit/s (fast-lane)
  -device="": Interface (device) to use (defaults to eth0 where applicable)
  -dry-run=false: Specifies whether or not to commit the rule changes
  -latency=-1: Latency to add in ms
  -mode="start": Start or stop packet controls
  -packet-loss="0": Packet loss percentage (eg: 0.1%%)
  -target-addr="": Target addresses, \
(eg: 10.0.0.1 or 10.0.0.0/24 or 10.0.0.1,192.168.0.0/24)
  -target-bw=-1: Target bandwidth limit in kbit/s (slow-lane)
  -target-port="": Target port(s) (eg: 80 or 1:65535 or 22,80,443,1000:1010)
  -target-proto="tcp,udp,icmp": \
Target protocol TCP/UDP (eg: tcp or tcp,udp or icmp)
```

The tweaks we added provide the -cont option, which allows you to refer to a container rather than having to find the name of a virtual interface. Note that we've had to add some special flags to the docker run command in order to give the container more permissions—this is so Comcast is freely able to examine and apply changes to network interfaces.

In order to see the difference Comcast can make, we'll first find out what a normal network connection looks like. Open a new terminal and run the following commands to set your expectations for baseline network performance:

```
$ docker run -it --name c1 ubuntu:14.04.2 bash
root@0749a2e74a68:/# apt-get update && apt-get install -y wget
[...]
root@0749a2e74a68:/# ping -q -c 5 www.docker.com
PING www.docker.com (104.239.220.248) 56(84) bytes of data.

--- www.docker.com ping statistics ---
5 packets transmitted, 5 received, 0% packet loss,
time 4005ms
rtt min/avg/max/mdev = 98.546/101.272/106.424/2.880 ms
root@0749a2e74a68:/# time wget -o /dev/null https://www.docker.com

real    0m0.680s
user    0m0.012s
sys     0m0.006s
root@0749a2e74a68:/#
```

The connection between this machine and www.docker.com seems to be reliable, with no packets lost.

The total time taken to download the HTML homepage of www.docker.com is about 0.7s.

The average round trip time is about 100 ms for www.docker.com.

Once you've done this, leave the container running and you can apply some network conditions to it:

```
$ comcast -cont c1 -default-bw 50 -latency 100 -packet-loss 20%
2015/07/29 02:28:13 Found interface vetha7b90a7 for container 'c1'
sudo tc qdisc show | grep "netem"
sudo tc qdisc add dev vetha7b90a7 handle 10: root htb
sudo tc class add dev vetha7b90a7 parent 10: classid 10:1 htb rate 50kbit
sudo tc class add dev vetha7b90a7 parent 10:1 classid 10:10 htb rate 50kbit
sudo tc qdisc add dev vetha7b90a7 parent 10:10 handle 100:
➥ netem delay 100ms loss 20.00%
sudo iptables -A POSTROUTING -t mangle -j CLASSIFY --set-class 10:10 -p tcp
sudo iptables -A POSTROUTING -t mangle -j CLASSIFY --set-class 10:10 -p udp
sudo iptables -A POSTROUTING -t mangle -j CLASSIFY --set-class 10:10 -p icmp
2015/07/29 02:28:13 Packet rules setup...
2015/07/29 02:28:13 Run `sudo tc -s qdisc` to double check
2015/07/29 02:28:13 Run `comcast --mode stop` to reset
```

The preceding command applies three different conditions: 50 KBps bandwidth cap for all destinations (to bring back memories of dial-up), an added latency of 100 ms (on top of any inherent delay), and a packet percentage of 20%.

Comcast first identifies the appropriate virtual network interface for the container and then invokes a number of standard Linux command-line networking utilities to apply the traffic rules, listing what it's doing as it goes along. Let's see how our container reacts to this:

```
root@0749a2e74a68:/# ping -q -c 5 www.docker.com
PING www.docker.com (104.239.220.248) 56(84) bytes of data.

--- www.docker.com ping statistics ---
5 packets transmitted, 2 received, 60% packet loss, time 4001ms
rtt min/avg/max/mdev = 200.163/200.164/200.789/0.100 ms
root@0749a2e74a68:/# time wget -o /dev/null https://www.docker.com

real    0m9.673s
user    0m0.011s
sys     0m0.011s
```

Success! An additional 100 ms of latency is reported by ping, and the timing from wget shows a slightly greater than 10x slowdown, approximately as expected (the bandwidth cap, latency addition, and packet loss will all impact on this time). But there's something odd about the packet loss—it seems to be three times greater than expected. It's important to bear in mind that the ping is sending a few packets and that packet loss is not a precise "one in five" counter—if you increase the ping count to 50, you'll find that the resulting loss is much closer to what's expected.

Note that the rules we've applied apply to *all* network connections via this network interface. This includes connections to the host and other containers.

Let's now instruct Comcast to remove the rules. Comcast is sadly not yet able to add and remove individual conditions, so altering anything on a network interface means completely removing and re-adding rules on the interface. You also need to remove the rules if you want to get your normal container network operation back. Don't worry about removing them if you exit the container, though—they'll be automatically deleted when Docker deletes the virtual network interface:

```
$ comcast -cont c1 -mode stop
2015/07/29 02:31:34 Found interface vetha7b90a7 for container 'c1'
[...]
2015/07/29 02:31:34 Packet rules stopped...
2015/07/29 02:31:34 Run `sudo tc -s qdisc` to double check
2015/07/29 02:31:34 Run `comcast --mode start` to start
```

If you want to get your hands dirty, you can dig into Linux traffic control tools, possibly using Comcast to generate example sets of commands to use. A full treatment of the possibilities is outside the scope of the technique, but remember, if you can put it in a container, and it hits the network, you can toy with it.

TECHNIQUE 72   Simulating troublesome networks with Blockade

Comcast is an excellent tool with a number of applications, but there's an important use case it doesn't solve—how do you apply network conditions to containers en masse? Manually running Comcast against tens of containers would be painful, hundreds would be unthinkable! This is a particularly relevant problem for containers, because they're so cheap to spin up—if you're trying to run a large network simulation on a single machine with hundreds of VMs rather than containers, you may find you have bigger problems, like a lack of memory!

On the subject of simulating a network with many machines, there's a particular kind of network failure that becomes interesting at this scale—a network partition. This is when a group of networked machines splits into two or more parts, such that all machines in the same part can talk to each other, but different parts can't communicate. Research indicates that this happens more than you might think, particularly on consumer-grade clouds!

Going down the classic Docker microservices route brings these problems into sharp relief, and having the tools to do experiments is crucial for understanding how your service will deal with it.

PROBLEM

You want to orchestrate setting network conditions for large numbers of containers, including creating network partitions.

SOLUTION

Use Blockade.

DISCUSSION

Blockade (https://github.com/dcm-oss/blockade.git) is an open source piece of software from a division of Dell, created for "testing network failures and partitions." Looks like exactly what we need.

BEWARE A BROKEN REPOSITORY As of the time of writing, the official Blockade repository doesn't work with any version of Docker after 1.6.2 without some tweaking. For the purposes of this technique, we made some modifications that we hope to contribute back. Bear this in mind if you want to dig into Blockade yourself.

Blockade works by reading a configuration file (blockade.yml) in your current directory that defines how to start containers and what conditions to apply to them. The full configuration details are available in the Blockade documentation, so we'll only cover the essentials.

First you need to create a blockade.yml:

```
containers:
  server:
    image: ubuntu:14.04.2
    command: /bin/sleep infinity
    expose: [10000]

  client1:
    image: ubuntu:14.04.2
    command: sh -c "ping $SERVER_PORT_10000_TCP_ADDR"
    links: ["server"]

  client2:
    image: ubuntu:14.04.2
    command: sh -c "ping $SERVER_PORT_10000_TCP_ADDR"
    links: ["server"]

network:
  flaky: 50%
  slow: 100ms
```

The containers in the preceding configuration are set up to represent a server being connected to by two clients. In practice, this could be something like a database server with client applications, and there's no inherent reason you have to limit the number of components you want to model. Chances are, if you can represent it in a compose.yml file (see technique 68), you can probably model it in Blockade.

In the configuration for server, we've specified a port to be exposed but we don't serve anything there or connect to it—this is to enable Docker's linking functionality and to expose the relevant environment variables in the client containers so they know what IP address to ping. If you use an alternative IP discovery technique, like the DNS technique covered in this chapter (see technique 70), the links may be unnecessary.

Don't worry about the network section for now; we'll come back to it shortly.

As usual, the first step in using Blockade is to pull the image:

```
$ IMG=dockerinpractice/blockade
$ docker pull $IMG
latest: Pulling from dockerinpractice/blockade
[...]
```

```
Status: Downloaded newer image for dockerinpractice/blockade:latest
$ alias blockade="docker run --rm --pid=host --privileged \
-v \$PWD:/blockade -v /var/run/docker.sock:/var/run/docker.sock $IMG"
```

You'll notice that the arguments we passed to docker run are identical to the arguments in the previous technique, with one exception—Blockade mounts the current directory into the container to access blockade.yml and store state in a hidden folder.

PAIN WITH NETWORKED FILESYSTEMS If you're running on a networked filesystem, you may encounter strange permission issues when you start Blockade for the first time—this is likely because Docker is trying to create the hidden state folder as root, but the networked filesystem isn't cooperating. The solution is to use a local disk.

Finally we come to the moment of truth—running Blockade. Make sure you're in the directory you've saved blockade.yml into:

```
$ blockade up
NODE        CONTAINER ID     STATUS   IP             NETWORK     PARTITION
client1     8c4d956cf9cf     UP       172.17.0.53    NORMAL
client2     fcd9af2b0eef     UP       172.17.0.54    NORMAL
server      b8f9f179a10d     UP       172.17.0.52    NORMAL
```

DEBUGGING TIPS On startup, Blockade may sometimes give cryptic errors about files in /proc not existing. The first thing to check is whether a container has immediately exited on startup, preventing Blockade from checking its network status. Additionally, try to resist any temptation to use the Blockade -c option to specify a custom path to the config file—only subdirectories of the current directory are available inside the container.

All of the containers defined in our config file have been started and we've been given a bunch of helpful information about the started containers. Let's now apply some basic network conditions. Tail the logs of client1 in a new terminal (with docker logs -f 8c4d956cf9cf) so you can see what happens as you change things:

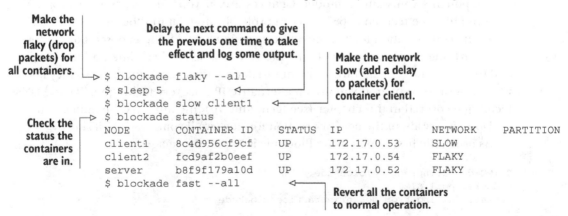

The flaky and slow commands use the values defined in the network section of the previous configuration file above—there's no way to specify a limit on the command line. If you want, it's possible to edit blockade.yml while containers are running and then selectively apply the new limits to containers. Be aware that a container can either be on a slow *or* flaky network, not both. These limitations aside, the convenience of running this against hundreds of containers is fairly significant.

If you look back at your logs from client1, you should now be able to see when the different commands took effect:

icmp_seq has taken a big jump—the flaky command has taken effect.

icmp_seq is sequential (no packets being dropped) and time is low (a small delay).

```
64 bytes from 172.17.0.52: icmp_seq=638 ttl=64 time=0.054 ms  ←
64 bytes from 172.17.0.52: icmp_seq=639 ttl=64 time=0.098 ms
64 bytes from 172.17.0.52: icmp_seq=640 ttl=64 time=0.112 ms
64 bytes from 172.17.0.52: icmp_seq=645 ttl=64 time=0.112 ms
64 bytes from 172.17.0.52: icmp_seq=652 ttl=64 time=0.113 ms
64 bytes from 172.17.0.52: icmp_seq=654 ttl=64 time=0.115 ms
64 bytes from 172.17.0.52: icmp_seq=660 ttl=64 time=100 ms   ←
64 bytes from 172.17.0.52: icmp_seq=661 ttl=64 time=100 ms
64 bytes from 172.17.0.52: icmp_seq=662 ttl=64 time=100 ms
64 bytes from 172.17.0.52: icmp_seq=663 ttl=64 time=100 ms
```

time has taken a big jump—the slow command has taken effect.

All this is useful, but it's nothing we couldn't have done already with some (likely painful) scripting on top of Comcast, so let's take a look at the killer feature of Blockade—network partitions:

```
$ blockade partition server client1,client2
$ blockade status
NODE          CONTAINER ID    STATUS    IP            NETWORK    PARTITION
client1       8c4d956cf9cf    UP        172.17.0.53   NORMAL     2
client2       fcd9af2b0eef    UP        172.17.0.54   NORMAL     2
server        b8f9f179a10d    UP        172.17.0.52   NORMAL     1
```

This has put our three nodes in two boxes—the server in one and clients in the other—with no way of communicating between them. You'll see that the log for client1 has stopped doing anything because all of the ping packets are being lost! The clients can still talk to each other, though, and you can verify this by sending a few ping packets between them:

```
$ docker exec 8c4d956cf9cf ping -qc 3 172.17.0.54
PING 172.17.0.54 (172.17.0.54) 56(84) bytes of data.

--- 172.17.0.54 ping statistics ---
3 packets transmitted, 3 received, 0% packet loss, time 1999ms
rtt min/avg/max/mdev = 0.065/0.084/0.095/0.015 ms
```

No packet loss, low delay…looks like a good connection. Partitions and other network conditions operate independently, so you can play with packet loss while your apps are partitioned. There's no limit to the number of partitions you can define, so you can play with complex scenarios to your heart's content.

One final suggestion if you need more power than Blockade and Comcast can individually provide is to combine the two. Blockade is excellent at creating partitions and doing the heavy lifting of starting up containers; adding Comcast to the mix gives you fine-grained control over the network connections of each and every container!

8.3 *Docker and virtual networks*

Docker's core functionality is all about isolation. Previous chapters have shown some of the benefits of process and filesytem isolation, and in this chapter you've seen network isolation.

You could think of there being two aspects to network isolation:

- *Individual sandbox*—Each container has its own IP and set of ports to listen on without stepping on the toes of other containers (or the host).
- *Group sandbox*—This is a logical extension of the individual sandbox— all of the isolated containers are grouped together in a private network, allowing you to play around without interfering with the network your machine lives on (and incurring the wrath of your company network administrator!).

The previous two techniques provide some practical examples of these two aspects of network isolation—Comcast manipulated individual sandboxes to apply rules to each container, whereas partitioning in Blockade relied on the ability to have complete oversight of the private container network to split it into pieces.

Behind the scenes, it looks a bit like figure 8.2.

The exact details of how the bridge works aren't important. Suffice it to say that the bridge creates a flat network between containers (it allows direct communication with no intermediate steps) and it forwards requests to the outside world to your external connection.

The flexibility permitted by this virtual network spurred efforts from third parties to extend the networking system in various ways to permit more complex use cases. Docker, Inc. is using these efforts to inform the ongoing (at the time of writing) work to permit network extensions to plug directly into Docker rather then working around it.

TECHNIQUE 73 **Setting up a substrate network with Weave**

A substrate network is a software-level network layer built on top of another network. In effect, you end up with a network that appears to be local, but under the hood it's communicating across other networks. This means that performance-wise, the network will behave less reliably than a local network, but from a usability point of view it can be a great convenience: you can communicate with nodes in completely different locations as though they are in the same room.

Achieving this is particularly interesting for Docker containers—containers can be seamlessly connected across hosts in the same way as connecting hosts across

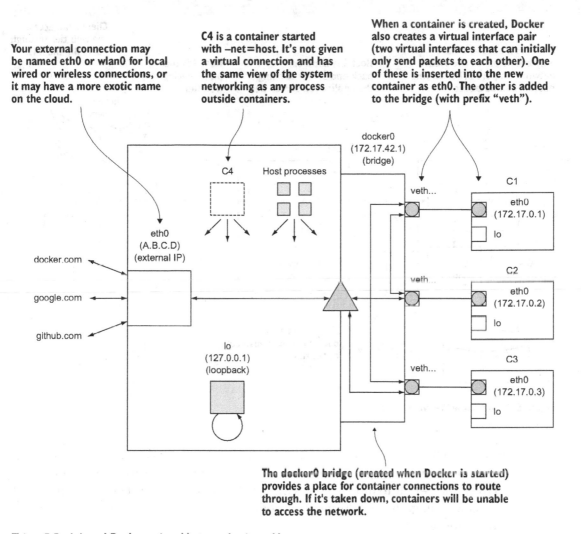

Your external connection may be named eth0 or wlan0 for local wired or wireless connections, or it may have a more exotic name on the cloud.

C4 is a container started with –net=host. It's not given a virtual connection and has the same view of the system networking as any process outside containers.

When a container is created, Docker also creates a virtual interface pair (two virtual interfaces that can initially only send packets to each other). One of these is inserted into the new container as eth0. The other is added to the bridge (with prefix "veth").

The docker0 bridge (created when Docker is started) provides a place for container connections to route through. If it's taken down, containers will be unable to access the network.

Figure 8.2   Internal Docker networking on a host machine

networks. Doing this removes any urgent need to plan how many containers you can fit on a single host.

PROBLEM

You want to seamlessly communicate between containers across hosts.

SOLUTION

Use a substrate network.

DISCUSSION

We're going to demonstrate the principle of a substrate network with Weave (http://weave.works/), a tool designed for this purpose. Figure 8.3 shows an overview of a typical Weave network.

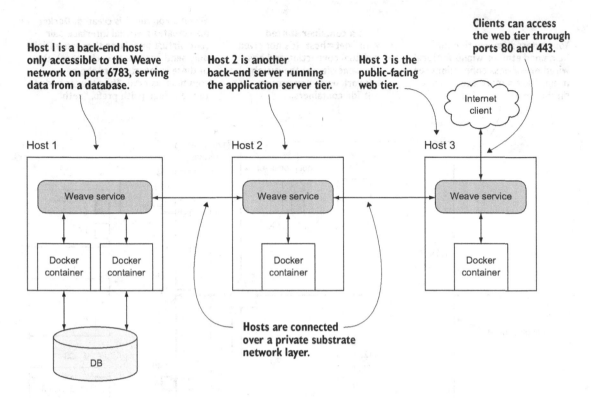

Host 1 is a back-end host only accessible to the Weave network on port 6783, serving data from a database.

Host 2 is another back-end server running the application server tier.

Host 3 is the public-facing web tier.

Clients can access the web tier through ports 80 and 443.

Hosts are connected over a private substrate network layer.

Figure 8.3   A typical Weave network

In figure 8.3, host 1 has no access to host 3, but they can talk to each other over the Weave network as though they were locally connected. The Weave network isn't open to the public—only to those containers started up under Weave. This makes the development, testing, and deployment of code across different environments relatively straightforward, because the network topology can be made the same in each case.

INSTALLING WEAVE

Weave is a single binary. You can find installation instructions at https://github.com/zettio/weave.

These instructions worked for us. Weave needs to be installed on every host that you want to be part of your Weave network:

```
$ sudo wget -O /usr/local/bin/weave \
https://github.com/zettio/weave/releases/download/latest_release/weave
$ sudo chmod +x /usr/local/bin/weave
```

CONFLICTING WEAVE BINARY   If you experience problems with this technique, there may already be a Weave binary on your machine that's part of another software package.

SETTING UP WEAVE

To follow this example, you'll need two hosts. We'll call them host1 and host2. Make sure they can talk to each other by using ping. You'll need both hosts' IP addresses.

> **HOW DO YOU GET YOUR IP ADDRESS?** A quick way to get a host's IP address is by accessing http://ip-addr.es with a browser, or by running curl http://ip-addr.es.

> **NETWORK FIREWALLS** If you experience problems with this technique, it's likely that the network is firewalled in some way. If you're not sure, talk to your network administrator. Specifically, you'll need to have port 6783 open for both TCP and UDP.

On the first host, you can run the first Weave router:

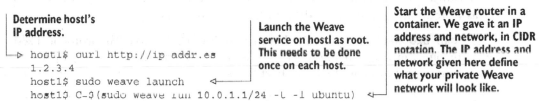

Determine host1's IP address.

Launch the Weave service on host1 as root. This needs to be done once on each host.

Start the Weave router in a container. We gave it an IP address and network, in CIDR notation. The IP address and network given here define what your private Weave network will look like.

```
host1$ curl http://ip-addr.es
1.2.3.4
host1$ sudo weave launch
host1$ C=$(sudo weave run 10.0.1.1/24 -t -i ubuntu)
```

> **WHAT IS CIDR?** CIDR stands for *Classless Inter-Domain Routing*. It's a method of allocating IP addresses and routing IP network packets. CIDR notation consists of an IP address with a forward slash and a number following that. The trailing number indicates the number of leading bits in the routing prefix. The remaining bits become the route's address space. The smaller the trailing number, therefore, the bigger the address space. For example, a 192.168.2.0/24 network would have an 8-bit address space of 256 addresses, whereas a 16.0.0.0/8 network would have an address space of 16,777,216 addresses.

You can perform similar steps on host2, but telling Weave about the location of host1 and assigning it a different IP address:

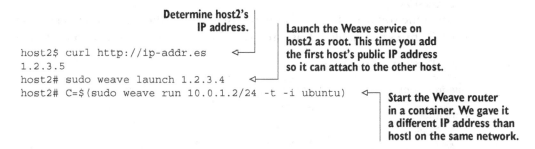

Determine host2's IP address.

Launch the Weave service on host2 as root. This time you add the first host's public IP address so it can attach to the other host.

```
host2$ curl http://ip-addr.es
1.2.3.5
host2# sudo weave launch 1.2.3.4
host2# C=$(sudo weave run 10.0.1.2/24 -t -i ubuntu)
```

Start the Weave router in a container. We gave it a different IP address than host1 on the same network.

The only difference on host2, apart from the choice of IP address for the application container, is that you tell your Weave that it should peer with the Weave on host1 (specified with the IP address or hostname, and optional :port, by which host2 can reach it).

TESTING YOUR CONNECTION

Now that you've got everything set up, you can test whether your containers can talk to each other:

```
host1# docker attach $C          ◄────────   Attach to the container
root@28841bd02eff:/# ping -c 1 -q 10.0.1.2   ◄──   ID returned earlier in
PING 10.0.1.2 (10.0.1.2): 48 data bytes         this interactive session.
--- 10.0.1.2 ping statistics ---
1 packets transmitted, 1 packets received, 0% packet loss
round-trip min/avg/max/stddev = 1.048/1.048/1.048/0.000 ms
```

Attach to the container ID returned earlier in this interactive session.

Ping the other server's assigned IP address.

A successful ping response

If you get a successful ping, you've proven connectivity within your self-assigned private network. You can now assign (as a convention within your own organization) 10.0.1.1 as your application server and 10.0.1.2 as your web server.

> **ICMP BLOCKED?**   It's possible that this won't work due to ICMP protocol (used by ping) messages being blocked by a firewall. If this doesn't work, try telnetting to port 6783 on the other host to test whether connections can be made.

TECHNIQUE 74   **Docker networking and service features**

Weave is an excellent tool, but it requires a tool outside of Docker and therefore may not integrate well with other tools in the ecosystem.

    Because of the popularity of tools like Weave, Docker, Inc. took feedback from a number of companies interested in networking solutions within Docker and came up with a plan to try and serve the most pressing needs, while not locking people into a one-size-fits-all solution. This work is ongoing, but it's getting closer to release!

PROBLEM

You want a solution supported by Docker, Inc. for creating virtual networks.

SOLUTION

Use the experimental networking and service features.

DISCUSSION

By the time you read this, Docker may have released the (currently) experimental network features in a stable release. You can check by running the following command:

```
$ docker network --help

Usage: docker network [OPTIONS] COMMAND [OPTIONS] [arg...]

Commands:
  create                      Create a network
  rm                          Remove a network
  ls                          List all networks
  info                        Display information of a network

Run 'docker network COMMAND --help' for more information on a command.

  --help=false        Print usage
```

If it says something like 'network' is not a docker command, you'll need to install an experimental version of Docker. To install experimental features, refer to the Docker Experimental Features page on GitHub: https://github.com/docker/docker/tree/master/experimental.

> **EXPERIMENTAL FEATURES CHANGE UNDERFOOT** We have endeavoured to keep this technique as up-to-date as possible, but experimental features tend to change. The instructions in this technique may need to be altered slightly by the time you come to follow them.

The high-level aim of this functionality is to abstract away the creation of virtual networks by permitting the use of network plugins within Docker. These are either built-in or provided by third parties and provide you with a virtual network. Behind the scenes, the plugin should do all the necessary work to wire up the network, letting you get on with using it. In theory, tools like Weave should be able to become network plugins, along with more exotic use cases. In practice, the design of this feature is likely to be an iterative process.

You can see the list of networks Docker always has available:

```
$ docker network ls
NETWORK ID          NAME              TYPE
04365ecf2eaa        none              null
c82bde52597d        host              host
7e8c8a0eab7d        bridge            bridge
```

You'll recognize these as the options you can pass to Docker run's --net option when starting a container. Let's add a new bridge network (a flat network for containers to freely communicate in):

```
$ docker network create --driver=bridge mynet
3265097deff3847cb1f7b8e8bc924bae1c439d8bf6247458400e620b35447292
$ docker network ls | grep mynet
3265097deff3          mynet                    bridge
$ ip addr | grep mynet
34: mynet: <NO-CARRIER,BROADCAST,MULTICAST,UP> mtu 1500 qdisc noqueue
 state DOWN
    inet 172.18.42.1/16 scope global mynet
$ ip addr | grep docker
4: docker0: <NO-CARRIER,BROADCAST,MULTICAST,UP> mtu 1500 qdisc noqueue
 state DOWN
    inet 172.17.42.1/16 scope global docker0
```

This has created a new network interface that will use a different IP address range than the normal Docker bridge.

Let's now start up two containers that will advertise a service into the network. The concept of a *service* is tightly integrated in the networking features at present, and a container must have a service name to participate in a particular network:

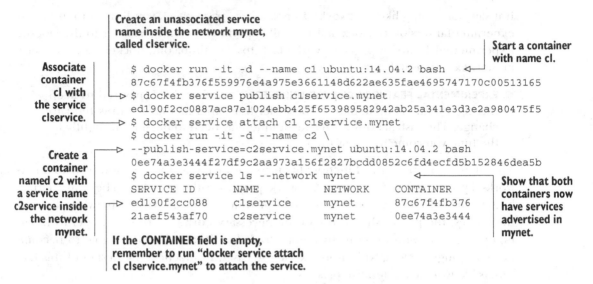

Create an unassociated service
name inside the network mynet,
called c1service.

Start a container
with name c1.

Associate
container
c1 with
the service
c1service.

```
$ docker run -it -d --name c1 ubuntu:14.04.2 bash
87c67f4fb376f559976e4a975e3661148d622ae635fae4695747170c00513165
$ docker service publish c1service.mynet
ed190f2cc0887ac87e1024ebb425f653989582942ab25a341e3d3e2a980475f5
$ docker service attach c1 c1service.mynet
$ docker run -it -d --name c2 \
--publish-service=c2service.mynet ubuntu:14.04.2 bash
0ee74a3e3444f27df9c2aa973a156f2827bcdd0852c6fd4ecfd5b152846dea5b
$ docker service ls --network mynet
SERVICE ID        NAME           NETWORK         CONTAINER
ed190f2cc088      c1service      mynet           87c67f4fb376
21aef543af70      c2service      mynet           0ee74a3e3444
```

Create a
container
named c2 with
a service name
c2service inside
the network
mynet.

Show that both
containers now
have services
advertised in
mynet.

If the **CONTAINER** field is empty,
remember to run "docker service attach
c1 c1service.mynet" to attach the service.

The preceding commands demonstrate two different ways of registering a service— creating a container and then attaching the service, and creating and attaching in one step.

There's a difference between these two. The first will join the default network on startup (usually the Docker bridge, but this is customizable with an argument to the Docker daemon), and then will add a new interface so it can access mynet as well. The second will *just* join mynet—any containers on the normal Docker bridge will be unable to access it.

Let's do some connectivity checks:

List the interfaces
and IP addresses
for c1.

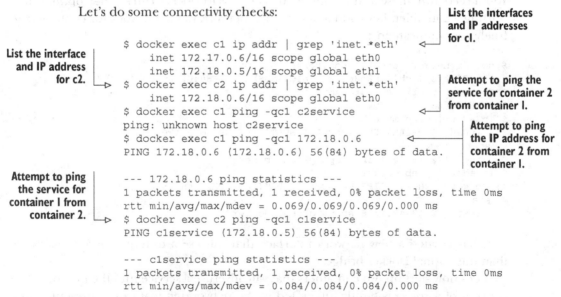

List the interface
and IP address
for c2.

```
$ docker exec c1 ip addr | grep 'inet.*eth'
    inet 172.17.0.6/16 scope global eth0
    inet 172.18.0.5/16 scope global eth1
$ docker exec c2 ip addr | grep 'inet.*eth'
    inet 172.18.0.6/16 scope global eth0
$ docker exec c1 ping -qc1 c2service
ping: unknown host c2service
$ docker exec c1 ping -qc1 172.18.0.6
PING 172.18.0.6 (172.18.0.6) 56(84) bytes of data.

--- 172.18.0.6 ping statistics ---
1 packets transmitted, 1 received, 0% packet loss, time 0ms
rtt min/avg/max/mdev = 0.069/0.069/0.069/0.000 ms
$ docker exec c2 ping -qc1 c1service
PING c1service (172.18.0.5) 56(84) bytes of data.

--- c1service ping statistics ---
1 packets transmitted, 1 received, 0% packet loss, time 0ms
rtt min/avg/max/mdev = 0.084/0.084/0.084/0.000 ms
```

Attempt to ping the
service for container 2
from container 1.

Attempt to ping
the IP address for
container 2 from
container 1.

Attempt to ping
the service for
container 1 from
container 2.

There's a lot going on here! We've found that although the actual IP addresses of the containers are definitely available to each other, container c1 can't find the service for c2. This is because of the way services work—/etc/hosts gets updated inside containers when services are added and removed, but this doesn't happen for c1 because it was initially started on the default docker0 bridge. This unexpected behaviour may or may not change in the future.

For simplicity, we recommend sticking to --publish-service where possible, though you may find a setup of two networks connected by a single container useful for emulating a real-world bastion host setup.

One thing we haven't covered here (since work is still ongoing) is the built-in overlay network plugin—depending on your use case, this may be worth some research as a possible replacement for Weave.

8.4   Summary

The networking possibilities provided by Docker can initially be overlooked when evaluating other aspects, so we've investigated using networking features both to complement other Docker features and to provide value in their own right.

We've covered

- How to use Docker Compose
- An alternative to using linking
- Putting containers through their paces in bad networking environments
- Stringing containers together across hosts

This marks the end of using Docker in a development pipeline—it's time to see how we can use it for real in production, starting with an exploration of how to actually manage all your containers.

Part 4

Docker in production

At last we're ready to contemplate running Docker in production. In part 4 we address the key operational considerations when running Docker on live environments. Chapter 9 covers the burgeoning area of orchestration. As soon as you run any number of containers in the same environment, you'll need to think about how they're managed in a consistent and reliable way, so we'll look at some of the most popular tools currently available. Security is the focus of chapter 10. Through practical techniques you'll get a real understanding of the security challenges Docker brings and how you might want to address them. Backups, logging and resource management are considered in chapter 11, where we show you how these traditional sysadmin tasks can be managed with in a Docker context. Finally, in chapter 12 we look at what to do when things go wrong, covering some common areas where Docker can get into trouble, as well as how to debug containers in production.

Container orchestration: managing multiple Docker containers

The technology Docker is built on has existed for a while in different forms, but Docker is the solution that's managed to grab the interest of the technology industry. This puts Docker in an enviable position—the mindshare did the initial job of kickstarting an ecosystem of tools, which became a self-perpetuating cycle of people being drawn into the ecosystem and contributing back to it.

This is particularly evident when it comes to orchestration. After seeing a list of company names with offerings in this space, you'd be forgiven for thinking that everyone has their own opinion on how to do things and has developed their own tool.

Although the ecosystem is a huge strength of Docker (which is why we've been drawing from it so much in this book), the sheer quantity of possible orchestration tools can be overwhelming to novices and veterans alike. This chapter will take you on a tour through some of the most notable tools available and give you a feel for the high-level offerings so you're better informed when it comes to evaluating what you want a framework to do for you.

There are many ways of arranging family trees of the orchestration tools. Figure 9.1 shows some of the tools we're familiar with.

At the root of the tree is docker run, the most common way to start a container. Everything inspired by Docker is an offshoot of this. On the left side are the tools that treat groups of containers as a single entity. The middle shows the tools focused on managing containers under the umbrella of systemd and service files. Finally, the right side treats individual containers as just that. As you move down the branches, the tools end up doing more for you, be it working across multiple hosts or taking the tedium of manual container deployment away from you.

You'll note two seemingly isolated areas on the diagram—Mesos and the Consul/etcd/Zookeeper group. Mesos is an interesting case—it existed before Docker and the support it has for Docker is an added feature rather than core functionality. It works very well, though, and should be evaluated carefully, if only to see what features from it you might want in other tools. By contrast, Consul, etcd, and Zookeeper aren't orchestration tools at all. Instead, they provide the important complement to orchestration: service discovery.

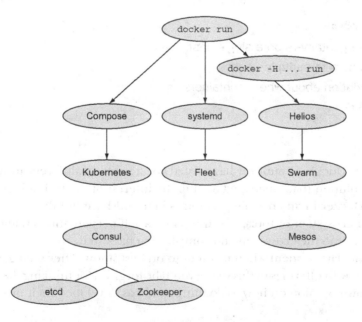

Figure 9.1 Orchestration tools in the Docker ecosystem

As you read this chapter, it might be helpful to take a step back as you come to each orchestration tool and try and come up with a scenario it would be useful in. This will help clarify whether a particular tool is relevant for you. We'll give you some examples along the way to get you started.

We'll start slow by turning our gaze inwards to a single computer.

9.1 Simple single-host Docker

Managing the containers on your local machine can be a painful experience. The features provided by Docker for managing long-running containers are relatively primitive, and starting up containers with links and shared volumes can be a frustratingly manual process.

In chapter 8 we looked at using Docker Compose to make managing links easier, so we'll deal with the other pain point now and see how the management of long-running containers on a single machine can be made more robust.

TECHNIQUE 75 Managing your host's containers with systemd

In this technique we'll take you through setting up a simple Docker service with systemd. If you're already familiar with systemd, this chapter will be relatively easy to follow, but we assume no prior knowledge of the tool.

Using systemd to control Docker can be useful for a mature company with an operations team that prefers to stick to proven technologies that they already understand and have the tooling for.

PROBLEM

You want to manage the running of Docker container services on your host.

SOLUTION

Use systemd to manage your container services.

DISCUSSION

systemd is a system-management daemon that replaced SysV init scripts in Fedora some time ago. It manages services on your system—everything from mount points to processes to one-shot scripts—as individual *units*. It's growing in popularity as it spreads to other distributions and operating systems, though some systems (Gentoo being an example at time of writing) may have problems installing and enabling it. It's worth looking around for experiences other people have had with systemd on a setup similar to yours.

In this technique we'll demonstrate how the startup of your containers can be managed by systemd by running the to-do app from chapter 1.

INSTALLING SYSTEMD

If you don't have systemd on your host system (you can check by running `systemctl status` and seeing whether you get a coherent response), you can install it directly on your host OS using your standard package manager. If you're not comfortable interfering with your host system in this way, the recommended way to play with it is to use Vagrant to provision a systemd-ready VM, as shown in the following listing. We'll cover it briefly here, but see appendix C for more advice on installing Vagrant.

Listing 9.1   A Vagrant setup

```
$ mkdir centos7_docker
$ cd centos7_docker
$ vagrant init jdiprizio/centos-docker-io
$ vagrant
$ vagrant ssh
```

Create and enter a new folder.

Initialize the folder for use as a Vagrant environment, specifying the Vagrant image.

Bring up the VM.

SSH into the VM.

JDIPRIZIO/CENTOS-DOCKER-IO NO LONGER AVAILABLE?   At the time of writing, jdiprizio/centos-docker-io is a suitable and available VM image. If it's no longer available when you're reading this, you can replace that string in the preceding listing with another image name. You can search for one on Atlas's "Discover Vagrant Boxes" page: https://atlas.hashicorp.com/boxes/search (*box* is the terminology Vagrant uses to refer to a VM image). To find this image, we searched for "docker centos". You may need to look up help for the command-line vagrant box add command to figure out how to download your new VM before attempting to start it.

SETTING UP A SIMPLE DOCKER APPLICATION UNDER SYSTEMD

Now that you have a machine with systemd and Docker on it, we're going to use it to run the to-do application from chapter 1.

systemd works by reading configuration files in the simple INI file format.

INI FILES   INI files are simple text files with a basic structure composed of sections, properties, and values.

First you create a service file as root in /etc/systemd/system/todo.service, as shown in the next listing. In this file you tell systemd to run the Docker container with the name todo on port 8000 on this host.

Listing 9.2   /etc/systemd/system/todo.service

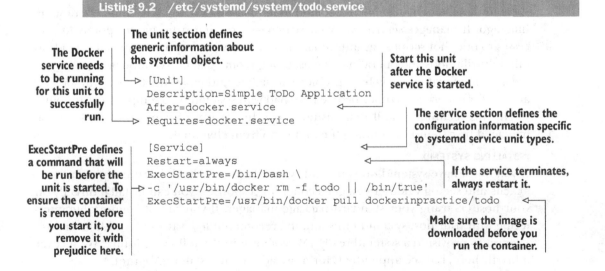

The Docker service needs to be running for this unit to successfully run.

The unit section defines generic information about the systemd object.

Start this unit after the Docker service is started.

```
[Unit]
Description=Simple ToDo Application
After=docker.service
Requires=docker.service

[Service]
Restart=always
ExecStartPre=/bin/bash \
-c '/usr/bin/docker rm -f todo || /bin/true'
ExecStartPre=/usr/bin/docker pull dockerinpractice/todo
```

The service section defines the configuration information specific to systemd service unit types.

ExecStartPre defines a command that will be run before the unit is started. To ensure the container is removed before you start it, you remove it with prejudice here.

If the service terminates, always restart it.

Make sure the image is downloaded before you run the container.

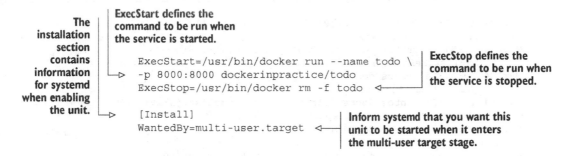

The installation section contains information for systemd when enabling the unit.

ExecStart defines the command to be run when the service is started.

```
ExecStart=/usr/bin/docker run --name todo \
-p 8000:8000 dockerinpractice/todo
ExecStop=/usr/bin/docker rm -f todo

[Install]
WantedBy=multi-user.target
```

ExecStop defines the command to be run when the service is stopped.

Inform systemd that you want this unit to be started when it enters the multi-user target stage.

This configuration file should make it clear that systemd offers a simple declarative schema for managing processes, leaving the details of dependency management up to the systemd service. This doesn't mean that you can ignore the details, but it does put a lot of tools at your disposal for managing Docker (and other) processes.

DOCKER RESTART POLICIES AND PROCESS MANAGERS Docker doesn't set any container restart policies by default, but be aware that any you set will conflict with most process managers. Don't set restart policies if you're using a process manager.

Enabling a new unit is just a matter of invoking the systemctl enable command. If you want this unit to start automatically when the system boots, you can also create a symlink in the multi-user.target.wants systemd directory. Once done, you can start the unit with systemctl start:

```
$ systemctl enable /etc/systemd/system/todo.service
$ ln -s '/etc/systemd/system/todo.service' \
'/etc/systemd/system/multi-user.target.wants/todo.service'
$ systemctl start todo.service
```

Then just wait for it to start. If there's a problem, you'll be informed.

To check that all is OK, use the systemctl status command. It will print out some general information about the unit, such as how long it's been running and the process ID, followed by a number of log lines from the process. In this case, seeing Swarm server started port 8000 is a good sign:

```
[root@centos system]# systemctl status todo.service
todo.service - Simple ToDo Application
   Loaded: loaded (/etc/systemd/system/todo.service; enabled)
   Active: active (running) since Wed 2015-03-04 19:57:19 UTC; 2min 13s ago
  Process: 21266 ExecStartPre=/usr/bin/docker pull dockerinpractice/todo
➡ (code=exited, status=0/SUCCESS)
  Process: 21255 ExecStartPre=/bin/bash -c /usr/bin/docker rm -f todo ||
➡ /bin/true (code=exited, status=0/SUCCESS)
  Process: 21246 ExecStartPre=/bin/bash -c /usr/bin/docker kill todo ||
➡ /bin/true (code=exited, status=0/SUCCESS)
 Main PID: 21275 (docker)
   CGroup: /system.slice/todo.service
           ??21275 /usr/bin/docker run --name todo
➡ -p 8000:8000 dockerinpractice/todo
```

```
Mar 04 19:57:24 centos docker[21275]: TodoApp.js:117:
➡ // TODO scroll into view
Mar 04 19:57:24 centos docker[21275]: TodoApp.js:176:
➡ if (i>=list.length()) { i=list.length()-1; } // TODO .length
Mar 04 19:57:24 centos docker[21275]: local.html:30:
➡ <!-- TODO 2-split, 3-split -->
Mar 04 19:57:24 centos docker[21275]: model/TodoList.js:29:
➡ // TODO one op - repeated spec? long spec?
Mar 04 19:57:24 centos docker[21275]: view/Footer.jsx:61:
➡ // TODO: show the entry's metadata
Mar 04 19:57:24 centos docker[21275]: view/Footer.jsx:80:
➡ todoList.addObject(new TodoItem()); // TODO create default
Mar 04 19:57:24 centos docker[21275]: view/Header.jsx:25:
➡ // TODO list some meaningful header (apart from the id)
Mar 04 19:57:24 centos docker[21275]: > todomvc-swarm@0.0.1 start /todo
Mar 04 19:57:24 centos docker[21275]: > node TodoAppServer.js
Mar 04 19:57:25 centos docker[21275]: Swarm server started port 8000
```

The principles in this technique can be applied to more than just systemd—most process managers, including other init systems, can be configured in a similar way.

In the next technique, we'll take this further by implementing in systemd the SQLite server we created in technique 69.

TECHNIQUE 76   Orchestrating your host's containers with systemd

Unlike docker-compose (at the time of writing), systemd is a mature technology ready for production. In this technique we'll show you how to achieve local orchestration functionality that's similar to docker-compose using systemd.

If you run into trouble with this technique, you may need to upgrade your version of Docker. Anything from 1.7.0 up should work fine.

PROBLEM
You want to manage more complex container orchestration on one host in production.

SOLUTION
Use systemd with dependent services to manage your containers.

DISCUSSION
To demonstrate the use of systemd for a more complex scenario, we're going to re-implement the SQLite TCP server example from technique 69 in systemd.

Figure 9.2 illustrates the dependencies for our planned systemd service unit configuration.

This is a similar schema to what you saw with the Docker Compose example in technique 69. A key difference here is that rather than the SQLite service being treated as a single monolithic entity, each container here is a discrete entity. In this scenario, the SQLite proxy can be stopped independently of the SQLite server.

Listing 9.3 shows the code for the sqliteserver service. As before, it depends on the Docker service, but it has a couple of differences from the to-do example in the previous technique.

All the services ultimately depend on the Docker service unit. If it's not running, none of the other services can run.

The SQLite service unit depends on the Docker service unit to run.

The todo service unit depends only on the Docker service unit.

The SQLite proxy service depends on the SQLite service unit to run.

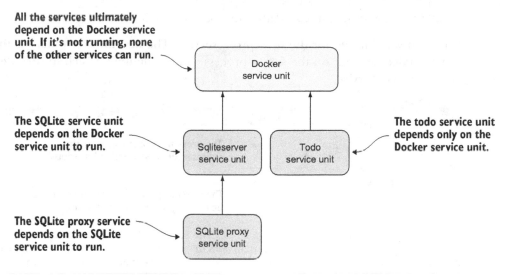

Figure 9.2 systemd unit dependency graph

Listing 9.3 /etc/systemd/system/sqliteserver.service

The Docker service needs to be running for this unit to successfully run.

Start this unit after the Docker service is started.

The unit section defines generic information about the systemd object.

These lines ensure that the SQLite database files exist before the service starts up. The dash before the touch command indicates to systemd that startup should fail if the command returns an error code.

ExecStartPre defines a command that will be run before the unit is started. To ensure the container is removed before you start it, you remove it with prejudice here.

ExecStart defines the command to be run when the service is started. Note that we've wrapped the socat command in a /bin/bash -c call to avoid confusion, as the ExecStart line is run by systemd.

Make sure the image is downloaded before you run the container.

ExecStop defines the command to be run when the service is stopped.

```
[Unit]
Description=SQLite Docker Server
After=docker.service
Requires=docker.service

[Service]
Restart=always
ExecStartPre=-/bin/touch /tmp/sqlitedbs/test
ExecStartPre=-/bin/touch /tmp/sqlitedbs/live
ExecStartPre=/bin/bash \
-c '/usr/bin/docker kill sqliteserver || /bin/true'
ExecStartPre=/bin/bash \
-c '/usr/bin/docker rm -f sqliteserver || /bin/true'
ExecStartPre=/usr/bin/docker \
pull dockerinpractice/docker-compose-sqlite
ExecStart=/usr/bin/docker run --name sqliteserver \
-v /tmp/sqlitedbs/test:/opt/sqlite/db \
dockerinpractice/docker-compose-sqlite /bin/bash -c \
'socat TCP-L:12345,fork,reuseaddr \
EXEC:"sqlite3 /opt/sqlite/db",pty'
ExecStop=/usr/bin/docker rm -f sqliteserver

[Install]
WantedBy=multi-user.target
```

ABSOLUTE PATHS REQUIRED   Paths must be absolute in systemd!

Now comes the listing for the sqliteproxy service. The key difference here is that the proxy service depends on the server process you just defined, which in turn depends on the Docker service.

Listing 9.4   /etc/systemd/system/sqliteproxy.service

```
[Unit]
Description=SQLite Docker Proxy
After=sqliteserver.service
Requires=sqliteserver.service

[Service]
Restart=always
ExecStartPre=/bin/bash -c '/usr/bin/docker kill sqliteproxy || /bin/true'
ExecStartPre=/bin/bash -c '/usr/bin/docker rm -f sqliteproxy || /bin/true'
ExecStartPre=/usr/bin/docker pull dockerinpractice/docker-compose-sqlite
ExecStart=/usr/bin/docker run --name sqliteproxy \
-p 12346:12346 --link sqliteserver:sqliteserver \
dockerinpractice/docker-compose-sqlite /bin/bash \
-c 'socat TCP-L:12346,fork,reuseaddr TCP:sqliteserver:12345'
ExecStop=/usr/bin/docker rm -f sqliteproxy

[Install]
WantedBy=multi-user.target
```

The proxy unit must run after the sqliteserver service defined previously.

The proxy requires that the server instance be running before you start it up.

The command used to run the container

With these two configuration files, we've laid the groundwork for installing and running our SQLite service under systemd's control. Now we can enable these services...

```
$ sudo systemctl enable /etc/systemd/system/sqliteserver.service
ln -s '/etc/systemd/system/sqliteserver.service' \
'/etc/systemd/system/multi-user.target.wants/sqliteserver.service'
$ sudo systemctl enable /etc/systemd/system/sqliteproxy.service
ln -s '/etc/systemd/system/sqliteproxy.service' \
'/etc/systemd/system/multi-user.target.wants/sqliteproxy.service'
```

...and start them up:

```
$ sudo systemctl start sqliteproxy
$ telnet localhost 12346
[vagrant@centos ~]$ telnet localhost 12346
Trying ::1...
Connected to localhost.
Escape character is '^]'.
SQLite version 3.8.2 2013-12-06 14:53:30
Enter ".help" for instructions
Enter SQL statements terminated with a ";"
sqlite> select * from t1;
select * from t1;
test
```

Note that because the sqliteproxy service depends on the sqliteserver service to run, you only need to start the sqliteproxy service—dependencies are started automatically.

9.2   *Multi-host Docker*

Now that you're comfortable with some fairly complicated arrangements of Docker containers on a machine, it's time to think bigger—let's move into the world of multiple hosts to enable us to use Docker on a larger scale.

The best process for moving Docker containers to target machines and starting them up is a matter of much debate in the Docker world. A number of well-known companies have created their own ways of doing things and have released them to the world. A user can benefit massively from this, if they can decide what tools to use.

This is a fast moving topic—we've seen the birth and death of multiple orchestration tools for Docker and recommend caution when considering whether to move over to using a brand new tool. As a result, we've tried to select tools with significant stability or momentum (or both).

TECHNIQUE 77   Manual multi-host Docker with Helios

It can be intimidating to hand over all control of provisioning a group of machines to an application, so it doesn't hurt to ease yourself in with a more manual approach.

Helios is ideal for companies that have mostly static infrastructures and are interested in using Docker for their critical services but (understandably) want human oversight in the process.

PROBLEM
You want to be able to provision multiple Docker hosts with containers but retain manual control over what runs where.

SOLUTION
Use the Helios tool from Spotify.

DISCUSSION
Helios is the tool Spotify currently uses to manage their servers in production, and it has the pleasing property of being both easy to get started with and stable (as you'd hope). Helios allows you to manage the deployment of Docker containers across multiple hosts. It gives you a single command-line interface that you can use to specify what you want to run and where to run it, as well as the ability to take a look at the current state of play.

Because we're just introducing Helios, we're going to run everything on a single node inside Docker for simplicity—don't worry, anything relevant to running on multiple hosts will be clearly highlighted. The high-level architecture of Helios is outlined in figure 9.3.

As you can see, there's only one additional service required when running Helios: Zookeeper. Helios uses Zookeeper to track the state of all of your hosts and as a communication channel between the masters and agents.

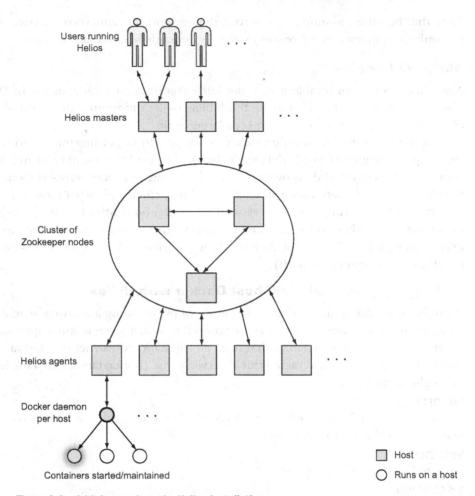

Figure 9.3   A birds-eye view of a Helios installation

WHAT IS ZOOKEEPER?   Zookeeper is a lightweight distributed database optimized for storing configuration information written in Java. It's part of the Apache suite of open source software products. It's similar in functionality to etcd (which you learned about in chapter 7, and you'll see again in this chapter).

All you need to know for this technique is that Zookeeper stores data so that it can be distributed across multiple nodes (for both scalability and reliability) by running multiple Zookeeper instances. This may sound similar to our description of etcd in chapter 7—these two tools have significant overlap.

To start the single Zookeeper instance we'll use in this technique, run the following:

```
$ docker run --name zookeeper -d jplock/zookeeper:3.4.6
cd0964d2ba18baac58b29081b227f15e05f11644adfa785c6e9fc5dd15b85910
$ docker inspect -f '{{.NetworkSettings.IPAddress}}' zookeeper
172.17.0.9
```

PORTS ON HOSTS AND OTHER NODES When starting a Zookeeper instance on its own node, you'll want to expose ports to make it accessible to other hosts, and use volumes to persist data. Take a look at the Dockerfile on the Docker Hub for details about which ports and folders you should use (https://hub.docker.com/r/jplock/zookeeper/~/dockerfile/). It's also likely you'll want to run Zookeeper on multiple nodes, but configuring a Zookeeper cluster is beyond the scope of this technique.

You can inspect the data Zookeeper has stored by using the zkCli.sh tool, either interactively or by piping input to it. The initial startup is quite chatty, but it'll drop you into an interactive prompt where you can run commands against the file-tree-like structure Zookeeper stores data in:

```
$ docker exec -it zookeeper bin/zkCli.sh
Connecting to localhost:2181
2015-03-07 02:56:05,076 [myid:] - INFO  [main:Environment@100] - Client
 environment:zookeeper.version=3.4.6-1569965, built on 02/20/2014 09:09 GMT
2015-03-07 02:56:05,079 [myid:] - INFO  [main:Environment@100] - Client
 environment:host.name=917d0f8ac077
2015-03-07 02:56:05,079 [myid:] - INFO  [main:Environment@100] - Client
 environment:java.version=1.7.0_65
2015-03-07 02:56:05,081 [myid:] - INFO  [main:Environment@100] - Client
 environment:java.vendor=Oracle Corporation
[...]
2015-03-07 03:00:59,043 [myid:] - INFO  [main-SendThread(localhost:2181):
 ClientCnxn$SendThread@1235] - Session establishment complete on server
 localhost/0:0:0:0:0:0:0:1:2181, sessionid = 0x14bf223e159000d, negotiated
 timeout = 30000

WATCHER::

WatchedEvent state:SyncConnected type:None path:null
[zk: localhost:2181(CONNECTED) 0] ls /
[zookeeper]
```

Nothing's running against Zookeeper yet, so the only thing currently being stored is some internal Zookeeper information. Leave this prompt open and we'll revisit it as we progress.

Helios itself is split into three parts:

- *The master*—This is used as an interface for making changes in Zookeeper.
- *The agent*—This runs on every Docker host, starts and stops containers based on Zookeeper, and reports state back.
- *The command-line tools*—These are used to make requests to the master.

Figure 9.4 shows how our final system is strung together when we perform an operation against it (the arrows indicate data flow).

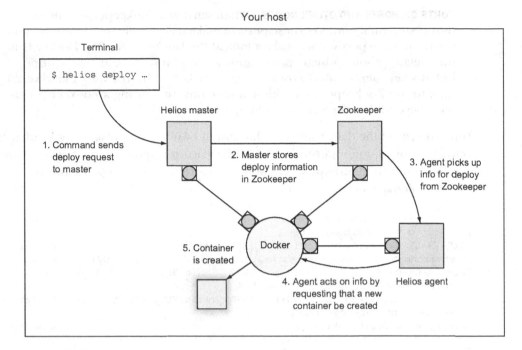

Figure 9.4   Starting a container on a single-host Helios installation

Now that Zookeeper is running, it's time to start Helios. We need to run the master while specifying the IP address of the Zookeeper node we started earlier:

```
$ IMG=dockerinpractice/docker-helios
$ docker run -d --name hmaster $IMG helios-master --zk 172.17.0.9
896bc963d899154436938e260b1d4e6fdb0a81e4a082df50043290569e5921ff
$ docker logs --tail=3 hmaster
03:20:14.460 helios[1]: INFO  [MasterService STARTING] ContextHandler:
➥ Started i.d.j.MutableServletContextHandler@7b48d370{/,null,AVAILABLE}
03:20:14.465 helios[1]: INFO  [MasterService STARTING] ServerConnector:
➥ Started application@2192bcac{HTTP/1.1}{0.0.0.0:5801}
03:20:14.466 helios[1]: INFO  [MasterService STARTING] ServerConnector:
➥ Started admin@28a0d16c{HTTP/1.1}{0.0.0.0:5802}
$ docker inspect -f '{{.NetworkSettings.IPAddress}}' hmaster
172.17.0.11
```

Now let's see what's new in Zookeeper:

```
[zk: localhost:2181(CONNECTED) 1] ls /
[history, config, status, zookeeper]
[zk: localhost:2181(CONNECTED) 2] ls /status/masters
[896bc963d899]
[zk: localhost:2181(CONNECTED) 3] ls /status/hosts
[]
```

It looks like the Helios master has created a bunch of new pieces of configuration, including registering itself as a master. Unfortunately we don't have any hosts yet. Let's solve this by starting up an agent that will use the current host's Docker socket to start containers on:

```
$ docker run -v /var/run/docker.sock:/var/run/docker.sock -d --name hagent \
dockerinpractice/docker-helios helios-agent --zk 172.17.0.9
5a4abcb271070d0171ca809ff2beafac5798e86131b72aeb201fe27df64b2698
$ docker logs --tail=3 hagent
03:30:53.344 helios[1]: INFO   [AgentService STARTING] ContextHandler:
➡ Started i.d.j.MutableServletContextHandler@774c71b1{/,null,AVAILABLE}
03:30:53.375 helios[1]: INFO   [AgentService STARTING] ServerConnector:
➡ Started application@7d9e6c27{HTTP/1.1}{0.0.0.0:5803}
03:30:53.376 helios[1]: INFO   [AgentService STARTING] ServerConnector:
➡ Started admin@2bceb4df{HTTP/1.1}{0.0.0.0:5804}
$ docker inspect -f '{{.NetworkSettings.IPAddress}}' hagent
172.17.0.12
```

Again let's check back in Zookeeper:

```
[zk: localhost:2181(CONNECTED) 4] ls /status/hosts
[5a4abcb27107]
[zk: localhost:2181(CONNECTED) 5] ls /status/hosts/5a4abcb27107
[agentinfo, jobs, environment, hostinfo, up]
[zk: localhost:2181(CONNECTED) 6] get /status/hosts/5a4abcb27107/agentinfo
{"inputArguments":["-Dcom.sun.management.jmxremote.port=9203", [...]
[...]
```

You can see here that /status/hosts now contains one item. Descending into the Zookeeper directory for the host reveals the internal information Helios stores about the host.

> **HOSTNAMES REQUIRED IN MULTI-HOST SETUPS** When running on multiple hosts, you'll want to pass --name $(hostname -f) as an argument to both the Helios master and agent. You'll also need to expose ports 5801 and 5802 for the master and 5803 and 5804 for the agent.

Let's make it a bit easier to interact with Helios:

```
$ alias helios="docker run -i --rm dockerinpractice/docker-helios \
helios -z http://172.17.0.11:5801"
```

The alias above means that invoking helios will start a throwaway container to perform the action you want, pointing at the correct helios cluster to begin with. Note that the cli needs to be pointed at the Helios master rather than Zookeeper.

Everything is now set up. We're able to easily interact with our Helios cluster, so it's time to try an example:

```
$ helios create -p nc=8080:8080 netcat:v1 ubuntu:14.04.2 -- \
sh -c 'echo hello | nc -l 8080'
Creating job: {"command":["sh","-c","echo hello | nc -l 8080"],
```

```
➥ "creatingUser":null,"env":{},"expires":null,"gracePeriod":null,
➥ "healthCheck":null,"id":
➥ "netcat:v1:2067d43fc2c6f004ea27d7bb7412aff502e3cdac",
➥ "image":"ubuntu:14.04.2","ports":{"nc":{"externalPort":8080,
➥ "internalPort":8080,"protocol":"tcp"}},"registration":{},
➥ "registrationDomain":"","resources":null,"token":"","volumes":{}}
Done.
netcat:v1:2067d43fc2c6f004ea27d7bb7412aff502e3cdac
$ helios jobs
JOB ID             NAME   VERSION HOSTS COMMAND              ENVIRONMENT
netcat:v1:2067d43 netcat v1      0     sh -c "echo hello | nc -l 8080"
```

Helios is built around the concept of *jobs*—everything to be executed must be expressed
as a job before it can be sent to a host to be executed. At a minimum, you need an image
with the basics Helios needs to know to start the container: a command to execute and
any port, volume, or environment options. You may also want a number of other
advanced options, including health checks, expiry dates, and service registration.

The previous command creates a job that will listen on port 8080, print `hello` to
the first thing that connects to the port, and then terminate.

You can use `helios hosts` to list hosts available for job deployment, then perform
the deployment with `helios deploy`. The `helios status` command will then show you
that the job has successfully started:

```
$ helios hosts
HOST           STATUS          DEPLOYED RUNNING CPUS MEM  LOAD AVG MEM USAGE
➥ OS                          HELIOS  DOCKER
5a4abcb27107.Up 19 minutes 0       0       4    7 gb 0.61     0.84
➥ Linux 3.13.0-46-generic 0.8.213 1.3.1 (1.15)
$ helios deploy netcat:v1 5a4abcb27107
Deploying Deployment{jobId=netcat:v1:
➥ 2067d43fc2c6f004ea27d7bb7412aff502e3cdac, goal=START, deployerUser=null}
➥ on [5a4abcb27107]
5a4abcb27107: done
$ helios status
JOB ID             HOST          GOAL   STATE    CONTAINER ID PORTS
netcat:v1:2067d43 5a4abcb27107.START RUNNING b1225bc    nc=8080:8080
```

Of course, we now want to verify that the service works:

```
$ curl localhost:8080
hello
$ helios status
JOB ID             HOST          GOAL   STATE          CONTAINER ID PORTS
netcat:v1:2067d43 5a4abcb27107.START PULLING_IMAGE b1225bc      nc=8080:8080
```

The result of `curl` clearly tells us that the service is working, but `helios status` is now
showing something interesting. When defining the job, we noted that after serving
`hello` the job would terminate, but the preceding output shows a `PULLING_IMAGE` status. This is down to how Helios manages jobs—once you've deployed to a host, Helios
will do its best to keep the job running. The status you can see here is Helios going

through the complete job startup process, which happens to involve ensuring the image is pulled.

Finally, we need to clean up after ourselves:

```
$ helios undeploy -a --yes netcat:v1
Undeploying netcat:v1:2067d43fc2c6f004ea27d7bb7412aff502e3cdac from
➥ [5a4abcb27107]
5a4abcb27107: done
$ helios remove --yes netcat:v1
Removing job netcat:v1:2067d43fc2c6f004ea27d7bb7412aff502e3cdac
netcat:v1:2067d43fc2c6f004ea27d7bb7412aff502e3cdac: done
```

We asked for the job to be removed from all nodes (terminating it if necessary and stopping any more automatic restarts), and then we deleted the job itself, meaning it can't be deployed to any more nodes.

Helios is a simple and reliable way of deploying your containers to multiple hosts. Unlike a number of techniques we'll come to later on, there's no "magic" going on behind the scenes to determine appropriate locations—Helios starts containers exactly where you want them with minimal fuss.

TECHNIQUE 78   A seamless Docker cluster with Swarm

It's great having complete control over your cluster, but sometimes the micromanagement isn't necessary. In fact, if you have a number of applications with no complex requirements, you can take full advantage of the Docker promise of being able to run anywhere—there's no reason you shouldn't be able to throw containers at a cluster and let the cluster decide where to run them.

Swarm could be useful for a research lab if the lab was able to split up a computationally intensive problem into bite-size chunks. This would allow them to very easily run their problem on a cluster of machines.

PROBLEM

You have a number of hosts with Docker installed, and you want to be able to start containers without needing to micromanage where they'll run.

SOLUTION

Use Docker Swarm to treat a cluster of hosts as a single Docker daemon, and run Docker commands as normal.

DISCUSSION

A Docker Swarm consists of three parts: agents, a discovery service, and a master. Figure 9.5 shows how these three parts would interact with each other on a Docker Swarm with three nodes—hosts with agents installed on them.

The agents are programs running on each host you want to be part of your cluster; they report connection information to the discovery service and turn the host into a node in the Docker Swarm. Each host with an agent needs to have the Docker daemon exposed on an external port—we covered how to do this in technique 1 with the -H option to the Docker daemon, and we'll assume we're using the default port of 2375.

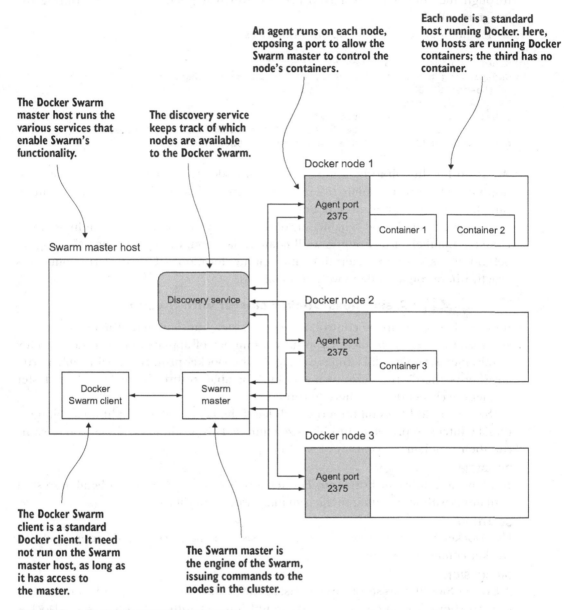

An agent runs on each node, exposing a port to allow the Swarm master to control the node's containers.

Each node is a standard host running Docker. Here, two hosts are running Docker containers; the third has no container.

The Docker Swarm master host runs the various services that enable Swarm's functionality.

The discovery service keeps track of which nodes are available to the Docker Swarm.

Docker node 1

Agent port 2375

Container 1   Container 2

Swarm master host

Discovery service

Docker node 2

Agent port 2375

Container 3

Docker Swarm client

Swarm master

Docker node 3

Agent port 2375

The Docker Swarm client is a standard Docker client. It need not run on the Swarm master host, as long as it has access to the master.

The Swarm master is the engine of the Swarm, issuing commands to the nodes in the cluster.

Figure 9.5   A Docker Swarm with three nodes

ONE MASTER ONLY   By default there can only be one master running against a Swarm. If you want to make your Swarm resilient in the event of a master failure, you'll need to look at Docker's documentation for high availability at https://docs.docker.com/swarm/multi-manager-setup/.

When the master is started, it will contact the discovery service to find the list of nodes in the cluster. From that point on, you can run commands against the cluster by directly connecting to the master, which will forward requests to an agent.

> **MINIMUM REQUIREMENTS FOR DOCKER CLIENTS** All versions of Docker used by both agents and clients in a cluster must be at least 1.4.0. You should try to keep all versions exactly the same, but the cluster should work as long as your clients are not newer than your agents.

The first step in setting up any Swarm cluster is to decide on the discovery service you want to use. There are a few options for this, ranging from a list of IP addresses in a file to Zookeeper (remember Helios?). For this technique, we're going to use a discovery service built into the Docker Hub that uses tokens.

> **DISCOVERY SERVICE BACK ENDS** Everything in this technique can be done with services you host yourself—the ability to register your nodes with the Docker Hub discovery service is provided as a convenience to get you going quickly. But if you aren't comfortable with putting the IP addresses of your nodes in a potentially public place (though someone would have to guess your cluster ID), you should read the documentation on alternative back ends: http://docs.docker.com/swarm/discovery/.

The Docker Hub discovery service requires you to obtain a token to identify your cluster. Because this is a service provided by Docker, Inc., Swarm has built-in functionality to make this easier. The Swarm binary is (naturally) available as a Docker image, so you can get going with the following commands:

```
h1 $ docker pull swarm
h1 $ docker run swarm create
126400c309dbd1405cd7318od3f1a35o
h1 $ CLUSTER_ID=126400c309dbd1405cd7218ed3f1a25e
```

The long string after the `swarm create` command is the token you're going to use to identify your cluster. It's important—jot it down! For the rest of this technique we'll use the `CLUSTER_ID` variable to refer to it.

You can now inspect your newly created Swarm:

```
h1 $ docker run swarm list token://$CLUSTER_ID
h1 $ curl https://discovery-stage.hub.docker.com/v1/clusters/$CLUSTER_ID
[]
```

As you can see, there's not much going on at the moment. The `swarm list` command returns nothing, and (to go behind the scenes a little) querying the Docker Hub discovery service directly for the hosts in the cluster returns an empty list.

DOCKER DAEMON WITH TLS ENABLED   Some cloud services provide access to a Docker daemon with TLS enabled, or you can enable it yourself. You should refer to the Swarm documentation for the latest information on generating certificates and using them for a Swarm connection: https://docs.docker.com/v1.5/swarm/#tls.

You can start up your first agent on your current machine as follows:

```
h1 $ ip addr show eth0 | grep 'inet '
    inet 10.194.12.221/20 brd 10.194.15.255 scope global eth0
h1 $ docker run -d swarm join --addr=10.194.12.221:2375 token://$CLUSTER_ID
9bf2db849bac7b33201d6d258187bd14132b74909c72912e5f135b3a4a7f4e51
h1 $ docker run swarm list token://$CLUSTER_ID
10.194.12.221:2375
h1 $ curl https://discovery-stage.hub.docker.com/v1/clusters/$CLUSTER_ID
["10.194.12.221:2375"]
```

The first step is to identify the IP address that the master will use to connect to the agent via whatever method you're most comfortable with. The IP address is used when starting the agent and will be reported to the discovery service, which means that the swarm `list` command will be updated with the new agent information.

There's no way to do anything with the node yet—we need a master to be running. Because we're going to run the master on the same machine as an agent, with the standard Docker port already exposed, we need to use an arbitrary different port for the master:

```
h1 $ docker run -d -p 4000:2375 swarm manage token://$CLUSTER_ID
04227ba0c472000bafac8499e2b67b5f0629a80615bb8c2691c6ceda242a1dd0
h1 $ docker -H tcp://localhost:4000 info
Containers: 10
Strategy: spread
Filters: affinity, health, constraint, port, dependency
Nodes: 1
 h1: 10.194.12.221:2375
  ? Containers: 2
  ? Reserved CPUs: 0 / 4
  ? Reserved Memory: 0 B / 7.907 GiB
```

We've started up the master and run docker info against it to retrieve some details about our cluster. The two containers listed as running are the master and agent.

Now let's start an agent on a completely different node:

```
h2 $ docker run -d swarm join --addr=10.194.8.7:2375 token://$CLUSTER_ID
h2 $ docker -H tcp://10.194.12.221:4000 info
Containers: 3
Strategy: spread
Filters: affinity, health, constraint, port, dependency
```

```
Nodes: 2
 h2: 10.194.8.7:2375
  ? Containers: 1
  ? Reserved CPUs: 0 / 4
  ? Reserved Memory: 0 B / 3.93 GiB
 h1: 10.194.12.221:2375
  ? Containers: 2
  ? Reserved CPUs: 0 / 4
  ? Reserved Memory: 0 B / 7.907 GiB
```

Another node has been added to our cluster. Note that we're taking advantage of the ability to access the master from another machine here.

> **SWARM STRATEGIES AND FILTERS** In the output of docker info, you may have noted the lines starting with Strategy and Filters. These hint at some more advanced things you can do with Swarm, which won't be covered here. Filters allow you to define conditions that must be met for a node to be considered for running a container. The choice of strategy then defines how Swarm will select from the possible nodes to start the container up. You can read more about strategies and filters in the Docker Swarm documentation at https://docs.docker.com/swarm/scheduler/.

Finally, let's start a container:

```
h2 $ docker -H tcp://10.194.12.221:4000 run -d ubuntu:14.04.2 sleep 60
0747c14774c70bad00bd7e2bcbf583d756ffe6d61459ca920887894b33734d3a
h2 $ docker -H tcp://localhost:4000 ps
CONTAINER ID  IMAGE          COMMAND   CREATED         STATUS
➥ PORTS        NAMES
0747c14774c7  ubuntu:14.04   sleep 60  19 seconds ago  Up Less than a second
➥            h1/serene_poitras
h2 $ docker -H tcp://10.194.12.221:4000 info | grep Containers
Containers: 4
  ? Containers: 1
  ? Containers: 3
```

There are a few things to note here. The most important is that the Swarm has automatically selected a machine to start the container on. You can see which node has been selected in the container name (h1 here) and the container count has increased correspondingly. As you can see, Swarm automatically hides any Swarm-related containers, though you can list them with the -a argument to ps.

As an optional final step, you may want to delete your cluster from the discovery service:

```
h1 $ curl -X DELETE https://discovery.hub.docker.com/v1/clusters/$CLUSTER_ID
OK
```

TECHNIQUE 79   Using a Kubernetes cluster

You've now seen two extremes in approaches to orchestration—the conservative approach of Helios and the much more free-form approach of Docker Swarm. But some users and companies will expect a little more sophistication from their tooling. This need for customizable orchestration can be fulfilled by many options, but there are a few that are used and discussed more than the others. In one case, that's undoubtedly partially due to the name behind it, but one would hope that Google knows how to build orchestration software.

Kubernetes is for companies that prefer to have clear guidance and best practices on how to arrange applications and state relationships between them. It allows you to use specially designed tools to manage a dynamic infrastructure based on a specified structure.

PROBLEM
You want to manage Docker services across hosts.

SOLUTION
Use Kubernetes.

DISCUSSION
Before we get going with Kubernetes, let's take a quick look at Kubernetes' high-level architecture in figure 9.6.

Kubernetes has a master-minion architecture. Master nodes are responsible for receiving orders about what should be run on the cluster and orchestrating its resources. Each minion has Docker installed on it, along with a *kubelet* service, which manages the pods (sets of containers) running on each node. Information about the cluster is maintained in etcd, a distributed key-value data store (see technique 66), and this is the cluster's source of truth.

> **WHAT IS A POD?** We'll go over it again later in this technique, so don't worry about it too much now, but a pod is a grouping of related containers. The concept exists to facilitate the management and maintenance of Docker containers.

The end goal of Kubernetes is to make running your containers at scale a simple matter of declaring what you want and letting Kubernetes ensure the cluster meets your needs. In this technique you'll see how to scale a simple service to a given size by running one command.

> **HOW KUBERNETES CAME INTO BEING** Kubernetes was originally developed by Google as a means for managing containers at scale. Google has been running containers for over a decade at scale, and it decided to develop this container orchestration system when Docker became popular. Kubernetes builds on the lessons learned from Google's extensive experience. Kubernetes is also known as K8s.

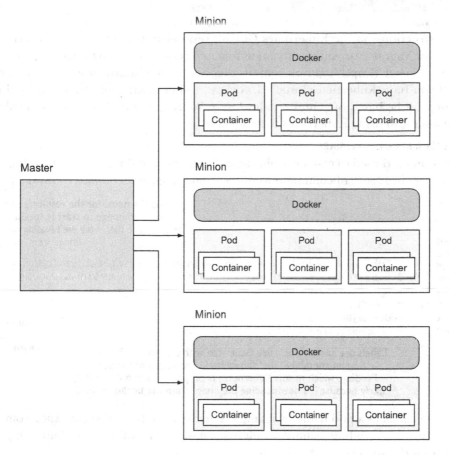

Figure 9.6 Kubernetes high-level view

A full treatment of Kubernetes' installation, setup, and features is a big and fast-changing topic that's beyond the scope of this book (and no doubt will become a book in itself, before too long). Here we're going to focus on Kubernetes' core concepts and set up a simple service so you can get a feel for it.

INSTALLING KUBERNETES

You can either install Kubernetes directly on your host, which will give you a single-minion cluster, or use Vagrant to install a multi-minion cluster managed with VMs.

To install a single-minion cluster on your host, run the following:

```
export KUBERNETES_PROVIDER=vagrant
curl -sS https://get.k8s.io | bash
```

> **GETTING THE LATEST INSTRUCTIONS** These instructions were correct at the time of printing. For the latest instructions for getting started with Kubernetes, see the documentation on GitHub at http://mng.bz/62ZH.

If you want to install a multi-minion cluster, you have another choice. Either follow the instructions on the Kubernetes GitHub repository (as outlined in the preceding note) for Vagrant, or you can try an automated script we maintain that sets up a two-minion cluster (https://github.com/docker-in-practice/shutit-kubernetes-vagrant).

If you have Kubernetes installed, you can follow along from here. The following output will be based on a multi-node cluster. We're going to start by creating a single container and using Kubernetes to scale it up.

SCALING A SINGLE CONTAINER

The command used to manage Kubernetes is `kubectl`. In this case, you're going to use the `run-container` subcommand to run a given image as a container within a pod:

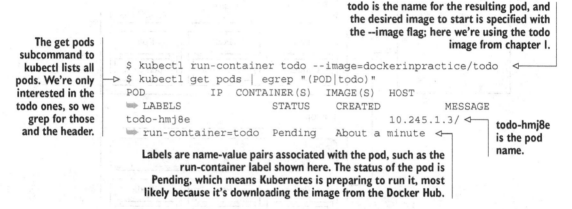

The get pods subcommand to kubectl lists all pods. We're only interested in the todo ones, so we grep for those and the header.

todo is the name for the resulting pod, and the desired image to start is specified with the --image flag; here we're using the todo image from chapter I.

```
$ kubectl run-container todo --image=dockerinpractice/todo
$ kubectl get pods | egrep "(POD|todo)"
POD            IP   CONTAINER(S)   IMAGE(S)   HOST
   LABELS           STATUS      CREATED            MESSAGE
todo-hmj8e                              10.245.1.3/
   run-container=todo  Pending   About a minute
```

todo-hmj8e is the pod name.

Labels are name-value pairs associated with the pod, such as the run-container label shown here. The status of the pod is Pending, which means Kubernetes is preparing to run it, most likely because it's downloading the image from the Docker Hub.

Kubernetes picks a pod name by taking the name from the `run-container` command (todo in the preceding example), adding a dash, and adding a random string. This ensures it doesn't clash with other pod names.

After waiting a few minutes for the todo image to download, you'll eventually see that its status has changed to `Running`:

```
$ kubectl get pods | egrep "(POD|todo)"
POD          IP            CONTAINER(S)   IMAGE(S)
   HOST                LABELS          STATUS     CREATED       MESSAGE
todo-hmj8e  10.246.1.3
   10.245.1.3/10.245.1.3  run-container=todo  Running   4 minutes
                        todo            dockerinpractice/todo

                                        Running    About a minute
```

This time the IP, CONTAINER(S), and IMAGE(S) columns are populated. The IP column gives the address of the pod (in this case 10.246.1.3), and the container column has one row per container in the pod (in this case we have only one, todo). You can test that the container (todo) is indeed up and running and serving requests by hitting the IP address and port directly:

```
$ wget -qO- 10.246.1.3:8000
<html manifest="/todo.appcache">
[...]
```

At this point we haven't seen much difference from running a Docker container directly. To get your first taste of Kubernetes, you can scale up this service by running a resize command:

```
$ kubectl resize --replicas=3 replicationController todo
resized
```

This command tells Kubernetes that we want the todo replication controller to ensure that there are three instances of the todo app running across the cluster.

> **WHAT IS A REPLICATION CONTROLLER?** A replication controller is a Kubernetes service that ensures that the right number of pods is running across the cluster.

You can check that the additional instances of the todo app have been started with the kubectl get pods command:

```
$ kubectl get pods | egrep "(POD|todo)"
POD          IP             CONTAINER(S)    IMAGE(S)
 HOST                       LABELS           STATUS     CREATED         MESSAGE
todo-2ip3n   10.246.2.2
 10.245.1.4/10.245.1.4     run-container=todo  Running   10 minutes
                           todo             dockerinpractice/todo
                                             Running    8 minutes
todo-4os5b   10.246.1.3
 10.245.1.3/10.245.1.3     run-container=todo  Running   2 minutes
                           todo             dockerinpractice/todo
                                             Running    48 seconds
todo-cuggp   10.246.2.3
 10.245.1.4/10.245.1.4     run-container=todo  Running   2 minutes
                           todo             dockerinpractice/todo
                                             Running    2 minutes
```

Kubernetes has taken the resize instruction and the todo replication controller and ensured that the right number of pods is started up. Notice that it placed two on one host (10.245.1.4) and one on another (10.245.1.3). This is because Kubernetes' default scheduler has an algorithm that spreads pods across nodes by default.

> **WHAT IS A SCHEDULER?** A scheduler is a piece of software that decides where and when items of work should be run. The Linux kernel has a scheduler, for example, that decides what task should be run next. Schedulers range from the stupidly simple to the incredibly complex.

You've started to see how Kubernetes can make managing containers easier across multiple hosts. Next we'll dive into the core Kubernetes concept of pods.

USING PODS

A *pod* is a collection of containers that are designed to work together in some way and that share resources.

Each pod gets its own IP address and shares the same volumes and network port range. Because a pod's containers share a localhost, the containers can rely on the different services being available and visible wherever they're deployed.

Figure 9.7 illustrates this with two containers that share a volume. In the figure, container 1 might be a web server that reads data files from the shared volume, which is in turn updated by container 2. Both containers are therefore stateless; state is stored in the shared volume.

This design of separated responsibilities facilitates a microservices approach by allowing you to manage each part of your service separately; you can upgrade one image without needing to be concerned with the others.

The pod specification in listing 9.5 defines a complex pod with one container that writes random data (simple-writer) to a file every five seconds, and another container that reads from the same file. The file is shared via a volume (pod-disk).

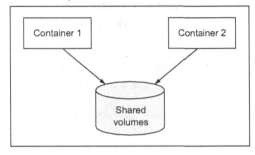

Kubernetes pod

Figure 9.7   A two-container pod

Listing 9.5   complexpod.json

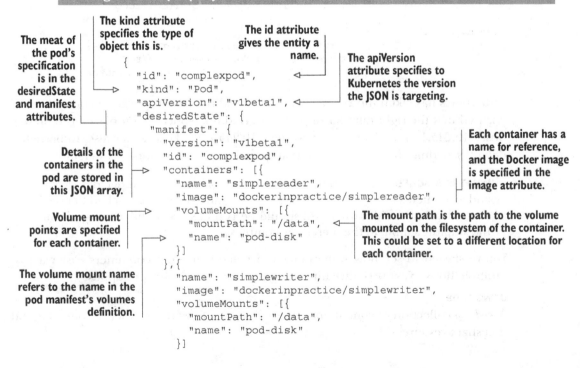

The meat of the pod's specification is in the desiredState and manifest attributes.

The kind attribute specifies the type of object this is.

The id attribute gives the entity a name.

The apiVersion attribute specifies to Kubernetes the version the JSON is targeting.

Details of the containers in the pod are stored in this JSON array.

Each container has a name for reference, and the Docker image is specified in the image attribute.

Volume mount points are specified for each container.

The mount path is the path to the volume mounted on the filesystem of the container. This could be set to a different location for each container.

The volume mount name refers to the name in the pod manifest's volumes definition.

```
{
    "id": "complexpod",
    "kind": "Pod",
    "apiVersion": "v1beta1",
    "desiredState": {
        "manifest": {
            "version": "v1beta1",
            "id": "complexpod",
            "containers": [{
                "name": "simplereader",
                "image": "dockerinpractice/simplereader",
                "volumeMounts": [{
                    "mountPath": "/data",
                    "name": "pod-disk"
                }]
            }, {
                "name": "simplewriter",
                "image": "dockerinpractice/simplewriter",
                "volumeMounts": [{
                    "mountPath": "/data",
                    "name": "pod-disk"
                }]
```

The name of the volume is referred to in the previous volumeMounts entries.

The volumes attribute defines the volumes created for this pod.

A temporary directory that shares a pod's lifetime

To load this pod specification, create a file with the preceding listing and run the following:

```
$ kubectl create -f complexpod.json
pods/complexpod
```

After waiting a minute for the images to download, you'll see the log output of the container by running `kubectl log` and specifying first the pod and then the container you're interested in:

```
$ kubectl log complexpod simplereader
2015-08-04T21:03:36.535014550Z '? U
[2015-08-04T21:03:41.537370907Z] h(^3eSk4y
[2015-08-04T21:03:41.537370907Z] CM(@
[2015-08-04T21:03:46.542871125Z] qm>5
[2015-08-04T21:03:46.542871125Z] {Vv_
[2015-08-04T21:03:51.552111956Z] KH+74        f
[2015-08-04T21:03:56.556372427Z] j?p+!\
```

WHAT NEXT?

We've only scratched the surface of Kubernetes' capabilities and potential here, but this should give you a sense of what can be done with it and how it can make orchestrating Docker containers simpler. You'll see Kubernetes again when we show you OpenShift, an application platform as a service that uses Kubernetes as its orchestration engine (see technique 87).

TECHNIQUE 80   Building a framework on Mesos

When discussing the multitude of orchestration possibilities, you'll probably find one in particular mentioned as an alternative to Kubernetes: Mesos. Typically this is followed by opaque statements like "Mesos is a framework for a framework" and "Kubernetes can be run on top of Mesos"!

The most apt analogy we've come across is to think of Mesos as providing the kernel for your data center. You can't do anything useful with it alone—the value comes when combining it with an init system and applications.

For a low-tech explanation, imagine you have a monkey sitting in front of a panel that controls of all of your machines and has the power to start and stop applications at will. Naturally, you'll need to give the monkey a *very* clear list of instructions about what to do in particular situations, when to start an application up, and so on. You could do it all yourself, but that's time-consuming and monkeys are cheap.

Mesos is the monkey!

Mesos is ideal for a company with a highly dynamic and complex infrastructure, likely with experience at rolling their own production orchestration solutions. If you don't meet these conditions, you may be better served by an off-the-shelf solution rather than spending time tailoring Mesos.

PROBLEM

You have a number of rules for controlling the startup of applications and jobs, and you want to enforce them without manually starting them on remote machines and keeping track of their status.

SOLUTION

Use Apache Mesos with a custom framework.

DISCUSSION

Mesos is a mature piece of software for providing an abstraction of resource management on multiple machines. It's been battle-tested in production by companies you've heard of, and, as a result, it's stable and reliable.

> **DOCKER 1.6.2+ REQUIRED**   You need Docker 1.6.2 or later for this technique for Mesos to be able to use the correct Docker API version.

Figure 9.8 shows a generic production Mesos setup.

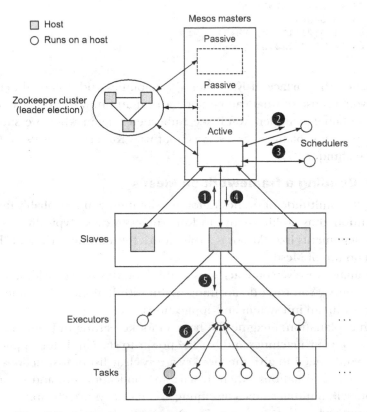

Figure 9.8   A generic production Mesos setup

With reference to this image, you can see what the basic Mesos lifecycle for starting a task looks like:

1. A slave runs on a node, tracking resource availability and keeping the master informed.
2. The master receives information from one or more slaves about available resources and makes resource offers to schedulers.
3. A scheduler receives resource offers from the master, decides where it wants to run tasks, and communicates this back to the master.
4. The master passes on the task information to the appropriate slaves.
5. Each slave passes the task information to an existing executor on the node or starts a new one.
6. The executor reads the task information and starts the task on the node.
7. The task runs.

The Mesos project provides the master and slave, as well as a built-in shell executor. It's your job to provide a *framework* (or *application*), which consists of a scheduler (the "list of instructions" from our monkey analogy) and, optionally, a custom executor.

Many third-party projects provide frameworks you can drop into Mesos (and we'll look at one in more detail in the next technique), but to get a better understanding of how you can fully harness the power of Mesos with Docker, we're going to build our own framework consisting only of a scheduler. If you have highly complex logic for starting applications, this may be your final chosen route.

> **JUST THE ESSENTIALS OF MESOS WITH DOCKER** You don't have to use Docker with Mesos, but since that's what the book is about, we will. There's a lot of detail we won't go into because Mesos is so flexible. We're also going to be running Mesos on a single computer, but we'll try to keep it as realistic as possible and point out what you need to do to go live.

We've not yet explained where Docker fits into the Mesos lifecycle—the final piece to this puzzle is that Mesos provides support for *containerizers*, allowing you to isolate your executors or tasks (or both). Docker isn't the only tool that can be used here, but it's so popular that Mesos has some Docker-specific features to get you started.

Our example will only containerize the tasks we run because we're using the default executor. If you had a custom executor only running a language environment, where each task involves dynamically loading and executing some code, you might want to consider containerizing the executor instead. As an example use case, you might have a JVM running as an executor that loads and executes pieces of code on the fly, avoiding JVM startup overhead for potentially very small tasks.

Figure 9.9 shows what will be going on behind the scenes in our example when a new Dockerized task is created.

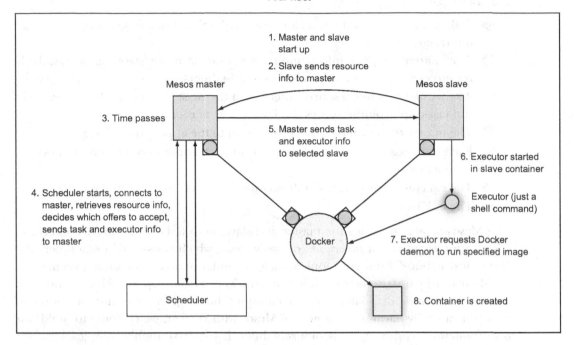

Figure 9.9 A single-host Mesos setup starting a container

Without any further ado, let's get started! First we need to start up a master in the next listing.

Listing 9.6 Starting a master

```
$ docker run -d --name mesmaster redjack/mesos:0.21.0 mesos-master \
--work_dir=/opt
24e277601260dcc6df35dc20a32a81f0336ae49531c46c2c8db84fe99ac1da35
$ docker inspect -f '{{.NetworkSettings.IPAddress}}' mesmaster
172.17.0.2
$ docker logs -f mesmaster
I0312 01:43:59.182916    1 main.cpp:167] Build: 2014-11-22 05:29:57 by root
I0312 01:43:59.183073    1 main.cpp:169] Version: 0.21.0
I0312 01:43:59.183084    1 main.cpp:172] Git tag: 0.21.0
[...]
```

The master startup is a little verbose, but you should find it stops logging quickly. Keep this terminal open so you can see what happens when you start the other containers.

MULTIPLE-MASTER MESOS SETUP   Usually a Mesos setup will have multiple Mesos masters (one active and several backups), along with a Zookeeper cluster. Setting this up is documented on the "Mesos High-Availability Mode" page on the Mesos site (http://mesos.apache.org/documentation/latest/high-availability). You'd also need to expose port 5050 for external communications and use the work_dir folder as a volume to save persistent information.

We also need a slave. Unfortunately this is a little fiddly. One of the defining characteristics of Mesos is the ability to enforce resource limits on tasks, which requires the slave to have the ability to freely inspect and manage processes. As a result, the command to run the slave needs a number of outer system details to be exposed inside the container, as shown in the next listing.

Listing 9.7 Starting a slave

```
$ docker run -d --name messlave --pid=host \
  -v /var/run/docker.sock:/var/run/docker.sock -v /sys:/sys \
  redjack/mesos:0.21.0 mesos-slave \
  --master=172.17.0.2:5050 --executor_registration_timeout=5mins \
  --isolation=cgroups/cpu,cgroups/mem --containerizers=docker,mesos \
  --resources="ports(*):[8000-8100]"
1b88c414527f63e24241691a96e3e3251fbb24996f3bfba3ebba01d7a541a9f5
$ docker inspect -f '{{.NetworkSettings.IPAddress}}' messlave
172.17.0.3
$ docker logs -f messlave
I0312 01:46:43.341621 32398 main.cpp:142] Build: 2014-11-22 05:29:57 by root
I0312 01:46:43.341789 32398 main.cpp:144] Version: 0.21.0
I0312 01:46:43.341795 32398 main.cpp:147] Git tag: 0.21.0
[...]
I0312 01:46:43.554498 32429 slave.cpp:627] No credentials provided.
➥ Attempting to register without authentication
I0312 01:46:43.554633 32429 slave.cpp:638] Detecting new master
I0312 01:46:44.419646 32424 slave.cpp:756] Registered with master
➥ master@172.17.0.2:5050; given slave ID 20150312-014359-33558956-5050-1-S0
[...]
```

At this point you should also have seen some activity in the Mesos master terminal, starting with a couple of lines like these:

```
I0312 01:46:44.332494     9 master.cpp:3068] Registering slave at
➥ slave(1)@172.17.0.3:5051 (8c6c63023050) with id
➥ 20150312-014359-33558956-5050-1-S0
I0312 01:46:44.333772     8 registrar.cpp:445] Applied 1 operations in
➥ 134310ns; attempting to update the 'registry'
```

The output of these two logs shows that your slave has started and is connected to the master. If you don't see these, stop and double-check your master IP address. It can be frustrating later on to try and debug why a framework isn't starting any tasks, when there are no connected slaves to start them on.

Anyway, there's a lot going on in the command in listing 9.7. The arguments after run and before `redjack/mesos:0.21.0` are all Docker arguments, and they mainly consist of giving the slave container lots of information about the outside world. The arguments after `mesos-slave` are more interesting. `master` tells your slave where to find your master (or your Zookeeper cluster). The next three arguments, `executor_registration_timeout`, `isolation`, and `containerizers`, are all tweaks to Mesos settings that should always be applied when working with Docker. Last, but certainly not least, you need to let the Mesos slave know what ports are acceptable to hand out as resources. By default, Mesos offers 31000–32000, but we want something a bit lower and more memorable.

Now the easy steps are out of the way, and we come to the final stage of setting up Mesos—creating a scheduler.

Happily, we have an example framework ready for you to use. Let's try it out, see what it does, and then explore how it works. Keep your two `docker logs -f` commands open on your master and slave containers so you can see the communication as it happens.

The following commands will get the source repository for the example framework from GitHub and start it up.

Listing 9.8   Downloading and starting the example framework

```
$ git clone https://github.com/docker-in-practice/mesos-nc.git
$ docker run -it --rm -v $(pwd)/mesos-nc:/opt redjack/mesos:0.21.0 bash
# apt-get update && apt-get install -y python
# cd /opt
# export PYTHONUSERBASE=/usr/local
# python myframework.py 172.17.0.2:5050
I0312 02:11:07.642227    182 sched.cpp:137] Version: 0.21.0
I0312 02:11:07.645598    176 sched.cpp:234] New master detected at
➥ master@172.17.0.2:5050
I0312 02:11:07.645800    176 sched.cpp:242] No credentials provided.
➥ Attempting to register without authentication
I0312 02:11:07.648449    176 sched.cpp:408] Framework registered with
➥ 20150312-014359-33558956-5050-1-0000
Registered with framework ID 20150312-014359-33558956-5050-1-0000
Received offer 20150312-014359-33558956-5050-1-O0. cpus: 4.0, mem: 6686.0,
➥ ports: 8000-8100
Creating task 0
Task 0 is in state TASK_RUNNING
[...]
Received offer 20150312-014359-33558956-5050-1-O5. cpus: 3.5, mem: 6586.0,
➥ ports: 8005-8100
Creating task 5
Task 5 is in state TASK_RUNNING
Received offer 20150312-014359-33558956-5050-1-O6. cpus: 3.4, mem: 6566.0,
➥ ports: 8006-8100
Declining offer
```

You'll note that we've mounted the Git repository inside the Mesos image. This is because it contains all the Mesos libraries we need. Unfortunately, it can be a little painful to install them otherwise.

Our `mesos-nc` framework is designed to run `echo 'hello <task id>' | nc -l <port>` on all available hosts, on all available ports between 8000 and 8005. Because of how netcat works, these "servers" will terminate as soon as you access them, be it by curl, Telnet, nc, or your browser. You can verify this by running `curl localhost:8003` in a new terminal. It will return the expected response, and your Mesos logs will show the spawning of a task to replace the terminated one. You can also keep track of which tasks are running with `docker ps`.

It's worth pointing out here the evidence of Mesos keeping track of allocated resources and marking them as available when a task terminates. In particular, when you accessed `localhost:8003` (feel free to try it again), take a close look at the `Received offer` line—it shows two port ranges (as they're not connected), including the freshly freed one:

```
Received offer 20150312-014359-33558956-5050-1-045. cpus: 3.5, mem: 6586.0,
➥ ports: 8006-8100,8003-8003
```

> **MESOS SLAVE NAMING CLASHES**   The Mesos slave names all the containers it starts with the prefix mesos-, and it assumes anything like that can be freely managed by the slave. Be careful with your container naming, or you might end up with the Mesos slave killing itself.

The framework code (myframework.py) is well commented in case you're feeling adventurous. We'll go through some of the high-level design:

```
class TestScheduler(mesos.interface.Scheduler):
[...]
    def registered(self, driver, frameworkId, masterInfo):
[...]
    def statusUpdate(self, driver, update):
[...]
    def resourceOffers(self, driver, offers):
[...]
```

All Mesos schedulers subclass the base Mesos scheduler class and they implement a number of methods that Mesos will call at appropriate points to let your framework react to events. Although we've implemented three in the preceding snippet, two of those are optional and have been implemented to add extra logging for demonstration purposes. The only method you *must* implement is `resourceOffers`—there's not much point in a framework that doesn't know when it can launch tasks. You're free to add any additional methods for your own purposes, such as `init` and `_makeTask`, as long as they don't conflict with any of the methods Mesos expects to use, so make sure you read the documentation (http://mesos.apache.org/documentation/latest/app-framework-development-guide/).

BUILDING YOUR OWN FRAMEWORK?   If you end up writing your own framework, you'll want to look at some documentation of methods and structures. Unfortunately, at time of writing, the only generated documentation is for Java methods. Readers looking for a starting point for digging into the structures may wish to begin with the include/mesos/mesos.proto file in the Mesos source code. Good luck!

Let's look in a bit more detail at the main method of interest: resourceOffers. This is where the decision happens to launch tasks or decline an offer. Figure 9.10 shows the execution flow after resourceOffers in our framework is called by Mesos (usually because some resources have become available for use by the framework).

resourceOffers is given a list of offers, where each offer corresponds to a single Mesos slave. The offer contains details about the resources available to a task launched on the slave, and a typical implementation will use this information to identify the most appropriate places to launch the tasks it wants to run. Launching a task sends a message to the Mesos master, which then continues with the lifecycle outlined in figure 9.8.

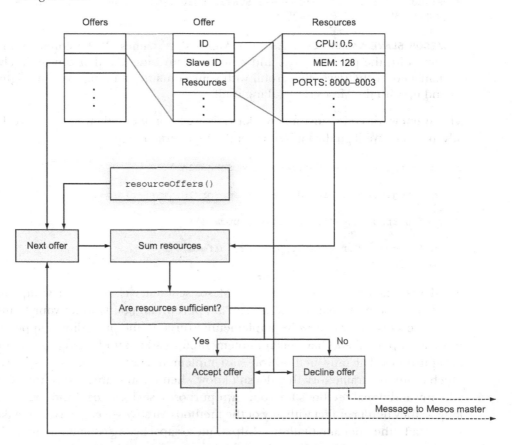

Figure 9.10   Execution flow of framework during a call to resourceOffers

It's important to note the flexibility here—your task-launching decisions can depend on any criteria you choose, from health checks of external services to the phase of the moon! This flexibility can be a burden, so pre-made frameworks exist to take some of this low-level detail away and simplify Mesos usage. One of these frameworks is covered in the next technique.

You may want to consult Roger Ignazio's *Mesos in Action* (Manning Publications, 2016) for more details on what you can do with Mesos—we've only scratched the surface here, and you've seen how easily Docker slots in.

TECHNIQUE 81 Micromanaging Mesos with Marathon

By now you'll have realized that there's a lot you need to think about with Mesos, even for an extremely simple framework. Being able to rely on applications being deployed correctly is extremely important—the impact of a bug in a framework could range from the inability to deploy new applications to a full service outage.

The stakes get higher as you scale up, and unless your team is used to writing reliable dynamic deployment code, you might want to consider a more battle-tested approach—Mesos itself is very stable, but an in-house bespoke framework may not be as reliable as you'd want.

Marathon is suitable for a company without in-house deployment tooling experience, but that needs a well-supported and easy-to-use solution for deploying containers in a somewhat dynamic environment.

PROBLEM

You need a reliable way to harness the power of Mesos without getting bogged down in writing your own framework.

SOLUTION

Use Marathon.

DISCUSSION

Marathon is an Apache Mesos framework built by Mesosphere for managing long-running applications. The marketing materials describe it as the `init` or `upstart` daemon for your data center (where Mesos is the kernel). This is not an unreasonable analogy.

Marathon makes it easy to get started by allowing you to start a single container with a Mesos master, Mesos slave, and Marathon itself inside. This is useful for demos, but it isn't suitable for production Marathon deployments. To get a realistic Marathon setup, you'll need a Mesos master and slave (from the previous technique) as well as a Zookeeper instance (from technique 77). Make sure you have all this running and we'll get started by running the Marathon container:

```
$ docker inspect -f '{{.NetworkSettings.IPAddress}}' mesmaster
172.17.0.2
$ docker inspect -f '{{.NetworkSettings.IPAddress}}' messlave
172.17.0.3
$ docker inspect -f '{{.NetworkSettings.IPAddress}}' zookeeper
172.17.0.4
```

```
$ docker pull mesosphere/marathon:v0.8.2
[...]
$ docker run -d -h $(hostname) --name marathon -p 8080:8080 \
mesosphere/marathon:v0.8.2 --master 172.17.0.2:5050 --local_port_min 8000 \
--local_port_max 8100 --zk zk://172.17.0.4:2181/marathon
accd6de46cfab65572539ccffa5c2303009be7ec7dbfb49e3ab8f447453f2b93
$ docker logs -f marathon
MESOS_NATIVE_JAVA_LIBRARY is not set. Searching in /usr/lib /usr/local/lib.
MESOS_NATIVE_LIBRARY, MESOS_NATIVE_JAVA_LIBRARY set to
➥ '/usr/lib/libmesos.so'
[2015-06-23 19:42:14,836] INFO Starting Marathon 0.8.2
➥ (mesosphere.marathon.Main$:87)
[2015-06-23 19:42:16,270] INFO Connecting to Zookeeper...
➥ (mesosphere.marathon.Main$:37)
[...]
[2015-06-30 18:20:07,971] INFO started processing 1 offers,
➥ launching at most 1 tasks per offer and 1000 tasks in total
➥ (mesosphere.marathon.tasks.IterativeOfferMatcher$:124)
[2015-06-30 18:20:07,972] INFO Launched 0 tasks on 0 offers,
➥ declining 1 (mesosphere.marathon.tasks.IterativeOfferMatcher$:216)
```

Like Mesos itself, Marathon is fairly chatty, but (also like Mesos) it stops fairly quickly. At this point, it will enter the loop you're familiar with from writing your own framework—considering resource offers and deciding what to do with them. Because we haven't launched anything yet, you should see no activity, hence the declining 1 in the preceding log.

Marathon comes with a nice-looking web interface, which is why we exposed port 8080 on the host—visit http://localhost:8080 in your browser to pull it up.

We're going to dive straight into Marathon, so let's create a new application. To clarify a bit of terminology—an "app" in the Marathon world is a group of one or more tasks with exactly the same definition.

Click the New App button at the top right to bring up a dialog box you can use to define the app you want to start up. We'll continue in the vein of the framework we created ourselves by setting the ID to marathon-nc, leaving CPU, memory, and disk space at their defaults (to match the resource limits imposed on our mesos-nc framework), and setting the command to echo "hello $MESOS_TASK_ID" | nc -l $PORT0 (using environment variables available to the task—note, that's the number zero). Set the Ports field to 8000 as an indication of where we want to listen. For now we're going to skip over the other fields. Click Create.

Your newly defined application will now be listed on the web interface. The status will briefly show as Deploying before showing as Running. Your app is now started!

If you click on the /marathon-nc entry in the Apps list, you'll see the unique ID of your app. You can get the full configuration from the REST API, as shown in the following code, and also verify that it's running by curling the Mesos slave container on the appropriate port. Make sure you save the full configuration as returned by the REST API, because it'll come in handy later—it's been saved to app.json in the following example:

```
$ curl http://localhost:8080/v2/apps/marathon-nc/versions
{"versions":["2015-06-30T19:52:44.649Z"]}
$ curl -s \
http://localhost:8080/v2/apps/marathon-nc/versions/2015-06-30T19:52:44.649Z \
> app.json
$ cat app.json
{"id":"/marathon-nc",
➡ "cmd":"echo \"hello $MESOS_TASK_ID\" | nc -l $PORT0",[...]
$ curl http://172.17.0.3:8000
hello marathon-nc.f56f140e-19e9-11e5-a44d-0242ac110012
```

Note the text following `hello` in the output from curl`ing the app—it should match
the unique ID in the interface. Be quick with checking, though— running that `curl
command will make the app terminate, Marathon will relaunch it, and the unique ID
in the web interface will change. Once you've verified all this, go ahead and click the
Destroy App button to remove `marathon-nc`.

This works OK, but you may have noticed that we've not achieved what we set out
to do with Marathon—orchestrate Docker containers. Although our application is
within a container, it's been launched in the Mesos slave container rather than in a
container of its own. Reading the Marathon documentation reveals that creating tasks
inside Docker containers requires a little more configuration (as it did when writing
our own framework).

Happily, the Mesos slave we started previously has both the required settings, so we
need to alter some Marathon options—in particular, app options. By taking the Marathon API response from before (saved in app.json), we can focus on just adding the
Marathon settings that enable Docker usage. To perform the manipulation here, we'll
use the handy `jq` tool, though it's equally easy to do it via a text editor:

```
$ JQ=https://github.com/stedolan/jq/releases/download/jq-1.3/jq-linux-x86_64
$ curl -Os $JQ && mv jq-linux-x86_64 jq && chmod +x jq
$ cat >container.json <<EOF
{
  "container": {
    "type": "DOCKER",
    "docker": {
      "image": "ubuntu:14.04.2",
      "network": "BRIDGE",
      "portMappings": [{"hostPort": 8000, "containerPort": 8000}]
    }
  }
}
$ # merge the app and container details
$ cat app.json container.json | ./jq -s add > newapp.json
```

We can now send the new app definition to the API and see Marathon launch it:

```
$ curl -X POST -H 'Content-Type: application/json; charset=utf-8' \
--data-binary @newapp.json http://localhost:8080/v2/apps
{"id":"/marathon-nc",
```

```
➥ "cmd":"echo \"hello $MESOS_TASK_ID\" | nc -l $PORT0",[...]
$ sleep 10
$ docker ps --since=marathon
CONTAINER ID   IMAGE         COMMAND             CREATED
➥ STATUS           PORTS               NAMES
284ced88246c   ubuntu:14.04  "\"/bin/sh -c 'echo  About a minute ago
➥ Up About a minute  0.0.0.0:8000->8000/tcp  mesos-
➥ 1da85151-59c0-4469-9c50-2bfc34f1a987
$ curl localhost:8000
hello mesos-nc.675b2dc9-1f88-11e5-bc4d-0242ac11000e
$ docker ps --since=marathon
CONTAINER ID   IMAGE         COMMAND             CREATED
➥ STATUS           PORTS               NAMES
851279a9292f   ubuntu:14.04  "\"/bin/sh -c 'echo  44 seconds ago
➥ Up 43 seconds             0.0.0.0:8000->8000/tcp  mesos-
➥ 37d84e5e-3908-405b-aa04-9524b59ba4f6
284ced88246c   ubuntu:14.04  "\"/bin/sh -c 'echo  24 minutes ago
➥ Exited (0) 45 seconds ago
➥ mesos-1da85151-59c0-4469-9c50-2bfc34f1a987
```

As with our custom framework, Mesos has launched a Docker container for us with the application running. Running `curl` terminates the application and container, and a new one is automatically launched.

There are some significant differences between these frameworks. For example, in the custom framework, we had extremely fine-grained control over accepting resource offers, to the point where we could pick and choose individual ports to listen on. In order to do a similar thing in Marathon, you'd need to impose the setting on each individual slave.

By contrast, Marathon comes with a lot of built-in features that would be error-prone to build yourself, including health checking, an event notification system, and a REST API. These aren't trivial things to implement, and using Marathon lets you operate with the assurance that you aren't the first one trying it. If nothing else, it's a lot easier to get support for Marathon than for a bespoke framework, and we've found that the documentation for Marathon is more approachable than that for Mesos.

We've covered the basics of setting up and using Marathon, but there are many more things to see and do. One of the more interesting suggestions we've seen is to use Marathon to start up other Mesos frameworks, potentially including your own bespoke one! We encourage you to explore—Mesos is a high-quality tool for orchestration, and Marathon provides a usable layer on top of it.

9.3   *Service discovery: what have we here?*

This chapter's introduction referred to service discovery as the flip side of orchestration—being able to deploy your applications to hundreds of different machines is fine, but if you can't then find out which applications are located where, you won't be able to actually *use* them.

While not nearly as saturated an area as orchestration, the service-discovery field still has a number of competitors. It doesn't help that they all offer slightly different feature sets.

There are two pieces of functionality that are typically desirable when it comes to service discovery: a generic key-value store and a way of retrieving service endpoints via some convenient interface (likely DNS). etcd and Zookeeper are examples of the former, whereas SkyDNS (a tool we won't go into) is an example of the latter. In fact, SkyDNS uses etcd to store the information it needs.

TECHNIQUE 82 Using Consul to discover services

etcd is a highly popular tool, but it does have one particular competitor that gets mentioned alongside it a lot: Consul. This is a little strange, because there are other tools more similar to etcd (Zookeeper has a similar feature set to etcd but is implemented in a different language), whereas Consul differentiates itself with some interesting additional features, like service discovery and health checks.

In fact, if you squint, Consul might look a bit like etcd, SkyDNS, and Nagios all in one.

PROBLEM

You need to be able to distribute information to, discover services within, and monitor a collection of containers.

SOLUTION

Start a container with Consul on each Docker host to provide a service directory and configuration communication system.

DISCUSSION

Consul tries to be a generic tool for doing some important tasks required when you need to coordinate a number of independent services. These tasks can be performed by other tools, but configuring them in one place can be useful. From a high level, Consul provides the following:

- *Service configuration*—A key-value store for storing and sharing small values, like etcd and Zookeeper
- *Service discovery*—An API for registering services and a DNS endpoint for discovering them, like SkyDNS
- *Service monitoring*—An API for registering health checks, like Nagios

You can use all, some, or one of these features, as there's no tie-in. If you have existing monitoring infrastructure, there's no need to replace that with Consul.

This technique will cover the service-discovery and service-monitoring aspects of Consul, but not key-value storage. The strong similarities between etcd and Consul in this aspect make the two final techniques in chapter 7 transferable with some perusal of the Consul documentation.

Figure 9.11 shows a typical Consul setup.

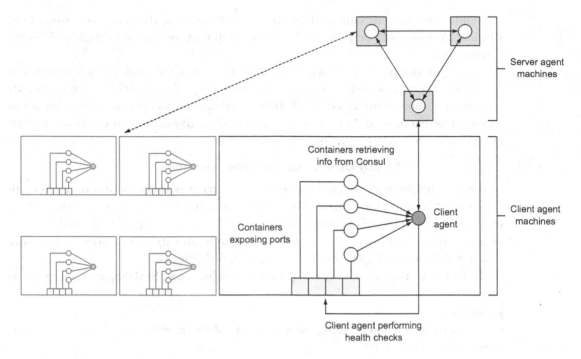

Figure 9.11 A typical Consul setup

The data stored in Consul is the responsibility of *server* agents. These are responsible for forming a *consensus* on the information stored—this concept is present in most distributed data-storage systems. In short, if you lose under half of your server agents, you're guaranteed to be able to recover your data (see an example of this with etcd in technique 66). Because these servers are so important and have greater resource requirements, keeping them on dedicated machines is a typical choice.

> **KEEPING DATA AROUND** Although the commands in this technique will leave the Consul data directory (/data) inside the container, it's generally a good idea to specify this directory as a volume for at least the servers, so you can keep backups.

It's recommended that all machines under your control that may want to interact with Consul should run a client agent. These agents forward requests on to the servers and run health checks:

The first step in getting Consul running is to start a server agent:

```
c1 $ IMG=dockerinpractice/consul-server
c1 $ docker pull $IMG
[...]
c1 $ ip addr | grep 'inet ' | grep -v 'lo$\|docker0$\|vbox.*$'
    inet 192.168.1.87/24 brd 192.168.1.255 scope global wlan0
```

```
c1 $ EXTIP1=192.168.1.87
c1 $ echo '{"ports": {"dns": 53}}' > dns.json
c1 $ docker run -d --name consul --net host \
-v $(pwd)/dns.json:/config/dns.json $IMG -bind $EXTIP1 -client $EXTIP1 \
-recursor 8.8.8.8 -recursor 8.8.4.4 -bootstrap-expect 1
88d5cb48b8b1ef9ada754f97f024a9ba691279e1a863fa95fa196539555310c1
c1 $ docker logs consul
[...]
    Client Addr: 192.168.1.87 (HTTP: 8500, HTTPS: -1, DNS: 53, RPC: 8400)
    Cluster Addr: 192.168.1.87 (LAN: 8301, WAN: 8302)
[...]
==> Log data will now stream in as it occurs:

    2015/08/14 12:35:41 [INFO] serf: EventMemberJoin: mylaptop 192.168.1.87
[...]
    2015/08/14 12:35:43 [INFO] consul: member 'mylaptop' joined, marking
➥ health alive
    2015/08/14 12:35:43 [INFO] agent: Synced service 'consul'
```

Because we want to use Consul as a DNS server, we've inserted a file into the folder Consul reads the configuration from to request it listen on port 53 (the registered port for the DNS protocol). We've then used a command sequence you may recognize from earlier techniques to try to find the external-facing IP address of the machine for both communicating with other agents and listening for client requests.

> **DNS PORT CONFLICTS** The IP address 0.0.0.0 is typically used to indicate that an application should listen on all available interfaces on the machine. We've deliberately not done this because some Linux distributions have a DNS caching daemon listening on 127.0.0.1, which disallows listening on 0.0.0.0:53.

There are three items of note in the previous docker run command:

- We've used --net host. Although this can be seen as a faux pas in the Docker world, the alternative is to expose up to eight ports on the command line—it's a matter of personal preference, but we feel it's justified here. It also helps bypass a potential issue with UDP communication. If you were to go the manual route, there'd be no need to set the DNS port—you could expose the default Consul DNS port (8600) as port 53 on the host.
- The two recursor arguments tell Consul what DNS servers to look at if a requested address is unknown by consul itself.
- The -bootstrap-expect 1 argument means the Consul cluster will start operating with only one agent, which is not robust. A typical setup would set this to three (or more) to make sure the cluster doesn't start until the required number of servers has joined. To start the additional server agents, add a -join argument, as we'll discuss when we start a client.

Now let's go to a second machine, start a client agent, and add it to our cluster.

STEPPING ON TOES   Because Consul expects to be able to listen on a particular set of ports when communicating with other agents, it's tricky to set up multiple agents on a single machine while still demonstrating how it would work in the real world. We'll use a different host now—if you decide to use an IP alias, ensure you pass a -node newAgent, because by default the hostname will be used, which will conflict.

```
c2 $ IMG=dockerinpractice/consul-agent
c2 $ docker pull $IMG
[...]
c2 $ EXTIP1=192.168.1.87
c2 $ ip addr | grep docker0 | grep inet
    inet 172.17.42.1/16 scope global docker0
c2 $ BRIDGEIP=172.17.42.1
c2 $ ip addr | grep 'inet ' | grep -v 'lo$\|docker0$'
    inet 192.168.1.80/24 brd 192.168.1.255 scope global wlan0
c2 $ EXTIP2=192.168.1.80
c2 $ echo '{"ports": {"dns": 53}}' > dns.json
c2 $ docker run -d --name consul-client --net host \
-v $(pwd)/dns.json:/config/dns.json $IMG -client $BRIDGEIP -bind $EXTIP2 \
-join $EXTIP1 -recursor 8.8.8.8 -recursor 8.8.4.4
5454029b139cd28e8500922d1167286f7e4fb4b7220985ac932f8fd5b1cdef25
c2 $ docker logs consul-client
[...]
    2015/08/14 19:40:20 [INFO] serf: EventMemberJoin: mylaptop2 192.168.1.80
[...]
    2015/08/14 13:24:37 [INFO] consul: adding server mylaptop
⇒ (Addr: 192.168.1.87:8300) (DC: dc1)
```

REFUTING MESSAGES   The images we've used are based on gliderlabs/consul-server:0.5 and gliderlabs/consul-agent:0.5, and they come with a newer version of Consul to avoid possible problems with UDP communication, indicated by the constant logging of lines like "Refuting a suspect message." When version 0.6 of the images are released, you can switch back to the images from gliderlabs.

All client services (HTTP, DNS, and so on) have been configured to listen on the Docker bridge IP address. This gives containers a known location from which they can retrieve information from Consul, and it only exposes Consul internally on the machine, forcing other machines to directly access the server agents rather than taking a slower route via a client agent to a server agent. To ensure the bridge IP address is consistent across all your hosts, you can look at the --bip argument to the Docker daemon—this may be familiar from setting up Resolvable in technique 70.

As before, we've found the external IP address and bound cluster communication to it. The -join argument tells Consul where to initially look to find the cluster. Don't worry about micromanaging the cluster formation—when two agents initially meet each other, they'll *gossip*, transferring information about finding the other agents in the cluster. The final -recursor arguments tell Consul what upstream DNS servers to use for DNS requests that aren't trying to look up registered services.

Let's verify that the agent has connected to the server with the HTTP API on the client machine. The API call we'll use will return a list of members the client agent currently thinks are in the cluster (in large, quickly changing clusters, this may not always match the members of the cluster—there's another, slower API call for that):

```
c2 $ curl -sSL $BRIDGEIP:8500/v1/agent/members | tr ',' '\n' | grep Name
[{"Name":"mylaptop2"
{"Name":"mylaptop"
```

Now that the Consul infrastructure is set up, it's time to see how you can register and discover services. The typical process for registration is to get your app to make an API call against the local client agent after initializing, prompting the client agent to distribute the information to the server agents. For demonstration purposes, we'll perform the registration step manually:

```
c2 $ docker run -d --name files -p 8000:80 ubuntu:14.04.2 \
python3 -m http.server 80
96ee81148154a75bc5c8a83e3b3d11b73d738417974eed4e019b26027787e9d1
c2 $ docker inspect -f '{{.NetworkSettings.IPAddress}}' files
172.17.0.16
c2 $ /bin/echo -e 'GET / HTTP/1.0\r\n\r\n' | nc -i1 172.17.0.16 80 \
| head -n 1
HTTP/1.0 200 OK
c2 $ curl -X PUT --data-binary '{"Name": "files", "Port": 8000}' \
$BRIDGEIP:8500/v1/agent/service/register
c2 $ docker logs consul-client | tail -n 1
    2015/08/15 03:44:30 [INFO] agent: Synced service 'files'
```

Here we've set up a simple HTTP server in a container, exposing it on port 8000 on the host, and checked that it works. Then we used curl and the Consul HTTP API to register a service definition. The only thing absolutely necessary here is the name of the service—the port, along with the other fields listed in the Consul documentation, are all optional. The ID field is worth a mention—it defaults to the name of the service but must be unique across all services. If you want multiple instances of a service, you'll need to specify it.

The log line from Consul has told us that the service is synced, so we should be able to retrieve the information about it from the service DNS interface. This information comes from the server agents, so it acts as validation that the service has been accepted into the Consul catalog. You can use the dig command to query service DNS information and check that it's present:

Look up the IP address of the files service from the client agent DNS. If using $BRIDGEIP fails, you may wish to try with $EXTIPI.

Look up the IP address of the files service from the server agent DNS. This DNS service is available to arbitrary machines not in your Consul cluster, allowing them to benefit from service discovery as well.

Request the SRV record of the files service from the client agent DNS. SRV records are a way of communicating service information by DNS, including protocol, port, and other entries. Two items worth noting are that you can see the port number in the response, and you've been given the canonical hostname of the machine providing the service rather than the IP address.

Start a container configured to use the local client agent as the only DNS server. If you've familiarized yourself with the technique on Resolvable we mentioned earlier (technique 70), you'll recall that you can set this as a default for all containers. Remember to override the defaults for the Consul agent, or you may end up with unexpected behavior.

```
c2 $ EXTIP1=192.168.1.87
c2 $ dig @$EXTIP1 files.service.consul +short
192.168.1.80
c2 $ BRIDGEIP=172.17.42.1
c2 $ dig @$BRIDGEIP files.service.consul +short
192.168.1.80
c2 $ dig @$BRIDGEIP files.service.consul srv +short
1 1 8000 mylaptop2.node.dc1.consul.
c2 $ docker run -it --dns $BRIDGEIP ubuntu:14.04.2 bash
root@934e9c26bc7e:/# ping -c1 -q www.google.com
PING www.google.com (216.58.210.4) 56(84) bytes of data.

--- www.google.com ping statistics ---
1 packets transmitted, 1 received, 0% packet loss, time 0ms
rtt min/avg/max/mdev = 25.358/25.358/25.358/0.000 ms
root@934e9c26bc7e:/# ping -c1 -q files.service.consul
PING files.service.consul (192.168.1.80) 56(84) bytes of data.

--- files.service.consul ping statistics ---
1 packets transmitted, 1 received, 0% packet loss, time 0ms
rtt min/avg/max/mdev = 0.062/0.062/0.062/0.000 ms
```

Verify that lookup of external addresses still works.

Verify that service lookup works automatically inside the container.

The similarities between Resolvable and the Consul DNS service are striking. The key difference is that Consul lets you find containers across multiple nodes. However, as mentioned at the beginning of this technique, Consul has another interesting feature we'll take a look at: health checks.

Health checking is a big topic, so we'll leave the minutiae for the comprehensive Consul documentation and look at one of the options for monitoring—a script check. This runs a command and sets the health based on the return value, with 0 for success, 1 for warning, and any other value for critical. You can register a health check when initially defining the service, or in a separate API call, as we'll do here.

```
c2 $ cat >check <<'EOF'
#!/bin/sh
set -o errexit
set -o pipefail
```

Create check script verifying that the HTTP status code from the service is 200 OK. The service port is looked up from the service ID passed to the script as an argument.

```
SVC_ID="$1"
SVC_PORT=\
"$(wget -qO - 172.17.42.1:8500/v1/agent/services | jq ".$SVC_ID.Port")"
wget -qsO - "localhost:$SVC_PORT"
echo "Success!"'
EOF
c2 $ cat check | docker exec -i consul-client sh -c \
'cat > /check && chmod +x /check'
c2 $ cat >health.json <<'EOF'
{
    "Name": "filescheck",
    "ServiceID": "files",
    "Script": "/check files",
    "Interval": "10s"
}
EOF
c2 $ curl -X PUT --data-binary @health.json \
172.17.42.1:8500/v1/agent/check/register
c2 $ sleep 300
c2 $ curl -sSL 172.17.42.1:8500/v1/health/service/files | \
python -m json.tool | head -n 13
[
    {
        "Checks": [
            {
                "CheckID": "filescheck",
                "Name": "filescheck",
                "Node": "mylaptop2",
                "Notes": "",
                "Output": "/check: line 6: jq: not \
found\nConnecting to 172.17.42.1:8500 (172.17.42.1:8500)\n",
                "ServiceID": "files",
                "ServiceName": "files",
                "Status": "critical"
            },
c2 $ dig @$BRIDGEIP files.service.consul srv +short
c2 $
```

Copy the check script into the Consul agent container.

Create a health check definition to send to the Consul HTTP API. The service ID has to be specified in both the ServiceID field and the script command line.

Submit the health check JSON to the Consul agent.

Wait for the check output to be communicated to the server agents.

Retrieve health check information for the check you've registered.

Attempt to look up the files service, with no results.

AVOIDING CHECK STATUS CHURN Because output from health checks can change on every execution (if it includes timestamps, for example) Consul only synchronizes check output with the server on a status change, or every five minutes (though this interval is configurable). Because statuses start as critical, there's no initial status change in this case, so you'll need to wait out the interval to get output.

We added a health check for the files service to be run every 10 seconds, but checking it shows the service as having a critical status. Because of this, Consul has automatically taken the failing endpoint out of the entries returned by DNS, leaving us with no servers. This is particularly helpful for automatically removing servers from a multiple-backend service in production.

The root cause of the error we've hit is an important one to be aware of when running Consul inside a container. All checks are also run inside the container, so as the check script had to be copied into the container, you also need to make sure any commands you need are installed in the container. In this particular case, we're missing the jq command (a helpful utility for extracting information from JSON), which we can install manually, though the correct approach for production would be to add layers to the image:

```
c2 $ docker exec consul-client sh -c 'apk update && apk add jq'
fetch http://dl-4.alpinelinux.org/alpine/v3.2/main/x86_64/APKINDEX.tar.gz
v3.2.3 [http://dl-4.alpinelinux.org/alpine/v3.2/main]
OK: 5289 distinct packages available
(1/1) Installing jq (1.4-r0)
Executing busybox-1.23.2-r0.trigger
OK: 14 MiB in 28 packages
c2 $ docker exec consul-client sh -c \
'wget -qO - 172.17.42.1:8500/v1/agent/services | jq ".files.Port"'
8000
c2 $ sleep 15
c2 $ curl -sSL 172.17.42.1:8500/v1/health/service/files | \
python -m json.tool | head -n 13
[
    {
        "Checks": [
            {
                "CheckID": "filescheck",
                "Name": "filescheck",
                "Node": "mylaptop2",
                "Notes": "",
                "Output": "Success!\n",
                "ServiceID": "files",
                "ServiceName": "files",
                "Status": "passing"
            },
```

We've now installed jq onto the image using the Alpine Linux package manager (see technique 51), verified that it works by manually executing the line that was previously failing in the script, and then waited for the check to rerun. It's now successful!

By covering script health checks in the previous examples, you now have a vital building block for constructing monitoring around your application—if you can express a health check as a series of commands you'd run in a terminal, you can get Consul to automatically run it. If you find yourself wanting to check the status code returned by an HTTP endpoint, you're in luck—this is such a common task that one of the three types of health checking in Consul is dedicated to it. The final type of health check, Time to Live, requires a deeper integration with your application. The status must be periodically set to healthy, or the check will automatically be set to failing. Combining these three types of health checks gives you the power to build comprehensive monitoring on top of your system.

To round off this technique, we'll look at the optional Consul web interface that comes with the server agent image. It provides a helpful insight into the current state of your cluster. You can visit this by going to port 8500 on the external IP address of a server agent. In this case you'd want to visit $EXTIP1:8500. Remember that even if you're on a server agent host, localhost or 127.0.0.1 will not work.

We've covered a lot in this technique—Consul is a big topic! Fortunately, just as the knowledge you gained about utilizing key-value stores with etcd is transferable to other key-value stores (like Consul), this service-discovery knowledge is transferable to other tools offering DNS interfaces (SkyDNS being one you may come across). The subtleties we covered related to using the host network stack and using external IP addresses are also transferable. Most containerized distributed tools requiring discovery across multiple nodes have similar problems.

TECHNIQUE 83 Automatic service registration with Registrator

The obvious downside of Consul (and any service discovery tool) so far is the overhead of having to manage the creation and deletion of service entries. If you integrate this into your applications, you'll have multiple implementations and multiple places it could go wrong.

Integration also doesn't work for applications you don't have complete control over, so you'll end up having to write wrapper scripts when starting up your database and the like.

PROBLEM
You don't want to manually manage service entries and health checks in Consul.

SOLUTION
Use Registrator.

DISCUSSION
This technique will build on top of the previous one and will assume you have a two-part Consul cluster available, as described previously. We'll also assume there are no services in it, so you may want to recreate your containers to start from scratch.

Registrator (http://gliderlabs.com/registrator/latest/) takes away much of the complexity of managing Consul services—it watches for containers to start and stop, registering services based on exposed ports and container environment variables. The easiest way to see this in action is to jump in.

Everything we do will be on the machine with the client agent. As discussed previously, no containers except the server agent should be running on the other machine.

The following commands are all you need to start up Registrator:

```
$ IMG=gliderlabs/registrator:v6
$ docker pull $IMG
[...]
$ ip addr | grep 'inet ' | grep -v 'lo$\|docker0$'
    inet 192.168.1.80/24 brd 192.168.1.255 scope global wlan0
$ EXTIP=192.168.1.80
$ ip addr | grep docker0 | grep inet
    inet 172.17.42.1/16 scope global docker0
$ BRIDGEIP=172.17.42.1
$ docker run -d --name registrator -h $(hostname)-reg \
-v /var/run/docker.sock:/tmp/docker.sock $IMG -ip $EXTIP -resync \
```

```
60 consul://$BRIDGEIP:8500 # if this fails, $EXTIP is an alternative
b3c8a04b9dfaf588e46a255ddf4e35f14a9d51199fc6f39d47340df31b019b90
$ docker logs registrator
2015/08/14 20:05:57 Starting registrator v6 ...
2015/08/14 20:05:57 Forcing host IP to 192.168.1.80
2015/08/14 20:05:58 consul: current leader  192.168.1.87:8300
2015/08/14 20:05:58 Using consul adapter: consul://172.17.42.1:8500
2015/08/14 20:05:58 Listening for Docker events ...
2015/08/14 20:05:58 Syncing services on 2 containers
2015/08/14 20:05:58 ignored: b3c8a04b9dfa no published ports
2015/08/14 20:05:58 ignored: a633e58c66b3 no published ports
```

The first couple of commands here—for pulling the image and finding the external IP address—should look familiar. This IP address is given to Registrator so it knows what IP address to advertise for the services. The Docker socket is mounted to allow Registrator to be automatically notified of container starts and stops as they happen. We've also told Registrator how it can connect to a Consul agent and that we want all containers to be refreshed every 60 seconds. Registrator should automatically be notified of container changes, so this final setting is helpful in mitigating the impact of Registrator possibly missing updates.

Now that Registrator is running, it's extremely easy to register a first service:

```
$ curl -sSL 172.17.42.1:8500/v1/catalog/services | python -m json.tool
{
    "consul": []
}
$ docker run -d -e "SERVICE_NAME=files" -p 8000:80 ubuntu:14.04.2 python3 \
-m http.server 80
3126a8668d7a058333d613f7995954f1919b314705589a9cd8b4e367d4092c9b
$ docker inspect 3126a8668d7a | grep 'Name.*/'
    "Name": "/evil_hopper",
$ curl -sSL 172.17.42.1:8500/v1/catalog/services | python -m json.tool
{
    "consul": [],
    "files": []
}
$ curl -sSL 172.17.42.1:8500/v1/catalog/service/files | python -m json.tool
[
    {
        "Address": "192.168.1.80",
        "Node": "mylaptop2",
        "ServiceAddress": "192.168.1.80",
        "ServiceID": "mylaptop2-reg:evil_hopper:80",
        "ServiceName": "files",
        "ServicePort": 8000,
        "ServiceTags": null
    }
]
```

The only effort we've had to put in when registering the service is passing an environment variable to tell Registrator what service name to use. By default, Registrator uses a name based on the container name component after the slash and before the tag: mycorp.com/myteam/myimage:0.5 would have the name myimage. Whether this is useful or you want to specify something manually will depend on your naming conventions.

The rest of the values are pretty much as you'd hope. Registrator has discovered the port being listened on, added it to Consul, and set a service ID that tries to give a hint about where you can find the container (which is why the hostname was set in the Registrator container).

Registrator will pick up a number of other details from environments if they're present, including tags, service names per port (if multiple), and using health checks (if using Consul as the data storage). All three types of Consul health checks can be enabled by specifying the check details in the environment in JSON——you can read more about this in the Consul section of the "Registrator Backends" documentation at http://gliderlabs.com/registrator/latest/user/backends/#consul.

Registrator is excellent at giving you a handle on a swiftly changing environment with a high churn of containers, making sure you don't need to worry about your service creation checks being created.

9.4 *Summary*

This chapter is probably the most unopinionated in the book. We've tried to give you a glimpse into the world of orchestration with Docker so you can go out and make a decision for yourself—there's definitely no one-size-fits-all solution here.

Even with this survey of the tools available, actually committing to one can be daunting. Our advice is to keep it as simple as possible for as long as possible, and to keep the tradeoffs in mind if you're considering moving down the branches in figure 9.1 at the beginning of the chapter. For example, you may not need dynamic provisioning and service discovery right now if your traffic growth indicates two servers will be sufficient for the next year.

The topics we looked at included

- Using a mature solution from outside the Docker world to control container execution on a single machine
- Simple multi-host orchestration solutions
- The two heavyweights in the Docker orchestration field
- Automatically inserting your applications into your service discovery backend of choice

The next chapter will turn to more sober matters—keeping Docker secure.

Docker and security

As Docker makes clear in its documentation, access to the Docker API implies access to root privileges, which is why Docker must often be run with sudo, or the user must be added to a user group (which might be called docker or dockerroot) that allows access to the Docker API.

In this chapter we're going to look at the issue of security in Docker.

10.1 Docker access and what it means

You may be wondering what sort of damage a user can do if they can run Docker. As a simple example, this command (don't run it!) would delete all the binaries in /sbin on your host machine (if you took out the bogus --donotrunme flag):

```
docker run --donotrunme -v /sbin:/sbin busybox rm -rf /sbin
```

It's worth pointing out that this is true even if you're a non-root user. This command will show you the contents of the secure shadow password file from the host system:

```
docker run -v /etc/shadow:/etc/shadow busybox cat /etc/shadow
```

Docker's insecurity is often misunderstood, partly due to a misunderstanding of the benefits of namespaces in the kernel. Linux namespaces provide isolation from other parts of the system, but the level of isolation you have in Docker is at your discretion (as seen in the preceding `docker run` examples). Furthermore, not all parts of the Linux OS have the ability to be namespaced. Devices and kernel modules are two examples of core Linux features that aren't namespaced.

> **LINUX NAMESPACES** Linux namespaces were developed to allow processes to have a different view of the system than other processes have. For example, *process namespacing* means that containers can only see processes associated with that container—other processes running on the same host are effectively invisible to them. *Network namespacing* means that containers appear to have their own network stack available to them. Namespaces have been part of the Linux kernel for a number of years.

Also, because you have the ability to interact with the kernel as root from within the container through syscalls, any kernel vulnerability could be exploited by root within the Docker container. Of course, VMs also have the same class of attack service through access to the hypervisor, albeit a smaller one. Hypervisors have security vulnerabilities reported against them also.

Another way to understand it is to think of running a Docker container as being no different (from a security perspective) from being able to install any package via a package manager.

In other words, your requirement for security when running Docker containers should be the same as for installing packages. If you have Docker, you can install software as root. This is part of the reason why some argue that Docker is best understood as a software packaging system.

> **USER NAMESPACING** Work is underway to remove this risk through user namespacing, which maps root in the container to a non-privileged user on the host.

10.1.1 Do you care?

Given that access to the Docker API is equivalent to root access, the next question is "Do you care?" Although this might seem an odd line to take, security is all about trust, and if you trust your users to install software in the environment in which they operate, there should be no barrier to them running Docker containers there. Security difficulties primarily arise when considering multi-tenant environments. Because the root user inside your container is in key respects the same as root outside your container, having lots of different users being root on your system is a potentially worrying place to be.

MULTI-TENANCY   A multitenant environment is one in which many different users share the same resources. For example, two teams might share the same server with two different VMs. Multi-tenancy offers cost savings through sharing hardware rather than provisioning hardware for specific applications. But it can bring other challenges related to service reliability and security isolation that can offset the cost savings.

Some organizations take the approach of running Docker on a dedicated VM for each user. The VM can be used for security, operational, or resource isolation. Within the VM trust boundary, users run Docker containers for the performance and operational benefits they bring. This is the approach taken by Google Compute Engine, which places a VM between the user's container and their underlying infrastructure for an added level of security and some operational benefits. Google has more than a little compute resources at their disposal, so they don't mind the overhead of doing this.

10.2   *Security measures in Docker*

Various measures have already been taken by the Docker maintainers to reduce the security risks of running containers. For example,

- Certain core mount points (such as /proc and /sys) are now mounted as read-only.
- Default Linux capabilities have been reduced.
- Support for third-party security systems like SELinux and AppArmor now exists.

In this section, we'll look more deeply at these and at some of the measures you can take to reduce the risks of running containers on your system.

TECHNIQUE 84   Constraining capabilities

As we've already mentioned, the root user on the container is the same user as root on the host. But not all root users are created equal. Linux provides you with the ability to assign more fine-grained privileges to the root user within a process. These fine-grained privileges are called *capabilities*, and they allow you to limit the damage a user can do even if they're root. This technique shows you how to manipulate these capabilities when running Docker containers.

PROBLEM
You want to reduce the ability of containers to perform damaging actions on your host machine.

SOLUTION
Use the --drop-cap flag to reduce the privileges a container has access to.

DISCUSSION
If you don't fully trust the content of containers running on your system, you can reduce the risk of issues arising by dropping the capabilities available to the container.

THE UNIX TRUST MODEL
To understand what this means and does, a little bit of background is required. When the Unix system was designed, the trust model wasn't sophisticated. You had admins

who were trusted (root users) and users who weren't. Root users could do anything, whereas standard users could only affect their own files. Because the system was typically used in a university lab and was small, this model made sense.

As the Unix model grew and the internet arrived, this model made less and less sense. Programs like web servers needed root permissions to serve content on port 80, but were also acting effectively as proxies for running commands on the host. Standard patterns were established to handle this, such as binding to port 80 and dropping the effective user ID to a non-root user. Users performing all sorts of roles, from sysadmins to database administrators through to application support engineers and developers, could all potentially need fine-grained access to different resources on a system. Unix groups alleviated this to some degree, but modeling these privilege requirements—as any systems admin will tell you—is a non-trivial problem.

LINUX CAPABILITIES

In an attempt to support a more fine-grained approach to privileged user management, the Linux kernel engineers developed *capabilities*. This was an attempt to break down the monolithic root privilege into slices of functionality that could be granted discretely. You can read about them in more detail by running `man 7 capabilities` (assuming you have the man page installed).

Docker has helpfully switched off certain capabilities by default. This means that even if you have root in the container, there are things you won't be able to do. For example, the `CAP_NET_ADMIN` capability, which allows you to affect the network stack of the host, is disabled by default.

Table 10.1 lists Linux capabilities, gives a brief description of what they allow, and indicates whether they're permitted by default in Docker containers. Remember that each capability relates to the root user's ability to affect other users' objects on the system—a root user within a container could still chown root's files on the host if the files were made available as a volume in the container, for example.

Table 10.1 Linux capabilities in Docker containers

Capability	Description	Switched on?
CHOWN	Make ownership changes to any files.	Y
DAC_OVERRIDE	Override read, write, and execution checks.	Y
FSETID	Don't clear suid and guid bits when modifying files.	Y
FOWNER	Override ownership checks when saving files.	Y
KILL	Bypass permission checks on signals.	Y
MKNOD	Make special files with mknod.	Y
NET_RAW	Use raw and packet sockets, and bind to ports for transparent proxying.	Y
SETGID	Make changes to group ownership of processes.	Y

Table 10.1 Linux capabilities in Docker containers *(continued)*

Capability	Description	Switched on?
SETUID	Make changes to user ownership of processes.	Y
SETFCAP	Set file capabilities.	Y
SETPCAP	If file capabilities aren't supported, then apply capability limits to and from other processes.	Y
NET_BIND_SERVICE	Bind sockets to ports under 1024.	Y
SYS_CHROOT	Use chroot.	Y
AUDIT_WRITE	Write to kernel logs.	Y
AUDIT_CONTROL	Enable/disable kernel logging.	N
BLOCK_SUSPEND	Employ features that block the ability of the system to suspend.	N
DAC_READ_SEARCH	Bypass file permission checks on reading files and directories.	N
IPC_LOCK	Lock memory.	N
IPC_OWNER	Bypass permissions on interprocess communication objects.	N
LEASE	Establish leases (watches on attempts to open or truncate) on ordinary files.	N
LINUX_IMMUTABLE	Set the FS_APPEND_FL and FS_IMMUTABLE_FL i-node flags.	N
MAC_ADMIN	Override mandatory access control (related to the Smack Linux Security Module (SLM)).	N
MAC_OVERRIDE	Mandatory access control changes (related to SLM).	N
NET_ADMIN	Various network-related operations, including IP firewall changes and interface configuration.	N
NET_BROADCAST	Unused.	N
SYS_ADMIN	A range of administrative functions. See man capabilities for more information.	N
SYS_BOOT	Rebooting.	N
SYS_MODULE	Load/unload kernel modules.	N
SYS_NICE	Manipulate nice priority of processes.	N
SYS_PACCT	Turn on or off process accounting.	N
SYS_PTRACE	Trace processes' system calls and other process manipulation capabilities.	N

Table 10.1 Linux capabilities in Docker containers (continued)

Capability	Description	Switched on?
SYS_RAWIO	Perform I/O on various core parts of the system, such as memory and SCSI device commands.	N
SYS_RESOURCE	Control and override various resource limits.	N
SYS_TIME	Set the system clock.	N
SYS_TTY_CONFIG	Privileged operations on virtual terminals.	N

ASSUMES LIBCONTAINER ENGINE If you aren't using Docker's default container engine (libcontainer), these capabilities may be different on your installation. If you have a sysadmin and want to be sure, ask them.

Unfortunately the kernel maintainers only allocated 32 capabilities within the system, so capabilities have grown in scope as more and more fine-grained root privileges have been carved out of the kernel. Most notably, the vaguely named CAP_SYS_ADMIN capability covers actions as varied as changing the host's domain name to exceeding the system-wide limit on the number of open files.

One extreme approach is to remove all the capabilities that are switched on in Docker by default from the container, and see what stops working. Here we start up a bash shell with the capabilities that are enabled by default removed:

```
$ docker run -ti --cap-drop=CHOWN --cap-drop=DAC_OVERRIDE \
--cap-drop=FSETID --cap-drop=FOWNER --cap-drop=KILL --cap-drop=MKNOD \
--cap-drop=NET_RAW --cap-drop=SETGID --cap-drop=SETUID \
--cap-drop=SETFCAP --cap-drop=SETPCAP --cap-drop=NET_BIND_SERVICE \
--cap-drop=SYS_CHROOT --cap-drop=AUDIT_WRITE debian /bin/bash
```

If you run your application from this shell, you can see where it fails to work as desired, and re-add the required capabilities. For example, you may need the capability to change file ownership, so you'll need to lose the dropping of the FOWNER capability in the preceding code to run your application:

```
$ docker run -ti --cap-drop=CHOWN --cap-drop=DAC_OVERRIDE \
--cap-drop=FSETID  --cap-drop=KILL --cap-drop=MKNOD \
--cap-drop=NET_RAW --cap-drop=SETGID --cap-drop=SETUID \
--cap-drop=SETFCAP --cap-drop=SETPCAP --cap-drop=NET_BIND_SERVICE \
--cap-drop=SYS_CHROOT --cap-drop=AUDIT_WRITE debian /bin/bash
```

DROP/ENABLE ALL CAPABILITIES If you want to enable or disable all capabilities, you can use all instead of a specific capability, such as docker run -ti --cap-drop=all ubuntu bash.

If you run a few basic commands in the bash shell, you'll see that it's quite usable. Your mileage may vary when running more complex applications, though.

ROOT IS STILL ROOT!   It's worth making clear that many of these capabilities relate to the root capabilities to affect other users' objects on the system, not root's own objects. A root user could still chown root's files on the host if they were host in the container and had access to the host's files through a volume mount, for example. Therefore, it's still worth ensuring that applications drop to a non-root user as soon as possible to protect the system, even if all these capabilities are switched off.

This ability to fine-tune the capabilities of your container means that using the `--privileged` flag to `docker run` should be unnecessary. Processes that require capabilities will be auditable and under the control of the administrator of the host.

TECHNIQUE 85   **HTTP auth on your Docker instance**

In technique 1 you saw how to open up access to your daemon to the network, and in technique 4 you saw how to snoop the Docker API using socat.

This technique combines those two: you'll be able to access your daemon remotely and view the responses. Access is restricted to those with a username/password combination, so it's slightly safer. As a bonus, you don't have to restart your Docker daemon to achieve it—start up a container daemon!

PROBLEM

You'd like basic authentication with network access available on your Docker daemon.

SOLUTION

Set up HTTP authentication.

DISCUSSION

In this technique we're going to show you how to share your Docker daemon with others in a temporary way. Figure 10.1 lays out the architecture.

DOCKER'S DEFAULT SETTING ASSUMED   This discussion assumes your Docker daemon is using Docker's default Unix socket method of access in /var/run/docker.sock.

The code in this technique is available at https://github.com/docker-in-practice/docker-authenticate. The following listing shows the contents of the Dockerfile in this repository, used to create the image for this technique.

Listing 10.1   Dockerfile used to create dockerinpractice/docker-authenticate image

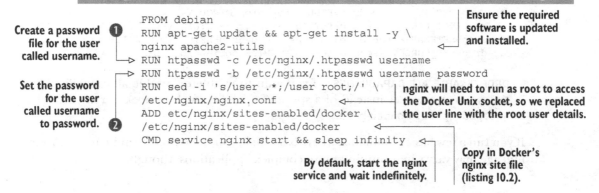

Create a password file for the user called username. ❶

Set the password for the user called username to password. ❷

```
FROM debian
RUN apt-get update && apt-get install -y \
nginx apache2-utils
RUN htpasswd -c /etc/nginx/.htpasswd username
RUN htpasswd -b /etc/nginx/.htpasswd username password
RUN sed -i 's/user .*;/user root;/' \
/etc/nginx/nginx.conf
ADD etc/nginx/sites-enabled/docker \
/etc/nginx/sites-enabled/docker
CMD service nginx start && sleep infinity
```

Ensure the required software is updated and installed.

nginx will need to run as root to access the Docker Unix socket, so we replaced the user line with the root user details.

By default, start the nginx service and wait indefinitely.

Copy in Docker's nginx site file (listing 10.2).

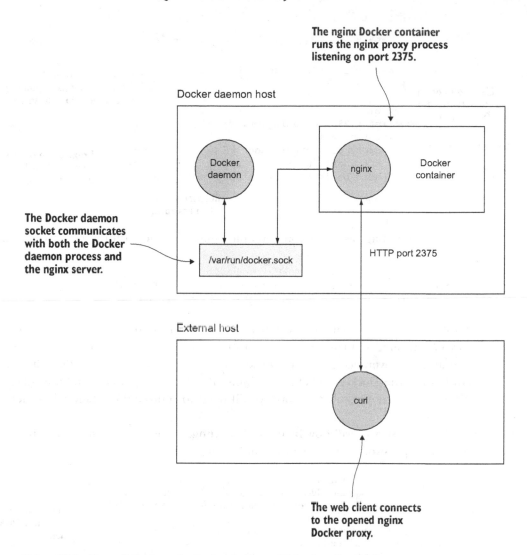

Figure 10.1   The architecture of a Docker daemon with basic authentication

The password file set up in ❶ and ❷ contains the credentials to be checked before allowing (or rejecting) access to the Docker socket. If you're building this image yourself, you'll probably want to alter username and password in those two steps to customize the credentials with access to the Docker socket.

> **KEEP THIS IMAGE PRIVATE**   Be careful not to share this image, as it will contain the password you've set!

The nginx site file for Docker is shown in the following listing.

Listing 10.2 /etc/nginx/sites-enabled/docker

```
upstream docker {
  server unix:/var/run/docker.sock;
}

server {
  listen 2375 default_server;
  location / {
    proxy_pass http://docker;
    auth_basic_user_file /etc/nginx/.htpasswd;
    auth_basic "Access restricted";
  }
}
```

Define the "docker" location in nginx as pointing to Docker's domain socket.

Listen on port 2375 (the standard Docker port).

Define the password file to use.

Proxy these requests to and from the "docker" location defined earlier.

Restrict access by password.

Now run the image as a daemon container, mapping the required resources from the host machine:

```
$ docker run -d --name docker-authenticate -p 2375:2375 \
  -v /var/run:/var/run dockerinpractice/docker-authenticate
```

This will run the container in the background with the name `docker-authenticate` so you can refer to it later. Port 2375 of the container is exposed on the host, and the container is given access to the Docker daemon by mounting the default directory containing the Docker socket as a volume. If you're using a custom-built image with your own username and password, you'll need to replace the image name here with your own.

The web service will now be up and running. If you curl the service with the username and password you set, you should see an API response:

Put the username:password in the URL to curl, and the address after the @ sign. This request is to the /info endpoint of the Docker daemon's API.

The JSON response from the Docker daemon

```
$ curl http://username:password@localhost:2375/info
{"Containers":115,"Debug":0,
 "DockerRootDir":"/var/lib/docker","Driver":"aufs",
 "DriverStatus":[["Root Dir","/var/lib/docker/aufs"],
 ["Backing Filesystem","extfs"],["Dirs","1033"]],
 "ExecutionDriver":"native-0.2",
 "ID":"QSCJ:NLPA:CRS7:WCOI:K23J:6Y2V:G35M:BF55:OA2W:MV3E:RG47:DG23",
 "IPv4Forwarding":1,"Images":792,
 "IndexServerAddress":"https://index.docker.io/v1/",
 "InitPath":"/usr/bin/docker","InitSha1":"",
 "KernelVersion":"3.13.0-45-generic",
 "Labels":null,"MemTotal":5939630080,"MemoryLimit":1,
 "NCPU":4,"NEventsListener":0,"NFd":31,"NGoroutines":30,
 "Name":"rothko","OperatingSystem":"Ubuntu 14.04.2 LTS",
 "RegistryConfig":{"IndexConfigs":{"docker.io":
 {"Mirrors":null,"Name":"docker.io",
 "Official":true,"Secure":true}},
 "InsecureRegistryCIDRs":["127.0.0.0/8"]},"SwapLimit":0}
```

When you're done, remove the container with this command:

```
$ docker rm -f docker-authenticate
```

Access is now revoked!

USING THE DOCKER COMMAND?

Readers may be wondering whether other users will be able to connect with the docker command—for example, with something like this:

```
docker -H tcp://username:password@localhost:2375 ps
```

At the time of writing, authentication functionality is not built into Docker itself. But we have created an image that will handle the authentication and allow Docker to connect to a daemon. Simply use the image as follows:

```
$ docker run -d --name docker-authenticate-client \
  -p 127.0.0.1:12375:12375 \
  dockerinpractice/docker-authenticate-client \
  192.168.1.74:2375 username:password
```

Expose a port to connect a Docker daemon to, but only for connections from the local machine

Run the client container in the background and give it a name

The image we've made to allow authenticated connections with Docker

The two arguments to the image (a specification of where the other end of the authenticated connection should be, and the username and password) should be replaced as appropriate for your setup.

Note that `localhost` or `127.0.0.1` will not work for specifying the other end of the authenticated connection—if you want to try it out on one host, you must use `ip addr` to identify an external IP address of your machine.

You can now use the authenticated connection with the following command:

```
docker -H localhost:12375 ps
```

Be aware that interactive Docker commands (`run` and `exec` with the `-i` argument) won't work over this connection due to some implementation limitations.

> **DON'T RELY ON THIS FOR SECURITY**   This gives you a basic level of *authentication*, but it doesn't give you a serious level of *security* (in particular, someone able to listen to your network traffic could intercept your username and password). Setting up a server secured with TLS is rather more involved and is covered in the next technique.

TECHNIQUE 86   **Securing your Docker API**

In this technique we'll show how you can open up your Docker server to others over a TCP port while at the same time ensuring that only trusted clients can connect. This is achieved by creating a secret key that only trusted hosts will be given. As long as that trusted key remains a secret between the server and client machines, the Docker server should remain secure.

PROBLEM

You want your Docker API to be served securely over a port.

SOLUTION

Create a self-signed certificate and run the Docker daemon with the `--tls-verify` flag.

DISCUSSION

This method of security depends on so-called *key files* being created on the server. These files are created using special tools that ensure they are difficult to duplicate if you don't have the *server key.* Figure 10.2 gives an overview of this how this works.

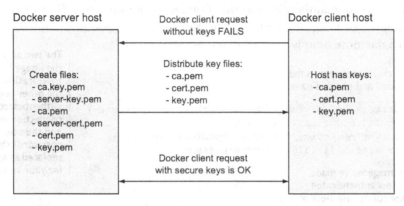

Figure 10.2   Key setup and distribution

WHAT ARE SERVER AND CLIENT KEYS?   The *server key* is a file that holds a secret number known only to the server, and which is required to read messages encrypted with the secret key files given out by the owner of the server (the so-called *client keys*). Once the keys have been created and distributed, they can be used to make the connection between client and server secure.

SETTING UP THE DOCKER SERVER CERTIFICATE

First you create the certificates and keys. Generating keys requires the OpenSSL package. Check whether it's installed by running `openssl` in a terminal. If it's not installed, you'll need to install it before generating the certificates and keys with the following code:

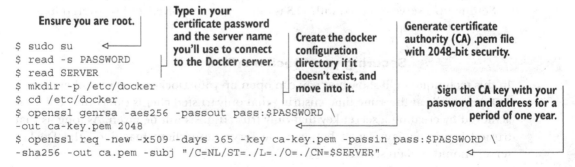

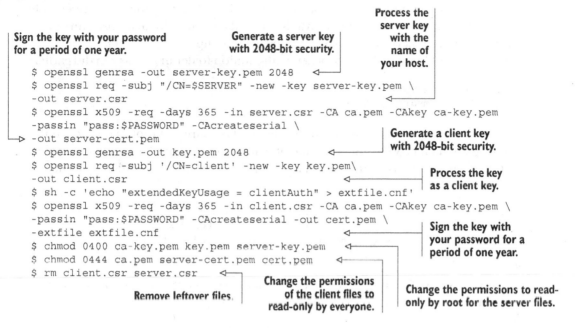

Sign the key with your password for a period of one year.

Generate a server key with 2048-bit security.

Process the server key with the name of your host.

```
$ openssl genrsa -out server-key.pem 2048
$ openssl req -subj "/CN=$SERVER" -new -key server-key.pem \
-out server.csr
$ openssl x509 -req -days 365 -in server.csr -CA ca.pem -CAkey ca-key.pem
-passin "pass:$PASSWORD" -CAcreateserial \
-out server-cert.pem
$ openssl genrsa -out key.pem 2048
$ openssl req -subj '/CN=client' -new -key key.pem\
-out client.csr
$ sh -c 'echo "extendedKeyUsage = clientAuth" > extfile.cnf'
$ openssl x509 -req -days 365 -in client.csr -CA ca.pem -CAkey ca-key.pem \
-passin "pass:$PASSWORD" -CAcreateserial -out cert.pem \
-extfile extfile.cnf
$ chmod 0400 ca-key.pem key.pem server-key.pem
$ chmod 0444 ca.pem server-cert.pem cert.pem
$ rm client.csr server.csr
```

Generate a client key with 2048-bit security.

Process the key as a client key.

Sign the key with your password for a period of one year.

Remove leftover files.

Change the permissions of the client files to read-only by everyone.

Change the permissions to read-only by root for the server files.

HELPER FUNCTIONS A script called CA.pl may be installed on your system that makes this process simpler. Here we've exposed the raw `openssl` commands because they're more instructive.

SETTING UP THE DOCKER SERVER

Next you need to set the Docker opts in your Docker daemon config file to specify which keys are used to encrypt the communications (see appendix B for advice on how to configure and restart your Docker daemon):

Specify the CA file for the Docker server.

Specify the private key used by the server.

Open the Docker daemon locally via a Unix socket in the normal way.

```
DOCKER_OPTS="$DOCKER_OPTS --tlsverify"
DOCKER_OPTS="$DOCKER_OPTS \
--tlscacert=/etc/docker/ca.pem"
DOCKER_OPTS="$DOCKER_OPTS \
--tlscert=/etc/docker/server-cert.pem"
DOCKER_OPTS="$DOCKER_OPTS \
--tlskey=/etc/docker/server-key.pem"
DOCKER_OPTS="$DOCKER_OPTS -H tcp://0.0.0.0:2376"
DOCKER_OPTS="$DOCKER_OPTS \
-H unix:///var/run/docker.sock"
```

Tell the Docker daemon that you want to use TLS security to secure connections to it.

Specify the certificate for the server.

Open the Docker daemon to external clients over TCP on port 2376.

DISTRIBUTING CLIENT KEYS

Next you need to send the keys to the client host so it can connect to the server and exchange information. You don't want to reveal your secret keys to anyone else, so this needs to be passed to the client securely. A relatively safe way to do this is to SCP (secure copy) them direct from the server to the client. The SCP utility uses essentially the same technique to secure the transmission of data that we're demonstrating here, only with different keys that will have already been set up.

On the client host, create the Docker configuration folder in /etc as you did earlier:

```
user@client:~$ sudo su
root@client:~$ mkdir -p /etc/docker
```

Then SCP the files from the server to the client. Make sure you replace `client` in the following commands with the hostname of your client machine. Also make sure that all the files are readable by the user that will run the `docker` command on the client.

```
user@server:~$ sudo su
root@server:~$ scp /etc/docker/ca.pem client:/etc/docker
root@server:~$ scp /etc/docker/cert.pem client:/etc/docker
root@server:~$ scp /etc/docker/key.pem client:/etc/docker
```

TESTING

To test your setup, first try making a request to the Docker server without any credentials. You should be rejected:

```
root@client~: docker -H myserver.localdomain:2376 info
FATA[0000] Get http://myserver.localdomain:2376/v1.17/info: malformed HTTP
➥ response "\x15\x03\x01\x00\x02\x02". Are you trying to connect to a
➥ TLS-enabled daemon without TLS?
```

Then connect with the credentials, which should return useful output:

```
root@client~: docker --tlsverify --tlscacert=/etc/docker/ca.pem \
--tlscert=/etc/docker/cert.pem --tlskey=/etc/docker/key.pem \
-H myserver.localdomain:2376 info
243 info
Containers: 3
Images: 86
Storage Driver: aufs
 Root Dir: /var/lib/docker/aufs
 Backing Filesystem: extfs
 Dirs: 92
Execution Driver: native-0.2
Kernel Version: 3.16.0-34-generic
Operating System: Ubuntu 14.04.2 LTS
CPUs: 4
Total Memory: 11.44 GiB
Name: rothko
ID: 4YQA:KK65:FXON:YVLT:BVVH:Y3KC:UATJ:I4GK:S3E2:UTA6:R43U:DX5T
WARNING: No swap limit support
```

This technique gives you the best of both worlds—a Docker daemon open to others to use, and one that's only accessible to trusted users. Make sure you keep those keys safe!

10.3   Security from outside Docker

Security on your host doesn't stop with the docker command. In this section you're going to see two other approaches to securing your Docker containers, this time from outside Docker.

The first approach demonstrates the application platform as a service (aPaaS) approach, which ensures Docker runs within a straightjacket set up and controlled by the administrator. As an example, we'll run an OpenShift Origin server (an aPaaS that deploys Docker containers in a managed way) using Docker commands. You'll see that the end user's powers can be limited and managed by the administrator, and access to the Docker runtime can be removed.

The second approach goes beyond this level of security to further limit the freedoms available within running containers using SELinux, a security technology that gives you fine-grained control over who can do what.

> **WHAT IS SELINUX?**   SELinux is a tool built and open-sourced by the United States' National Security Agency (NSA) that fulfils their need for strong access control. It has been a security standard for some time now, and it's very powerful. Unfortunately, many people simply switch it off when they encounter problems with it, rather than take the time to understand it. We hope the technique shown here will help make that approach less tempting.

TECHNIQUE 87   OpenShift—an application platform as a service

OpenShift is a product managed by Red Hat that allows an organization to run an application platform as a service (aPaas) and offer application development teams a platform on which to run code without needing to be concerned about hardware details. Version 3 of the product was a ground-up rewrite in Go, with Docker as the container technology and Kubernetes and etcd for orchestration. On top of this, Red Hat has added enterprise features that enable it to be more easily deployed in a corporate and security-focused environment.

Although OpenShift has many features we could cover, here we'll use it as a means of managing security by taking away the user's ability to run Docker directly, but retaining the benefits of using Docker.

OpenShift is available both as an enterprise-supported product and as an open source project called Origin, maintained at https://github.com/openshift/origin.

PROBLEM
You want to manage the security risk of untrusted users invoking docker run.

SOLUTION
Use an application platform as a service (aPaaS) tool like OpenShift.

DISCUSSION
An aPaaS has many benefits, but the one we'll focus on here is its ability to manage user permissions and run Docker containers on the user's behalf, providing a secure audit point for users running Docker containers.

Why is this important? The users using this aPaaS have no direct access to the `docker` command, so they can't do any damage without subverting the security that OpenShift provides. For example, containers are deployed by non-root users by default, and overcoming this requires permission to be granted by an administrator. If you can't trust your users, using an aPaaS is a effective way of giving them access to Docker.

> **WHAT IS AN APAAS?**   An aPaaS provides users with the ability to spin up applications on demand for development, testing, or production. Docker is a natural fit for these services, as it provides a reliable and isolated application delivery format, allowing an operations team to take care of the details of deployment.

In short, OpenShift builds on Kubernetes (see technique 79) but adds features to deliver a full-fledged aPaaS. These additional features include

- User management
- Permissioning
- Quotas
- Security contexts
- Routing

INSTALLING OPENSHIFT

A complete overview of OpenShift installation is beyond the scope of this book.

If you'd like an automated install using Vagrant that we maintain, see https://github.com/docker-in-practice/shutit-openshift-origin. If you need help installing Vagrant, see appendix C.

Other options, such as a Docker-only installation (single-node only), or a full manual build are available and documented on the OpenShift Origin codebase at https://github.com/openshift/origin.git.

> **WHAT IS OPENSHIFT ORIGIN?**   OpenShift Origin is the "upstream" version of OpenShift. Upstream means that it's the codebase from which RedHat takes changes for OpenShift, its supported offering. Origin is open source and can be used and contributed to by anyone, but RedHat's curated version of it is sold and supported as "OpenShift." An upstream version is usually more cutting edge but less stable.

AN OPENSHIFT APPLICATION

In this technique we're going to show a simple example of creating, building, running, and accessing an application using the OpenShift web interface. The application will be a basic NodeJS application that serves a simple web page.

The application will use Docker, Kubernetes, and S2I under the hood. Docker is used to encapsulate the build and deployment environments. The Source to Image (S2I) build method from technique 48 is used to build the Docker container, and Kubernetes is used to run the application on the OpenShift cluster.

LOGGING IN

To get started, run `./run.sh` from the shutit-openshift-origin folder, and then navigate to https://localhost:8443, bypassing all the security warnings. You'll see the login

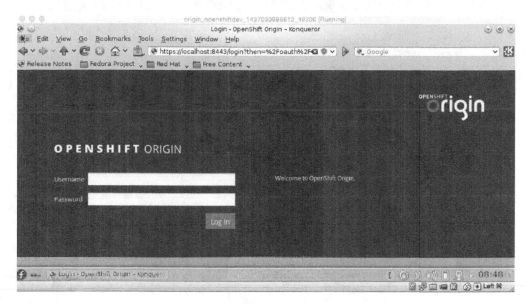

Figure 10.3   The OpenShift login page

page shown in figure 10.3. Note that if you're using the Vagrant install, you'll need to start up a web browser in your VM. (See Appendix C for help on getting a GUI with your VM.)

Log in as `hal-1` with any password.

BUILDING A NODEJS APP

You're now logged into OpenShift as a developer (see figure 10.4).

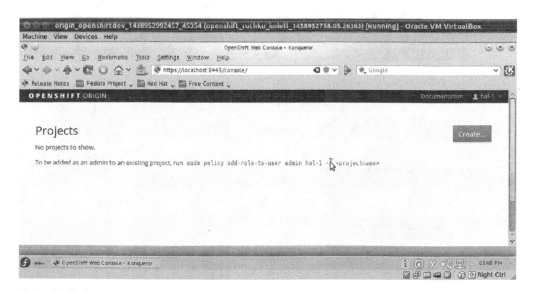

Figure 10.4   The OpenShift projects page

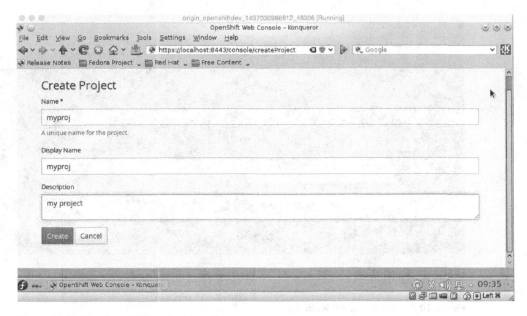

Figure 10.5   The OpenShift project creation page

Create a project by clicking Create. Fill out the form, as shown in figure 10.5. Then click Create again.

Once the project is set up, click on Create again and input the suggested GitHub repo (https://github.com/openshift/nodejs-ex), as shown in figure 10.6.

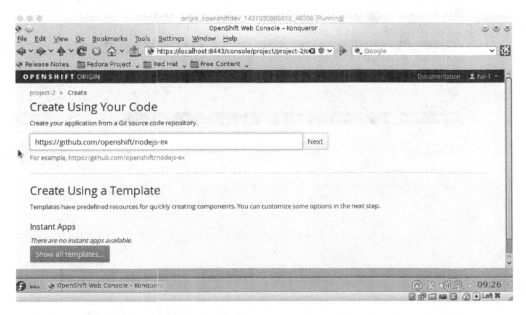

Figure 10.6   The OpenShift project source page

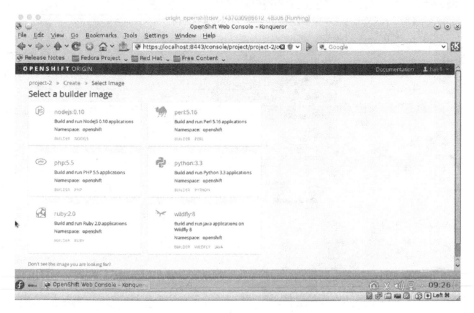

Figure 10.7   The OpenShift builder image selection page

Click Next, and you'll be given a choice of builder images, as shown in figure 10.7. The build image defines the context in which the code will be built. Choose the NodeJS builder image.

Now fill out the form, as shown in figure 10.8. Click Create on NodeJS at the bottom of the page as you scroll down the form.

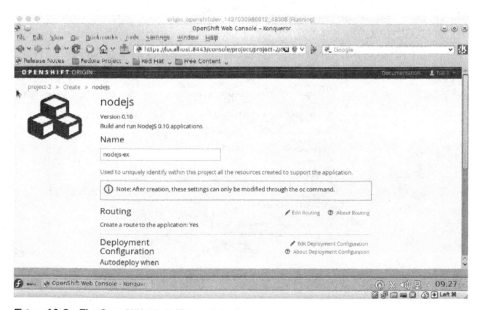

Figure 10.8   The OpenShift NodeJS template form

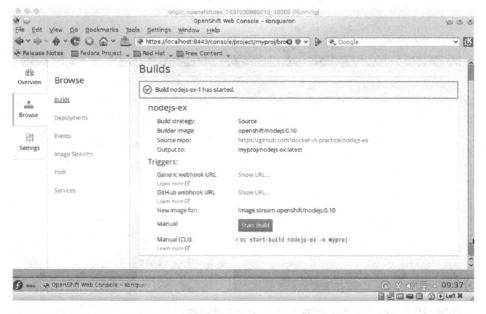

Figure 10.9   The OpenShift build started page

After a few minutes, you should see a screen like the one in figure 10.9.

In a few moments, if you scroll down, you'll see that the build has started, as shown in figure 10.10.

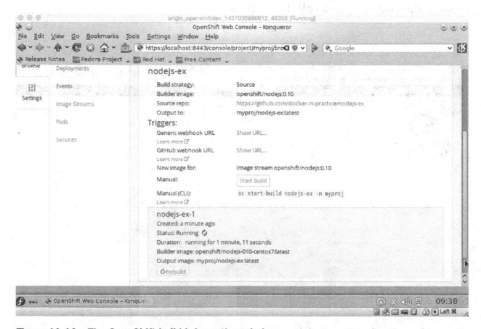

Figure 10.10   The OpenShift build information window

BUILD NOT STARTING? In early versions of OpenShift, the build would some-times not begin automatically. If this is the case, click the Start Build button after a few minutes.

After some time you'll see that the app is running, as in figure 10.11.

By clicking Browse and Pods, you can see that the pod has been deployed, as in fig-ure 10.12.

WHAT IS A POD? See technique 79 for an explanation of what a pod is.

How do you access your pod? If you look at the Services tab (see figure 10.13), you'll see an IP address and port number to access.

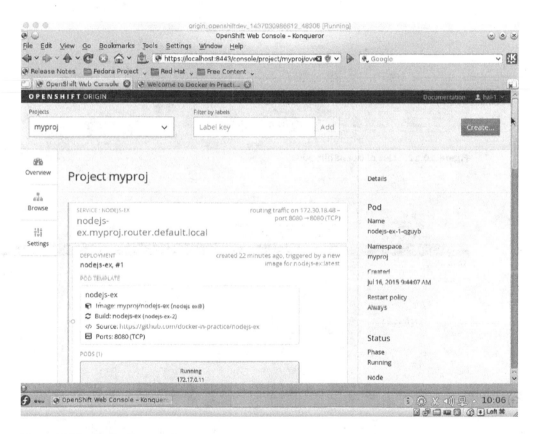

Figure 10.11 Application running page

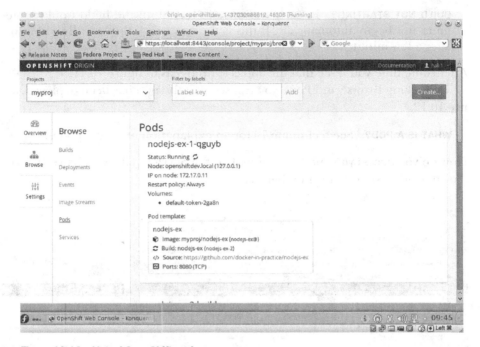

Figure 10.12   List of OpenShift pods

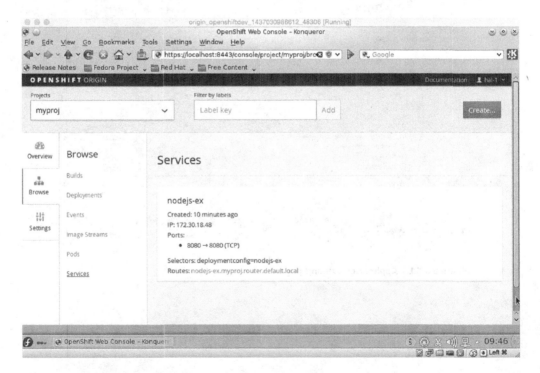

Figure 10.13   The OpenShift NodeJS application service details

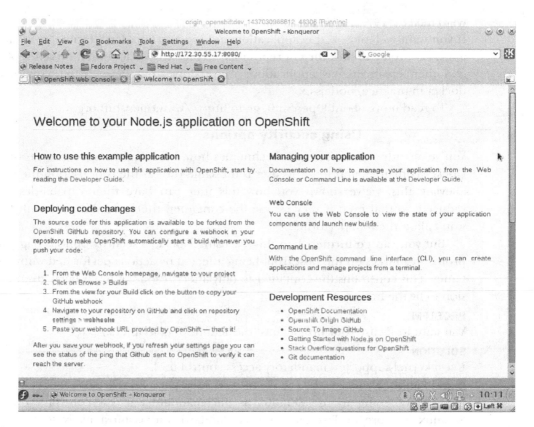

Figure 10.14 The NodeJS application landing page

Point your browser at that address, and voila, you'll have your NodeJS app, as in figure 10.14.

RECAP

Let's recap what we've achieved here, and why it's important for security.

From the point of view of the user, they logged into a web application and deployed an application using Docker-based technologies without going near a Dockerfile or the `docker run` command.

The administrator of OpenShift can

- Control user access
- Limit resource usage by project
- Provision resources centrally
- Ensure code is run with non-privileged status by default

This is far more secure than giving users direct access to `docker run`!

WHAT NEXT?

If you want to build on this application and see how an aPaaS facilitates an iterative approach, you can fork the Git repository, change the code in that forked repository, and then create a new application. We've done that here: https://github.com/docker-in-practice/nodejs-ex.

To read more about OpenShift, go to http://www.openshift.org.

TECHNIQUE 88   Using security options

You've already seen in previous techniques how, by default, you're given root in the Docker container, and that this user is the same root as the root user on the host. To alleviate this, we've shown you how this user can have their capabilities as root reduced, so that even if they escape the container, there are still actions the kernel won't allow them to perform.

But you can go further than this. By using Docker's security options flag you can protect resources on the host from being affected by actions performed within a container. This constrains the container to only affect resources it has been given permission to by the host.

PROBLEM

You want to secure your host against the actions of containers.

SOLUTION

Use a kernel-supported mandatory access control tool.

DISCUSSION

Here we're going to use SELinux as our mandatory access control (MAC) tool. SELinux is more or less the industry standard and is most likely to be used by organizations that particularly care about security. It was originally developed by the NSA to protect their systems and was subsequently open-sourced. It's used in Red Hat-based systems as a standard.

SELinux is a big subject, so we can't cover it in depth in this book. We're going to show you how to write and enforce a simple policy so that you can get a feel for how it works. You can take things further and experiment if you need to.

> **WHAT IS A MAC TOOL?** Mandatory access control (MAC) tools in Linux enforce security rules beyond the standard ones you may be used to. Put briefly, they ensure that not only are the normal rules of read-write-execute on files and processes enforced, but more fine-grained rules can be applied to processes at the kernel level. For example, a MySQL process may only be allowed to write files under specific directories, such as /var/lib/mysql. The equivalent standard for Debian-based systems is AppArmor.

This technique assumes you have an SELinux-enabled host. This means you must first install SELinux (assuming it's not already installed). If you're running Fedora or some other Red Hat-based system, you are likely to have it already.

To determine whether you have SELinux enabled, run the command `sestatus`:

```
# sestatus
SELinux status:                enabled
SELinuxfs mount:               /sys/fs/selinux
SELinux root directory:        /etc/selinux
Loaded policy name:            targeted
Current mode:                  permissive
Mode from config file:         permissive
Policy MLS status:             enabled
Policy deny_unknown status:    allowed
Max kernel policy version:     28
```

The first line of the output will tell you whether SELinux is enabled. If the command is not available, then you don't have SELinux installed on your host.

You'll also need to have the relevant SELinux policy-creation tools available. On a yum-capable machine, for example, you'll need to run yum -y install selinux-policy-devel.

SELINUX ON A VAGRANT MACHINE

If you don't have SELinux and want it to be built for you, you can use a ShutIt script to build a VM inside your host machine, with Docker and SELinux preinstalled. What it does is explained at a high level in figure 10.15.

> **WHAT IS SHUTIT?** ShutIt is a generic shell automation tool that we created to overcome some limitations of Dockerfiles. If you want to read more about it, see the GitHub page: http://ianmiell.github.io/shutit.

Figure 10.15 lists the steps required to get a policy set up. The script will do the following:

1 Set up VirtualBox
2 Start an appropriate Vagrant image
3 Log into the VM
4 Ensure the state of SELinux is correct
5 Install the latest version of Docker
6 Install the SELinux policy development tools
7 Give you a shell

Linux host machine

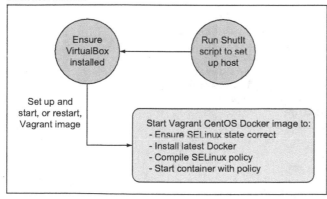

Figure 10.15 Script to provision an SELinux VM

Here are the commands to set up and run it (tested on Debian and Red Hat-based distributions):

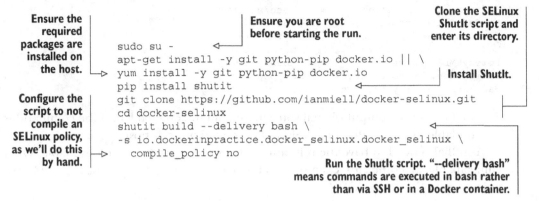

After running this script, you should eventually see output like this:

```
Pause point:
Have a shell:
You can now type in commands and alter the state of the target.
Hit return to see the prompt
Hit CTRL and ] at the same time to continue with build

Hit CTRL and u to save the state
```

You now have a shell running inside a VM with SELinux on it. If you type `sestatus`, you'll see that SELinux is enabled in permissive mode (as shown in listing 10.3). To return to your host's shell, press Ctrl-].

COMPILING AN SELINUX POLICY

Whether you used the ShutIt script or not, we assume you now have a host with SELinux enabled. Type `sestatus` to get a status summary (as shown in the next listing).

Listing 10.3   SELinux status summary

```
# sestatus
SELinux status:                 enabled
SELinuxfs mount:                /sys/fs/selinux
SELinux root directory:         /etc/selinux
Loaded policy name:             targeted
Current mode:                   permissive
Mode from config file:          permissive
Policy MLS status:              enabled
Policy deny_unknown status:     allowed
Max kernel policy version:      28
```

In this case we're in permissive mode, which means that SELinux is recording violations of security in logs, but isn't enforcing them. This is good for safely testing new policies without rendering your system unusable. To move your SELinux status to permissive, type `setenforce Permissive` as root. If you can't do this on your host for security reasons, don't worry; there's an option to set the policy as permissive outlined in listing 10.4.

> **SET –SELINUX-ENABLED ON THE DAEMON** If you're installing SELinux and Docker yourself on a host, ensure that the Docker daemon has `--selinux-enabled` set as a flag. You can check this with `ps -ef | grep 'docker -d.*--selinux-enabled`, which should return a matching process on the output.

Create a folder for your policy and move to it. Then create a policy file with the following content as root, named dockcr_apache.te. This policy file contains a policy we'll try to apply.

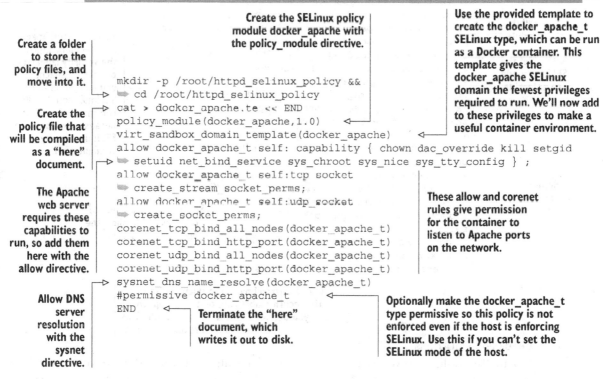

Listing 10.4   Creating an SELinux policy

Create a folder to store the policy files, and move into it.

Create the policy file that will be compiled as a "here" document.

The Apache web server requires these capabilities to run, so add them here with the allow directive.

Allow DNS server resolution with the sysnet directive.

Create the SELinux policy module docker_apache with the policy_module directive.

```
mkdir -p /root/httpd_selinux_policy &&
  cd /root/httpd_selinux_policy
cat > docker_apache.te << END
policy_module(docker_apache,1.0)
virt_sandbox_domain_template(docker_apache)
allow docker_apache_t self: capability { chown dac_override kill setgid
  setuid net_bind_service sys_chroot sys_nice sys_tty_config } ;
allow docker_apache_t self:tcp socket
  create_stream socket_perms;
allow docker_apache_t self:udp_socket
  create_socket_perms;
corenet_tcp_bind_all_nodes(docker_apache_t)
corenet_tcp_bind_http_port(docker_apache_t)
corenet_udp_bind_all_nodes(docker_apache_t)
corenet_udp_bind_http_port(docker_apache_t)
sysnet_dns_name_resolve(docker_apache_t)
#permissive docker_apache_t
END
```

Use the provided template to create the docker_apache_t SELinux type, which can be run as a Docker container. This template gives the docker_apache SELinux domain the fewest privileges required to run. We'll now add to these privileges to make a useful container environment.

These allow and corenet rules give permission for the container to listen to Apache ports on the network.

Terminate the "here" document, which writes it out to disk.

Optionally make the docker_apache_t type permissive so this policy is not enforced even if the host is enforcing SELinux. Use this if you can't set the SELinux mode of the host.

SELINUX POLICY DOCUMENTATION For more information on the preceding permissions, and to explore others, you can install the selinux-policy-doc package, and then use a browser to browse the documentation on file:///usr/share/doc/selinux-policy-doc/html/index.html. The docs are also available online at http://mcs.une.edu.au/doc/selinux-policy/html/templates.html.

Now you're going to compile your policy and see your application fail to start against this policy in enforcing mode. Then you'll restart it in permissive mode to check the violations and correct it later:

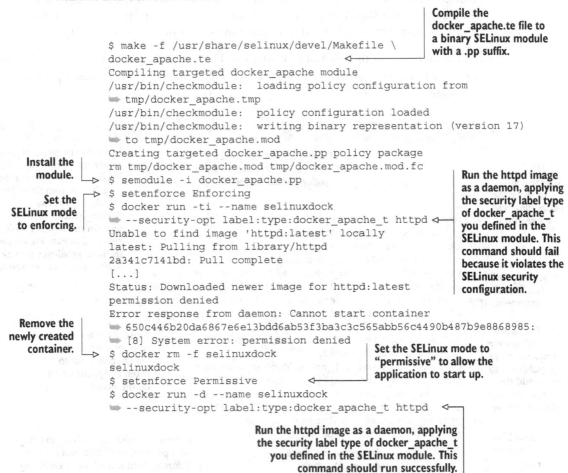

Compile the docker_apache.te file to a binary SELinux module with a .pp suffix.

```
$ make -f /usr/share/selinux/devel/Makefile \
docker_apache.te
Compiling targeted docker_apache module
/usr/bin/checkmodule:  loading policy configuration from
➥ tmp/docker_apache.tmp
/usr/bin/checkmodule:  policy configuration loaded
/usr/bin/checkmodule:  writing binary representation (version 17)
➥ to tmp/docker_apache.mod
Creating targeted docker_apache.pp policy package
rm tmp/docker_apache.mod tmp/docker_apache.mod.fc
$ semodule -i docker_apache.pp
$ setenforce Enforcing
$ docker run -ti --name selinuxdock
➥ --security-opt label:type:docker_apache_t httpd
Unable to find image 'httpd:latest' locally
latest: Pulling from library/httpd
2a341c7141bd: Pull complete
[...]
Status: Downloaded newer image for httpd:latest
permission denied
Error response from daemon: Cannot start container
➥ 650c446b20da6867e6e13bdd6ab53f3ba3c3c565abb56c4490b487b9e8868985:
➥ [8] System error: permission denied
$ docker rm -f selinuxdock
selinuxdock
$ setenforce Permissive
$ docker run -d --name selinuxdock
➥ --security-opt label:type:docker_apache_t httpd
```

Install the module.

Set the SELinux mode to enforcing.

Run the httpd image as a daemon, applying the security label type of docker_apache_t you defined in the SELinux module. This command should fail because it violates the SELinux security configuration.

Remove the newly created container.

Set the SELinux mode to "permissive" to allow the application to start up.

Run the httpd image as a daemon, applying the security label type of docker_apache_t you defined in the SELinux module. This command should run successfully.

CHECK FOR VIOLATIONS

Up to this point you've created an SELinux module and applied it to your host. Because the enforcement mode of SELinux is set to permissive on this host, actions that would be disallowed in enforcing mode are allowed with a log line in the audit log. You can check these messages by running the following command:

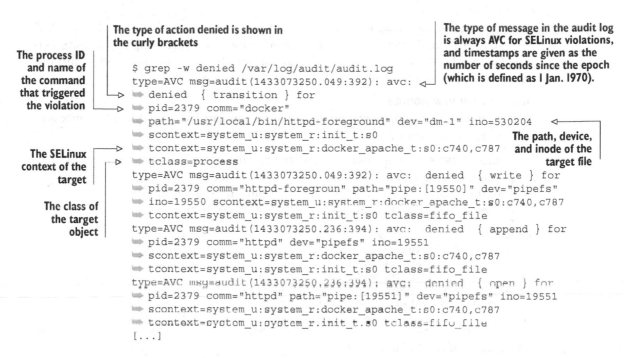

The type of action denied is shown in
the curly brackets

The process ID
and name of
the command
that triggered
the violation

The type of message in the audit log
is always AVC for SELinux violations,
and timestamps are given as the
number of seconds since the epoch
(which is defined as 1 Jan. 1970).

The SELinux
context of the
target

The class of
the target
object

The path, device,
and inode of the
target file

```
$ grep -w denied /var/log/audit/audit.log
type=AVC msg=audit(1433073250.049:392): avc:
denied { transition } for
pid=2379 comm="docker"
path="/usr/local/bin/httpd-foreground" dev="dm-1" ino=530204
scontext=system_u:system_r:init_t:s0
tcontext=system_u:system_r:docker_apache_t:s0:c740,c787
tclass=process
type=AVC msg=audit(1433073250.049:392): avc:  denied { write } for
pid=2379 comm="httpd-foregroun" path="pipe:[19550]" dev="pipefs"
ino=19550 scontext=system_u:system_r:docker_apache_t:s0:c740,c787
tcontext=system_u:system_r:init_t:s0 tclass=fifo_file
type=AVC msg=audit(1433073250.236:394): avc:  denied { append } for
pid=2379 comm="httpd" dev="pipefs" ino=19551
scontext=system_u:system_r:docker_apache_t:s0:c740,c787
tcontext=system_u:system_r:init_t:s0 tclass=fifo_file
type=AVC msg=audit(1433073250.236:394): avc:  denied { open } for
pid=2379 comm="httpd" path="pipe:[19551]" dev="pipefs" ino=19551
scontext=system_u:system_r:docker_apache_t:s0:c740,c787
tcontext=system_u:system_r:init_t:s0 tclass=fifo_file
[...]
```

Phew! There's a lot of jargon there, and we don't have time to teach you everything
you might need to know about SELinux. If you want to find out more, a good place to
start is with Red Hat's SELinux documentation: http://mng.bz/QyFh.

For now, you need to check that the violations are nothing untoward. What might
look untoward? If an application tries to open a port you didn't expect or a file you
didn't expect it to, then you might think twice about doing what we're going show you
next: patch these violations with a new SELinux module.

In this case, we're happy that the httpd can write pipes. We've worked out that this
is what SELinux was preventing from doing because the "denied" actions mentioned
are append, write, and open for pipefs files on the VM.

PATCHING SELINUX VIOLATIONS

Once you've decided that the violations you've seen are acceptable, there are tools
that can automatically generate the policy file you need to apply, so you don't need to
go through the pain and risk of writing one yourself. The following example uses the
audit2allow tool to achieve this:

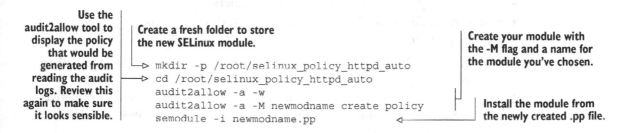

Use the
audit2allow tool to
display the policy
that would be
generated from
reading the audit
logs. Review this
again to make sure
it looks sensible.

Create a fresh folder to store
the new SELinux module.

Create your module with
the -M flag and a name for
the module you've chosen.

Install the module from
the newly created .pp file.

```
mkdir -p /root/selinux_policy_httpd_auto
cd /root/selinux_policy_httpd_auto
audit2allow -a -w
audit2allow -a -M newmodname create policy
semodule -i newmodname.pp
```

It's important to understand that this new SELinux module we've created "includes" (or "requires") and alters the one we created before by referencing and adding permissions to the docker_apache_t type. Combining the two into a complete and discrete policy in a single .te file is left as an exercise for the reader.

TESTING YOUR NEW MODULE

Now that you have your new module installed, you can try re-enabling SELinux and restarting the container.

> **COULDN'T SET ENFORCE MODE TO PERMISSIVE?**   If you couldn't set your host to permissive earlier (and you added the hashed-out line to your original docker _apache.te file), then recompile and reinstall the original docker_apache.te file (with the permissive line hashed-out) before continuing.

```
docker rm -f selinuxdock
setenforce Enforcing
docker run -d --name selinuxdock \
--security-opt label:type:docker_apache_t httpd
docker logs selinuxdock
grep -w denied /var/log/audit/audit.log
```

There should be no new errors in the audit log. Your application has started within the context of this SELinux regime.

SELinux has a reputation for being complex and hard to manage, with the most frequently heard complaint being that it's more often switched off than debugged. That's hardly secure at all. Although the finer points of SELinux do require serious effort to master, we hope this technique has shown you how to create something that a security expert can review—and ideally sign off on—if Docker isn't acceptable out of the box.

10.4   *Summary*

In this chapter we've approached the problem of security in Docker from various angles. We've covered the basic concerns with respect to security in Docker and shown ways of approaching them. What you'll need or want depends on the nature of your organization and how much you trust your users.

This chapter covered

- Reducing the danger of containers running as root with SELinux
- Authenticating the users of your Docker API over HTTP
- Encrypting your Docker API using certificates
- Limiting the power of root within your containers
- Using an application platform as a service (aPaaS) to control access to the Docker runtime

You should now be fully aware of the security concerns Docker raises, and how they can be alleviated.

Next we're going to take Docker into production, and look at some of the areas you should consider when running Docker as part of your live operation.

Plain sailing—Docker in production and operational considerations

This chapter covers

- Options for logging container output
- How to monitor your running containers
- Managing your containers' resource usage
- Using Docker's capabilities to help manage traditional sysadmin tasks

In this chapter we're going to cover some of the subjects that come up when running in production. Running Docker in production is a big subject, and production use of Docker is still an evolving area. Many major tools are in the early stages of development and were changing as we wrote this book. For example, while we were writing this chapter, Kubernetes went to version 1.0 and a revamped Registry was released by Docker.

In this chapter we focus on showing you some of the key things you should consider when going from volatile environments to stable ones.

11.1 Monitoring

When you run Docker in production, one of the first things you'll want to consider is how to track and measure what your containers are up to. In this section you're going to learn how you can get an operational view of both your live containers' logging activity and their performance.

This is still a developing aspect of the Docker ecosystem, but some tools and techniques are emerging as more mainstream than others. We'll look at redirecting application logs to the host's syslog, at redirecting the output of the docker logs command to a single place, and at Google's container-oriented performance monitoring tool, cAdvisor.

TECHNIQUE 89   Logging your containers to the host's syslog

Linux distributions typically run a *syslog* daemon. This daemon is the server part of the system-logging functionality—applications send messages to this daemon, along with metadata like the importance of the message, and the daemon will decide where to save the message (if at all). This functionality is used by a range of applications, from network connection managers to the kernel itself dumping information if it encounters an error.

Because it's so reliable and widely used, it's reasonable for applications you write yourself to log to syslog. Unfortunately, this will stop working once you containerize your application (because there's no syslog daemon in containers, by default). If you do decide to start a syslog daemon in all of your containers, you'll need to go to each individual container to retrieve the logs.

PROBLEM

You want to capture syslogs centrally on your Docker host.

SOLUTION

Create a central syslog daemon container on your host, and bind-mount syslog to a central location.

DISCUSSION

The basic idea of this technique is to run a service container that runs a syslog daemon, and share the logging touchpoint (/dev/log) via the host's filesystem. The log itself can be retrieved by querying the syslog Docker container, and it's stored in a volume. Figure 11.1 illustrates this.

Figure 11.1 illustrates how /tmp/syslogdev on the host's filesystem is used as a touchpoint for all syslogging taking place on containers on the host. The logging containers mount and write their syslog to that location, and the syslogger container collates all those inputs.

> **WHAT IS THE SYSLOG DAEMON?**   The syslog daemon is a process that runs on a server, collecting and managing messages sent to a central file, which is normally a Unix domain socket. It generally uses /dev/log as a file to receive log messages on, and logs out to /var/log/syslog.

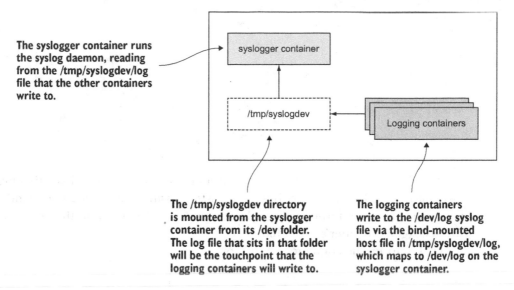

The syslogger container runs the syslog daemon, reading from the /tmp/syslogdev/log file that the other containers write to.

The /tmp/syslogdev directory is mounted from the syslogger container from its /dev folder. The log file that sits in that folder will be the touchpoint that the logging containers will write to.

The logging containers write to the /dev/log syslog file via the bind-mounted host file in /tmp/syslogdev/log, which maps to /dev/log on the syslogger container.

Figure 11.1 Overview of centralized syslogging of Docker containers

The syslogger container can be created with this straightforward Dockerfile:

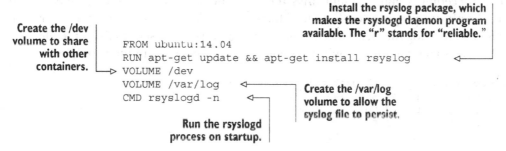

Create the /dev volume to share with other containers.

Install the rsyslog package, which makes the rsyslogd daemon program available. The "r" stands for "reliable."

```
FROM ubuntu:14.04
RUN apt-get update && apt-get install rsyslog
VOLUME /dev
VOLUME /var/log
CMD rsyslogd -n
```

Create the /var/log volume to allow the syslog file to persist.

Run the rsyslogd process on startup.

Next you build the container, tagging it with the syslogger tag, and run it:

```
docker build -t syslogger .
docker run --name syslogger -d -v /tmp/syslogdev:/dev syslogger
```

You bind-mounted the container's /dev folder to the host's /tmp/syslogdev folder so you can mount a /dev/log socket into each container as a volume, as you'll see shortly. The container will continue running in the background, reading any messages from the /dev/log file and handling them.

On the host, you'll now see that the /dev folder of the syslog container has been mounted to the host's /tmp/syslogdev folder:

```
$ ls -1 /tmp/syslogdev/
fd
full
fuse
```

```
kcore
log
null
ptmx
random
stderr
stdin
stdout
tty
urandom
zero
```

For this demonstration, you're going to start up 100 daemon containers that log their own starting order from 0 to 100 to the syslog, using the `logger` command. Then you'll be able to see those messages by running a `docker exec` on the host to look at the syslogger container's syslog file.

First, start up the containers:

```
for d in {1..100}
do
    docker run -d -v /tmp/syslogdev/log:/dev/log ubuntu logger hello_$d
done
```

The preceding volume mount links the container's syslog endpoint (/dev/log) to the host's /tmp/syslogdev/log file, which in turn is mapped to the syslogger container's /dev/log file. With this wiring, all syslog outputs are sent to the same file.

When that's complete, you'll see something similar to this (edited) output:

```
$ docker exec -ti syslogger tail -f /var/log/syslog
May 25 11:51:25 f4fb5d829699 logger: hello
May 25 11:55:15 f4fb5d829699 logger: hello_1
May 25 11:55:15 f4fb5d829699 logger: hello_2
May 25 11:55:16 f4fb5d829699 logger: hello_3
[...]
May 25 11:57:38 f4fb5d829699 logger: hello_97
May 25 11:57:38 f4fb5d829699 logger: hello_98
May 25 11:57:39 f4fb5d829699 logger: hello_99
```

You can use a modified `exec` command to archive these syslogs if you wish. For example, you could run the following command to get all logs for hour 11 on May 25th archived to a compressed file:

```
$ docker exec syslogger bash -c "cat /var/log/syslog | grep '^May 25 11'" | \
xz - > /var/log/archive/May25_11.log.xz
```

> **APPLICATIONS MUST LOG TO SYSLOG** For the messages to show up in the central syslog container, your programs need to log to syslog. We ensure this here by running the `logger` command, but your applications should do the same for this to work. Most modern logging methods have a means to write to the locally visible syslog.

You may be wondering how you can distinguish between different containers' log messages with this technique. You have a couple of options. You can change the application's logging to output the hostname of the container, or you can see the next
technique to have Docker do this heavy lifting for you.

> **SYSLOG DRIVERS ARE DIFFERENT!** This technique looks similar to the next one,
> which uses a Docker syslog driver, but is different. This technique keeps the
> output of containers' running processes as the output of the docker logs
> command, whereas the next one takes over the logs command, rendering
> this technique redundant.

TECHNIQUE 90 Sending Docker logs to your host's output system

As you've seen, Docker offers a basic logging system that captures the output of your
container's start command. If you're a system administrator running many services off
one host, it can be operationally tiresome to manually track and capture logs using
the docker logs command on each container in turn.

In this technique, we're going to cover Docker's log driver feature. This lets you
use the standard logging systems to track many services on a single (or even across
multiple) hosts.

PROBLEM
You want to capture docker logs output centrally on your Docker host.

SOLUTION
Set up a log driver to capture docker logs output elsewhere.

DISCUSSION
By default, Docker logs are captured within the Docker daemon, and you can access
these with the docker logs command. As you're probably aware, this shows you the
output of the container's main process.

At the time of writing, Docker gives you several choices for redirecting this output,
including

- syslog
- journald
- json-file

The default is json-file, but others can be chosen with the --log-driver command.
The syslog and journald options send the log output to their respective daemons of
the same name. You can find the official documentation on all available log drivers at
https://docs.docker.com/engine/reference/logging/.

> **VERSION DEPENDENCY** This technique requires Docker version 1.6.1 or
> higher.

The syslog daemon is a process that runs on a server, collecting and managing messages sent to a central file (normally a Unix domain socket). It generally uses /dev/
log as a file to receive log messages on, and logs out to /var/log/syslog.

Journald is a system service that collects and stores logging data. It creates and maintains a structured index of logs received from a variety of sources. The logs can be queried with the `journalctl` command.

LOGGING TO SYSLOG

To direct your output to the syslog, use the `--log-driver` flag:

```
$ docker run --log-driver=syslog ubuntu echo 'outputting to syslog'
outputting to syslog
```

This will record the output in the syslog file. If you have permission to access the file, you can examine the logs using standard Unix tools:

```
$ grep 'outputting to syslog' /var/log/syslog
Jun 23 20:37:50 myhost docker/6239418882b6[2559]: outputting to syslog
```

LOGGING TO JOURNALD

Outputting to a journal daemon looks similar:

```
$ docker run --log-driver=journald ubuntu echo 'outputting to journald'
outputting to syslog
$ journalctl | grep 'outputting to journald'
```

> **JOURNAL DAEMON RUNNING?** Ensure you have a journal daemon running on your host before running the preceding command.

APPLYING ACROSS ALL CONTAINERS

It can be laborious to apply this argument to all containers on your host, so you can change your Docker daemon to log by default to these supported mechanisms.

Change the daemon /etc/default/docker, or /etc/sysconfig/docker, or whichever Docker config file your distribution has set up, such that the `DOCKER_OPTS=""` line is activated and includes the log-driver flag. For example, if the line was

```
DOCKER_OPTS="--dns 8.8.8.8 --dns 8.8.4.4"
```

then change it to

```
DOCKER_OPTS="--dns 8.8.8.8 --dns 8.8.4.4 --log-driver syslog"
```

> **CONFIG CHANGES IN DOCKER** See appendix B for details on how to change the Docker daemon's configuration on your host.

If you restart your Docker daemon, containers should then log to the relevant service.

Another common choice (not covered here) worth mentioning in this context is that you can use containers to implement an ELK (Elasticsearch, Logstash, Kibana) logging infrastructure.

BREAKING THE DOCKER LOGS COMMAND Changing this daemon setting to anything other than `json-file` or `journald` will mean that the standard docker logs command will no longer work by default. Users of this Docker daemon may not appreciate this change, especially because the /var/log/syslog file (used by the `syslog` driver) is typically not accessible to non-root users.

TECHNIQUE 91 **Monitoring containers with cAdvisor**

Once you have a serious number of containers running in production, you'll want to be able to monitor their resource usage and performance exactly as you do when you have multiple processes running on a host.

The sphere of monitoring (both generally, and with respect to Docker) is a wide field with many candidates. cAdvisor has been chosen here as it's a popular choice. Open sourced by Google, it has quickly gained in popularity. If you already use a traditional host monitoring tool such as Zabbix or Sysdig, then it's worth seeing whether it already offers the functionality you need—many tools are adding container-aware functionality as we write.

PROBLEM

You want to monitor the performance of your containers.

SOLUTION

Use cAdvisor.

DISCUSSION

cAdvisor is a tool developed by Google for monitoring containers. It's open sourced on GitHub at https://github.com/google/cadvisor.

cAdvisor runs as a daemon that collects performance data on running containers. Among other things, it tracks

- Resource isolation parameters
- Historical resource usage
- Network statistics

cAdvisor can be installed natively on the host or run as a Docker container:

Give cAdvisor read-only access to the host's /sys folder, which contains information about the kernel subsystems and devices attached to the host.

Give cAdvisor read-only access to the root filesystem so it can track information about the host.

Mount the /var/run folder with read-write access. At most, one instance of cAdvisor is expected to run per host.

```
$ docker run \
--volume /:/rootfs:ro \
--volume /var/run:/var/run:rw \
--volume /sys:/sys:ro \
--volume /var/lib/docker/:/var/lib/docker:ro \
-p 8080:8080 -d --name cadvisor \
--restart on-failure:10 google/cadvisor
```

Give cAdvisor read-only access to Docker's host directory.

Restart the container on failure, up to a maximum of 10 times. The image is stored on the Docker Hub within Google's account.

cAdvisor's web interface is served on port 8080 of the container, and we publish it to the host on the same port. The standard Docker arguments to run the container in the background and give the container a name are also used.

Once you've started the image, you can visit: http://localhost:8080 with your browser to start examining the data output. There's information about the host, but by clicking on the Docker Containers link at the top of the homepage, you'll be able to examine graphs of CPU, memory, and other historical data by clicking on the running containers listed under the Subcontainers heading.

The data is collected and retained in memory while the container runs. There is documentation for persisting the data to an InfluxDB instance on the GitHub page. The GitHub repository also has details about the REST API and a sample client written in Go.

> **WHAT IS INFLUXDB?**   InfluxDB is an open source database designed to handle the tracking of time-series data. It's therefore ideal for recording and analyzing monitoring information that's provided in real time.

11.2   *Resource control*

One of the central concerns of running services in production is the fair and functional allocation of resources. Under the hood, Docker uses the core operating system concept of cgroups to manage containers' resource usage. By default, a simple and equal-share algorithm is used when containers contend for resources, but sometimes this isn't enough. You might want to reserve or limit resources for a container, or class of containers, for operational or service reasons.

In this section you'll learn how to tune containers' usage of CPU and memory.

TECHNIQUE 92   **Restricting the cores a container can execute on**

By default, Docker allows containers to execute on any cores on your machine. Containers with a single process and thread will obviously only be able to max out one core, but multithreaded programs in a container (or multiple single-threaded programs) will be able to use all your CPU cores. You might want to change this behavior if you have a container that's more important than others—it's not ideal for customer-facing applications to have to fight for the CPU every time your internal daily reports run! You could also use this technique to prevent runaway containers from locking you out of SSH to a server.

PROBLEM
You want a container to have a minimum CPU allocation, have a hard limit on CPU consumption, or otherwise want to restrict the cores a container can run on.

SOLUTION
Reserve a core for use by a container by using the --cpuset-cpus option.

DISCUSSION
To properly explore the --cpuset-cpus option, you'll need to follow this technique on a computer with multiple cores. This may not be the case if you're using a cloud machine.

> **FLAG RENAMED –CPUSET**   Older versions of Docker used the flag --cpuset, which is now deprecated. If you can't get --cpuset-cpus to work, try using --cpuset instead.

To look at the effects of the --cpuset-cpus option, we're going to use the htop command, which gives a useful graphical view of the core usage of your computer. Make sure this is installed before continuing—it's typically available as the htop package from your system package manager. Alternatively, you can install it inside an Ubuntu container started with the --pid=host option to expose process information from the host to the container.

If you now run htop, you'll probably see that none of your cores are busy. To simulate some load inside a couple of containers, run the following command in two different terminals:

```
docker run ubuntu:14.04 sh -c 'cat /dev/zero >/dev/null'
```

Looking back at htop, you should see that two of your cores now show 100% use. To restrict this to one core, docker kill the previous containers and then run the following command in two terminals:

```
docker run --cpuset-cpus=0 ubuntu:14.04 sh -c 'cat /dev/zero >/dev/null'
```

Now htop will show that only your first core is being used by these containers.

The --cpuset-cpus option permits multiple core specification as a comma-separated list (0,1,2), a range (0-2), or a combination of the two (0-1,3). Reserving a CPU for the host is therefore a matter of choosing a range for your containers that excludes a core.

You can use this functionality in numerous ways. For example, you can reserve specific CPUs for the host processes by consistently allocating the remaining CPUs to running containers. Or you could restrict specific containers to run on their own dedicated CPUs so they don't interfere with the compute used by other containers.

TECHNIQUE 93 Giving important containers more CPU

Containers on a host will normally share CPU usage equally when they compete for it. You've seen how to make absolute guarantees or restrictions, but these can be a little inflexible. If you want a process to be able to use more CPU than others, it's a waste to constantly reserve an entire core for it, and doing so can be limiting if you have a small number of cores.

Docker facilitates multi-tenancy for users who want to bring their applications to a shared server. This can result in the *noisy neighbor* problem well-known to those experienced with VMs, where one user eats up resources and affects another user's VM that happens to be running on the same hardware.

As a concrete example, while writing this book we had to use this functionality to reduce the resource use of a particularly hungry Postgres application that ate CPU cycles, robbing a web server on the machine of the ability to serve end users.

PROBLEM

You want to be able to give more important containers a bigger share of CPU or mark some containers as less important.

SOLUTION

Use the `-c/--cpu-shares` argument to the `docker run` command to define the relative share of CPU usage.

DISCUSSION

When a container is started up, it's given a number (1024 by default) of *CPU shares*. When only one process is running, it will have access to 100% of the CPU if necessary, no matter how many CPU shares it has access to. It's only when competing with other containers for CPU that the number is used.

Imagine we have three containers (A, B, and C) all trying to use all available CPU resources:

- If they've all been given equal CPU shares, they will each be allocated one third of the CPU.
- If A and B are given 512 and C is given 1024, C will get half of the CPU, and A and B will get a quarter each.
- If A is given 10, B is given 100, and C is given 1000, A will get under 1% of the available CPU resources and will only be able to do anything resource-hungry if A and B are idle.

All of this assumes that your containers can use all cores on your machine (or that you only have one core). Docker will spread the load from containers across all cores where possible. If you have two containers running single-threaded applications on a two-core machine, there's obviously no way to apply relative weighting while maximally using the available resources. Each container will be given a core to execute on, regardless of their weight.

If you want to try this out, run the following:

```
docker run --cpuset-cpus=0 -c 10000 ubuntu:14.04 \
sh -c 'cat /dev/zero > /dev/null' &
docker run --cpuset-cpus=0 -c 1 -it ubuntu:14.04 bash
```

Now see how doing anything in the bash prompt is sluggish. Note that these numbers are relative—you can multiply them all by 10 (for example) and they would mean exactly the same thing. However, the default granted is still 1024, so once you start changing these numbers, it's worth considering what will happen to processes that start without a CPU share specified in the command and that run on the same CPU set.

> **CHOOSING YOUR SETTINGS**   Finding the right CPU share levels for your use case is something of an art. It's worth looking at the output of programs such as top and vmstat to determine what's using CPU time. When using top, it's particularly useful to hit the "1" key to display what each CPU core is doing separately.

TECHNIQUE 94   **Limiting the memory usage of a container**

When you run a container, Docker will allow it to allocate as much memory from the host as possible. Usually this is desirable (and a big advantage over virtual machines, which have an inflexible way of allocating memory). But sometimes applications can go out of control, allocate too much memory, and bring a machine grinding to a halt as it starts swapping. It's annoying, and it's happened to us many times in the past. We want a way of limiting a container's memory consumption to prevent this.

PROBLEM

You want to be able to limit the memory consumption of a container.

SOLUTION

Use the -m/--memory parameter to docker run.

DISCUSSION

If you're running Ubuntu, chances are that you don't have the memory-limiting capability enabled by default. To check, run docker info. If one of the lines in the output is a warning about No swap limit support, there's unfortunately some setup work you need to do. Be aware that making these changes can have performance implications on your machine for all applications—see the Ubuntu installation documentation for more information (http://docs.docker.com/engine/installation/ubuntulinux/#adjust-memory-and-swap-accounting).

In short, you need to indicate to the kernel at boot that you want these limits to be available. To do this, you'll need to alter /etc/default/grub as follows. If GRUB_CMDLINE_LINUX already has values in it, add the new ones at the end:

```
-GRUB_CMDLINE_LINUX=""
+GRUB_CMDLINE_LINUX="cgroup_enable=memory swapaccount=1"
```

You now need to run sudo update-grub and restart your computer. Running docker info should no longer give you the warning, and you're now ready to proceed with the main attraction.

First, let's crudely demonstrate that the memory limit does work by using a limit of 4 MB, the lowest possible:

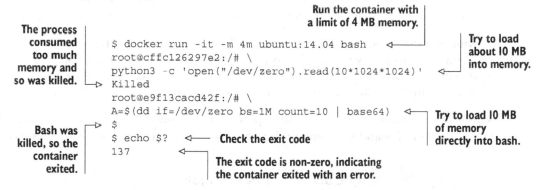

There's a gotcha with this kind of constraint. To demonstrate this, we'll use the jess/stress image, which contains stress, a tool designed for testing the limits of a system.

EASY STRESS TESTING   jess/stress is a helpful image for testing any resource limits you impose on your container. Try out the previous techniques with this image if you want to experiment more.

If you run the following command, you might be surprised to see that it doesn't exit immediately:

```
docker run -m 100m jess/stress --vm 1 --vm-bytes 150M --vm-hang 0
```

You've asked Docker to limit the container to 100 MB, and you've instructed stress to take up 150 MB. You can verify that stress is operating as expected by running this command:

```
docker top <container_id> -eo pid,size,args
```

The size column is in KB and shows that your container is indeed taking about 150 MB of memory…raising the question of why it hasn't been killed! It turns out that Docker double-reserves memory—half for physical memory and half to swap. If you try the following command, the container will terminate immediately:

```
docker run -m 100m jess/stress --vm 1 --vm-bytes 250M --vm-hang 0
```

This double reservation is just a default and can be controlled with the --memory-swap argument, which specifies the total virtual memory size (memory + swap). For example, to completely eliminate swap usage, you should set --memory and --memory-swap to be the same size. You can see more examples in the Docker run reference at https://docs.docker.com/engine/reference/run/#user-memory-constraints.

11.3   *Sysadmin use cases for Docker*

In this section we're going to take a look at some of the surprising uses to which Docker can be put. Although it may seem strange at first glance, Docker can be used to make your cron job management easier and can be used as a form of backup tool.

WHAT'S A CRON JOB?   A cron job is a timed, regular command that's run by a daemon included as a service with almost all Linux systems. Each user can specify their own schedule of commands to be run. It's heavily used by sysadmins to run periodic tasks, such as cleaning up log files or running backups.

This is by no means an exhaustive list of potential uses, but it should give you a taste of Docker's flexibility and some insight into how its features can be used in unexpected ways.

TECHNIQUE 95   Using Docker to run cron jobs

If you've ever had to manage cron jobs across multiple hosts, you may have come across the operational headache of having to deploy the same software to multiple places and ensuring the crontab itself has the correct invocation of the program you want to run.

Although there are other solutions to this problem (such as using Chef, Puppet, Ansible, or some other configuration management tool to manage the deployment of software across hosts), one option can be to use a Docker registry to store the correct invocation.

This is not always the best solution to the problem outlined, but it's a striking illustration of the benefits of having an isolated and portable store of your applications' runtime configuration, and one that comes for free if you already use Docker.

PROBLEM

You want your cron jobs to be centrally managed and auto-updated.

SOLUTION

Pull and run your cron job scripts as Docker containers.

DISCUSSION

If you have a large estate of machines that need to run jobs regularly, you typically will use crontabs and configure them by hand (yes, that still happens), or you'll use a configuration management tool such as Puppet or Chef. Updating their recipes will ensure that when a machine's config management controller next runs, the changes are applied to the crontab, ready for the run following that.

> **WHAT IS A CRONTAB?** A *crontab* file is a special file maintained by a user that specifies the times scripts should be run. Typically these will be maintenance tasks, like compressing and archiving log files, but they could be business-critical applications, such as a credit card payment settler.

In this technique, we'll show you how to replace this scheme with Docker images delivered from a registry with Docker pull.

In the normal case shown in figure 11.2, the maintainer updates the configuration management tool, which is then delivered to the servers when the agent is run. Meanwhile, the cron jobs are running with the old and new code while the systems update.

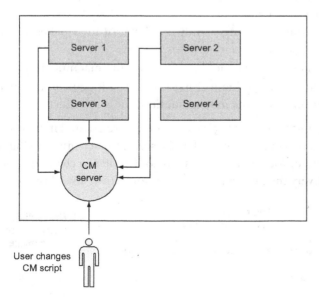

Figure 11.2 Each server updates cron scripts during CM agent scheduled run.

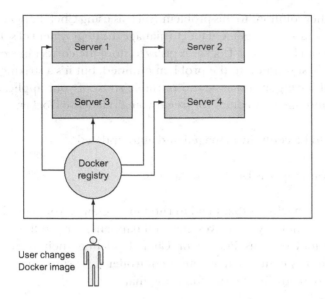

User changes
Docker image

**Figure 11.3   Each server pulls
latest image on every cron job run.**

In the Docker scenario illustrated in figure 11.3, the servers pull the latest version of
the code before the cron jobs run.

At this point you may be wondering why it's worth bothering with this, if you
already have a solution that works. Here are some advantages of using Docker as the
delivery mechanism:

- Whenever a job is run, the job will update itself to the latest version from the
  central location.
- Your crontab files become much simpler, because the script and the code are
  encapsulated in a Docker image.
- For larger or more complex changes, only the deltas of the Docker image need
  be pulled, speeding up delivery and updates.
- You don't have to maintain the code or binaries on the machine itself.
- You can combine Docker with other techniques, such as logging output to the syslog, to simplify and centralize the management of these administration services.

For this example we're going to use the log_cleaner image we created in technique 40.
You'll no doubt recall that this image encapsulated a script that cleaned up log files on
a server and took a parameter for the number of days of log files to clean up. A crontab
that uses Docker as a delivery mechanism would look something like this:

**Run the log
cleaner over
a day's worth
of log files.**

**Run this at
midnight every day.**

**First pull the
latest version
of the image.**

```
0 0 * * * \
docker pull dockerinpractice/log_cleaner && \
docker run \
-v /var/log/myapplogs:/log_dir dockerinpractice/log_cleaner 1
```

NOT FAMILIAR WITH CRON? If you're not familiar with cron, you may want to know that to edit your crontab you can run `crontab -e`. Each line specifies a command to be run at a time specified by the five items at the start of the line. Find out more by looking at the crontab man page.

If there's a failure, the standard cron mechanism of sending an email should kick into effect. If you don't rely on this, then add a command with an or operator. In the following example, we assume your bespoke alerting command is `my_alert_command`:

```
0 0 * * * (docker pull dockerinpractice/log_cleaner && \
docker run -d -v /var/log/myapplogs:/log_dir \
dockerinpractice/log_cleaner 1) \
|| my_alert_command 'log_cleaner failed'
```

WHAT IS AN OR OPERATOR? An or operator (in this case, the double pipe: ||) ensures that one of the commands on either side will be run. If the first command fails (in this case, either of the two commands within the parentheses after the cron specification 0 0 * * * joined by the and operator, &&), then the second will be run.

The || operator ensures that if any part of the log-cleaning job run failed, the alert command gets run.

TECHNIQUE 96 The "save game" approach to backups

If you've ever run a transactional system, you'll know that when things go wrong, the ability to infer the state of the system at the time of the problem is essential for a root-cause analysis.

Usually this is done through a combination of means:

- Analysis of application logs
- Database forensics (determining the state of data at a given point in time)
- Build history analysis (working out what code and config was running on the service at a given point in time)
- Live system analysis (for example, did anyone log onto the box and change something?)

For such critical systems, it can pay to take the simple but effective approach of backing up the Docker service containers. Although your database is likely to be separate from your Docker infrastructure, the state of config, code, and logs can be stored in a registry with a couple of simple commands.

PROBLEM

You want to keep backups of Docker containers.

SOLUTION

Commit the containers while running, and push as a dedicated repository.

DISCUSSION

Following Docker best practices and taking advantage of some Docker features can help you avoid the need to store container backups. As one example, using a logging driver as described in technique 90 instead of logging to the container filesystem means logs don't need to be retrieved from the container backups.

But sometimes reality dictates that you can't do everything the way you'd like, and you really need to see what a container looked like. The following commands show the entire process of committing and pushing a backup container:

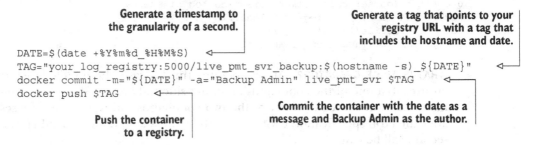

```
DATE=$(date +%Y%m%d_%H%M%S)
TAG="your_log_registry:5000/live_pmt_svr_backup:$(hostname -s)_${DATE}"
docker commit -m="${DATE}" -a="Backup Admin" live_pmt_svr $TAG
docker push $TAG
```

> **Generate a timestamp to the granularity of a second.**

> **Generate a tag that points to your registry URL with a tag that includes the hostname and date.**

> **Push the container to a registry.**

> **Commit the container with the date as a message and Backup Admin as the author.**

> **TAKES CONTAINER OUT OF SERVICE** This technique will pause the container while it runs, effectively taking it out of service. Your service should either tolerate outages, or you should have other nodes running at the time that can service requests in a load-balanced fashion.

If this is done in a staggered rotation across all your hosts, you'll have an effective backup system and a means to restore the state for support engineers with as little ambiguity as possible.

Figure 11.4 illustrates a simplified view of such a setup.

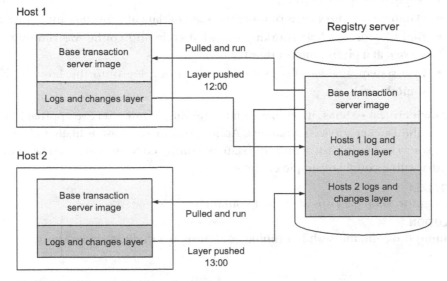

Figure 11.4 Two-host backup of a service

The backups only push the differences between the base image and the state of the container at the time it's backed up, and the backups are staggered to ensure that the service stays up on at least one host. The registry server only stores one copy of the base image and the diffs at each commit point, saving disk space.

COMBINING WITH PHOENIX DEPLOYMENT

You can take this technique one step further by combining this technique with a Phoenix deployment model. Phoenix deployment is a model for deployment that emphasizes replacing as much of the system as possible rather than upgrading a deployment in-place. It's a central principle of many Docker tools.

In this case, rather than committing the container and letting it continue on afterwards, you can do the following:

1 Pull a fresh copy of the latest image from your registry
2 Stop the running container
3 Start up a new container
4 Commit, tag, and push the old container to the registry

Combining these approaches gives you even more certainty that the live system has not drifted from the source image. One of the authors uses this approach to manage a live system on his home server.

11.4 Summary

In this chapter you've seen some of the topics that come up when running Docker in production. As with much of Docker, this is a fast-changing field, not least because organizations are still discovering the use cases and pain points of using Docker in production as they move workloads there.

The main areas we covered were

- Capturing logging from your containers to your host's syslog daemon
- Capturing your Docker log output to a host-level service
- Monitoring the performance of your containers with cAdvisor
- Constraining container resource usage on CPU, core, and memory
- Surprising uses for Docker, such as a cron delivery tool and a backup system

Now that we've covered what Docker can and should be in production, we'll look at debugging Docker when things go wrong.

Docker in production—
dealing with challenges

This chapter covers

- Bypassing Docker's namespace functionality and using the host's resources directly
- Making more room by resizing your storage
- Debugging a container's network directly, using your host's tooling
- Tracing system calls to determine why a container isn't working on your host

In this chapter we'll discuss what you can do when Docker's abstractions aren't working for you. These topics necessarily involve getting under the hood of Docker to understand how such solutions can be needed, and in the process we aim to provide you with a deeper awareness of what can go wrong when using Docker and how to go about fixing it.

12.1 Performance—you can't ignore the tin

Although Docker seeks to abstract the application from the host it's running on, one can never completely ignore the host. In order to provide its abstractions,

Docker must add layers of indirection. These layers can have implications for your running system, and they sometimes need to be understood in order for operational challenges to be fixed or worked around.

In this section we'll look at how you can bypass some of these abstractions, ending up with a Docker container that has little of Docker left in it. We'll also show that although Docker appears to abstract away the details of the storage you use, this can sometimes come back to bite you.

<hr>

TECHNIQUE 97 **Accessing host resources from the container**

We covered volumes, the most commonly used Docker abstraction bypass, in technique 19. They're convenient for sharing files from the host and keeping larger files out of image layers. They can also be significantly faster for filesystem access than the container filesystem, as some storage backends impose significant overheads for certain workloads—this isn't important for all applications, but it's important in some cases.

Another performance hit comes about as a result of the network interfaces Docker sets up to give each container its own network. As with filesystem performance, network performance is definitely not a bottleneck for everyone, but it's something you may wish to benchmark for yourself (although the fine details of network tuning are very much outside the scope of this book). Alternatively, you may have other reasons to want to bypass Docker networking entirely—a server that opens random ports to listen on may not be well served by listening on port ranges with Docker, especially because exposing a range of ports will allocate them on the host whether they're in use or not.

Regardless of your reason, sometimes Docker abstractions get in the way, and Docker does offer the ability to opt out if you need to.

PROBLEM

You want to allow access to the host's resources from the container.

SOLUTION

Use the host options and volumes flags to docker run.

DISCUSSION

Docker offers several ways to bypass the kernel namespace functionality that Docker uses.

> **WHAT IS A NAMESPACE?** Kernel namespaces are a service the kernel offers to programs, allowing them to get views of global resources in such a way that they appear to have their own separate instances of that resource. For example, a program can request a network namespace that will give you what appears to be a complete network stack. Docker uses and manages these namespaces to create its containers.

Table 12.1 summarizes how Docker uses namespaces, and how you can effectively switch them off.

> **FLAGS NOT AVAILABLE?** If any of these flags aren't available, it will likely be due to your version of Docker being out of date.

Table 12.1   Namespaces and Docker

Kernel namespace	Description	Used in Docker?	"Switch off" option
Network	The network subsystem	Yes	`--net=host`
IPC	Inter-process communication: shared memory, semaphores, and so on	Yes	`--ipc=host`
UTS	Hostname and NIS domain	Yes	`--uts=host`
PID	Process IDs	Yes	`--pid=host`
Mount	Mount points	Yes	`--volume, --device`
User	User and group IDs	No	`N/A`

If your application is a heavy user of shared memory, for example, and you want to have your containers share this space with the host, you can use the `--ipc=host` flag to achieve this. This use is relatively advanced, so we'll focus on the other more common ones.

Docker doesn't at present use the Linux kernel's user namespace functionality, although efforts are ongoing in that area.

NETWORK AND HOSTNAME

To use the host's network, you run your container with the `--net` flag set to host, like this:

```
user@yourhostname:/$ docker run -ti --net=host ubuntu /bin/bash
root@yourhostname:/#
```

You'll notice that this immediately differs from a network-namespaced container in that the hostname within the container is the same as the host's. On a practical level, this can cause confusion, as it's not so obvious that you're in a container.

In a network-isolated container, a quick `netstat` will show that there are no connections on startup:

```
host$ docker run -ti ubuntu
root@b1c4877a00cd:/# netstat
Active Internet connections (w/o servers)
Proto Recv-Q Send-Q Local Address          Foreign Address         State
Active UNIX domain sockets (w/o servers)
Proto RefCnt Flags       Type       State         I-Node   Path
root@b1c4877a00cd:/#
```

A similar run using the host's network shows the usual network-busy host of a similarly busy technical author:

```
$ docker run -ti --net=host ubuntu
root@host:/# netstat -nap | head
Active Internet connections (servers and established)
```

```
Proto Recv-Q Send-Q Local Address    Foreign Address State       PID/
      Program name
tcp        0      0 127.0.0.1:47116 0.0.0.0:*        LISTEN      -
tcp        0      0 127.0.1.1:53     0.0.0.0:*        LISTEN      -
tcp        0      0 127.0.0.1:631   0.0.0.0:*        LISTEN      -
tcp        0      0 0.0.0.0:3000     0.0.0.0:*        LISTEN      -
tcp        0      0 127.0.0.1:54366 0.0.0.0:*        LISTEN      -
tcp        0      0 127.0.0.1:32888 127.0.0.1:47116 ESTABLISHED -
tcp        0      0 127.0.0.1:32889 127.0.0.1:47116 ESTABLISHED -
tcp        0      0 127.0.0.1:47116 127.0.0.1:32888 ESTABLISHED -
root@host:/#
```

WHAT IS NETSTAT? netstat is a command that allows you to see information about networking on your local network stack. It's used most commonly to determine the state of network sockets.

The net=host flag is the most often used for a couple of reasons. First, it can make connecting containers much easier. But you lose the benefits of port mapping for your containers. If you have two containers that listen on port 80, for example, you can't run them on the same host in this way. The second reason is that network performance is significantly improved over Docker's when using this flag.

Figure 12.1 shows at a high level the layers of overhead a network packet must go through in Docker versus a native network. Whereas the native network need only go through the TCP/IP stack of the host to the network interface card (NIC), Docker has to additionally maintain a virtual Ethernet pair (a.k.a. a *veth pair*, a virtual representation of a physical connection via an Ethernet cable), a network bridge between this veth pair and the host network, and a layer of network address translation (NAT). This overhead can cause the Docker network to be half the speed of a native host network in normal use cases.

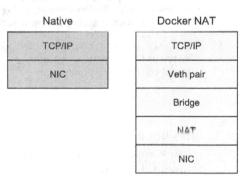

Figure 12.1 Docker networking vs native

PID

The PID namespace flag is similar to the others:

```
imiell@host:/$ docker run ubuntu ps -p 1
    PID TTY          TIME CMD
      1 ?        00:00:00 ps
imiell@host:/$ docker run --pid=host ubuntu ps -p 1
    PID TTY          TIME CMD
      1 ?        00:00:27 systemd
```

Run the ps command in a containerized environment, showing only the process that has a PID of 1.

The ps we're running is the only process in this container and is given the PID 1.

Run the same ps command with the PID namespace removed, giving us a view of the host's processes.

This time the PID of 1 is the systemd command, which is the startup process of the host's operating system. This may differ for you, depending on your distribution.

The preceding example demonstrates that the systemd process of the host has process ID 1 in the container that has a view of the host PIDs, whereas without that view the only process seen is the ps command itself.

MOUNT

If you want access to the host's devices, you can use the --device flag if you want to use a specific device, or you can mount the entire host's filesystem with the --volume flag:

```
docker run -ti --volume /:/host ubuntu /bin/bash
```

This command mounts the host's / directory to the container's /host directory. You may be wondering why you can't mount the host's / directory to the container's / directory. This is explicitly disallowed by the docker command.

You may also be wondering whether you can use these flags to create a container that's virtually indistinguishable from the host. That leads us to the next section...

A HOST-LIKE CONTAINER

You can use these flags to create a container that has an almost transparent view of the host:

Mount the root filesystem of the host to a directory /host on the container. Docker disallows the mounting of volumes to the / folder, so you must specify the /host subfolder volume.

Run a container with the three host arguments (net, pid, ipc).

```
host:/$ docker run -ti --net=host --pid=host --ipc=host \
   --volume /:/host \
   busybox chroot /host
```

Start up a BusyBox container. All you need is the chroot command, and this is a small image that contains that. chroot is executed to make the mounted filesystem appear as the root to you.

It's ironic that Docker has been characterized as "chroot on steroids," and here we're using something characterized as a framework to run chroot in a way that subverts one of the principal purposes of chroot, which is to protect a host filesystem. It's usually at this point that we try not to think about it too hard.

In any case, it's hard to imagine a real-world use of that command (instructive as it is). If you think of one, please drop us a line.

That said, you might want to use it as a basis for more useful commands like this:

```
$ docker run -ti --workdir /host \
   --volume /:/host:ro ubuntu /bin/bash
```

--workdir /host sets the working directory on container startup to be the root of the host's filesystem, as mounted with the --volume argument. The :ro part of the volume specification means the host filesystem will be mounted as read-only.

With this command, you can give yourself a read-only view of the filesystem while having an environment where you can install tools (with the standard Ubuntu package manager) to inspect it. For example, you could use an image that runs a nifty tool that reports security problems on your host's filesystem, without having to install it on your host.

> **INSECURE!** As the preceding discussion implies, using these flags opens you up to more security risks. In security terms, using them should be considered equivalent to running with the --privileged flag.

In this technique you've learned how to bypass Docker's abstractions within the container. The next technique looks at how you can bypass a restriction of Docker's underlying disk storage.

TECHNIQUE 98 Device Mapper storage driver and default container size

Docker comes with a number of supported *storage drivers*. These offer a few different approaches to handling layers, each with their own advantages and disadvantages. You can find more Docker documentation on each of these at https://docs.docker.com/engine/userguide/storagedriver/.

The default storage driver on CentOS and Red Hat is devicemapper, chosen by Red Hat as a more supportable alternative to AUFS (the default on Ubuntu) because it had fewer bugs and more flexible features at the time.

> **DEVICE MAPPER TERMINOLOGY** *Device Mapper* refers to a Linux technology that abstracts away physical device access by providing virtual devices that map onto the physical devices in some user-defined way. In this technique we're talking about *devicemapper*, the name of the Docker storage driver built on top of Device Mapper.

The devicemapper driver's default behavior is to allocate a single file, which is treated as a "device" to read and write from. Unfortunately, this file has a fixed maximum capacity that's not automatically increased when it runs out of space.

PROBLEM

You've run out of space on a Docker container when using the Device Mapper storage driver.

SOLUTION

Change the maximum size of Docker containers.

DISCUSSION

To demonstrate the problem, you can try running the following Dockerfile:

```
FROM ubuntu:14.04
RUN truncate --size 11G /root/file
```

If you haven't changed any of the default configuration of your Docker daemon in relation to storage drivers, you should see output like the following:

```
$ docker build .
Sending build context to Docker daemon 24.58 kB
Sending build context to Docker daemon
Step 0 : FROM ubuntu:14.04
```

```
Pulling repository ubuntu
d2a0ecffe6fa: Download complete
83e4dde6b9cf: Download complete
b670fb0c7ecd: Download complete
29460ac93442: Download complete
Status: Downloaded newer image for ubuntu:14.04
 ---> d2a0ecffe6fa
Step 1 : RUN truncate --size 11G /root/file
 ---> Running in 77134fcbd040
INFO[0200] ApplyLayer exit status 1 stdout:  stderr: write /root/file:
no space left on device
```

This build eventually failed because the attempt to create the 11 GB file failed with a "no space left" error message. Note that when this was run, there were over 200 GB of disk space on our machine, so it wasn't a machine-wide limit that was hit.

> **HOW CAN YOU TELL WHETHER YOU'RE USING DEVICEMAPPER?** If you run `docker info`, it will tell you which storage driver you're using in the output. If yours says `devicemapper` in the output, then you're using devicemapper, and this technique may be relevant to you.

By default, the space limit for devicemapper containers was 10 GB. To change this, you need to wipe your Docker folder, reconfigure your Docker daemon, and then restart it. For details on how to reconfigure your Docker daemon on your distribution, see appendix B.

> **SPACE LIMIT HAS BEEN CHANGED** Around the time of going to press, the devicemapper limit was upped to 100 GB, so your limit may be higher by the time you read this.

To make the configuration change, you need to add or replace the `dm.basesize` item in your Docker options so that it's larger than the 11 GB file you're trying to create:

```
--storage-opt dm.basesize=20G
```

A typical file might look like this:

```
DOCKER_OPTIONS="-s devicemapper --storage-opt dm.basesize=20G"
```

Once you've restarted your Docker daemon, you can rerun the `docker build` command you ran earlier:

```
# docker build --no-cache -t big .
Sending build context to Docker daemon 24.58 kB
Sending build context to Docker daemon
Step 0 : FROM ubuntu:14.04
 ---> d2a0ecffe6fa
Step 1 : RUN truncate --size 11G /root/file
 ---> Running in f947affe7900
 ---> 39766546a1a5
Removing intermediate container f947affe7900
Successfully built 39766546a1a5
```

You'll see that the 11 GB file can be created without issue.

This is a runtime constraint of the devicemapper storage driver, whether you're building an image with a Dockerfile or running a container.

12.2 *When containers leak—debugging Docker*

In this section we'll cover some techniques that will help you understand and fix issues with applications running in Docker containers. We'll cover how to "jump into" a container's network while using tools from your host to debug issues, and look at a more "in-action" solution by monitoring network interfaces directly.

Finally, we'll demonstrate how the Docker abstraction can break down, leading to containers working on one host and not another, and how to debug this on live systems.

TECHNIQUE 99   **Debugging a container's network with nsenter**

In an ideal world, you'd be able to use socat (see technique 4) in an *ambassador container* to diagnose issues. You'd start the extra container and make sure connections go to this new container, which acts as a proxy. The proxy allows you to diagnose and monitor the connections, and then forwards them on to the right place. Unfortunately it's not always convenient (or possible) to set up a container like this only for debugging purposes.

> **AMBASSADOR CONTAINER PATTERN**   See technique 66 for a description of the ambassador pattern.

You've already read about docker exec in technique 14. This technique discusses *nsenter*, a tool that looks similar but allows you to use tools from your machine inside the container, rather than being limited to what the container has installed.

PROBLEM

You want to debug a network problem in a container, but the tools aren't in the container.

SOLUTION

Use nsenter to jump into the container's network but retain your host's tooling.

DISCUSSION

If you don't already have nsenter available on your Docker host, you can build it with the following command:

```
$ docker run -v /usr/local/bin:/target jpetazzo/nsenter
```

This will install nsenter in /usr/local/bin, and you'll be able to use it immediately. Nsenter might also be available in your distro (in the util-linux package).

You may have noticed by now that the generally useful BusyBox image doesn't come with bash by default. As a starter demo, we're going to show how you can enter a container with your host's bash program:

Start up a BusyBox container and save the container ID (CID).

Run nsenter, specifying the container to enter with the --target flag. The "sudo" may not be required.

```
$ docker run -ti busybox /bin/bash
FATA[0000] Error response from daemon: Cannot start container
➥ a81e7e6b2c030c29565ef7adb94de20ad516a6697deeeb617604e652e979fda6:
➥ exec: "/bin/bash": stat /bin/bash: no such file or directory
$ CID=$(docker run -d busybox sleep 9999)
$ PID=$(docker inspect --format {{.State.Pid}} $CID)
$ sudo nsenter --target $PID \
--uts --ipc --net /bin/bash
root@781c1fed2b18:~#
```

Inspect the container, extracting the process ID (PID) (see technique 27).

Specify the namespaces of the container to enter with the remaining flags (see technique 97 for more on namespaces). The critical point here is that you don't use the --mount flag, which would use the container's filesystem, in which bash wouldn't be available. /bin/bash is specified as the executable to start.

It should be pointed out that you don't get direct access to the container's filesystem. But you do get all the tools your host has.

Something that we've needed before is a way to find out which veth interface device on the host corresponds to which container. For example, sometimes it's desirable to quickly knock a container off the network without having to settle down with any of the tools from chapter 8 to simulate network breakage. But an unprivileged container can't bring a network interface down, so you need to do it from the host by finding out the veth interface name:

Verify that attempting to ping from inside a new container succeeds.

```
$ docker run -d --name offlinetest ubuntu:14.04.2 sleep infinity
fad037a77a2fc337b7b12bc484babb2145774fde7718d1b5b53fb7e9dc0ad7b3
$ docker exec offlinetest ping -q -c1 8.8.8.8
PING 8.8.8.8 (8.8.8.8) 56(84) bytes of data.

--- 8.8.8.8 ping statistics ---
1 packets transmitted, 1 received, 0% packet loss, time 0ms
rtt min/avg/max/mdev = 2.966/2.966/2.966/0.000 ms
$ docker exec offlinetest ifconfig eth0 down
SIOCSIFFLAGS: Operation not permitted
$ PID=$(docker inspect --format {{.State.Pid}} offlinetest)
$ nsenter --target $PID --net ethtool -S eth0
NIC statistics:
    peer_ifindex: 53
$ ip addr | grep '^53'
53: veth2e7d114: <BROADCAST,MULTICAST,UP,LOWER_UP> mtu 1500 qdisc noqueue
➥ master docker0 state UP
$ sudo ifconfig veth2e7d114 down
$ docker exec offlinetest ping -q -c1 8.8.8.8
PING 8.8.8.8 (8.8.8.8) 56(84) bytes of data.

--- 8.8.8.8 ping statistics ---
1 packets transmitted, 0 received, 100% packet loss, time 0ms
```

We're unable to bring an interface in the container down. Note that your interface may not be eth0, so if this doesn't work, you may wish to use iconfig to find out your principal interface name.

Enter into the network space of the container, using the ethtool command from the host to look up the peer interface index—the other end of the virtual interface.

Look through the list of interfaces on the host to find the appropriate veth interface for the container.

Verify that attempting to ping from inside the container fails.

Bring down the virtual interface.

One final example of a program you might want to use from within a container is tcp-dump, a tool that records all TCP packets on a network interface. To use it, you need to run nsenter with the `--net` command, allowing you to "see" the container's network from the host and therefore monitor the packets with tcpdump.

For example, the `tcpdump` command in the following code records all packets to the /tmp/google.tcpdump file (we assume you're still in the nsenter session you started above). Some network traffic is then triggered by retrieving a web page:

```
root@781c1fed2b18:/# tcpdump -XXs 0 -w /tmp/google.tcpdump &
root@781c1fed2b18:/# wget google.com
--2015-08-07 15:12:04--  http://google.com/
Resolving google.com (google.com)... 216.58.208.46, 2a00:1450:4009:80d::200e
Connecting to google.com (google.com)|216.58.208.46|:80... connected.
HTTP request sent, awaiting response... 302 Found
Location: http://www.google.co.uk/?gfe_rd=cr&ei=tLzEVcCXN7Lj8wepgarQAQ
➥ [following]
--2015-08-07 15:12:04--
➥ http://www.google.co.uk/?gfe_rd=cr&ei=tLzEVcCXN7Lj8wepgarQAQ
Resolving www.google.co.uk (www.google.co.uk)... 216.58.208.67,
➥ 2a00:1450:4009:80a::2003
Connecting to www.google.co.uk (www.google.co.uk)|216.58.208.67|:80...
➥ connected.
HTTP request sent, awaiting response... 200 OK
Length: unspecified [text/html]
Saving to: 'index.html'

index.html              [ <=>                ]  18.28K  --.-KB/s    in 0.008s

2015-08-07 15:12:05 (2.18 MB/s) - 'index.html' saved [18720]

root@781c1fed2b18:# 15:12:04.839152 IP 172.17.0.26.52092 >
➥ google-public-dns-a.google.com.domain: 7950+ A? google.com. (28)
15.12:04.844754 IP 172.17.0.26.52092 >
➥ google-public-dns-a.google.com.domain: 18121+ AAAA? google.com. (28)
15:12:04.860430 IP google-public-dns-a.google.com.domain >
➥ 172.17.0.26.52092: 7950 1/0/0 A 216.58.208.46 (44)
15:12:04.869571 IP google-public-dns-a.google.com.domain >
➥ 172.17.0.26.52092: 18121 1/0/0 AAAA 2a00:1450:4009:80d::200e (56)
15:12:04.870246 IP 172.17.0.26.47834 > lhr08s07-in-f14.1e100.net.http:
➥ Flags [S], seq 2242275586, win 29200, options [mss 1460,sackOK,TS val
➥ 49337583 ecr 0,nop,wscale 7], length 0
```

> **"TEMPORARY FAILURE IN NAME RESOLUTION" ERRORS** Depending on your network setup, you may need to temporarily change your resolv.conf file to allow the DNS lookup to work. If you get a "Temporary failure in name resolution" error, try adding the line `nameserver 8.8.8.8` to the top of your /etc/resolv.conf file. Don't forget to revert it when you're finished.

As an aside, this demonstrates another compelling use case for Docker—it's much easier to debug network issues in the isolated network environment Docker provides. Trying to remember the correct arguments for tcpdump to appropriately filter out irrelevant packets in the middle of the night is an error-prone process. Using the preceding method, you can forget about that and capture everything within the container, without tcpdump being installed (or having to install it) on the image.

Using tcpflow to debug in flight without reconfiguring

tcpdump is the de facto standard in network investigation, and it's likely the first tool most people reach for if asked to dive into debugging a network issue.

But tcpdump is typically used for displaying packet summaries and examining packet headers and protocol information—it's not quite as full-featured for displaying the application-level data flow between two programs. This can be quite important when investigating issues with two applications communicating.

PROBLEM

You need to monitor the communication data of a containerized application.

SOLUTION

Use tcpflow to capture traffic crossing an interface.

DISCUSSION

tcpflow is similar to tcpdump (accepting the same pattern-matching expressions) but it's designed to give you a better insight into application data flows. tcpflow may be available from your system package manager, but, if not, we've prepared a Docker image you can use, which should be virtually identical in functionality to an equivalent package manager install:

```
$ IMG=dockerinpractice/tcpflow
$ docker pull $IMG
$ alias tcpflow="docker run --rm --net host $IMG"
```

There are two ways you can use tcpflow with Docker: point it at the docker0 interface and use a packet-filtering expression to retrieve only the packets you want, or use the trick from the previous technique to find the veth interface for the container you're interested in, and capture on that.

Expression filtering is more powerful, letting you drill down to the traffic you're interested in, so we'll show a simple example to get you started:

```
$ docker run -d --name tcpflowtest alpine:3.2 sleep 30d
fa95f9763ab56e24b3a8f0d9f86204704b770ffb0fd55d4fd37c59dc1601ed11
$ docker inspect -f '{{ .NetworkSettings.IPAddress }}' tcpflowtest
172.17.0.1
$ tcpflow -c -J -i docker0 'host 172.17.0.1 and port 80'
tcpflow: listening on docker0
```

In the preceding example, you ask tcpflow to print a colorized stream of any traffic going to or from your container with a source or destination port of 80 (generally used for HTTP traffic). You can now try this by retrieving a web page in the container in a new terminal:

```
$ docker exec tcpflowtest wget -O /dev/null http://www.example.com/
Connecting to www.example.com (93.184.216.34:80)
null                100% |*****************************|  1270   0:00:00 ETA
```

You'll see colorized output in the tcpflow terminal! The cumulative output of the command so far will look something like this:

```
$ tcpflow -J -c -i docker0 'host 172.17.0.1 and (src or dst port 80)'
tcpflow: listening on docker0
172.017.000.001.36042-093.184.216.034.00080:
⇒ GET / HTTP/1.1                              ←——— Blue coloring starts
Host: www.example.com
User-Agent: Wget
Connection: close


093.184.216.034.00080-172.017.000.001.36042:
⇒ HTTP/1.0 200 OK                             ←——— Red coloring starts
Accept-Ranges: bytes
Cache-Control: max-age=604800
Content-Type: text/html
Date: Mon, 17 Aug 2015 12:22:21 GMT
[...]


<!doctype html>
<html>
<head>
    <title>Example Domain</title>
[...]
```

tcpflow is an excellent addition to your toolbox, given how unobtrusive it is. You can start it against long-running containers to get a bit of insight into what they're transferring right now, or use it alongside tcpdump to get a more complete picture of the kind of requests your application makes and what information is transferred.

TECHNIQUE 101   Debugging containers that fail on specific hosts

The previous two techniques have shown how you can start investigating issues caused by the interaction between your containers and other locations (whether those other locations are more containers or third parties on the internet).

If you've isolated a problem to one host, and you're sure that external interaction isn't the cause, the next step should be to try reducing the number of moving parts (removing volumes and ports) and to check the details of the host itself (free disk space, number of open file descriptors, and so on). It's probably also worth checking that each host is on the latest version of Docker.

In some cases, none of the above will help—you've got an image you can run with no arguments (such as docker run imagename), which should be perfectly contained, yet it runs differently on different hosts.

PROBLEM

You want to determine why a particular action within a container isn't working on a particular host.

SOLUTION

Strace the process to see what system calls it's making, and compare that to a working system.

DISCUSSION

Although Docker's stated aim is to allow apps to "run any app anywhere," the means by which it tries to achieve this are not always foolproof.

Docker treats the Linux kernel API as its *host* (the environment in which it can run). When they first learn how Docker works, many people ask how Docker handles changes to the Linux API. As far as we're aware, it doesn't yet. Fortunately the Linux API is backwards-compatible, but it's not difficult to imagine a scenario in the future where a new Linux API call is created and used by a Dockerized application, and is then deployed to a kernel recent enough to run Docker but old enough to not support that particular API call.

> **DOES THIS HAPPEN?** You may think that the Linux kernel API changing is something of a theoretical problem, but we came across this scenario while writing this book. A project we were working on used the memfd_create Linux system call, which only exists on kernels versioned 3.17 and above. Because some hosts we were working on had older kernels, our containers failed on some systems and worked on others.

That scenario is not the only way in which the Docker abstraction can fail. Containers can fail on particular kernels because assumptions may be made by the application about files on the host. Although rare, it does happen, and it's important to be alert to that risk.

SELINUX

An example of where the Docker abstraction can break down is with anything that interacts with SELinux. As discussed in chapter 10, SELinux is a layer of security implemented in the kernel that works outside the normal user permissions.

Docker uses this layer to allow container security to be tightened up by managing what actions can be performed from within a container. For example, if you're root within a container, you are the same user as root on the host. Although it's hard to break out of the container so you obtain root on the host, it's not impossible; exploits have been found, and others may exist that the community is unaware of. What SELinux can do is provide another layer of protection so that even if a root user breaks out of the container to the host, there are limits set on what actions they can perform on the host.

So far so good, but the problem for Docker is that SELinux is implemented on the host, and not within the container. This means that programs running in containers that query the status of SELinux and find it enabled might make certain assumptions about the environment in which they run, and fail in unexpected ways if these expectations aren't met.

In the following example, we're running a CentOS7 Vagrant machine with Docker installed, and within that an Ubuntu 12.04 container. If we run a fairly straightforward command to add a user, the exit code is 12, indicating an error, and indeed the user has not been created:

```
[root@centos vagrant]# docker run -ti ubuntu:12.04
Unable to find image 'ubuntu:12.04' locally
Pulling repository ubuntu
78cef618c77e: Download complete
b5da78899d3a: Download complete
87183ecb6716: Download complete
82ed8e312318: Download complete
root@afade8b94d32:/# useradd -m -d /home/dockerinpractice dockerinpractice
root@afade8b94d32:/# echo $?
12
```

The same command run on an ubuntu:14.04 container works just fine. If you want to try to reproduce this result, you'll need a CentOS 7 machine (or similar). But for learning purposes, following the rest of the technique with any command and container will be sufficient.

> **WHAT DOES $? DO?**   In bash, $? gives you the exit code of the last-run command. The meaning of the exit code varies from command to command, but typically an exit code of 0 means the call was successful, and a non-zero code indicates an error or exceptional condition of some kind.

DEBUGGING LINUX API CALLS

Because we know that the likely difference between the containers is due to differences between the kernel APIs running on the hosts, strace can help you determine the differences between calls to the kernel API.

> **WHAT IS STRACE?**   Strace is a tool that allows you to snoop on the calls made to the Linux API by a process (a.k.a. system calls). It's an extremely useful debugging and educational tool.

First, you need to install strace on your container using the appropriate package manager, and then run the command that differs, with the strace command prepended. Here's some example output for the failed useradd call:

Run strace on the command with the -f flag, which ensures that any process spawned by your command and any of its descendants are followed by strace.

Append the command you want to debug to the strace invocation.

Each line of the strace output starts with the Linux API call. The execve call here executes the command you gave strace. The 0 at the end is the return value from the call (successful).

```
# strace -f \
useradd -m -d /home/dockerinpractice dockerinpractice
execve("/usr/sbin/useradd", ["useradd", "-m", "-d",
➡ "/home/dockerinpractice", "dockerinpractice"], [/* 9 vars */]) = 0
```

```
[...]
open("/proc/self/task/39/attr/current",
➥ O_RDONLY) = 9
read(9, "system_u:system_r:svirt_lxc_net_"...,
4095) = 46
close(9)                                    = 0
[...]
```

The open system call opens a file for reading. The return value (9) is the file handle number used in subsequent calls to work on the file. In this case, the SELinux information is retrieved from the /proc filesystem, which holds information about running processes.

The close system call closes the file referenced with the file descriptor number.

The read system call works on the previously opened file (with the file descriptor 9) and returns the number of bytes read (46).

```
open("/etc/selinux/config", O_RDONLY)    =
➥ -1 ENOENT (No such file or directory)
open("/etc/selinux/targeted/contexts/files/
➥ file_contexts.subs_dist", O_RDONLY) = -1 ENOENT (No such file or directory)
open("/etc/selinux/targeted/contexts/files/
file_contexts.subs", O_RDONLY) = -1 ENOENT (No such file or directory)
open("/etc/selinux/targeted/contexts/files/
➥ file_contexts", O_RDONLY) = -1 ENOENT (No such file or directory)
[...]
exit_group(12)                              = ?
```

The process exits with the value 12, which for useradd means that the directory couldn't be created.

The program attempts to open the SELinux files it expects to be there but in each case fails. Strace helpfully tells you what the return value means: No such file or directory.

The preceding output may seem confusing at first, but after a few times it becomes relatively easy to read. Each line represents a call to the Linux kernel to perform some action in what's known as *kernel space* (as opposed to *user space*, meaning actions performed by programs without handing over responsibility to the kernel).

USE MAN 2 TO FIND OUT MORE ABOUT THE SYSTEM CALL If you want to learn more about a specific system call, you can run man 2 <callname> to find out more. You may need to install the man pages with apt-get install manpages-dev or a similar command for your packaging system. Alternatively, Googling man 2 <callname> will likely get you what you need.

This is an example of where Docker's abstractions break down. In this case, the action fails because the program expects SELinux files to be present, because SELinux appears to be enabled on the container, but the details of enforcement are kept on the host.

Although such situations are rare, the ability to debug and understand how your program is interacting by using strace is an invaluable technique, not only with Docker but for more general development.

READ THE MAN PAGES! It's incredibly useful to read over the man 2 pages for all the system calls if you're serious about being a developer. At first they might seem full of jargon you don't understand, but as you read around the various subjects, you'll learn a great deal about fundamental Linux concepts. At some point, you'll start to see how most languages derive from this root, and some of their quirks and oddities will make more sense. Be patient, though, as you won't understand it all immediately.

12.3 Summary

In this chapter we've covered what you can do when Docker doesn't work quite as you expected. While it's rare to find leaky abstractions when using Docker, such leaks can occur, and it's important to be prepared with an understanding of what can go wrong.

This chapter showed you how to

- Use docker's flags to use the host's resources directly for greater efficiency
- Resize your DeviceMapper disk to use your disk's space to its fullest
- Use nsenter to jump into the container's network.
- Run strace to determine why a Docker container doesn't work on a specific host

This concludes the book! We hope we've opened your eyes to some of the uses of Docker and given you some ideas for integrating it in your company or personal projects. If you'd like to get in touch with us or give us some feedback, please create a thread in the Manning *Docker in Practice* forum (https://forums.manning.com/forums/docker-in-practice) or raise an issue against one of the "docker-in-practice" GitHub repositories.

appendix A
Installing and using Docker

The techniques in this book sometimes require you to make files and clone repositories from GitHub. To avoid interference, we suggest you create a new empty folder for each technique when you need some working space.

Linux users have it relatively easy when it comes to installing and using Docker, though the fine details can vary significantly between different Linux distributions. Rather than enumerating the different possibilities here, we suggest you check the latest Docker documentation at https://docs.docker.com/installation/.

Although this book assumes that you're using a Linux distribution (containers are currently Linux-based, so this keeps things simple), many users interested in Docker work on either Windows or OS X (Mac) based machines. For these users it's worth pointing out that the techniques in this book will still work, as long as you use one of the following approaches to set up the Docker daemon.

> **CHANGES COMING FOR WINDOWS SERVER** Microsoft is committed to supporting the Docker container paradigm and management interface. Changes are coming to Windows Server to allow for the creation of Windows-based containers. This may be covered in future versions of this book, but it's not available at the time of writing.

A.1 The virtual machine approach

One approach to using Docker on Windows or Mac is to install a full Linux virtual machine. Once that's achieved, you can use the virtual machine exactly as you would any native Linux machine.

The most common way to achieve this is to install VirtualBox. See http://virtualbox.org for more information and installation guides.

A.2   Docker client connected to an external Docker server

If you already have a Docker daemon set up as a server, you can natively install a client that talks to it on your Windows or OS X machine. Be aware that exposed ports will be exposed on the external Docker server, not your local machine—you may need to alter IP addresses in order to access the exposed services.

See technique 1 for the essentials of this more advanced approach, and see technique 86 for details on making it secure.

A.3   Native Docker client and virtual machine

A common approach is to install a minimal virtual machine that runs Linux and Docker, and a Docker client that talks to Docker on that virtual machine. The standard way to do this is to use a Boot2Docker virtual machine, which uses a "Tiny Core Linux" distribution to provide an environment in which the Docker daemon can run as a server.

The Docker Toolbox can quickly get you started with Boot2Docker and is officially supported on Mac and Windows: https://www.docker.com/toolbox.

A.3.1   Docker on Windows

Windows is a very different operating system from Mac and Linux, so we'll go into a bit more detail here to highlight some common problems and solutions. You should follow the official installation documentation for the Docker Toolbox at https://docs.docker.com/engine/installation/windows/, and we'll emphasize some important parts here.

During the installation process, you should make sure to check the boxes for Docker Compose for Windows (used in technique 68, among others) and Git for Windows. The latter will allow you to git clone repositories mentioned throughout the book as well to use the bash shell and some Linux utilities like grep, sed, and curl. It even comes with ssh and perl. The scripting used throughout this book assumes that you're using bash (or a similar shell) and have these utilities available, so opting out of installing them and using the built-in Windows shell or Windows PowerShell instead will cause problems if you're following along. Feel free to also install the Kitematic GUI for Docker—it makes using images a matter of point and click, and you may find it interesting to experiment with, but we won't cover it in the book.

You should also select Add Docker Binaries to PATH during the installation process—this ensures that you can always run the docker command from your terminal.

If you've not already got Oracle VirtualBox installed, the Docker Toolbox will install it for you—all of your containers will run inside a VM as Linux containers can't run natively on Windows. Unlike the virtual machine approach discussed in section A.1, the VM created by the Docker Toolbox is very lightweight, as it only runs Docker, but you may still need to modify the memory of the VM in the VirtualBox interface settings if you're running resource-heavy programs.

To check that all is working correctly, open the Docker Quickstart Terminal from your programs list. It will start the virtual machine containing Docker if it's not already running and set up the environment so you can begin using Docker immediately. If you run `docker run hello-world`, Docker will automatically pull the hello-world image from the Docker Hub and run it. The output of this image gives a brief description of the steps that have just been taken regarding communication between the Docker client and daemon. Don't worry if it doesn't make much sense; there's more detail about what goes on behind the scenes in chapter 2.

Be aware that there will be some unavoidable oddities on Windows:

- Volumes need a double slash at the beginning, as discussed here: https://github.com/docker/docker/issues/12751.
- Because containers are running in a VM, if you want to access an exposed port from the host, you'll need to use `docker-machine ip default` in a shell to find the IP of the VM in order to visit it (this is covered in the Docker installation instructions for Windows: https://docs.docker.com/engine/installation/windows/).
- Some less popular tools may be more difficult to obtain than the "use your package manager" instructions we give in the techniques (for example, `socat` is best obtained by using Cygwin), and other tools (such as those that are significantly tied to Linux like `strace` and the `ip` command for using `ip addr`) may not be available directly on Windows at all.

WHAT IS CYGWIN? Cygwin, available at https://www.cygwin.com/, is a collection of tools from Linux made available on Windows. If you want a Linux-like environment to experiment with or want to obtain a Linux tool for use natively on Windows, Cygwin should be at the top of your list. It comes with a package manager so you can browse available software and see what's available.

A brief list of useful Windows replacements for some commands and components follows, but it's worth bearing in mind that some of these will be noticeably imperfect replacements. This book focuses on using Docker to run Linux containers, and it makes sense that a full Linux installation (be it a fat VM, a box in the cloud, or an installation on your local machine) will be more capable of teasing out the full potential of Docker:

- `ip addr`—We typically use this command in this book to find the IP of our machine on the local network. The Windows equivalent is `ipconfig`.
- `strace`—Take a look at the discussion of "A host-like container" in technique 97 for details on how to bypass Docker containerization and get host-like access inside the virtual machine running Docker. You'll want to start a shell rather than run `chroot` and use a Linux distribution with a package manager, like Ubuntu, rather than BusyBox. From there you can install and run commands as if you're running on the host. This tip applies to many commands, and almost lets you treat your Docker VM as a fat VM.

- Exposing ports to your host machine—Install Cygwin and install `socat` from the package list. You'll need to start the Cygwin shell from your application list to get access to these utilities. To forward ports with `socat` to provide access from outside your host, you can use `socat TCP-LISTEN:$PORT,reuseaddr,fork TCP:$DOCKERIP:$PORT`, where `$PORT` is the port you want to forward and `$DOCKERIP` is the output of `docker-machine ip default` in your Docker terminal.

GRAPHICAL APPLICATIONS ON WINDOWS

Running Linux graphical applications on Windows can be challenging—not only do you have to make all the code work on Windows, you also need to decide how to display it. The windowing system used on Linux (known as the *X Window System* or *X11*) isn't built into Windows. Fortunately, X allows you to display an application window over a network, so you can use an implementation of X on Windows to display applications running in a Docker container.

There are a few different implementations of X on Windows, so we're just going to cover the installation you can obtain with Cygwin. You should follow the official documentation at http://x.cygwin.com/docs/ug/setup.html#setup-cygwin-x-installing. When selecting packages to install, you must ensure xorg-server, xinit, and xhost are selected.

Once the installation has completed, open a Cygwin terminal and run `XWin :0 -listen tcp -multiwindow`. This will start an X server on your Windows machine with the ability to listen to connections from the network (`-listen tcp`) and display each application in its own window (`-multiwindow`), rather than a single window acting as a virtual screen to display applications on. Once it's started, you should see an "X" icon in your system tray area.

> **AUTHORIZATION PROBLEMS** Although this X server can listen to the network, it currently only trusts the local machine. In all cases we've seen, this allows access from your Docker VM, but if you have issues with authorization you may want to try running the insecure `xhost +` command to permit access from all machines. If you do this, be sure your firewall is configured to reject any connection attempts from the network!

It's time to try out your X server! Find out the IP address of your local machine with `ipconfig`. You want to look for an IP address on a VirtualBox Host-Only Network adapter—this is the IP address your Docker VM sees your host as. If you have multiple adapters like this, you may need to try the IP for each in turn. Starting your first graphical application should be as simple as running `docker run -e DISPLAY=$MY_IP:0 --rm fr3nd/xeyes` in a Docker Quickstart Terminal, where `$MY_IP` is the IP address of the adapter described previously.

A.4   *Getting help*

If you run a non-Linux operating system and want to get further help or advice, the Docker documentation (https://docs.docker.com/installation/) has the latest officially recommended advice for Windows and Mac users.

appendix B
Docker configuration

At various points in this book you're advised to change your Docker configuration to make changes permanent on starting up your Docker host machines. This appendix will advise you on the best practices for achieving this. The operating system distribution you use will be significant in this context.

The location of the config files for most mainstream distributions is listed in table B.1.

Table B.1   Docker configuration file locations

Distribution	Configuration
Ubuntu / Debian / Gentoo	/etc/default/docker
OpenSuse / CentOS / Red Hat	/etc/sysconfg/docker

Note that some distributions keep the configuration to a single file, whereas others use a directory and multiple files. For example, on Red Hat Enterprise License, there's a file called /etc/sysconfig/docker/docker-storage, which by convention contains the configuration relating to storage options for the Docker daemon.

If your distribution doesn't have any files that match the names in table B.1, it's worth checking for an /etc/docker folder, as there may be relevant files in there.

Within these files, arguments to the Docker daemon's startup command are managed. For example, when edited, a line such as the following allows you to set the starting arguments for the Docker daemon on your host:

```
DOCKER_OPTS=""
```

For example, if you want to change the location of Docker's root directory from the default (which is /var/lib/docker), you might change the preceding line as follows:

```
DOCKER_OPTS="-g /mnt/bigdisk/docker"
```

If your distribution uses systemd config files (as opposed to /etc), then you can also search for the ExecStart line in the docker file under the systemd folder, and change that if you want. This file might be located at /usr/lib/systemd/system/service/docker, for example. Here's an example file:

```
[Unit]
Description=Docker Application Container Engine
Documentation=http://docs.docker.io
After=network.target

[Service]
Type=notify
EnvironmentFile=-/etc/sysconfig/docker
ExecStart=/usr/bin/docker -d --selinux-enabled
Restart=on-failure
LimitNOFILE=1048576
LimitNPROC=1048576

[Install]
WantedBy=multi-user.target
```

The EnvironmentFile line refers the startup script to the file with the DOCKER_OPTS entry we discussed earlier. If you change the systemctl file directly, you'll need to run systemctl daemon-reload to ensure that the change is picked up by the systemd daemon.

B.1   Restarting Docker

Altering the configuration for the Docker daemon isn't sufficient—in order to apply the changes, the daemon must be restarted. Be aware that this will stop any running containers and cancel any in-progress image downloads.

B.1.1   Restarting with systemctl

Most modern Linux distributions use systemd to manage the startup of services on the machine. If you run systemctl on the command line and get pages of output, then your host is running systemd. If you get a "command not found" message, then try the approach in section B.1.2.

   If you want to make changes to your configuration, you can stop and start Docker as follows:

```
$ systemctl stop docker
$ systemctl start docker
```

Or you can just restart:

```
$ systemctl restart docker
```

Check the progress by running these commands:

```
$ journalctl -u docker
$ journalctl -u docker -f
```

The first line here outputs available logs for the docker daemon process. The second follows the logs for any new entries.

B.1.2 Restarting with service

If your system is running a System V-based set of init scripts, try running `service --status-all`. If that returns a list of services, you can use `service` to restart Docker with your new configuration:

```
$ service docker stop
$ service docker start
```

appendix C
Vagrant

At various points in this book we use virtual machines to demonstrate a technique for Docker that requires a full machine representation, or even multi-virtual-machine orchestration.

Vagrant offers a simple way to start, provision, and manage virtual machines from the command line, and it's available on multiple platforms.

C.1 Setting up

Go to https://www.vagrantup.com and follow the instructions there to get set up.

C.2 GUIs

When running vagrant up to start up a virtual machine, Vagrant reads the local file called Vagrantfile to determine the settings.

A useful setting that you can create or change within the section for your provider is the gui one:

```
v.gui = true
```

For example, if your provider is VirtualBox, a typical config section might look like this:

```
config.vm.provider "virtualbox" do |v, override|
      override.vm.box     = vagrant_openshift_config['virtualbox']
      ➥ ['box_name'] unless dev_cluster
      override.vm.box_url = vagrant_openshift_config['virtualbox']
      ➥ ['box_url'] unless dev_cluster
      override.ssh.insert_key = vagrant_openshift_config['insert_key']

      v.memory          = vagrant_openshift_config['memory'].to_i
      v.cpus            = vagrant_openshift_config['cpus'].to_i
```

```
    v.customize ["modifyvm", :id,
    ➡ "--cpus", vagrant_openshift_config['cpus'].to_s]
    v.gui             = false
  end if vagrant_openshift_config['virtualbox']
```

You could change the v.gui line's false setting to true (or add it if it wasn't already there) before running vagrant up to get a GUI for the running VM.

> **WHAT IS A PROVIDER?** A *provider* within Vagrant is the name of the program that provides the VM environment. For most users, this will be virtualbox, but it might also be libvirt, openstack, or vmware_fusion (among others).

C.3 *Memory*

Vagrant uses VMs to create its environments, and these can be very memory-hungry. If you're running a three-node cluster with each VM taking up 2 GB of memory, your machine will require 6 GB of available memory. If your machine is struggling to run, this lack of memory is most likely why—the only solutions are to stop any non-essential VMs or buy more memory. Being able to avoid this is one of the reasons Docker is more powerful than a VM. You don't need to preallocate resources to containers—they'll just consume what they need

index